The Fruits of Fascism

A volume in the series

Cornell Studies in Political Economy

EDITED BY PETER J. KATZENSTEIN

A full list of titles in the series appears at the end of the book

The Fruits of Fascism

POSTWAR PROSPERITY IN HISTORICAL PERSPECTIVE

SIMON REICH

CORNELL UNIVERSITY PRESS

Ithaca and London

First published 1990 by Cornell University Press.

International Standard Book Number 0–8014–2440–2 (cloth)
International Standard Book Number 0–8014–9729–9 (paper)
Library of Congress Catalog Card Number 90-55136
Printed in the United States of America
Librarians: Library of Congress cataloging information
appears on the last page of the book.

⊗ The paper used in this book meets the minimum requirements
of the American National Standard for Information Sciences–
Permanence of Paper for Printed Library Materials, ANSI Z39.48–1984.

In memory of my father

Erich Reich

who knew how to mix conflict and cooperation

"The new Germany's true foe is the old Germany."
—Hermann Kantorowicz, 1931

Contents

Preface

If the claim that books are never finished, merely discarded, is true, then I am fortunate in my timing. At the start of the 1990s the issue of continuity and change in Germany has returned to the forefront of public debate. Events in Eastern Europe have dramatically resurrected support for a united Germany, a support evident even among West Germany's most conservative politicians. More cautious observers may feel that some barriers to reunification are still impenetrable, but the speed of events in Europe has threatened to make any pronouncements instantly redundant.

No doubt historians and political scientists are now beginning to work on new projects about the division and reunification of Germany. Such a theme appears premature for this book—even as this preface is written at the turn of the decade. But this volume does stress a broader theme, one that was unpopular while I was writing but now has renewed vigor—that of twentieth-century German continuity. Specifically, it focuses on ideological and institutional continuities of the state in the fascist and postfascist periods, and their influence on postwar prosperity in the Federal Republic. I stress the influence of fascism on postwar economic prosperity. In doing so, I do not suggest that the Great Depression and two world wars had no bearing on the dynamics of postwar capitalism in the advanced industrial states. But fascism's influence on postwar prosperity has been neglected in the literature of political economy.

As I write this preface, in the context of ringing, euphoric West German demands that Germany be reconstituted, perhaps *The Fruits of Fascism* will serve as a reminder of what happened when Germany was last united—and why Germany was divided in the first place.

Books are written by one author but result from the cooperation and support of many institutions and individuals. Numerous administrators, teachers, colleagues, friends, and relations generously assisted me by contributing resources and patience—even though some considered the project doomed to failure. This book might still have been written without them, but it would not have been as good.

I received financial support for research and writing in the form of a Council of European Studies fellowship, a Sicca Foundation award, a National Resource Fellowship, and an award from the University Grants Program at the University of Pittsburgh. Brave archivists were helpful in putting up with my incessant demands, especially David Crippen of the Edison Institute, Darleen Flaherty of the Ford Industrial Archives, Philip Reed of the Imperial War Museum in London, Dr. Rest of the Bundesarchiv, Koblenz, Amy Schmidt of the National Archives in Washington, D.C., and Richard Storey of the Modern Records Center at the University of Warwick. The staffs of the Public Records Office in London and the Institute for Contemporary History in Munich were courteous and efficient.

Several individuals allowed me to ransack their personal collections of empirical material. Mira Wilkins allowed me to rummage through her collection of primary data and interview notes, retained after the completion of her and Frank Hill's book on Ford. Ian Turner gave me free rein over the data he had collected while writing on Allied policy toward Volkswagen during the Occupation. Hans Mommsen gave me access to the materials he and his staff are collecting for their study of Volkswagen. Heidrum Edelmann proved especially hospitable while I conducted research in Bochum. And Karl Heinz Roth allowed me to examine data from materials now deposited at the archive of the Hamburger Stiftung für Sozialgeschichte. Ulrich Jürgens and his colleagues at the Wissenschaftszentrum in Berlin helped me gain a sense of the location and nature of the available empirical materials at the outset of this project. I also thank Rainer Fröbe, who helped me get through the archival bureaucracy of Lower Saxony, helped develop my understanding of German fascism, and improved my chess game while eating currywurst in Hannover.

Over the last seven years I have built up hefty intellectual debts that I can never repay. Elliot Feldman, then at Brandeis University, played an important role when I originally conceived of this book; his loss from the ranks of political science is deeply regretted. Isabel Hull and Mitchell Abolafia helped me develop an understanding of German history and industrial sociology. I must mention the contribution of Sidney Tarrow, whose attempts to save me from myself, and this project, went unheeded but not unappreciated. T. J. Pempel and Jonas

Pontusson both proved extraordinarily helpful when faced with my disproportionate demands upon their time. Jonas's unabashed cynicism about this project has never abated (perhaps he will be proved right), but it was always presented constructively, forcing me to return to fundamentals, even if I do not see the world the same way as he does.

Several people read parts or all of this book. Steve Tolliday and Gary Marks read and provided valuable comments on the entire manuscript. Herrick Chapman, David Kaiser, Fritz Ringer, and Richard Smethurst all provided me with useful comments on my analysis of various historical debates. Furthermore, a group of friends provided me with valuable professional advice as well as intellectual criticism. Ellis Krauss has single-handedly made my first two years at the University of Pittsburgh a delight and taught me much about the world beyond Western Europe, academia, and state theory. Teaching a class with him proved to be a valuable intellectual experience. And Chris Allen has proved to me that is is possible simultaneously to have the deepest personal and professional respect for another human being—and to agree with him or her about nothing!

But there are three people whose intellectual contributions dominate this book. The first is Andrei Markovits. Before we had even met, Andy convinced a Council for European Studies committee that this project was worth funding. We finally met a year later, and ever since Andy has been a consistent source of intellectual criticism and professional advice. When they first coined the word "mensch," they must have had Andy in mind.

The second person is Theodore J. Lowi. Ted was instrumental in my gaining admission to Cornell University and securing the funding I desperately needed. Like many scholars before me, I am indebted to Ted Lowi for the enthusiasm with which he approached my work. Making a young scholar feel his or her work is interesting and significant bespeaks an attitude both rare and infectious. Most authors accept sole responsibility for a book. I refuse to do so. Ted Lowi played so essential a role in my professional development, and was so supportive, that he shares responsibility. For better or worse, Ted, this is the final product.

Beyond all these people stands Peter Katzenstein. At Cornell, Peter served as a constant source of both encouragement and criticism. He provides a model for both intellectual aspiration and professional behavior. This project had many initial drawbacks; while others were critical of the intellectual approach and feasibility, Peter had the patience to support it despite his many doubts—teaching me a valuable lesson in tolerance. His patience has proved inexhaustible. I have been a constant burden to him for the last six years—and very much doubt that I'll stop being one with the publication of this book. I can never repay him, I can only try to "send the elevator down."

In the final stages John Ackerman and Roger Haydon of Cornell University Press helped guide this manuscript through the publishing process. And as I made final revisions, Blaine Shiff provided valuable assistance.

My wife, Linda Myers Reich, played an ambivalent role in the development and completion of this book. She willingly provided the resources that made the book possible while she complained that the work often led me to neglect her (demonstrating one of the limits of classic rational choice theory). But I never diminished in my love and admiration for her. If nothing else, I hope that the appearance of this book in print will justify all the time I have not spent with her. My mother, Elisabeth Reich, constantly strengthened my resolve. She provided something generally missing in the lives of scholars—instant gratification—by telling me how proud she was of my efforts. And my daughter, Jamie Reich, often helped put this book into perspective while I worked on revisions. The arrival of my second daughter, Melissa, happily coincided with this book's completion. If they read it one day, I hope they'll not think their father's work outdated.

Finally I acknowledge the role of my late father in the completion of this manuscript. It is impossible to recall a specific date when work on a research project really commences. Maybe it is the first time one reads a formative article—in my case, by Barrington Moore—maybe the day one starts one's field research. Erich Reich died from a sudden heart attack at the age of sixty-two on the day I was to leave for Germany to begin mine. As is typical between father and son, we combined cooperation and conflict over the years in a relationship that was often resolved by compromise. In his latter years we grew to share a particularly close relationship. He supported me in periods of self-doubt and became a soothing influence in times of stress. My father gave me the intellect and character to begin this manuscript and the motive to complete it. I hope I have justified his efforts.

SIMON REICH

Pittsburgh, Pennsylvania

The Fruits of Fascism

CHAPTER ONE

Fascism and Prosperity in Advanced Industrial States

In the fall of 1989 Ford and General Motors competed for a valuable prize—the ownership of Jaguar, the British producer of luxury cars. Ford won the battle, outbidding General Motors, and the sale was approved by the shareholders in December. Jaguar was the last major, exclusively British-owned automobile company. Yet Margaret Thatcher, the British prime minister, encouraged both American firms to buy Jaguar, despite the Jaguar board's insistence that it wanted the firm to remain an independent producer. This foreign purchase of Jaguar was symptomatic of a broader trend. In the 1980s the British automobile industry had been transformed from a sector where British-owned firms and foreign direct investors competed against one another to one where the British firms were all either wholly or partially owned by foreign competitors.

That same fall, Thatcher vigorously reasserted her support for policies designed to lure Japanese automobile producers to invest in Britain. Newspapers chronicled the decision of Toyota and Nissan to locate production plants there as a springboard for sales throughout the Common Market. British pride at Thatcher's success was based on the belief that it would generate greater employment and renewed prosperity.

In the context of British economic policy there was nothing unusual or inconsistent about the Thatcher government's contrasting treatment of Jaguar and of Ford, General Motors, Toyota, and Nissan. At the heart of its strategy lay the government's promise that foreign investors would receive the same treatment as domestic firms. Fundamentally, this promise reflected a principle that had governed the behavior of both right-wing and left-wing British governments throughout the

I

twentieth century—a principle commonly termed "national treatment." No distinction would be made between firms on the basis of
foreign or domestic ownership, all government policies would be
nondiscriminatory.

In practice, however, national treatment is not egalitarian, because
first attracting and then keeping foreign investors often involves giving
them incentives not offered to domestic firms. The application of national treatment as a governing principle for policy making therefore
has differing implications for different firms.

Not all countries accept the principle of national treatment. While
Britain and the United States encourage foreign investment in industrial production facilities, other advanced industrial states deny foreign
firms local production rights or grant them such rights and then implement discriminatory policies that reduce their competitiveness. Governments in Japan, Italy, France, and West Germany never talk about
the advantages of attracting foreign investment or the application of
anything remotely resembling "national treatment." And the state in
these countries, this book will suggest, does not do so because it does
not believe in treating foreign direct investors equitably. Indeed,
in 1989 the Europeans expressed anger at Thatcher's cultivation of
Japanese investment. They wanted to subvert Japanese competition.

What is the source of this difference in state behavior? How are these
ideological differences reflected in the nature of state institutions and
in policy? The difference, I argue, is just one of the implications of a
basic bifurcation in the ideologies of advanced industrial states which
dates back to the fascist period. Foreign firms had been accorded national treatment in all advanced industrial states in the prefascist period, but a basic division developed between states that remained liberal
democracies and those that became fascist. In the fascist countries the
state revolutionized its attitude toward foreign direct investors. I focus
on three issues: how the contrasting ideologies of liberal and fascist
states initially developed; how these ideologies were effectively sustained in the postwar period; and, most important, how the state's
policies influenced the state's political autonomy and the relative prosperity of each economy.

I concentrate on the comparative development of the automobile
industry in Britain and West Germany. Both states implemented policies based on egalitarian principles in the first three decades of the
twentieth century, but there was a sharp ideological divergence in the
1930s and 1940s. The National Socialist state developed a new, aggressive ideology. It created new organs that used coercive measures.
These not only consciously and systematically discriminated against

2

foreign firms but also made distinctions among domestic firms. They dramatically affected the economic welfare of these firms. But, more important, this discriminatory ideology and the institutions it spawned survived the downfall of fascism and dominated the policies of the Allied powers and the Bonn Republic—with an equally dramatic effect on the relative prosperity of these firms in the first two decades of the postwar period.[1]

This book therefore has two major, controversial themes. The first concerns the influence of innovative fascist economic policies on postwar prosperity. Ideological divergence had a dramatic effect on the configuration of political relations between the state and individual auto firms, suggesting that some part of postwar German prosperity can be explained by the residual state ideology and institutional structures first adopted by the Nazi state. I therefore focus on a relationship oddly neglected in the disciplines of history and political science—the historical-political links between Germany's National Socialist, Occupational, and early Bonn periods. A second theme of this book involves the relative influence of political and economic factors on economic prosperity. Traditional economic theory about the influence of free market competition seems to be confounded by the historical pattern of development of the auto industry in Britain and West Germany. Indigenous British firms have been exposed to more intense, continuous competition from multinational corporations than have their German counterparts, yet the German firms have been more prosperous and dynamic since the war. British producers have all but disappeared, indigenous German firms have flourished. Economists might point to market imperfections to explain this apparent anomaly. But all markets have imperfections, and the source of the contrast in outcome, I believe, lies in the state's political choices—explicitly, its dominant ideological principles and how they influence what sort of firm dominates the domestic market. I assume, that is, that all states intervene; what matters is *how* they intervene.

In developing this argument, I question conventional theories and approaches to the study of history and political science. My argument establishes a link between the ideologies and institutions of fascist regimes and their post-fascist form. This form of analysis confronts the work of political economists such as Mancur Olson who have emphasized the lack of continuity between the fascist and the post-fascist period by emphasizing the purely destructive effects of fascist regimes

---

[1] In examining these countries I do not claim to explain conclusively the relative rates of prosperity for every industry in every advanced industrial state. Rather, I develop a more limited explanation that could plausibly be used in other contexts.

on their national economies.[2] It also poses a challenge to two forms of historical analysis. The first form has emphasized long-term structural factors, such as the relative timing of development, in explaining Britain's economic decline and West Germany's postwar prosperity. Instead of relating twentieth-century economic prosperity to eighteenth- or nineteenth-century structural changes in the international system, my argument emphasizes the importance of domestic ideological and institutional innovations in the twentieth century. The second form of historical analysis is expressed in a series of generally flattering, microeconomic studies of German automobile firms that insist these companies' achievements are unrelated to events in the fascist era, that each arose "like a phoenix from the ashes." Evidence presented here concerning individual companies casts doubt on these interpretations.

The theoretical discussion in this chapter stresses the systematic neglect of the influence of National Socialism on postwar German prosperity. Even if I confine my claims to relative prosperity in the auto industry, the importance of that sector to the postwar economy was so great that I can still account for a large percentage of prosperity. The second chapter describes the theoretical framework that explains the pattern of economic prosperity in the British and German automobile industries. And the four chapters that follow compare the treatment of domestic and foreign firms by the British and German states—and the implications of those differences for the individual firms, the industry, and the national economy. The seventh chapter, however, extends the argument's plausibility by comparing the pattern of development of the auto industry in Britain and West Germany with that in France, Italy, and Japan. In the concluding chapter I focus on two issues: the general one is the implications of state ideology for the pattern of national prosperity; and the parochial one is whether there are any lessons relevant to policies in the United States.

IDEOLOGIES, INSTITUTIONS, AND THE STUDY OF GERMANY

Scholars working on Germany have largely relied on structural analyses, even though they tend to insulate their debates according to discipline or subfield.[3] Historians have tended to employ structural theories that encompass great historical sweeps in an effort to instill coherence

[2]Mancur Olson, *The Rise and Decline of Nations: Stagflation and Social Rigidities* (New Haven: Yale University Press, 1982).
[3]For thinking on these issues I have found particularly helpful Emanuel Adler, *The Power of Ideology: The Quest for Technological Autonomy in Argentina and Brazil* (Berkeley: University of California Press, 1987), pp. 1–3.

in the study of German history. They have attempted, in general social and political terms, to link the domestic structure of the Second Empire to the preconditions of World War I and, eventually, the rise of German fascism. These historians have neglected the relationship of German fascism to the Bonn Republic. Conservative historians conceive of fascism as an aberration in German development. Liberals, operating largely from a sociological perspective, have suggested that German fascism was the culmination of a modernizing process—and thus presumably the end of an epoch—whereas Marxists, boxed in by a conception of fascism as the "ultimate stage of capitalism," have no effective way to explain the subsequent hegemony of liberal democracy in Germany (a development largely irreconcilable with Marxist theory). Similarly, political economists ignore the significance of the fascist period, tracing the development of the Bonn economy either to the origins of "organized capitalism" in the late nineteenth century or to the imposition of neoliberal values in the early postwar period. It is as if Germany learned or retained nothing from the Third Reich. The "no-legacy" view is taken to its extreme in Olson's *Rise and Decline of Nations*, where he credits German postwar prosperity to the complete destruction of traditional institutions and ideologies and suggests that this *tabula rasa* allowed entrepreneurial capitalism to generate high levels of growth.[4] Comparativists, finally, have largely devoted their energies to studying the causes rather than the consequences of fascism.

In this book I offer an alternative perspective. I assert that fascism revolutionized the attitudes of the German state about economic policy and how it conceived of the scope and domain of its power. These changes were sustained in the Bonn Republic and reflected in Bonn's behavior in the auto sector. The structure and unprecedented rate of growth of the automobile industry can therefore be explained only through a study of the fascist period. In Britain, by contrast, the state's ideology was not transformed, and the sustained hegemony of liberal values has led to both ideological and institutional stagnation.

The remainder of this chapter pulls together three separate debates demonstrating how the ideological and institutional innovations of the fascist state have been ignored. In three sections I systematically address the important questions discussed among three groups of scholars. First, I examine the historians' debate over continuity and change in the studies of Wilhelmine and fascist Germany. Historians have tended to focus on where responsibility lay for the outbreak of World War I and the preconditions for the rise of the fascism, and whether the two issues are related. A bitter argument has raged over whether

[4]Olson, *The Rise and Decline of Nations*, p. 76.

these developments were the inevitable outcome of the internal politics of Wilhelmine society or were simply the state's response to external factors beyond domestic influence. This, in turn, has given rise to further debate: can periods of German history be analytically insulated so that the events of one period can be used to explain developments in another, or are the patterns of German history too interwoven to make the attribution of causation a meaningful exercise? But among historians the issue of continuity and change ends with the defeat of fascism.

I then consider the utility of various explanations for postwar German prosperity. Political economists, I believe, have ignored the significance of the fascist period, exemplifying a historical insularity that the earlier work of Alexander Gerschenkron and Rudolf Hilferding, with their keen sense of the historical context, avoided. Subsequent work has paid homage to these theorists, but it has tended to be less contextual and has consigned historical factors to a few neat clichés such as "late development." I show where this book's form of explanation differs from that of most contemporary work and how a thesis linking German prosperity to Nazi state policy might be an appropriate avenue to explore.[5]

The third section considers how to define the liberal, fascist, and corporatist regimes examined in this book and the relationship between them—one ignored by more traditional comparativists, who have tended to decouple contemporary German corporatism from fascism. This exercise, though designed to distinguish the relationship of state and economy in the three regimes, is more immediately concerned with whether institutional and ideological attributes of German fascism are evident in German corporatism. I do not suggest that all fascist states become corporatist, or that all corporatist states were or are fascist. This section simply points out that fascist states which become corporatist may reflect the legacies of fascist policies—and that West Germany has done so.

CONTINUITY, CHANGE, AND FASCISM IN GERMAN HISTORY

The concepts of continuity and change have played a central role in interpretations of the pattern of German development. Their varying use largely explains why historians have profoundly disagreed whether

---

[5]See Alexander Gerschenkron, *Economic Backwardness in Historical Perspective* (Cambridge: Harvard University Press, Belknap Press, 1962); Rudolf Hilferding, *Finance Capital: A Study of the Latest Phase of Capitalist Development* (London: Routledge & Kegan Paul, 1981).

Germany was primarily responsible for the outbreak of World War I, what caused the rise of German fascism, and whether both can be attributed to the same cause. Although historians have generally debated these questions in a language different from that employed by political scientists, many of the issues reflect familiar disagreements, notably over the primacy of domestic or systemic factors, the influence of interest or ideology in determining behavior, and the relative autonomy of the state.

The nineteenth-century approach to the study of these issues emphasized the preeminence of the autonomous, deified state as the synthesis of *Macht* and *Geist* (power and spirit). Conservative German historians, notably Max Lenz, Erich Marcks, and Felix Rachfahl, fused principles derived from Georg Friedrich Hegel and Leopold von Ranke to develop a perspective consistent with contemporary realism. For Ranke, the state was the divine expression of the political spirit of its populace; its primary purpose was to survive in an amoral, anarchic international environment. Lacking any mechanism to impose international law, states were obliged to maximize their power. War was the natural outcome of their struggle, and states therefore had to emphasize the "primacy of foreign policy" to ensure survival. There was some ambivalence as to whether the state's eventual objective was to achieve hegemony or simply become a major actor in a balance of power system, but either result would reduce international conflict.[6] The corollary to these neo-Rankean assumptions was the development of the more parochial ideology of *Weltpolitik,* which justified German expansion as a means of securing national survival through its establishment among the Great Powers; it could use deterrence to "command the peace."[7]

The neo-Rankean school's methodology constituted, according to John A. Moses, a *Weltanschauung* that claimed to be impartial and objective but implicitly favored the belief that the historian's principal task was to provide ideological justifications for national policy that promoted the power and prestige of the German Reich. Fritz Fischer damns these conservative historians as "the mouthpieces of the decisive forces in the German Reich."[8] In application, the neo-Rankeans rejected explanations of the outbreak of war as a consequence of the

[6]For hegemony as the primary objective see Fritz Fischer, *The War of Illusions* (New York: Norton, 1975), p. 30. For the alternative claim that Germany merely sought to become an equal partner among world powers see John A. Moses, *The Politics of Illusion: The Fischer Controversy in German Historiography* (New York: Barnes & Noble, 1975), p. 24.

[7]See Gerschenkron, *Economic Backwardness,* p. 23.

[8]Moses, *The Politics of Illusion,* p. xiii; Fritz Fischer, *Germany's Aims in the First World War* (New York: Norton, 1967), p. 8.

nature of Germany's internal social structure. Like contemporary realism, neo-Rankeanism assumed the state was monolithic and decisions
were made by elites personified by the chancellor. Unlike contemporary realism, however, this approach was more or less consciously ideological, according to its critics, distinguished between states rather than
treated them as equals by discriminating between Germany and the
rest, and was explicitly prescriptive in intent. The neo-Rankeans promoted a perspective that recommended maximizing German power
through aggressive foreign policy. The prescription for German security lay in foreign expansion.[9] Specifically, this prescription called for
the defeat of France, the foundation of a Central European federation
under German leadership, and the development of Germany as a
world power through the acquisition of new colonies.[10]

This orthodox approach had tremendous utility in rationalizing Germany's foreign policies. In the prewar period it helped vindicate expansionist Wilhelmine foreign policies. In the Weimar period it de-
fused accusations of German responsibility for the outbreak of war in
1914. It suggested that Germany was no more responsible than other
powers, because it rejected the importance of domestic institutions and
the significance of international law or morality. Rather, it emphasized
the deterministic influences of systemic pressures—and therefore denied war guilt. Like other states, according to Gerhard Ritter and Golo
Mann, Germany had simply pursued foreign policies consistent with
the national interest. Miscalculation and conflicting interests had combined to spark a war, and lack of communication and failure of leadership explained Germany's defeat.[11]

Few historians challenged the method or conclusions of this orthodox analysis in the first half of the twentieth century. The major exception was Eckhart Kehr who in the 1920s "turned this thesis of the so-
called 'primacy of foreign policy' (*Primat der Aussenpolitik*) on its head
and argued instead for the 'primacy of internal policy' (*Primat der In-
nenpolitik*) in determining matters of peace and war."[12] Kehr took a
critical approach, emphasizing the modernist impulses of the Second
Empire by stressing the disjuncture between Germany's rapid economic modernization and its static, feudal political structure. Specifically, the sustained political power of preindustrial elites in the face of

---

[9]For the assumptions of Ranke and his successors see Moses, *The Politics of Illusion*,
foreword, preface, and pp. 1–29.

[10]Fischer, *Germany's Aims*, pp. 34–35.

[11]Moses, *The Politics of Illusion*, pp. 31–41.

[12]Richard J. Evans, "Introduction: Wilhelm II's Germany and the Historians," in
Evans, ed., *Society and Politics in Wilhelmine Germany* (New York: Barnes & Noble, 1978), p.
13.

economic modernization had created domestic tensions that could be ameliorated only by an aggressive, expansionist foreign policy. According to his interest-based argument, ideological trappings consistent with elite objectives had been developed. Kehr's views were soundly rejected by his contemporaries, but his radical approach was revived by Fritz Fischer four decades later in his landmark work *Griff nach der Weltmacht* (subsequently translated as *Germany's Aims in the First World War*). Fischer specified a causal linkage between the internal structure of the Bismarckian and Wilhelmine states, on the one hand, and both the outbreak of World War I and, more indirectly, the Nazi attainment of power, on the other.[13]

Fischer's analysis directly challenged the old orthodoxy by accepting German responsibility for the outbreak of war in 1914.[14] He claimed that German intellectuals, as representatives of elite conservative interests that dominated the state, prepared a climate conducive to an aggressive form of nationalism that increased the probability of war. Domestic institutions were dominated by an elite that had promulgated principles consistent with militaristic and nationalistic values because they considered foreign expansion a way of defusing internal tensions. Fischer explained that the German leadership's goal was to annex much of Europe and dominate the rest of it in a scheme conceived well before 1914.[15] Moses summarizes Fischer's position with the comment that "the war of 1914–1918 was therefore not the result of some tragic diplomatic error but a conscious, if nervous calculation by a power-deluded state which believed that her hour of destiny in world history had arrived."[16] In sum, Fischer echoed Hermann Kantorowicz's sentiment, expressed in 1931, that "the new Germany's true foe is the old Germany."[17]

Fischer's analysis prompted a historical debate that became known as the "Fischer controversy."[18] His radical treatment of late nineteenth- and early twentieth-century German history horrified traditional historians like Ritter and Mann who considered Wilhelmine Germany's internal political structure essentially healthy. In the often bitter debate Ritter and Mann conceded that German policies might have acted as the immediate catalyst for war, but they retained their neo-Rankean

[13]For example see Fischer, *Germany's Aims,* pp. 635–36; and his subsequent *War of Illusions,* pp. vii–ix.
[14]Fischer, *Germany's Aims,* pp. 637–38.
[15]Evans, "Introduction: Wilhelm II's Germany," p. 12.
[16]Moses, *The Politics of Illusion,* p. 47.
[17]Hermann Kantorowicz, *The Spirit of British Policy and the Myth of the Encirclement of Germany* (Cambridge: Cambridge University Press, 1931).
[18]Fischer's original work and his follow-up study have been translated as *Germany's Aims in the First World War* and *The War of Illusions* respectively.

assumptions in claiming that Germany's actions had constituted pre-emptive defensive measures in the face of imminent attack.[19] Furthermore, while both sides focused on the period preceding the outbreak of war in 1914, they recognized that Fischer's claims implicated much more than the issue of German culpability for the war. In attacking cherished values and institutions of the Wilhelmine period, Fischer was claiming that Germany's nationalist, imperialist, anti-Semitic, and Prussian statist traditions provided antecedent conditions for Hitler's emergence.[20] This claim was therefore not only about the causes of the war but a sweeping structural historical (historicist) analysis of German state and society that causally linked discrete periods of German history: the advent of the Third Reich could be explained by the structure of the Second Reich.[21]

Fischer's work revolutionized the study of the nation's history in Germany. The discipline became more pluralistic as an alternative, antistatist orthodoxy emerged, and Fischer's analysis provided a new research agenda for a generation of historians, notably Hans-Ulrich Wehler. Wehler's interest-based class analysis focused on the primacy of domestic politics in explaining German foreign and domestic policy. Wehler suggests that the internal structure of the German state was dominated by the vested interests of elites whose policies were legitimated by a manipulative ideology: "Pre-industrial value systems, creating a considerable and constant influence, contributed to the defense of the ruling elites' established positions. Through a process of mystification, the ideology of the German state continued to present the policies of the vested interests as motivated by impartial, above-party considerations. It nourished unfounded reservations against Germany's political parties and shielded the bureaucracy from criticism."[22]

This new approach focused on the governing coalition of iron and rye—the economic influence of the leaders of heavy industry coupled with the political dominance of the Prussian Junker class. The Junkers constituted an agrarian, preindustrial elite who owned large estates east of the Elbe and ran them on feudal principles. They dominated the ranks of the German bureaucracy, the officer corps of the armed forces, and the Prussian Diet (legislature).[23]

[19]Fischer, *Germany's Aims*, p. 637; and Hans-Ulrich Wehler, *The German Empire, 1871–1918* (Dover, N.H.: Berg, 1985), p. 192.

[20]For example, see Fischer, *War of Illusions*, p. 14.

[21]Perhaps the clearest statement is made by Wehler in *The German Empire, 1871–1918;* for his critical comments on Fischer see pp. 230–31. An interesting summary and effective critique of Kehr, Fischer, and Wehler is Wolfgang Mommsen, "Domestic Factors in German Foreign Policy before 1914," *Central European History* 6 (1973), pp. 3–43.

[22]Wehler, *The German Empire*, pp. 192–95, 238–39.

[23]Wehler takes a balanced approach when examining "organized capitalism" and the Junker class; Fischer places greater weight on the Junkers. See ibid., pp. 42–45, and Fischer, *War of Illusions*, p. 13.

Germany's unification was a result of Prussian conquest; Prussia and the Junkers, not surprisingly, dominated Germany's political institutions in the context of what Wehler identified as "pseudo-constitutional semi-absolutism."[24] This dominance was manifest in many ways. Under the terms of the constitution, the Prussian king was the German kaiser and acted as supreme commander of the armed forces, whereas the weak German Reichstag had limited powers. Second, the prime minister of Prussia acted as chancellor of the Reich. Third, the Prussian Diet was elected on the basis of a discriminatory three-tier, open-ballot voting system that guaranteed Junker control of the ruling Conservative party. This system proved tremendously important because two-thirds of the German population lived in Prussia, and Conservative party control of the Prussian legislature gave the Junkers an effective veto over national legislation.[25] These institutional privileges ensured that laws maintained agricultural tariffs and feudal privileges to protect the Junkers' economic base. Volker Berghahn succinctly captures the spirit of Fischer's conception of political power in Bismarckian and Wilhelmine Germany: "Prussia and the German Empire as a whole was, in effect, ruled by an elite, led by the crown and a 'strategic clique,' whose social and economic power base was the German countryside."[26] As Geoff Eley, perhaps caricaturing both Fischer and Wehler, stated: "The continuity of German imperialist ambition across the two world wars was seen to reflect a more basic continuity of dominant socio-economic interests at home."[27]

Although this form of analysis of Germany was new to domestic historians in the early 1960s, it had found expression two decades earlier in the United States in the work of Alexander Gerschenkron. *Bread and Democracy in Germany* explicitly linked the philosophy, designs, and strategies of the Junkers to the downfall of the Weimar Republic and the rise of fascism. According to Gerschenkron, important elements of the fascist *Weltanschauung*, including praise of the rural life, the promise of a kingdom of "blood and soil," the emphasis on economic autarky and political autarchy, the hatred of Jews, the emphasis on nationalism, and a contempt for international obligations can all be traced from the Junkers to the Nazis. He states that "the basic element of what was to become the *Weltanschauung* of Nazism can be perceived distinctly in the policy of an agriculture politically and spir-

---

[24]Evans, "Introduction: Wilhelm II's Germany," p. 16; and Wehler, *The German Empire*, pp. 52–55.

[25]See Alexander Gerschenkron, *Bread and Democracy in Germany* (1943; Ithaca: Cornell University Press, 1989), p. 25.

[26]Volker Berghahn, *Germany and the Approach of War in 1914* (New York: St. Martin's Press, 1973), p. 9.

[27]Geoff Eley, *From Unification to Nazism: Reinterpreting the German Past* (Boston: Allen & Unwin, 1986), p. 3.

itually dominated by the aristocratic landowners in the eastern half of the German Reich" and, in ascribing cause, adds: "It is impossible to overestimate the momentous role which the economic and political interests of the Junkers played in the long process of disintegration of democracy leading to the untimely end of the Weimar Republic, and in the initiation of a system which, barely seven years later, destroyed the peace of the world and came close to destroying its freedom."[28]

The new German orthodoxy of scholars like Wehler went beyond Gerschenkron and Fischer, according to Richard Evans, in elaborating on the role of such organizations as the Agrarian League, Navy League, Colonial Society, and Society for Eastern Marches as instruments of Junker power. Evans suggests that, in the new orthodoxy's view, the successful aim of the Junker strategy was to divert emancipatory and reformist impulses into an enthusiasm for foreign conquest, empire, and generally greater international prestige. This mobilization technique was given the name "social imperialism." Wehler suggests that "the intentions behind Germany's overseas expansion, and the function it performed, served the interests of a 'social imperialism.' This amounted to a conservative 'taming' policy. . . . It made use of modern propaganda techniques but aimed at preserving the inherited pre-industrial social and political structures of the Greater Prussian Empire, while defending the industrial and educated middle classes against the rising proletariat."[29]

Weltpolitik, according to this analysis, was an ideology specifically designed to encourage the creation of a large navy for competition with the British. Social imperialism and *Weltpolitik* shared a reciprocal if not symbiotic relationship, according to Wehler, in the functions they performed: "A successful social policy alongside an increase in parliamentary influence would make it possible to conduct a powerful *Weltpolitik* by first satisfying the workers. In this case internal reform would underpin imperialism as the main priority, for the integration of the social classes was seen as the prerequisite of strength abroad. *Weltpolitik* would, moreover, facilitate an effective social policy through tangible material concessions. Successes abroad were expected to lead to a kind of truce on the home fronts." Diversion of this type was only one method employed by the Junkers. Others included repression by outlawing opposition parties, manipulation of other parties that could be coopted, compensation through the development of a comprehensive welfare system, indoctrination through the education system, and what

[28]Gerschenkron, *Bread and Democracy,* pp. 16–17, 53, 153.
[29]Evans, "Introduction: Wilhelm II's Germany," p. 19; Wehler, *The German Empire,* p. 173.

became known as "negative integration"—enforcing a community of social interests by discriminating against outsiders (mainly Jews and foreigners) depicted as subversives.[30]

The new historians consciously rejected the view that the state constituted an autonomous entity. They emphasized political relationships among the dominant classes as opposed to the continuity of the state bureaucracy. However, the new and traditional orthodoxies did have some similarities. The new approach did maintain the view that the German decision-making elite was monolithic—even if that elite, the Junkers, was analyzed as a social class rather than a bureaucratic hierarchy. Both sides, moreover, agreed about the authoritarian character of the state (although they differed about whether it was desirable).

After old and new orthodoxies had exchanged bitter blows, a third, more complex literature emerged. This work rejects the structural or "historicist" analysis employed by both the old neo-Rankeans and the new radicals. Instead, it emphasizes the evolving nature of a fragmented governing coalition. Some of this literature has tended to be grounded in assumptions supporting the new orthodoxy. For example, Volker Berghahn's *Germany and the Approach of War in 1914* elaborated on Fischer's and Wehler's simple structural approach by emphasizing *Sammlungspolitik,* literally the politics of "concentration" or "rallying together"—the attempt to negotiate a compromise and thereby generate governing coalitions out of diverse interests. His analysis of Wilhelmine society focused on the struggle to create a coalition of the right. According to Berghahn the basis for the restitution of a governing coalition of the right lay in a series of Navy Bills beginning in 1898. These bills, intent on commissioning a large navy, were designed to be the keystone of an economic and political coalition between agrarian Junkers concerned with achieving foreign expansion and leaders of heavy industry who would benefit financially from construction orders. The Von Tirpitz Plan for naval development would build a domestic coalition at home while simultaneously deterring Britain and bullying the other nations of Europe into recognizing Germany's need for an empire. According to Berghahn, the one primary concern was the stabilization of the Prusso-German political system.

> The more direct and immediate consolidation of the Navy Bill was to come from the unifying effects of the naval armaments program at home. More indirect and more long-range were the stabilizing benefits which the government hoped to derive from the Navy as an instrument of foreign policy and German imperialism in the twentieth century. But it is not

[30]Wehler, *The German Empire*, pp. 17–19.

difficult to see that, in the final analysis, the result would be the same. It is in this sense that the decision to build a large battle-fleet represented an "inner-political crisis strategy" designed to contribute to the survival of the Prusso-German political system: with the help of the Navy, the monarchy wanted to overthrow the status quo internationally in order to preserve it at home.[31]

In developing this analysis Berghahn highlighted a point significant to our discussion—that the dominant coalition lacked continuity. Apparently there was no natural Junker dominance or sustained community of interest among the German right. The coalition had to be created and reconstituted as rapid industrialization militated against the monarchy and created potential conflicts between industrial and agricultural elites. Berghahn concludes that "at a time when the internal crisis appeared to be reaching a new peak, Tirpitz's program was designed to unite these forces against an embittered and restrictive proletariat and aimed at upsetting the international status quo in order to preserve the domestic balance of power."[32]

Berghahn emphasizes the importance of process but retains the view that the structural relationship between Wilhelmine state and society, and consequent government policies, explicitly explain the outbreak of war: "What the Kaiser's armaments policy had failed to do in peacetime, namely to destroy the international balance of power in order to maintain an antiquated political structure at home, was now to be achieved by the German armed forces in wartime. The immediate effect of the outbreak of war was no doubt to unite the nation internally." In passing, furthermore, Berghahn suggests that after 1918 this reconstituted coalition allied itself with the National Socialists to restore the traditional power structure at home by bringing down the Weimar Constitution and establishing the Reich as the dominant European power.[33] He thus retains the domestic basis of Fischer's analysis and so links the preconditions for Bismarck's and Hitler's rise to power.

Other contemporary analyses have mounted a more critical challenge to Fischer. Possibly the best example is the work of Geoff Eley whose work combines aspects of a Marxist theoretical analysis with a bourgeois historian's more fundamentalist methodological approach. Eley concludes there is an unmistakable commitment by Fischer and Wehler to the notion of structural continuity in Germany's historical development.[34] Reinterpreting rather than echoing their argument

---

[31]Berghahn, *Germany and the Approach of War*, p. 40.
[32]Ibid., p. 212.
[33]Ibid., pp. 213, 214.
[34]Eley, *From Unification to Nazism*, pp. 4, 6.

(and so risking the accusation that he creates two "straw men"), Eley suggests that Fischer and Wehler are claiming that both World War I and the onset of fascism were a consequence of delayed national unification and delayed industrialization. The effects of these delays were complicated by the absence of a bourgeois revolution, which would have created a parliamentary tradition. The link between these three factors was expressed in Bismarck's and Hitler's common war annexation programs through the primacy of "social imperialism."[35] *Sammlungspolitik* played a crucial role, creating a decisive alliance of capitalists and landowners united by a fear of foreign competition and democratic reform.

Eley criticizes this argument for a large degree of structural determinism and a willingness effectively to redefine the problem of fascism as a more general problem of political backwardness while avoiding the issue of how fascism is itself defined (an issue I address later in this chapter). More specifically, he states that the general belief that the Wilhelmine period was characterized mainly by

> the defence of inherited ruling positions by pre-industrial elites against the assault of new forces, establishing a continuity which culminated in 1933, is not without its problems. It raises difficulties at both a theoretical and an empirical level. Most fundamentally it contains a number of assumptions about the efficacy of "pre-industrial traditions," the "aristocratic" character of the dominant class and the "feudalized" subordination of the bourgeoisie, which can only be tackled properly at a level of theory; in contrast to this historicist approach I have preferred to emphasize the specific features of the Wilhelmine conjuncture after 1890 and the new structure of politics determined by the capitalist mode of production.[36]

Eley has two further criticisms of Fischer. First, Fischer's simplified notion of political mobilization and the role of ideology produces a subordinated, manipulated peasantry unable to define its own self-interest as a class. Eley suggests that empirical evidence does not support this view; from the early 1890s the emergence of a single agrarian interest was predicated on an explicit set of agreements that brought real advantages to the peasants.[37] The new orthodoxy, he suggests, was therefore content to employ "an extraordinary crude view of how polit-

---

[35]Geoff Eley, *Reshaping the German Right: Radical Nationalism and Political Change after Bismarck* (New Haven: Yale University Press, 1980), pp. 2–3.

[36]Ibid., pp. 7–8, 9.

[37]This constitutes an explicit criticism of both Fischer and Berghahn. Eley contends that Berghahn's analysis of the Tirpitz plan as central to the development of a new coalition is incorrect. He suggests that it played no role in the creation of a new *Sammlung*. See Eley, *From Unification to Nazism*, p. 10.

ical mobilization occurs, how ideology is constructed, and how consciousness is formed."[38] Second, Eley has problems identifying the continuity of Fischer's argument over six decades. Clearly, he suggests, the pivotal issue is the use of the concept of the *Sammlung,* but Eley contends that the evolving right-wing coalition at the turn of the century demanded a reassessment of the concept's utility. Both Fischer and Wehler's use of the concept may conveniently aggregate different coalitions that had little in common.[39] Similarly, Eley implicitly dissents from Gerschenkron, stressing the evolutionary process taking place in a series of coalitions that struggled for control of state policy in the Second Empire.

In sum, Eley suggests that Fischer and his successors have made choices: they have chosen to study structure instead of process, parsimony and generality instead of accuracy, and thematic unity instead of interpretative caution. The result, he says, is a static analysis that misses processes of "decomposition and regroupment" between the 1860s and the late 1920s. Eley tries, he says, to recapture some of the complexities lost in the new orthodoxy, particularly structural changes taking place among right-wing elements, by focusing on the dynamics of political change. He places far less emphasis on the sustained influence of the Junkers from 1871 to 1944. However, he contends that when the old industrial-agrarian power alliance was fragmenting, various complicated factors prevented industrial, mercantile, and financial capital from forming an alternative coalition. The economic privileges of the agrarian elite were therefore preserved not by the elite's sustained power as much as the inability of other economic groups to form a coalition forceful enough to deprive the Junkers of their historic rights.[40]

Eley's conclusions challenged both orthodoxies by suggesting there were only two sources of continuity in Germany. The first was the unevenly developing capitalist mode of production, with its social relations of subordination and exploitation and processes of reproduction. The second was the recurrence of problems in a tumultuous process of change. By Eley's admission, the state in this pluralistic analysis is a framework for containing and negotiating antagonisms. It was an "arena of power" rather than an "instrument of domination."[41]

One can make the same criticism of Eley that he leveled against Wehler—that he has created more problems than he has solved.[42]

[38]Eley, *Reshaping the German Right,* p. 11.
[39]Ibid., pp. 11–13.
[40]Ibid., pp. 13, 301, 308, 351.
[41]Ibid., pp. 353–54.
[42]Eley, *From Unification to Nazism,* p. 11.

Eley's refusal to concede more than minimal significance to the concept of continuity leaves little room for the development of broad theoretical insights. Yet he does point to one factor important to our concerns: the tendency among historians to stress the structural relationship between the Second and Third Empires and thereby, in effect, subdivide German history into discrete periods.[43] The result has been a literature that neglects the relationship—structural or otherwise—between the Third Reich and the Bonn Republic. Eley recommends an alternative focus, the consequences of the *embourgeoisement* of German society. He thus replaces an emphasis on the continuity of the authoritarian political process with one that stresses the continuity of capitalist development.

The issue of continuity and change has been central to the historical debate about war and the rise of fascism, but there has been no comparable debate about continuity between fascist rule and post-fascist Germany. Two factors helped analytically sever the Bonn Republic from its fascist past. First, Fischer, Gerschenkron, and Wehler all accept the central role of the Junker class as upholders of the authoritarian tradition. All three scholars assume, Gerschenkron most explicitly, that the destruction of the Junkers destroyed the social basis of German authoritarianism and therefore removed a major impediment to the development of German democracy.[44] Soviet tanks achieved what the Weimar Republic could not, and so the Bonn Republic began anew. This approach is consistent with contemporary discussions about German reunification that seek to allay security concerns by stressing the new character of the German right. Second, a common belief in Allied success in the 4 Ds—denazification, decartelization, democratization, and demilitarization—also helped popularize the view that the Bonn Republic had been decoupled from its fascist past.[45] East German historians contributed to this tendency by treating fascist Germany as an entity distinct from the German Democratic Republic's new socialism. Both arguments contain elements of truth. The Junker class was destroyed, and some 4 D policies were successfully implemented. But in accepting change in the transition from fascism to occupation and then corporatism, the current historical literature fails to identify continuities that transcend the Bonn Republic and the Third Reich. The Junker class may have been completely destroyed, but the same cannot

---

[43]Eley, *Reshaping the German Right,* pp. 3, 254.
[44]Gerschenkron, *Bread and Democracy,* p. vii.
[45]See John Montgomery, *Forced to Be Free: The Artificial Revolution in Germany and Japan* (Chicago: University of Chicago Press, 1957); and Robert Wolfe, *Americans as Proconsuls: United States Military Government in Germany and Japan, 1944–1952* (Carbondale: Southern Illinois University Press, 1984).

be said of the industrial bourgeoisie upon whom Eley places so much emphasis. Similarly, some 4 D policies were unsuccessful (as is evident in the studies of German automobile firms in Chapters 4 and 5). The automobile industry exhibits continuities in the nature and structure of capitalism and the industrial bourgeoisie; so does the dominant state ideology, as reflected in some critical state institutions and the policies those institutions generate; and thus in the state's segmentation of producers. By adopting Eley's approach we can identify the interactive process by which both the ideology and the institutions of the Bonn state retained structural elements initially introduced under fascism.

But historians have not done so. Instead, the contemporary debate, collectively termed the *Historikerstreit,* has focused on whether the Holocaust, the "Final solution of the Jewish question," is an event open to comparative analysis.[46] This debate is about whether German nationhood is forever tainted amid charges "that prestigious German historians were seeking to 'relativize' the Final Solution as part of a new nationalist and conservative search for a usable past."[47] It is neither prudent nor appropriate for this book to join this debate. Suffice it to note that the contemporary focus on this issue partially explains why historians and political scientists neglect explicitly to examine the issue of continuity between the Third Reich and what Edwin Hartrich has referred to as "the Fourth and Richest Reich."[48]

This brief review of the treatment of continuity and change in the study of German political history reveals some interesting conclusions. Proponents of both Ranke's and Fischer's views have embraced structural arguments and encountered significant criticisms from a British historian adopting a more typically individualistic, antistructural approach. Eley implies the structuralists demonstrate a willingness to ignore complexity for the sake of simplicity and detail for the sake of parsimony, thus maintaining thematic unity or ideological coherence at the risk of ignoring or distorting empirical evidence. Eley provides some lessons that inform this book's analysis. First, scholars who stress the notion of continuity in the study of Germany need to integrate clear theoretical links with sound empirical evidence. Second, the inte-

[46]The conservative position is presented in Rudolph Augstein et al., *Historikerstreit: Die Dokumentation der Kontroverse um die Einzigartigkeit der nationalsozialistischen Judenvernichtung* (Munich: Piper, 1987). For a summary of the debate see Norbert Kampe, "Normalizing the Holocaust? The Recent Historians' Debate in the Federal Republic of Germany," *Holocaust and Genocide Studies* 2 (1987), pp. 61–90.

[47]Charles Maier, *The Unmasterable Past: History, Holocaust, and the German National Identity* (Cambridge: Harvard University Press, 1988), pp. 1–2.

[48]Edwin Hartrich, *The Fourth and Richest Reich* (New York: Macmillan, 1980).

grative reciprocity of ideologies and institutions alerts one to possible continuities marking the transition from the Third Reich to the Bonn Republic—one area neglected by this literature.

Critics of the neo-Rankeans rejected the ideological, autonomous state in favor of a class-based analysis of social forces and thus collapsed two concepts—the capacity of the state to think independently (its degree of coherence) and its relative capacity to implement policy (its autonomy). Certainly the state may not be perfectly autonomous or coherent, but state coherence and autonomy are relative and separable concepts that vary with context. For example, states may be able to formulate policy goals without effectively implementing them or be able to implement the policies of a coalition of social forces effectively but not formulate independent policies. Coherence and autonomy do not move in "lock step." By implication, a focus on the ideological strands, resulting policies, and structural legacies of the Nazi state identify continuities—in ideas, structures, and policies—with post-fascist Germany. This book does so, but unlike these orthodoxies, it employs microhistorical analysis and confines its generalizations to the empirical evidence.

How do the political economists explain the origins of the Bonn economy's structure and prosperity? The next section considers the argument that this prosperity can be traced to the Wilhelmine economic structure and then justifies an alternative explanation that focuses on state policy in the fascist period.

POLITICAL ECONOMY AND THE BONN REPUBLIC

Political economists attempting to account for either the structure or the relative prosperity of the Bonn economy have generally ignored the importance of the Third Reich. The most popular line of argument traces continuities in the capitalist structure of the German economy from unification in the 1870s to the present, holding that within those antecedent conditions lies the explanation of contemporary prosperity. Much of this line of argument recalls the work of two noted political sociologists who focused on this earlier period, Alexander Gerschenkron and Rudolf Hilferding, although as we shall see, historians have argued that their concepts have a limited utility.

Gerschenkron offers the famous "advantages of backwardness" thesis. This perspective emphasizes the significance of the relative lateness of economic development in Germany compared to other advanced industrial states. To compensate for not being the first to industrialize, the thesis holds, the state had to act as financier and entrepreneur. As a result, in Germany the state developed close contacts with industrial leaders. According to Gerschenkron, this pattern differed from other states that industrialized earlier, notably Britain, where the state was less interventionist.[49] Interestingly, according to Gerschenkron, in order to perform many of these functions the state develops both directive and authoritarian characteristics.[50] The evidence amassed by historians questions this explanation. John Gillingham's description of business-government relations in the Ruhr and Peter Hayes's account of the chemical industry in the Bismarckian and Wilhelmine periods suggest that the government's role was generally facilitative and integrative rather than directive.[51]

Nonetheless, the idea that the state's character is functionally defined at the time of entry into the world political economy has tremendous utility, and it has been widely adapted and expanded in political economy.[52] The "advantages of backwardness" thesis purportedly explains, parsimoniously, variations among domestic structures in advanced industrial states and why some economies seem better suited to the contemporary demands of an evolving capitalist system. The logic of Gerschenkron's argument suggests that as the state's organizational form becomes outmoded, the state has less capacity to facilitate the organization of an efficient economy. The state's lack of institutional adaptation reduces its capacity to generate economic prosperity.[53] Such an argument parsimoniously explains Britain's twentieth-century economic decline. Gerschenkron's approach is one from which, David Calleo suggests, Kehr (and presumably Eley) would dissent because it emphasizes the structure of power relations prior to and during the early stages of unification—and thus discounts the importance of the interactive process since unification.[54] Scholars who stress the impulses of the Second Empire (as Kehr or Eley do) or the Third empire (as I

[49]For a study employing Gerschenkron's basic theme see John Zysman, *Governments, Markets, and Growth: Financial Systems and the Politics of Industrial Change* (Ithaca: Cornell University Press, 1983), particularly pp. 289–92.

[50]Gerschenkron, *Economic Backwardness*, pp. 5–30.

[51]John Gillingham, *Industry and Politics in the Third Reich: Ruhr Coal, Hitler, and Europe* (London: Methuen, 1985); and Peter Hayes, *Industry and Ideology: IG Farben in the Nazi Era* (New York: Cambridge University Press, 1987).

[52]On timing of entry into the world political economy as critical to state and economy see Fernando Henrique Cardoso and Enzo Faletto, *Dependency and Development in Latin America* (Berkeley: University of California Press, 1979); and Peter J. Katzenstein, *Small States in World Markets* (Ithaca: Cornell University Press, 1985), pp. 201–3.

[53]A notable application of this concept is Peter J. Katzenstein, "Conclusion: Domestic Structures and the Strategies of Foreign Economic Policy," in his edited volume *Between Power and Plenty: Foreign Economic Policies of Advanced Industrial States* (Madison: University of Wisconsin Press, 1978), pp. 324–25.

[54]David P. Calleo, *The German Problem Reconsidered: Germany and the World Order, 1870 to the Present* (New York: Cambridge University Press, 1978), pp. 73–84.

do) at least begin to dilute the validity of Gerschenkron's analysis as a comprehensive explanation of Germany's contemporary economic structure.

In many dimensions Rudolf Hilferding's analysis is consistent with Gerschenkron. His radical perspective, developed in the Wilhelmine period, focuses on the relationship between the state, heavy industry, and the banks (as representatives of finance capital) in Germany before World War I. He suggests their close relationship facilitated an increasing economic concentration based on the development of cartels and trusts in which the banks proved dominant, organizing industry into a coordinated group of large corporations.[55] These corporations, in a process of vertical and horizontal integration, increasingly planned the process of economic development, and small industry and the working class shared a disproportionately high burden of the costs of these economic policies.[56] Hilferding identified this pattern as a system of "organized capitalism." Richard Evans suggests that the concept

> has been developed in an effort to work out an alternative model to that put forward by East German historians under the term "state monopoly capitalism." Organized capitalism has been described as "a concentrated and bureaucratized economic order, organized in voluntary associations (*Verbände*) and assured the capacity to function by a variety of governmental measures." In place of free competition, industry constructed cartels and monopolies. These were backed by controls introduced by an increasingly interventionist state in an attempt to manage the economy so as to minimize social tensions created by economic crises.[57]

Wehler, for one, was much taken with the concept. In describing the motive, structure, principles, and goals of the corporations that favored "organized capitalism," he suggests that

> this new form of "cartel capitalism" of big business, which emerged from the end of the 1870s onwards, strove to ensure, to an unprecedented degree, economic stability, the rational calculation of commercial opportunities and prosperity by means of secure profits for the individual firm or, on a larger scale, through cooperation between members of the oligopoly. . . . The effects of irregular growth, inherent in the economic system with all its consequences, were to be ameliorated by forms of short-term substitute planning worked out by the interested parties. There remained less and less room in this "organized capitalism" for liberal

[55]Hilferding, *Finance Capital*, pp. 162–63, 213, and, most critically, 368.
[56]See Tom Bottomore, "Introduction to the Translation," in Hilferding, *Finance Capital*, pp. 5–6.
[57]Evans, "Introduction: Wilhelm II's Germany," p. 26.

competition, which acted as a price regulator, for the autonomy of industrial enterprises, or for the acquisition of profit as a reward for individual risk-taking. In many ways this new brand of capitalist organization was influenced by the general view that modern industrial development could no longer be left to the self-regulation of the market in the sense of Adam Smith's "Invisible Hand." At the same time, however, the camouflage of a liberal market economy was retained.[58]

Cartels, designed to achieve productive efficiency, became commonplace, initially as a temporary protective measure during the depression of the late nineteenth century and then as a permanent feature in the Bismarckian and Wilhelmine economies. Contemporary adaptation and application of Hilferding's theories tend to focus on the centrality of cartels and combines, particularly as post-Keynesian scholars seek to offer a prescriptive rival vision to monetarism.[59] Yet both the concept and its usage raise interesting issues and have to bear criticism.

One fundamental issue, already raised in this chapter, concerns the distribution of power between state and social actors—specifically, the state's relative autonomy. Fischer, Gerschenkron, Hilferding, and Wehler all conceived of the state as an instrument of social forces rather than as the more autonomous state implicitly identified by the neo-Rankeans. The former view created a paradoxical image: an authoritarian state in which the state was an instrument subject to the discipline of a certain social coalition or class. Private interests, in the form of corporations and banks, held decision-making power over an authoritarian state in the area of economic policy. One study consistent with this perspective is Richard Owen's examination of Gustav Krupp's relationship with the Imperial Navy Office. Owen reveals that Krupp felt powerful enough to explicitly threaten withdrawal of his company's support for Germany's shipbuilding program if Tirpitz, secretary of the navy, did not prove more cooperative. Owen suggests it is difficult to judge who used whom, but he concludes that armaments firms exploited the state's dependence on them to full effect—suggesting a maldistribution of power in favor of the private sector.[60]

A second issue raised by Hilferding's analysis is identified by historians critical of the empirical utility of "organized capitalism" and its application to Germany's prefascist history. Richard Evans notes that

---

[58]Wehler, *The German Empire*, pp. 43–44.

[59]For explicit reference to Hilferding's contribution see Christopher S. Allen, "The Underdevelopment of Keynesianism in the Federal Republic of Germany," in Peter A. Hall, ed., *The Political Power of Economic Ideas: Keynesianism across Nations* (Princeton: Princeton University Press, 1989).

[60]Richard Owen, "Military-Industrial Relations: Krupp and the Imperial Navy Office," in Evans, *Society and Politics*, pp. 79, 84.

most of those scholars "who have developed the idea of 'organized capitalism' have used it as a general theory encompassing the whole development of the German economy over a long period, rather than actually carrying out any detailed research with its aid or selecting any specific problem of state-industry relations as a test case of its value and utility."[61] Hayes's examination of IG Farben is one of the few to escape this criticism. Interestingly, although it supports the notion that the chemical industry formed cartels to protect firms against the effects of the Depression, Hayes does not explicitly employ the concept of organized capitalism.[62] Gerald Feldman did consciously attempt to apply the concept, to the German iron and steel industry between 1916 and 1923. He concluded the concept was too vague to be useful, noting two sources of continued tension: conflicts of interest between major firms and the cartel's other members, and between the major firms and the state. Furthermore, while Feldman confirmed Hilferding's claim that the state could not impose its wishes on the leaders of heavy industry, it specifically rejected the notion that the representatives of finance capital dominated heavy industry.[63]

Evans and Feldman therefore pose questions about the utility of the concept of organized capitalism in the prefascist era. But given the destruction of cartels as a basis of private power by the Nazi government, a third issue needs to be squarely addressed: the sustained explanatory utility of the concept of organized capitalism for the postwar period.

Let us for a moment accept that Hilferding was correct. Cartels, as the institutional basis for organized capitalism, were the dominant economic force in the Weimar Republic and therefore provided the legitimating basis for self-regulation. Proponents of this view stress the codification of the 1923 Cartel Law, which granted firms voluntary membership in a cartel and therefore allowed them the luxury of choosing among exit, voice, and loyalty. Yet the nature and functions of these cartels changed immediately and drastically when the Nazi party took power. A postwar Military Government discussion paper captures this dramatic change:

> The National Socialists' conception of a cartel was quite different from that of their predecessors. To them the cartel was not merely a medium whereby the leaders of a certain branch of industry exerted control over individual producers; it was also a tool to be used by the state for its own

[61]Evans, "Introduction: Wilhelm II's Germany," p. 26.
[62]See, for example, Hayes, *Industry and Ideology*, pp. 32–46.
[63]Gerald Feldman, *Iron and Steel in the German Inflation, 1916–1923* (Princeton: Princeton University Press, 1977), pp. 5–40.

purposes, whether political or economic. Formerly cartels had existed to
fix sales prices, production and territorial quotas, or to pool patents, exchange technology information and the like. Cartel agreements were
everywhere accepted as binding on the contracting parties (although not
on outsiders) until nullified by competent authority. But the new centralized Third Reich, determined to rule untroubled by any sort of rival
authority, viewed with alarm any large concentration of economic power
in the hands of privately controlled, independent associations, whether
they be political parties or cartels; so, under the Nazis, cartels were converted into instruments of economic planning to be used only with the
consent and under the supervision of the state. Regulation of prices, quantities, and the kinds of material to be produced, to say nothing of controlling capital investment, were being considered in the interest of a new
military economy, and cartels were to be one of the instruments for their
effectuation. This policy was to be implemented by forced consolidation,
compulsory membership features, application of the leadership principle,
withdrawal of former marketing functions, and imposition of government
administrative duties.[64]

This process began on 15 July 1933 when the new Nazi government
amended the 1923 Cartel Law. Henceforth the reichminister of economics could unilaterally invalidate all cartel agreements without referring the matter to the Cartel Court, which had hitherto been authorized to void specific cartel contracts if petitioned to do so by the
minister. This new measure gave the state a greater potential to integrate its control over cartels, enhancing both secrecy in negotiations
and rapid decision making. Furthermore, it introduced a new, powerful discretionary tool, permitting the reichminister to constrain the
economic freedom of action of any firm he deemed to be managed by
"commercially unreliable" individuals. Characteristically, no definite
criteria were established for the evaluation of cases, no legal directives
established to regulate sentences. Judgement was on an individual
basis, and punishment was essentially arbitrary.[65]

A simultaneous decree augmented state power by authorizing the
creation of compulsory cartels to replace the old voluntary ones. It
allowed the minister of economics to combine firms into syndicates or
cartels or to affiliate them with existing associations. The criterion for
evaluation was vaguely defined as the welfare of the general economy,
and the decree specified that no indemnification was to be paid by the

[64]"Report on German Cartels and Combines 1946, Volume 1," Office of Military
Government of the U.S. (OMGUS) Files, German Economic Decartelization, Prepared by
the Decartelization Branch, 1 March 1947. Files in the Military Field Branch, National
Archives and Records Administration, Washington, D.C.
[65]Ibid., 1:41.

government to any firm for losses resulting from the law's application. A firm's choice among exit, voice, and loyalty therefore ended. As the Allied government report stated, "while recognizing the validity of the 1923 decree, it [the 1933 decree] practically nullified its value by revoking the paragraph permitting withdrawal from cartel contracts."[66]

The rules governing a cartel could be modified only with the reichminister's consent. He could decide the rights and duties of individual members of a cartel, even if they conflicted with previously negotiated contractual arrangements, and could therefore make decisions about the type or quantity of production of individual firms. Again, punishment for violation was unspecified and, in practice, unlimited. The Nazis claimed these decrees were temporary and coercion was to be the last resort, but a further decree on 5 September 1934 strengthened the state's power over both cartel members and "outsiders."[67] The Nazis claimed they were intervening in the public interest to avoid the otherwise inevitable evils of surplus capacity, market competition, and uneconomic pricing policies that were considered counterproductive to the establishment of a prosperous economy. In sum:

> The introduction of governmental price controls, of the quota system in raw materials and other commodities (administered by supervisory agencies and Foreign Exchange Control Boards), of the new hierarchical machinery controlling industry and agriculture, combined to rob the cartels of much of their former power and influence. Little by little the cartels were transformed into agents of a totalitarian government suffering from claustrophobia, bawling for "*Lebensraum*," and not averse to employing the organizational patterns of the cartel form to attain its ends. . . . In most cases, at least in the early years of the decree, the Ministers of the Third Reich preferred to force outsiders into existing cartels rather than create new ones. But despite this, and even though approximately a dozen cartels were dissolved, the number of cartels actually increased during the next few years.[68]

These early decrees were the forerunners of integrative state policies

---

[66]Ibid., 1:42.

[67]Ibid. This interesting term is instructive for my claim that a core and a periphery were formed in this period. Fordwerke was definitely treated as an outsider and was effectively excluded from the German Automobile-Treuhandgesellschaft Berlin (DAT) until 1937. This cartel was funded by the Reichsverband der Automobilindustrie E.V. and the Reichsverband des Kraftfahrzeughandels und Gewerbes E.V. For the role of the DAT see "From Law 56: The Report of the Daimler-Benz Aktiengesellschaft, Stuttgart-Unterturkheim," OMGUS, Economic Decartelization Branch, 775092, Box 305, Military Field Branch, National Archives and Records Administration, Washington, D.C.

[68]"Report on German Cartels and Combines," 1:42.

that shifted the form and locus of political and economic power rather more permanently than the Nazis had originally suggested. They destroyed the old voluntary cartels, and with them the power base of private vested interests.[69] This destruction has implications for the validity of the concepts of continuity and change in the study of contemporary German prosperity. The Nazis' comprehensive destruction of these private institutions and the simultaneous formation of new organizations based on public sector power seem to create a problem for drawing parallels between prefascist and post-fascist Germany. Historical data indicate that the destruction of the cartels complicates the assumption that the pattern of relations evident in Wilhelmine Germany could be used to explain the relative durability or prosperity of individual firms, whole sectors, or the aggregate national economy in the Bonn Republic. Political economists have effectively ignored such data.

A final, more parochial issue concerns how appropriate Hilferding's concept of organized capitalism is to the empirical focus of this book? Can Wehler's explicit description of organized capitalism—both the institutionalization of cartels and the structure of power that supposedly was its foundation—have any relevance to the development of the automobile industry and, more specifically, its degree and distribution of prosperity after 1945? Historical studies of the chemical, electronics, optical, and coal industries all approximate the pattern of cartelization consistent with Hilferding's principles of organized capitalism, but the auto industry does not reflect this pattern of development.[70]

Four important factors distinguish the automobile industry from sectors that conform to Hilferding's organized capitalism. The first is the timing of the industry's development. The chemical, electronics, optical, and coal industries all developed rapidly under Bismarck and provided much of the basis for the German economy's expansion in the Wilhelmine period. The German automobile industry did not begin to develop until the Weimar period and did not significantly expand until the Nazi period.[71] If we extend Gerschenkron's claim that the timing of a country's entry into the world capitalist economy influences its inter-

[69]Some cartel members favored these coercive measures because they forced competitors to either join the cartel or face closure. Firms that favored such schemes were therefore coopted by the state into designing and enforcing such policies. The Allied military government claimed that while these policies strengthened the state in relation to the cartel as a whole, they systematically strengthened some members of the market relative to others—a point illustrated in the German auto industry. See ibid.

[70]Fischer, *Germany's Aims,* pp. 14–16; Hayes, *Industry and Ideology,* pp. 2–46; and Gillingham, *Industry and Politics,* pp. 5–38.

[71]See Richard J. Overy, *The Nazi Economic Recovery, 1932–1938* (London: Macmillan, 1982).

nal economic structure to the sectoral level, we can assume that a sector's development is similarly influenced by timing. The industries that emerged in the Bismarckian period did so in fields where German firms acted as pioneers, and these firms expanded with the industry. The German auto firms, however, entered a sector where other producers, notably Americans, were pioneers of large-scale production.[72]

A second feature of the auto sector, also possibly related to timing of development, was its small scale in the prefascist period relative to the chemical, electronics, and coal industries. Officials of the Wilhelmine and Weimar governments shared the concerns of large corporations in these industries that they be protected from an economic downturn because the sustained economic prosperity of these individual firms was central to the nation's economic welfare. The state saw critical firms in fulcrum sectors that warranted careful nurturing and regular contact between state officials and business leaders.[73] This was not true of an automobile sector composed of small firms that wielded no political influence, had little economic leverage, and therefore could do little to influence government policy. Given the sector's minimal impact on the economy, and its reduced impact on national defense after the conclusion of the Versailles Treaty, it was generally neglected by successive governments who considered its welfare of trivial importance.

The third factor distinguishing the automobile industry from other sectors was the nature of the product. As dealers in a consumer durable rather than extractors of a raw material or producers of machine tools, automobile producers competed in an area where logic demanded that they differentiate their product from their competitors'. For coal producers differentiation was not an issue; they had an incentive to act collectively to raise coal's market price. But one of the secrets of selling cars is to take a product that may be no different from a competitor's and to create the illusion of superiority. This prerequisite militated against the formation of cartels, as did an excessive number of firms in a small domestic market without a large export outlet. According to Fischer, the alternative pattern of industrial development of the German textile industry, another consumer products sector, resembled that evident in the automobile industry.[74]

---

[72]For the technically underdeveloped state of domestic German firms before 1933 see Anita Kugler, "Von der Werkstatt zum Fliessband: Etappen der frühen Automobilproduktion in Deutschland," *Geschichte und Gesellschaft* 13 (1987), pp. 304–39.

[73]Fischer, *Germany's Aims*, p. 17. See also David Abraham, *Collapse of the Weimar Republic* (Princeton: Princeton University Press, 1981). Despite the controversy surrounding Abraham's interpretation, he does support the claim that business and government shared a close relationship.

[74]Fischer, *Germany's Aims*, p. 14. For the textile industry and innovations under fascism see Werner Hagemann, "Zur Entwicklung der Bekleidungsindustrie," in Ernst Melzer, ed., *Die Bekleidungsindustrie* (Darmstadt: Elsner, 1955), pp. 1–15.

The fourth and probably critical feature of the auto industry was the presence of foreign firms with extensive domestic manufacturing facilities. Ford formed its own subsidiary and began local production in 1926, and General Motors purchased Opel in 1929. These subsidiaries were two of the larger and more dynamic firms producing in Germany, and for four reasons their presence created an impenetrable barrier to the formation of a cartel. First, as by far the largest, most efficient, and most profitable firm, Opel had no interest in subjugating itself to the discipline of a cartel. The firm could outproduce and undercut the price of any domestic competitor, so it made little economic sense to subject itself to the constraints of a cartel. Second, American subsidiaries enjoyed technological advantages over firms under domestic ownership, such as the use of mass production principles, and so would derive little benefit from the normal cartel agreements that generated joint technical research and development agreements. Third, cartels were designed to protect firms against the vagaries of the product cycle and political instability. The Detroit owners and managers of these firms, relatively small subsidiaries of large, wealthy multinational corporations, were not as risk-averse as the family owners of smaller, poorer domestic competitors. These subsidiaries had relatively greater resources, so their Detroit owners were far less concerned about cyclical sales patterns. Furthermore, as foreigners not immersed in Germany's political history or culture, the owners were less sensitive to concerns about economic or political instability. Finally, and probably most important, the guiding philosophy behind both parent companies was classic entrepreneurial capitalism and free market competition. Ford's and General Motors' owners wanted their German subsidiaries to avoid every possible nonmarket limitation.

The presence of foreign ownership was rare among Germany's leading economic sectors. Foreign owners existed in other sectors, for example French owners of coal and steel plants, but these firms were responsible for a very small percentage of output. They were subject to economic and political pressure from other producers in their sector and therefore had to conform to cartel agreements. The auto industry was unique because it was the only major German economic sector where foreign firms were the dominant producers. The effect of their presence, bearing in mind their attitude toward voluntary cartels, was to fragment the potential unity of owners. Cartels may have developed in other sectors because of the influence of the banks, but here the German banks had little leverage. Thus the auto sector did not follow the classic pattern of German industrial development. To consider the traditional explanation of organized capitalism as responsible for the auto industry's postwar prosperity therefore seems inappropriate.

Four factors distinguish the automobile sector from other traditional, large economic sectors, so it is reasonable to question the relevance of the auto sector at all. I will emphasize first that this book seeks to make no generalizations about the relationship between Nazi state policy and subsequent German prosperity beyond evidence relating to the automobile industry. I therefore do not intend to draw broad conclusions about other sectors based on my study of a single sector. If, however, I can justifiably demonstrate that the degree and distribution of prosperity in Germany's postwar auto industry was dependent on Nazi state policies, then I will have gone a long way toward explaining the Federal Republic's economic vitality in the 1950s, because the domestic auto industry in the late 1940s, the 1950s, and the 1960s constituted the new Federal Republic's elite economic sector—largely due to its growth under the Third Reich.[75] Between 1933 and 1939 alone, German motor truck output grew by 263 percent, car output by 74 percent, and motorcycle output by 176 percent. The industry, in aggregate, generated the second largest income from sales after coal mining.[76] The Adenauer and Erhard governments considered the postwar economic welfare of the domestically owned auto firms (primarily Volkswagen and Daimler-Benz) to be critically important because those firms were two of Germany's most profitable, its largest exporters, and, correspondingly, its highest earners of critical foreign currency.[77] Political importance in the early Bonn Republic was enhanced by new status as major employers. If we then include the smaller auto firms and foreign-owned subsidiaries and consider the sector as a whole, the auto industry was clearly the dominant postwar German sector. If I can present evidence to sustain the claim that Nazi state policies are critical to the auto industry's degree and distribution of power in the postwar period, I will have done much to explain the basis of German postwar prosperity without making a claim about other sectors.

In many ways the discussion among historians and political econo-

---

[75]For the significance of the auto sector to the general economy see Overy, *The Nazi Economic Recovery*, pp. 36, 49; and his "Cars, Roads, and Economic Recovery in Germany, 1932–8" in *Economic History Review*, 2d ser., 28 (1975), pp. 467–83. For its postwar strategic significance see Glen Yago, *The Decline of Transit* (New York: Cambridge University Press, 1984).

[76]United States Strategic Bombing Survey (USSBS), Munitions Division Report, "German Motor Vehicles Industry," 3 November 1945, p. 3; and Maurice Olley, "The Motor Car Industry in Germany during the Period 1939–1945," British Intelligence Objectives Sub-committee (BIOS) Report 21, Imperial War Museum (henceforth IWM), p. 7.

[77]For indicative figures on Volkswagen's and Daimler-Benz's profits, sales, export, investment, and employment figures see, for example, *Wall Street Journal*, 5 July and 6 and 20 August 1956 and 10 October 1962.

mists about the development of the German economy echoes broader tendencies to emphasize traditional structural factors and ignore modernist impulses. Contemporary political economists have used Gerschenkron and Hilferding to form structural explanations based on data from the late nineteenth and early twentieth centuries and ignored data on the Third Reich. The resulting conventional explanation links the late nineteenth century to the durability and success of the German economy in the second half of the twentieth century. It transcends the fascist period. Yet those who have tried to apply the concept of organized capitalism to Wilhelmine Germany have found its assumptions are unconfirmed by empirical data. If historians have difficulty applying the concept of organized capitalism to the early decades of this century, when it was supposedly most applicable, what chance do political scientists have in understanding the contemporary period?

Even if this criticism is discounted, the concept of organized capitalism still has little applicability to the auto industry, which was reorganized by an autonomous state, legitimated by a nationalist ideology, that employed a discriminatory set of policies. Yet despite this fundamental difference from other sectors, its focal importance is clear. It stems from its centrality to post-fascist German prosperity.

Contemporary work that heavily relies on Hilferding and Gerschenkron lacks an important historical dimension. Hilferding's analysis preceded the rise of fascism and the timing of Gerschenkron's writing meant he could effectively analyze the political and economic causes of fascism but was in no position to analyze its consequences. More recent scholars have accepted Gerschenkron's and Hilferding's analyses without recognizing fascism's contribution to an evolving context: both analyses are partial in the context of the post-fascist economy. Would Hilferding or Gerschenkron have employed the same analysis to study the economy of the Bonn Republic?

DEFINING AND LINKING REGIME TYPES

Both historians and political economists have neglected the relationship between the Third Reich and the Bonn Republic. Political scientists have developed typologies that deemphasize the link between fascist and corporatist regimes. It is as if regimes are simply typologies that are static, suggesting there is no relationship between a country now governed by a liberal democracy and its authoritarian past. In this section I examine how the three regimes (corporatism, fascism and liberalism) that have governed Germany and Britain have been, and can be, defined. Britain is generally characterized as having had a sustained liberal form of government; Germany, as having variants of corporatism punctuated by twelve years of fascist rule. I consider to what extent and how corporatism and fascism have been institutionally and ideologically related in the Bonn Republic.

So far in this book I have avoided a definition of liberal, fascist, and corporatist regimes. Neglecting operational distinctions risks interpretation of my argument as the vulgar claim that all countries once governed by fascist regimes are still in some sense "fascist" and that I somehow regard their contemporary democratic characteristics as ephemeral. This is not so, although one consequence of this discussion may be to balance some benign descriptions of contemporary corporatism in central, northern, and Western European states with recognition of some coercive aspects of state policies in postfascist, corporatist regimes that find their historical origins in the fascist period.[78] Nor do I want to be accused of drawing a caricature of these three political regimes. It is not my intention to provide a holistic definition of what constitutes a liberal, fascist, or corporatist regime. Rich literatures address these definitional questions, and I note them only briefly in the following pages. Rather, I concentrate on providing operational definitions that distinguish these three types of regimes in terms of the economic policy of the state. I recognize the incomplete nature of this exercise, but only this aspect of these literatures is relevant to my line of enquiry. I make fundamental distinctions between state economic policies in different regimes by focusing on the state's attitude to central planning and the marketplace; its willingness and capacity to intervene at macro, sectoral, and individual corporate levels; its capacity to articulate policy goals and its willingness and capacity to use coercive policies to achieve those goals; and finally, and most important, the state's willingness to discriminate among domestic firms in its economy.

Liberalism

Half this book purports to explain the driving motives for and consequences of state policies in Britain; half of the empirical material is devoted to the study of Britain. Yet as this chapter is concerned with the themes of continuity and change in Germany, and as what distinguishes postwar Germany from Britain are changes instituted by the fascist state, we risk ignoring the importance of continuity in explaining British economic development. The relationships between state

---

[78]For examples of benign views see Katzenstein on the "seven dwarfs" in *Small States*, pp. 136–90, and Wolfgang Streeck in *Industrial Relations in West Germany: A Case Study of the Car Industry* (New York: St. Martin's, 1984).

and individual firms in the British and German auto sectors were converging in the early 1920s as both governments relied on a nondiscriminatory ideology as the basis for allowing a free flow of investment capital. As a result, American subsidiaries became the most dynamic firms in both countries and, despite their varying problems, were poised to become the leading producers on the eve of the Nazi seizure of power. In sum, despite many national differences between Britain and Germany in the early 1930s, the nature of state policies and the structure of the market in the automobile sector looked surprisingly similar, converging toward what I will define as liberalism. The German economy never made an aggregate shift to a liberal economy, only to a societal corporatism. But for reasons already discussed, the auto industry differed from other sectors and its characteristics resembled those found in a liberal regime. Historically, the 1920s and early 1930s, and analytically liberalism itself, form the benchmark for this book. Both auto sectors looked remarkably alike in the early 1930s and very different by the late 1940s. I argue that this difference was the result of fascist state policies. If the German state had sustained liberal policies in the automobile sector instead of shifting toward discriminatory, fascist economic policies, then presumably the sector would have looked a lot more like the British auto sector in the postwar period.

Classical Ricardian liberalism is an economistic theory that focuses on the market as the determinant of consumer behavior. Individuals or firms are the consumers, and the state has a minimal role as upholder of the "rules of the game" in an analysis that emphasizes social forces. In a world exclusively defined in terms of consumers and producers, significance is heavily weighted toward the rights of consumers, as reflected in the justifications for antimonopoly legislation. The objective of society is to maximize economic efficiency and thus social welfare. Thus, as Robert Gilpin notes, "Property rights are said to be created or abandoned depending on their social utility and especially their contribution to the efficient economic organization of society." As liberalism has evolved, its political dimensions, specifically the roles of the state, have taken on greater significance. Contemporary liberalism, and scholars working in the tradition, recognize that even the most devoted liberals do not pursue policies consistent with pure open-market principles. Even such scholars as Douglass North and Robert Thomas recognize the significance of the state's role in defining and protecting property relations so that a society's private rate of return approaches its social rate of return.[79] Pluralist theorists have adapted

[79]Robert Gilpin, *War and Change in World Politics* (New York: Cambridge University Press, 1981), p. 74; Douglass C. North and Robert P. Thomas, *The Rise of the Western*

liberal theory to the political realm and depicted the state as an umpire who facilitates competitive interaction among interest groups.[80] Yet, the state must exercise some limited degree of autonomy in formulating and adapting these rules, making choices that are reflected in state policy and have major economic consequences for consumers, whether individuals or firms.[81]

The state's choices stem from a combination of the dominance of a particular ideology and a developing institutional context. Although liberal states may have fewer instruments for the formulation, articulation, and implementation of policy than other sorts of states, and therefore may reasonably be adjudged to have less autonomy in relation to social actors, they still derive a degree of policy coherence from a combination of institutional limits and ideological preferences. Even in this limited sense, liberal states are therefore active and interventionist. Yet governmental options in a liberal state on matters such as trade policy are constrained by three sets of factors. The first set is institutional; they relate to the fragmentation of power and decentralization of decision making. The second set is ideological, specifically the dominance of liberal assumptions about state structure, the positive-sum nature of open markets, and the key role of multinational firms in generating and distributing global wealth. Liberal ideology provides intellectual justification for the free movement of capital, thus encouraging direct investment by foreigners, and is buttressed by the claim that the postwar global economy is now an interdependent system from which it is both practically unfeasible and normatively undesirable to extricate a national economy.[82] The third set of constraints are pragmatic concerns about employment and balance of payments figures. Liberal economic theory assumes that short-term economic costs of adjustment, such as the bankruptcy of firms, increased unemployment, or an enlarged balance of payments deficit caused by unprotected trade, are tolerable if they are exchanged for greater long-term efficiency. This logic also dictates that foreign firms be encouraged to invest domestically because they provide jobs and stimulate competi-

---

World: A New Economic History (Cambridge: Cambridge University Press, 1973), pp. 1–15. The definitive critique of this liberal approach is Karl Polanyi, *The Great Transformation: The Political and Economic Origins of Our Time* (Boston: Beacon, 1957), pp. 33–129.

[80]For such traditional descriptions see David Truman, *The Governmental Process* (New York: Knopf, 1951); and Robert Dahl, *Who Governs?* (New Haven: Yale University Press, 1961).

[81]For an early critique of pluralist analysis see Elmer E. Schattschneider, *The Semi-Sovereign People: A Realist's View of Democracy in America* (New York: Holt, Rinehart & Winston, 1960).

[82]For example see Richard Cooper, "Economic Interdependence and Foreign Policy in the 1970s," *World Politics* 24 (January 1972), pp. 159–81.

tion. The economic logic of liberalism is therefore to accept short-term adjustment costs caused by the free flow of capital or of finished products in order to achieve a long-term remedy.

Yet the incentive structure created by the political process in a liberal state pushes politicians to seek short-term solutions that effectively ignore long-term costs because the comprehensive economic change often advocated by liberal economic theory is politically destabilizing. The fragmented nature of the political system ensures that change is incremental. In the United States, in contrast to small European corporatist states that successfully link short-term economic flexibility to long-term political stability, economic objectives and the political process therefore pull in different directions. This is because the dominant liberal economic ideology calls for long-term, market-oriented solutions while the democratic political process demands some form of short-term, circumscribed government intervention that emphasizes the benefits of job protection and an improved balance of payments but leads to accusations that politics poisons the economic process. As a result, a free flow of capital investment is encouraged but a free flow of goods discouraged.

Focusing on the political and economic behavior of liberal states, rather than liberal economic theory, prompts some assertions that contradict traditional expectations. Foremost, liberal states do not let markets operate autonomously as the determinant of political behavior, because the political costs of extreme, dislocating market forces would be too destabilizing. Instead, political decisions determine the structure of markets by defining the nature of property relations and, therefore, limit the array of economic outcomes.[83] Most pointedly, socioeconomic groups and states in liberal regimes profess devotion to market forces, but they seek to curb excessive effects. Liberal states can intervene to manipulate market forces in very few ways, however, because ideological and institutional factors combine to limit state capacity. The principles of liberal ideology lead to the development of few interventionist

[83]Thus I explicitly assume that an economic system is not the autonomous entity of neoclassical economics. See North and Thomas, *Rise of the Western World*. Rather, the predominant form of economic exchange in any society is embedded in a system of property rights that are determined by the political system. The nature of class relations and the sustained development of the capitalist system therefore are not economically determined, as suggested by classical Marxism, nor are markets autonomous, as suggested by neoclassical economics. State institutions have the capacity politically and economically to structure and restructure both economic classes and political coalitions. This view of the state as more than "the executive committee of the bourgeoisie" is discussed in Polanyi, *The Great Transformation*. It is by no means incompatible with a Marxist position; see Timothy Mason, "The Primacy of Politics: Politics and Economics in National Socialist Germany," in S. J. Woolf, ed., *The Nature of Fascism* (London: Weidenfield & Nicholson, 1969), pp. 165–95.

instruments, and the absence of examples of effective intervention sustains a belief in the efficacy of limited intervention. One practical effect is that liberal states lack the apparatus to reverse a sector's economic decline. The familiar response is to reduce the immediate effects of a loss of competitiveness by pushing the cost of adjustment on to foreign competitors.

If a strategy designed to externalize adjustment fails, the state must decide how to distribute the burden among domestic actors. Perhaps the single most characteristic feature of liberal states is their willingness to try to ensure the equitable distribution of costs among all producers in any sector. Egalitarian distribution of burdens is predicated on a cornerstone of liberalism: the protection of fair markets, commonly termed the "level playing field." This nondiscriminatory policy is important in three ways. First, liberal states, although they regulate against the import of finished products, do allow all domestically located producers access to domestic markets free of formal and informal barriers. Neither formally nor informally do they favor domestic producers over multinational subsidiaries that site production within their borders.[84] Second, foreign firms generally benefit from the political sensitivity of liberal states to the issue of unemployment. Liberal states are willing to "bail out" potentially bankrupt firms, regardless of whether they are under foreign or domestic ownership. Third, liberal regimes ironically constrain firms from becoming too successful, by legislating against monopolies through extensive antitrust legislation and specifically avoiding favoritism. Under these conditions, no firm will ever dominate, but those firms with the greatest access to resources will benefit from equal state treatment.

When the concept of national treatment is invoked, domestic firms operate under numerous political and economic constraints that foreign firms escape because they have the option of going elsewhere. Domestic firms seem to be burdened with all the obligations and few of the rights and privileges. It is not that states seek intentionally to discriminate against domestic firms. But knowing that domestic firms have few options, states can afford to make them conform to numerous obligations associated with citizenry. States, however, often believe that too many demands on foreign firms may provoke the withdrawal of domestic investment. The position of a subsidiary of a foreign multinational corporation is reminiscent of a grandparent's relationship to a newborn child; like grandparents, foreign firms receive all the rights

---

[84]See Daniel T. Jones, *Industrial Adjustment and Policy: 1. Maturity and Crisis in the European Car Industry* (Lewes: Sussex European Research Center, 1981), p. 45; and A. Black, "Neomercantilism in the Automobile Industry," Discussion Paper IIVG (Berlin: Wissenschaftszentrum, n.d.), pp. 6–12.

and privileges associated with citizenry and few of the obligations. Policies based on egalitarian treatment, therefore, often encourage a maldistribution of resources. If a large foreign multinational corporation competes against a smaller domestic firm, the multinational will always dominate the domestic market. Furthermore, in the development of what Theodore J. Lowi refers to as "irresponsible government," states in liberal regimes are unwilling to pick winners but, paradoxically, are willing to underwrite what Daniel Jones calls "the risk of all those who produce within their borders."[85]

Yet the consequence of their policies is that they effectively do pick winners. The governing philosophy may be egalitarian, but the distributive effects are different: some actors gain more than others. Indeed, one of the major claims I examine later is that British policies based on egalitarian principles created an advantage for the subsidiaries of American firms. The commitment to what the current American government terms "national treatment" extends to unlimited access to markets and information, as well as financial aid.[86] Some firms still fare better than others because of the technological, financial, and strategic advantages that distinguish competitors in any sector. Equal treatment therefore does not guarantee equal performance, but the system discriminates against winners by limiting rewards. However, this pattern of unequal distribution of wealth is generally the outcome not of a noninterventionist government policy but of a nondiscriminatory government policy. Liberal states therefore cannot serve the "national interest" in the broader manner defined by dirigiste states because they cannot control social actors or market forces. At best they can only distribute the burden of market forces.

Given these institutional and ideological limitations, liberal states avoid involvement in central planning whenever possible. Jack Hayward says that British governments are effectively unable to plan, in contrast to their European counterparts, because they hold a pluralistic conception of power and authority and lack a suitable institutional apparatus. British governments have few forums for articulating policy. When they do intervene, they simply try to persuade socioeconomic actors of the efficacy of their policies, whereas European governments employ comprehensive, discriminatory policies.[87] Studies of British at-

---

[85]Theodore J. Lowi, *The End of Liberalism* (New York: Norton, 1979); Jones, *Industrial Adjustment,* pp. 49–50. This is the term used by Jones to describe the Labour government's decision in the Chrysler case of 1975.

[86]Jones claims that the nature of intervention makes British governments capable only of reinforcing the weaknesses of a company like British Leyland, not its strengths. *Industrial Adjustment,* p. 51.

[87]Jack Hayward, "Change and Choice: The Agenda of Planning," in Hayward and Michael Watson, *Planning, Politics, and Public Policy* (Cambridge: Cambridge University Press, 1975), pp. 5–6, 17.

tempts to develop central planning reveal some of the limitations facing British governments from their ideology, internal institutional structure, and relationship with the private sector.[88] The limited success of prices and incomes policies in Britain since 1945 exemplifies the failure of the state to sustain tripartite institutions. As Hayward suggests, "the consensus that existed in Britain until the 1970s that price control by government was inconceivable and impracticable, despite the fact that it had been practiced for decades in France, mainly by governments of the Right, was a typical example of the self-restraining manner in which British government has worked to circumscribe both the range of problems to be faced and the kinds of action where use could be contemplated."[89] Consistent with this dislike of central planning, liberal states prefer to use macro-economic policies, whether monetarist or Keynesian, rather than sectoral or firm-level policies.[90] The result in Britain has been, according to Andrew Shonfield, that vague, generalized, aggregate-level objectives have been combined with inexact, macro-level policies to produce a "stop-go" cycle of policies harmful to the British economy in general. Peter Dunnett maintains that the macro-level policies of successive governments have proved particularly detrimental to the automotive industry and have provided the basis for that sector's economic decline.[91]

Liberal states clearly prefer to use a minimum of coercion, encouraging action through the promise of reward rather than the threat of sanction.[92] Indeed, Hayward suggests that a greater reliance on non-

[88]See Stephen Young and A. V. Lowe, *Intervention in the Mixed Economy: The Evolution of British Industrial Policy, 1964–1972* (London: Croom Helm, 1974); and Keith Middlemass, *Industry, Unions, and Government: Twenty-One Years of the NEDC* (London: Macmillan, 1983).

[89]Jack Hayward, "Institutional Inertia and Political Impetus in France and Britain," paper presented at the Political Studies Association Conference, Oxford, March 1975, p. 3.

[90]Stephen Young, "A Comparison of Industrial Experiences," in Hayward and Watson, *Planning, Politics, and Public Policy*, especially pp. 142–47. According to Middlemass, corporatist institutional forms are incompatible with a political regime that relies heavily on macro-economic instruments for policy implementation. Middlemass, *Industry, Unions, and Government*, p. 4.

[91]Andrew Shonfield, *Modern Capitalism: The Changing Face of Public and Private Power* (New York: Oxford University Press, 1980), p. 65; Peter J. S. Dunnett, *The Decline of the British Motor Industry: The Effects of Government Policy, 1945–1979* (London: Croom Helm, 1980), pp. 11–16. Note that the statistical study by Jones and Prais strongly contradicts this position and claims that demand was more stable than Dunnett supposed. Stable demand suggests that inconsistent use of macro-economic policy could not explain poor performance by British auto producers. However, consistently poor use of macro-economic tools, or a consistent reliance on only macro-economic tools, could provide an explanation—the latter version is consistent with my claims. See Daniel T. Jones and S. J. Prais, "Plant Size and Productivity in the Motor Industry: Some International Comparisons," *Oxford Bulletin of Economics and Statistics* 40 (May 1978).

[92]For the limits on coercive use of power by the British state see Middlemass, *Industry, Unions, and Government*, pp. 1–2.

coercive instruments, such as persuasion and incentives, has encouraged the British state to ignore its coercive capacities in the realm of economic policy.[93] I am not suggesting that state policies are not harmful or violent; as Andrew Friedman points out, such policies can lead to unconscious, nonvoluntaristic "structural violence."[94] But liberal states use coercion as little as possible, thereby avoiding direct confrontation.

I conclude that the liberal state's relationship with the economy has evolved over the last two centuries in a way not foreseen by classical liberalism. The liberal state is coherent even if it can exercise only a limited degree of autonomy. Liberal states are ill-equipped to plan an economy's development or to implement sectoral policies. Yet despite changes in the global economy from entrepreneurial to state capitalism, liberal states have retained a great proportion of their ideology and institutional base in the twentieth century, because they have not encountered revolutionary changes. Relative political stability and military victory have limited the breadth and scope of development. The result has been that liberal states have incrementally evolved in ways that are ambivalent—both consistent with and contrary to the principles of classical liberalism—thus avoiding the sweeping, violent changes experienced by central and Western continental Europe. They remain ideologically opposed to, and institutionally incapable of, discriminatory economic policies. This point is illustrated by the dominant, egalitarian "national treatment" principle that governs contemporary American policies concerning direct investment by foreigners.

Fascism

Social and economic policies in liberal democracies are predicated on different principles and more limited notions about public power than are fascist policies. Yet the idea of trying to provide a general definition of fascism is daunting. According to Eley, many historians who have pursued explanations of the causes of German fascism have systematically avoided any attempt to define the critical characteristics of fascist regimes. They have been content to define the German fascist state entirely in terms of its origins. Ernst Nolte is more explicit in suggesting that fascism is a time-bound concept. He specifies that the development of fascism was a response to Bolshevism and can be considered only within the historical era of imperialism dating from 1917 until

[93]In Hayward and Watson, *Planning, Politics, and Public Policy*, p. 6.
[94]Andrew L. Friedman, *Industry and Labor: Class Struggle at Work and Monopoly Capitalism* (London: Macmillan, 1977), pp. 8–9.

1945. What binds examples of fascist governance together, Nolte contends, was a unity based on kinship within a particular time period. This stress on uniqueness is counterproductive to the development of more general typologies and escapes the awkward task of differentiating between fascist regimes and other types of regimes. By contending that all major, mass, nationalist movements opposed to Bolshevism that over three decades claimed the title of fascist were indeed fascist, Nolte avoids awkward questions about generalization and operationalization.[95]

Political sociologists have proved more accomplished in defining fascism. Barrington Moore's analysis of the alternative routes to modernity is not as rigid as Nolte's historical analysis, but Moore does limit the possible universe of cases by contending that fascism is a response to the weakness of democracy, building on top of—rather than destroying—the old order. Seymour Lipset differentiates regimes by the social basis of their support and the content of their appeal. He suggests that fascist movements are an expression of a reactionary middle-class extremism, and their guiding principles include a profound antiliberalism in the glorification of the state, opposition to big business, trade unionism, and socialism, and dislike for religion. Their aim is to restore economic security and social prestige to the middle classes, most notably to the self-employed petty bourgeoisie. In contrast to sociological analyses that look at the social forces responsible for the onset of fascism, Carl Friedrich and Zbigniew Brzezinski adopt a broad institutional approach that focuses on the characteristics of the state within totalitarian regimes and then subdivides fascist and communist systems. Juan Linz's subsequent modifications refines this analysis by introducing the "cult of the individual" as a fascist characteristic. But none of these theorists can escape two problems relevant to this book: first, how to apply their conceptual frameworks to empirical research, and second, why they omit any substantial discussion of the relationship between state and economy in fascist regimes.[96]

Conversely, the empirical study of state-economy relations in fascist

[95]Eley, *Reshaping the German Right*, p. 8; Ernst Nolte, *The Three Faces of Fascism* (New York: Mentor, 1965), pp. 18–20, 567. For a succinct if uncritical summary of Nolte's position see Klaus Epstein, "A New Study of Fascism," in Henry A. Turner, ed., *Reappraisals of Fascism* (New York: New Viewpoints, 1975), pp. 2–25.

[96]Barrington Moore, Jr., *The Social Origins of Dictatorship and Democracy: Lord and Peasant in the Making of the Modern World* (Boston: Beacon, 1966), p. 438; Seymour Martin Lipset, *Political Man: The Social Bases of Politics* (New York: Doubleday, 1963), pp. 127–34; Carl Friedrich and Zbigniew Brzezinski, *Totalitarian Dictatorship and Autocracy* (Cambridge: Harvard University Press, 1956); and Juan Linz, "Totalitarian and Authoritarian Regimes," in Fred Greenstein and Nelson Polsby, *The Handbook of Political Science—Volume 3* (Reading, Mass.: Addison-Wesley, 1975). Linz himself describes his discussion of the relationship between state and economy as "sketchy." See p. 232.

regimes has been undertaken by scholars, generally historians, who address important issues—most commonly the relationship between interest and ideology—but generally are not concerned with broad definitional issues.[97] Perhaps the quintessential example of this focused, inductive approach is Roland Sarti's study of the relationship between the state and the major representative organization of industrial leaders in Italy in which he fails to define a fascist regime. Much of the more deductive, abstract, Marxist literature, meanwhile, simply consigns fascism to the role of the ultimate stage of capitalism in crisis and spends little time distinguishing fascism from other types of regimes. Marxist analysis has, according to Henry Turner, contributed little to attempts to define fascism.[98]

Ultimately, confusion and ambiguity over the definitional features of fascism abound, and my discussion is not a definitive attempt to fill that void.[99] Yet three sets of characteristics emerge from a synthesis of the overlapping features of the sociological, institutional, and historical literatures as necessary for a regime to be defined as fascist. The first two sets are general factors not concerned with the relationship between state and economy; I note them briefly as helpful in recognizing a fascist regime. The third set directly addresses this book's concerns with economic policy.[100]

The first set of characteristics, heavily emphasized by Nolte, relates to ideological aspects governing the behavior of fascist states. Fascist states have a comprehensive ideology that, unlike communist regimes, is specifically nationalistic in tone and substance. The fascist state generally defines the elite racial or national group through heavy (although not exclusive) emphasis on what Wehler called "negative integration." This process differentiates the in-group of community interests from the out-group, which may be composed of people who reside inside or outside the nation's territorial borders.[101] Fascist ideology has a well-developed *Weltanschauung* (world-view) for selecting and interpreting information. Its characteristic goals are antiliberal, antirational, racial, and nationalistic; spiritually, it seeks to reify the

[97]The best example of this is Hayes, *Industry and Ideology.*

[98]Roland Sarti, *Fascism and the Industrial Leadership in Italy, 1919–1940* (Berkeley: University of California Press, 1971). Turner makes this criticism in his editor's preface to *Reappraisals of Fascism.*

[99]The ambiguity and confusion surrounding attempts to define the term "fascism" are most lucidly captured by A. James Gregor, *Interpretations of Fascism* (Morristown, N.J.: General Learning Press, 1974), pp. 2–23.

[100]For revealing analyses of the properties of fascist regimes see Pierre Aycoberry, *The Nazi Question: An Essay on the Interpretations of National Socialism* (New York: Pantheon, 1981); Renzo De Felice, *Fascism: An Informal Introduction to Its Theory and Practice* (New Brunswick, N.J.: Transaction, 1976); and Gregor, *Interpretations of Fascism.*

[101]Wehler, *The German Empire,* p. 91.

state in the Hegelian and neo-Rankean traditions and glorifies the concept of the collectivity in a manner misappropriated from democratic theorists.

The second set of characteristics relates to the institutional structure of fascist regimes and the relationship between state and society. Fascist regimes have a single, mass-mobilizing party. Indeed, the party and the state become indistinguishable as the party monopolizes decision making over the means of coercion, if not physical control of the weaponry itself. The population is exhaustively encouraged, through heavy doses of coercion and propaganda, to provide active support to the state's aims and activities. The party (and thus the state) has a well-defined elite hierarchy at the very top permanently institutionalized around the concept of the "leadership principle." Contrary to fascist ideology, however, in practice fascist regimes had no well-defined hierarchy beyond the unquestioned authority of the leader over his immediate subordinates—and thus the distribution of power among subordinates often remained obscure. The development of the leadership principle among the political elite was mirrored in the structure of society. The most obvious example was in economic organization at the level of the firm, where the concept of the leadership principle recalled the traditional German *Herr im Haus* (master of the house) syndrome.

The third set of characteristics specifically relates to economic policy. Integrating this dimension of Marxist analysis into his work, Moore suggests that fascism and capitalism are complementary rather than mutually exclusive despite fascism's anticapitalist rhetoric. In common with Ralf Dahrendorf, Moore depicts fascism as one route to economic modernization and industrialization—in Germany's case a revolutionary, reactionary, conservative capitalism led mainly by the landed, aristocratic upper class. Moore therefore suggests that fascism and communism differ substantially in two respects: fascism as a political system can coexist with capitalism as an economic system; and fascism constitutes a reactionary, elite "revolution from above" rather than communism's "revolution from below" despite fascism's common image as a mass-participatory regime.[102]

Yet while fascist states and liberal democracies are both capitalist, their economic policies are very different. Much of this difference stems from their contrasting view of the role of the state, a contrast most marked in the relative distribution of power between the private and the public sector. Despite their rhetoric, fascist regimes surmount

[102]See Moore, *Social Origins of Dictatorship*, pp. 433–52; and Ralf Dahrendorf, *Society and Democracy in Germany* (New York: Norton, 1967), pp. 381–96. For an example of "Cold War" comparisons between fascism and communism see Carl Friedrich, *Constitutional Government and Democracy* (Waltham, Mass.: Blaisdell, 1968).

the tension between private ownership and public control by emphasizing the political importance of control. They reject liberalism's stress on the importance of private-sector ownership and control of the economy, and therefore liberalism's assumption that the ownership of private property will translate into economic or political power.[103] Sarti argues that fascism is unique in that it institutionalizes the relationship between public and private sectors in a mixed economy, although I shall argue that this institutionalization is one of the major characteristics shared by fascist and some corporatist regimes.[104] Like liberal democracy, fascism is therefore compatible with capitalism (if we define capitalism as ownership of the means of production rather than as the maintenance of autonomous market structures). Perhaps in a stronger form one can state that fascism ameliorates (or, in its strongest form, negates) the effects of market structures; as Hayes succinctly puts it, Hitler's "immediate plans did not entail revolutionizing the German economy so much as conscripting it."[105] It would be convenient to characterize the distinction between liberalism and fascism as a choice between market and state. Unfortunately, as I have already suggested, liberal states impose important limits on the power of markets and so the contrast is not symmetrical. But it is important to note that fascist states allow internal market structures no degree of latitude (and their goal of autarky is an attempt to impose the same insulation from the constraining effects of external markets) whereas liberal states exercise far less constraint on markets.

The differences between fascist and liberal states become more stark as we examine the broader issues of relative state coherence and autonomy. The state in liberal regimes is coherent but not autonomous. The fascist state, however, is ideologically coherent and has a powerful capacity for independent policy planning, articulation, and implementation. These monolithic capacities are partially explained by the centralization of power as a result of the leadership principle. As a result, the fascist state represents an extreme form of statism, being closest to the ideal type of the ideological (and possibly irrational) "strong state" despite the revisionist attempt to identify limitations in the fungibility of fascist state power.[106]

[103]Hayes, *Industry and Ideology*, p. xvii.
[104]See Sarti, *Fascism and Industrial Leadership*, p. 79.
[105]Hayes, *Industry and Ideology*, p. 73.
[106]For a summary of the characteristics of a strong state see Stephen D. Krasner, *Defending the National Interest: Raw Materials Investments and U.S. Foreign Policy* (Princeton: Princeton University Press, 1978), pp. 53–61. On the limitations of the fascist state see Sarti, *Fascism and Industrial Leadership*. One of the reasons I decided to study Nazi Germany was that there if anywhere was a state powerful enough to alter the economic structure of its society. If the "strong state" argument was going to effectively explain

The relationship between state and economy, and the specific features of fascist state economic policies, follow from this discussion. Fascist economic policies are derived from what A. James Gregor describes as its corporatist character where the state attempts to harmonize state, business, and worker organizations. They emphasize the importance of productive capital and technical expertise as distinct from the despised predatory capital and in contrast to liberalism's emphasis on consumers.[107] Yet these generalizations, which could be made about the state in a democratic corporatist regime, do not reflect the capacity or willingness of the fascist state to intervene in the workings of the economy. The fascist state plays a directive rather than integrative role, as Nazi Germany illustrates. To achieve its immediate goal of remaking the relationship between private economic and public political power, the Nazi state destroyed the old, voluntary cartels that were the basis of private economic power in Wilhelmine and Weimar Germany and created a new, involuntary system that, Hayes suggests, were "mere shells." In practice, the German fascist state used the reconstituted cartels as instruments for its economic policies. The new "estates" provided central forums for planning the implementation of the state's policy goals. The fact they were involuntary meant that no firm could escape the state's discipline and that the state could use them as instruments to discriminate among firms. Economic power therefore conclusively shifted from the private to the public sector in the Third Reich. Both the extent of the Nazi state's capacity to get the private sector to implement its political goals, and conversely the limited character of the private sector's economic and political power, are captured in Hayes's metaphor that for German private industry, "the emergent economic system was still capitalism, but only in the same sense that for a professional gambler poker remains poker, even when the house shuffles, deals, determines the ante and the wild cards, and can change them at will, even when there is a ceiling on winnings, which may be spent only as the casino permits and for the most part only on the premises."[108] The example of Hugo Junkers, whose refusal to produce warplanes for the Nazis resulted in his company's seizure by the state, illustrates the state's economic power over the private sector.[109] The

---

both economic policies *and changes in economic policies* (thus providing an explanation for modern German prosperity alternative to the literature tracing the contemporary German economy back to prefascist Germany), it would do so with Nazi Germany.

[107]See A. James Gregor, *Young Mussolini and the Intellectual Origins of Fascism* (Berkeley: University of California Press, 1979), pp. 203, 220. Perhaps similar fascist state policies explain the origins of the primacy of "the politics of productivity" in postwar Japan and Germany.

[108]Hayes, *Industry and Ideology*, p. 77.

[109]See Overy, *The Nazi Economic Recovery*, p. 40.

objectives of these new economic policies were governed primarily by nonrational, ideological concerns rather than by rational, economic ones. Indeed, fascism may provide the best example of political considerations that determine the nature and form of economic policies. This view is succinctly captured by Hayes in his citing of a *Völkischer Beobachter* editor who suggested that fascism is "capitalism harnessed to politics."[110]

Unlike the liberal state, whose policies are explicitly confined to the macro-economic level whenever possible, the fascist state predicates economic policies on the assumption that it is legitimate for state officials (who are often political appointees, lacking in technical training) to intervene pervasively and make authoritative decisions at the micro-level in both public- and private-sector enterprises. All allocative, employment, production, marketing, and supply decisions are legitimately within the state's authority. Fascist ideology accords the state the legitimate authority to impose its will without juridical, constitutional constraints. Where the state lacks an instrument to achieve its goal, it can contradict or supersede previous pronouncements or simply create governmental authority; its coercive capacities quell the possibility of dissent. Thus decrees replace the parliamentary process as mechanisms for authority. One classic example of the fascist state's unbridled authority and its effects on the distribution of economic power was the pronouncement of the new German Corporation Law of 30 January 1937, which ruthlessly substituted state authority for shareholder influence.[111] Where the state found no private-sector firm had the resources to fulfill its requirements, it simply created a new public-sector equivalent, whether that new entity was defined as a firm (IG Farben), a utility (Volkswagen), or a public-sector holding company (the Istituto per la Riconstruzione Industriale in Italy). The result in Germany was a plethora of instruments for state economic intervention. When used effectively, these instruments could have a revolutionizing effect on the economy's level of productivity—as demonstrated in Germany under Albert Speer's guidance between 1942 and 1944.[112]

[110]Hayes, *Industry and Ideology*, p. 79.

[111]Ibid., p. 168.

[112]See Joseph Borkin, *The Crime and Punishment of IG Farben* (New York: Free Press, 1978); or Alan S. Milward, *The German Economy at War* (London: Athlone, 1965). These comments are tempered by the realization that Gillingham claims important examples of what he terms "self-administration" existed in the Third Reich. Perhaps he conflates self-administration and autonomy too willingly. It is unclear that the two concepts share any explicit relationship, but Gillingham stresses that the state's willingness to let the coal industry "run itself" was predicated on the condition that it fully cooperate in implementing regime policy. Presumably any departure from state policy would have suspended "self-administration" in favor of direct state control. I doubt this was autonomy in any meaningful sense. Gillingham, *Industry and Politics in the Third Reich*, p. 163.

Within this structure the fascist state seeks to achieve economic autarky—an objective consistent with nationalist principles. The pursuit
of self-sufficiency has two effects. Externally, the state pursues aggressive foreign policies designed to incorporate more resources into
an enlarged nation. The result is usually a strategy of military conquest.
Internally, the state imposes adjustment on domestic socioeconomic
groups that are deprived of resources formerly imported from abroad.
In practice, Italian attempts at autarky failed, whereas German efforts
proved more effective. The fascist state contrasts with the liberal state
in that it tries partially to import, rather than wholly to export, the costs
of adjustment.

Unlike the liberal state, furthermore, the fascist state makes no effort
to distribute these costs equitably. Moore suggests that at the heart of
fascist ideology there is a violent rejection of humanitarian ideals, most
pointedly a rejection of the notion of potential human equality which is
reflected in its racial doctrines. Hayes may be correct that self-interest
dominated the behavior of big business in the Third Reich, but the
ideological impulses that dominated state behavior drove government
officials to implement discriminatory policies.[113] The fascist state's em-
brace of the concept of inequality in economic policy is reflected in
discriminatory treatment at four levels: classes, sectors, firms, and individuals. In the case of social and economic classes, despite a heroic
depiction of the peasant, fascism protected the landed aristocracy and
leaders of heavy industry at the expense of the agricultural laborer, the
small peasant, and the consumer.[114] At the sector level, the Nazis discriminated in their economic policies even before 1939, the automobile
and chemical industries benefiting from the Nazi government's maldistribution of resources. And this willingness to discriminate is powerfully evident in its treatment of individuals and firms. Here discrimination, based on ideological considerations such as the racial or national
composition of ownership rather than economic considerations such as
size of firm, critically influenced the state's policies and had a powerful,
negative impact on aggregate economic performance and military resources. The state discriminated between foreign-owned and domestic-
owned firms and curtailed the economic expansion of foreign firms.
Finally, the state discriminated between industrialists who were willing
to cooperate and those who were not. An extreme example is Hugo
Junkers, whom Hermann Göring stripped of ownership of his aircraft
company.[115] At all these levels the new cartels proved effective instru-

---

[113]Moore, *Social Origins of Dictatorship*, p. 447; Hayes, *Industry and Ideology*, p. xviii.
[114]Moore, *Social Origins of Dictatorship*, p. 452.
[115]See Overy, *The Nazi Economic Recovery*, p. 40.

ments for implementing discriminatory policies. Decisions about the inclusion or exclusion of firms from a particular cartel, the distribution of productive resources and the allocation of government contracts among cartel members, or simply which firms were to be included in a research and development scheme were governed by political considerations and had a powerful influence on the economy's aggregate development, the sector's structure, the firm's development and prosperity, and the individual industrialist's welfare and prestige. These comments about Nazi Germany can be extended to all fascist states, which are unprecedented among capitalist states in "picking winners and losers." In the absence of comprehensive structural reforms by subsequent regimes, a systematic policy of discrimination by fascist states can have durable effects.

Corporatism

Scholars of fascism have sought a definition generalizable to a diverse set of cases. Scholars of corporatism have focused their energies on dissecting it into various groups. Scholars studying fascism risk overgeneralization, but here the converse applies. Furthermore, definitions of corporatism focus on the institutional links of state to economy. Still the most inclusive definition of a corporatist regime is provided by Philippe Schmitter: "A system of interest and/or attitudinal representation, a particular model or ideal-typical institutional arrangement for linking the associationally organized interests of civil society with the decisional structure of the state." In institutional terms, "corporatism can be defined as a system of interest representation in which the constituent units are organized into a limited number of singular, compulsory, noncompetitive, hierarchically ordered and functionally differentiated categories, recognized or licensed (if not created) by the state and granted deliberate representative monopoly within their respective categories in exchange for observing certain controls on their selection of leaders and articulation of demands and supports."[116]

The corporatist state functions by exchanging licensing for monopoly representation. It expects the recognized representatives of economic groups to respect its priorities; policies are therefore the outcome of a process in which the state can formulate, articulate, and implement particular goals tempered by the priorities of societal actors. Compromise is not a subversion of policies, as in fascism, or the unforeseen consequence of "muddling through," as in liberalism, but an explicit attempt to constrain unpleasant effects of policies on social forces.

---

[116]Philippe Schmitter, "Still the Century of Corporatism?" *Review of Politics* 36 (January 1974), pp. 86, 93–94.

Policy outcomes are therefore more predictable than in liberalism. They are intended consequences of explicit state policy as negotiated with society's economic representatives in the corporatist system.

Schmitter's definition of corporatism contains a subdivision between state and societal corporatism. The state in state corporatism is more directive and creates representative institutions, whereas in societal corporatism the state is more responsive, negotiating policy with representatives of society's economic organizations. Among Schmitter's examples of state corporatist regimes are countries whose governments are described as authoritarian or fascist, notably Nazi Germany.[117] It would certainly be simpler to consign fascism to a subset of state corporatism, and I shall suggest that the two have common attributes. However, there are important distinctions between the two.

Beyond this typological distinction, Schmitter has little to say about the character of the state, the nature of state policies, or how these definitions can be applied in practice. He largely ignores attitudinal factors and so the importance of what Peter Katzenstein suggests is a definitive feature of corporatist regimes—an "ideology of social partnership."[118] Indeed, neither Schmitter nor Wolfgang Streeck develops a theoretical rationale for the alternating predominance of state and societal corporatist systems in Germany since 1871. Schmitter's analysis remains static, a typology rather than an explanation. It emphasizes continuity rather than change, leaving other scholars to provide the basis for operationalizing the concept of corporatism, explaining the causal link between different types of corporatism, and addressing major questions such as the effects of a corporatist system on a country's economic structure and its prospects for prosperity.

The concept of corporatism offers two temptations. The first, reflected in Schmitter's work, is to define corporatism so broadly as to include all advanced industrialized nations and many newly industrializing countries. The second, failing to find much in common among these abundant instances, is to subdivide corporatism into so many different types that one loses the capacity to generalize at all. For example, Katzenstein's *Small States in World Markets* provides the most recent comprehensive statement in the corporatist literature. In his acclaimed study of small European states that have corporatist systems—the "seven dwarfs"—Katzenstein recognizes that "corporatism is an ambiguous and evocative concept."[119] He claims that corporatism

---

[117]For studies of authoritarian corporatist regimes see Philippe Schmitter, *Interest Conflict and Political Change in Brazil* (Stanford: Stanford University Press, 1971); or *Corporatism and Public Policy in Authoritarian Portugal* (New York: Sage, 1975).
[118]Katzenstein, *Small States*, p. 88.
[119]Ibid., p. 30.

has three different meanings. The first is an antidemocratic one stemming from the political authoritarianism and fascism of the 1930s; the second (I would suggest more oblique) refers to the economic and political organization of modern capitalism expressed, for example, in discussions of "corporate capitalism"; and the third refers to the democratic corporatism of the postwar period. Elsewhere, in his comments on the third, democratic form, Katzenstein explicitly rejects the notion that West Germany bears any link to the authoritarian strand of corporatism.[120] Yet he devotes little effort to examining the historical origins of German corporatism. Instead, having subdivided corporatism, he concentrates in *Small States* on examples of democratic corporatism in the seven small corporatist states of central and northern Europe.

Katzenstein's book has been widely acclaimed, but there are some disconcerting features of his argument. First, it is explicitly functional in explaining policy in terms of structure and by examining only countries that are economically successful (although Katzenstein avoids explaining outcomes by focusing on policy choices). He suggests the relationship between policy choice and outcome is complex, contingent, overdetermined—and thus tenuous. Yet he only briefly compares his small corporatist states to liberal or statist ones, while his argument would be really strengthened by systematically comparing these countries to unsuccessful small states. A second concern is that Katzenstein's typology distinguishes democratic corporatist states from the authoritarian corporatist variant and rejects any link between them. While fascism plays an important role in small states—as a spur to the corporatist compromises of the 1930s and 1940s—a clear difference between indigenous fascism and the threat or imposition of fascism by an external power is reflected in a country's subsequent domestic structure. Yet paradoxically, Katzenstein suggests that modern West Germany provides the nearest thing to this "small state" political and economic structure among the large states, explained by its postwar openness, dependence, and sense of vulnerability. Whether fascism had domestic or external origins is critical to domestic structure, and is therefore a basic difference between the German and "small state" patterns of historical development; but a country that experienced profound indigenous fascism bears the clearest resemblance to small states whose structures were most influenced by its external threat. The critical missing link is Austria, the only one of the countries he examines that did experience indigenous fascism. Austria was racked by civil war rather than corporatist compromise in the 1930s, and its different historical evolution

---

[120]See Peter Katzenstein, *Policy and Politics in West Germany: The Growth of the Semi-Sovereign State* (Philadelphia: Temple University Press, 1987), pp. 3–35.

was reflected in a postwar structure that most closely resembles a large industrialized state.[121] Austria provides the missing link between the other small states and the Federal Republic, a point Katzenstein elsewhere concludes.[122] While the factors cited by Katzenstein may have proved important in influencing the structure of the Austrian economy in the postwar period, the influence of indigenous fascism in Austria cannot be discounted either there or in the FRG.

Thus the severing of the links between authoritarian and democratic corporatism is incomplete in both the German case and Katzenstein's description of Austria. Do these represent two forms of corporatism with common features, or is fascism a political regime whose characteristics might share common theoretical links to some types of corporatism? Corporatism in countries with a fascist legacy may reflect that legacy in state policy and economic structure. It is hard to ignore a country's historical pattern of authoritarian development and its present corporatist framework when considering the ease with which four centuries of Austrian authoritarianism were so easily transformed into the model of contemporary corporatism. Postwar West Germany has as much in common in this respect with France, Italy, or Japan as with the small states (see Chapter 7). Here, I attempt first to understand the relationship between state and societal corporatism; and second to recompose corporatism by generalizing about the behavior of the state in both democratic and authoritarian corporatist systems.

Some crucial distinctions undoubtedly exist between state corporatist and societal corporatist regimes. In practice the former exhibits a greater degree of centralization and a higher degree of cartelization. The propensity toward a concentration of industry is proportionally increased by the state's greater coercive capacities and the heightened nationalist tone of its ideology. Conversely, a more universalistic ideology and a fragmented state apparatus will increase the propensity toward societal corporatism. Regimes that oscillate back and forth do not achieve effective social transformation at the same rate. The directive state in state corporatist regimes can organize changes in institutional structure at a faster rate than the integrative state in societal corporatism, which is reliant on voluntary compliance. This claim suggests that attempts to link Wilhelmine Germany and the Bonn Republic need to be circumscribed. Comparisons may be more appropriate for the 1890s and the 1970s than the 1890s and the 1950s. It also explains why we can identify ideological and institutional remnants of state corporatist policies in the German auto industry more readily during

[121]Katzenstein, *Small States*, pp. 28–29, 131–32, 138–39, 200–201.
[122]Katzenstein, *Policy and Politics*, p. 368.

the 1950s than in the 1980s, and why, therefore, this book's claims are focused on the early postwar years.

What explicit economic features are common to states in corporatist regimes? One clear answer is their skepticism toward markets. Corporatist states may respond flexibly to markets they cannot control, but the other side of the coin is that they make every effort to control domestic markets. The institutionalization of a relationship between the public and the private sector in forums and quasi-public authorities controlled by members of the private sector through self-administration (most pointedly cartels) exemplifies the dominance of institutional compromise over market harmony. Furthermore, the semi-official and informal network of relations between state and private actors and among societal actors is complex because officials from banks and companies often hold supervisory positions on more than one company board. James Womack suggests these representatives are not earnest amateurs but have the incentive and technical knowledge to actively oversee the progress of the company with which they are involved. Again, these links tend to buffer the effects of market forces, as was demonstrated by the speed with which Volkswagen was able to generate loans amounting to $2.2 billion in the mid-1970s when a delay in securing financing might have led to a permanent loss of market share.[123] The state encourages its firms to be internationally competitive, but unlike liberal regimes it does not demand domestic competition, so it puts few limits on the concentration of ownership or joint projects. The state's central integrative role and sponsoring of a variety of formal, quasi-official, and informal networks reestablish the link between corporatism and the concept of "organized capitalism."

Correspondingly, the development of agendas and forums requires acceptance of the notion of central planning. The nature of this planning generally differs from that in fascist regimes (except in the most extreme case of state corporatism). It is generally integrative planning about what, where, and how an issue is to be discussed rather than directive planning about which policies are to be implemented. This form of planning tends to institutionalize and regulate conflict and to form a basis for maintaining informal networks where bilateral agreements can be reached. Yet the state's integrative role should not be mistaken as noncoercive or nondiscriminatory. Rather, in planning of this type the state plays two critical roles. It defines the parameters of negotiation and makes sure that all participants are subject to the discipline of the final negotiated agreement. These roles, in tandem, can

[123]James Womack, "The Competitive Significance of National Financial Systems in the Auto Sector," paper prepared for International Automobile Program, International Policy Forum, Hakone, Japan, May 1982, pp. 3–5.

prove to be oppressive and discriminatory. For example, firms can be forced into negotiations where they share few interests with other firms and then into agreements that conflict with their interests. Opel and Fordwerke, as mass producers, have consistently been forced to negotiate with German unions on wage agreements along with German specialist producers. Differing skill levels and vastly different profit per unit mean that Opel and Fordwerke have little in common with their supposed partners in negotiating with labor. The only domestic firm operating under similar conditions, Volkswagen, is allowed to negotiate a separate, generally more favorable agreement. Thus defining parameters and providing discipline can be just as effective as directive, fascist forms of central planning. Cartel membership may therefore be no more voluntary in corporatist regimes than it is in fascist ones—and can be just as oppressive.

In practice, corporatist states augment macro-economic policies with sectoral policies when necessary to tackle economic problems—no surprise, given a functional division of representation by sector and the existence of forums to negotiate sectoral policies. The state therefore makes a classic micro-level assumption, that the competitiveness of critical firms will determine the overall welfare of the economy. This assumption encourages a much tighter relationship between state and individual firms in strategic economic sectors, especially in periods of economic crisis.

These comments suggest that corporatist states will use coercion when it is the only available way to achieve their goals—unlike liberal states, which will often redefine goals rather than face conflict. This difference is reflected in the recent treatment of foreign workers in the British and German auto industries. British firms have fully integrated West Indians into the automobile industry's labor force whereas German firms still clearly distinguish domestic from foreign workers by rank. British Ford has attempted to hire immigrant workers at all levels of the company whereas foreign workers have remained in entry-level positions throughout the German industry.[124] Despite unprecedented

[124]Not surprisingly, data from the automobile companies is scarce, so the evidence is anecdotal. Wolfgang Streeck and Andreas Hoff, "Industrial Relations in the German Automobile Industry: Developments in the 1970s," in Streeck and Hoff, eds., *Industrial Relations in the World Automobile Industry: The Experiences of the 1970s*, research paper, "Future of the Automobile" program (Berlin: Wissenschaftszentrum, 1982), does provide aggregate data showing that 22.8 percent of manual workers in 1972 and 26.5 percent in 1975 and 1978 were foreign workers, overwhelmingly Turks, Yugoslavs, Italians, and Greeks (p. 316). But Streeck and Hoff provide no figures for foreign workers employed in supervisory positions. However, an anonymous interviewee in Berlin told me in July 1985 that in twenty years of inspecting German automobile plants he had come across only one foreign worker in a supervisory position—an Italian employed at Volkswagen.

levels of unemployment in the early 1980s, no British government attempted to repatriate immigrants.

In contrast, the German federal government has dealt harshly with foreign workers who bear all of the obligations and benefit from none of the advantages of citizenship. Bonn has always regarded foreign workers as a buffer against unemployment: their visas could be canceled and they (and in some cases their German-born children) thrown out of the country to relieve unemployment. The auto industry experienced its first real employment crisis in the mid-1970s, and the policies of the state and individual companies reflected the view that foreign workers were dispensable and had few rights. Nearly 60 percent of those who left Audi in 1974 and 1975 were foreign workers. At Volkswagen in the same years, the foreign labor force was reduced from 20,000 to 8,000, a 40 percent contribution to reduction of the labor force. The most spectacular departure of foreign workers occurred at BMW where foreigners accounted for 80 percent of labor force reductions in 1974. Wolfgang Streeck and Andreas Hoff point to incentives and the availability of other jobs in the Federal Republic or home countries to explain their departure. This explanation has three flaws. First, it ignores the coercive aspect of the process. Many foreign workers were forced either to take their DM 10,000 severance pay or risk being fired later without a lucrative settlement. Second, it cannot explain why foreign workers took advantage of the offer in numbers out of all proportion to their presence in the labor force, whereas German nationals were reluctant to accept.[125] And third, it ignores the fact that alternative employment was in fact scarce—a disincentive for rushing to accept severance pay. A more likely explanation of the behavior of these foreign workers would focus on the assumption that they were following a satisficing principle, voluntarily taking large severance payments rather than risk having their visas canceled and being fired without severance pay.

Although a spirit of collaboration exists, capital and labor have known instances of major conflict, rare times when the state has considered it acceptable to exclude one of the two groups from the decision-making process or to side explicitly with one against the other.[126] For example, the Management and Supervisory Boards overruled labor's representatives on the issue of firing workers during the crisis at Volkswagen in the mid-1970s; even with its relatively diluted and indirect

[125]Streeck and Hoff, "Industrial Relations," pp. 316–17.

[126]For a brief but valuable discussion of periods of industrial unrest in the Federal Republic, see Andrei Markovits and Christopher Allen, "Power and Dissent: The Trade Unions in the Federal Republic of Germany Reexamined," *West European Politics* 3 (January 1980), pp. 68–86.

role, the German state still has the will and capacity to act. Yet most conflict has been contained by the "ideology of social partnership."[127] The institutional structure effectively processes conflict, and the attitudinal structure supports an ideology that limits conflict.

Most important, for this book, corporatist states are, like fascist states, willing to pursue policies that discriminate among producers. They do not operate on the assumption that all actors should be equitably treated. Rather, they assume that one function of the state is to articulate and pursue a national interest, and they are willing to coordinate activities with specific firms in order to achieve their goals. Discrimination is not as crude or coercive in corporatist regimes as in fascist regimes, but is it nevertheless present. Distinctions between firms may be made on the basis of national or foreign ownership, or willingness to accommodate state policy. Perhaps a relatively high concentration of industry in critical sectors and an absence of major foreign subsidiaries competing with domestic firms in those same sectors explain the apparent lack of state discrimination in small states. But the German auto industry is a case where the relative fragmentation of an industry and the presence of foreign ownership in a critical sector bring out the corporatist state's more coercive side, and necessitates discriminatory intervention by the state at crucial junctures.

These three regimes can be differentiated mainly in terms of the nature of their state and its economic policies. I focus on those types relevant to the two countries examined in detail in this book. Over the last two centuries liberal states have evolved within limited parameters by avoiding revolutions and generally winning wars. Some of the principles upon which their twentieth-century economic policies are based have a tenuous link to classical liberalism, but the relationship remains recognizable. But both fascist and corporatist states have experienced more unstable, oscillating, violent forms of development in the twentieth century. As a result they have broader ideological and institutional parameters, to which fascism's contribution cannot be ignored.

Not all fascist regimes become corporatist in liberal democracies; not all corporatist regimes were once fascist. But where corporatist regimes were formerly fascist, a link still exists. Fascism and state corporatism are not the same thing, but they share common characteristics. The three forms of regime are not mutually exclusive. Viewed in this way,

[127]Katzenstein, *Small States*. Katzenstein implicitly recognizes this point when he suggests two types of corporatism among small states, liberal and democratic, the determinant of the type being the distribution of power among the central actors—capital, labor, and state. Presumably the balance of power determines the final arbitration on any policy issue; that is, the more powerful side's position endures in "zero-sum" conflicts.

state and societal corporatism are ideal types on a continuum of regimes; the primary distinction between them focuses on the legitimate boundaries of state coercion and discrimination. Fascism and extreme state corporatism, for example, overlap in the state's willingness to discriminate coercively in a pursuit of the national interest. Yet in other areas important differences divide them. The fascist state, for example, uses economic policy to pursue political goals, and the corporatist state uses its political structure to pursue economic goals. Scholars have proved too willing to rely on a static typology that in effect subsumes authoritarian, fascist, and liberal strands of corporatism under one title. This approach carries two risks. First, scholars may mistakenly identify a regime as corporatist because it has elements of corporatist policies in particular areas. Second, they ignore the fact that countries may simultaneously exhibit aspects of different types of regimes. Where corporatist regimes succeed fascist ones, for example, the effects of the prior regime can be discerned in the new regime's ideology and institutions—specifically, its state policies and economic structure.

CONCLUSION

All three debates examined in this chapter systematically neglect the effect of fascism on the Bonn Republic. The first discussion, among historians, focuses on the relationship between the Second and Third German Empires. Here structural arguments conflict with those stressing the interactive process of coalitional politics among interests groups and classes. The second discussion, generally confined to political economists, stresses links between the structure of Germany's economy in the late nineteenth and early twentieth centuries and in the Bonn Republic. Here scholars discount the significance of historians who have demonstrated the revolutionizing effects of Nazi state policies on the structure of the German economy. For example, political economists relate the Bonn Republic's tendencies toward concertation and a stress on peak associations to a benign nineteenth-century tradition, largely ignoring the oppressive use of cartels by the Nazis. Germany's "social market economy" in the 1950s has been described as liberal and as corporatist. Whichever description is more appropriate, that economy still reflected and retained elements of fascist state policy. The third discussion focuses on defining different types of political regimes, but it stresses static typologies. The result has been an attempt to find what distinguishes different types of regimes rather than what they have in common. Contrary to the conventional approach, I have tried to distill the ideological and institutional links between fascism and corporatism.

I recognize these links are not permanent; rather, they are diluted over time.[128] But it is unreasonable to suggest that Germany could undergo twelve years of fascist rule and not have those state policies affect the institutional structure and policies that followed its demise. The same generalization, I suggest, applies to the link between fascism and other forms of post-fascist liberal democracy. Aspects of postwar Japanese, Italian, and French statism may stem from the encounters of those countries with fascism—a possibility I apply to the auto industry in Chapter 7.

I am not suggesting that corporatism is fascism or that the postwar governments of these countries are in any sense fascist. But in the following chapters I try to demonstrate that the powerful impulses and extremist tendencies of the centralized, coercive fascist state had a revolutionizing impact on the structure of the German automobile industry. The state's ideology became more aggressive, and its range of coercive instruments expanded. Corporatist states that were once fascist retain both facets, and the policies they generated as a result heavily influenced the welfare of domestic and foreign firms. The liberal state intervened in a more limited way; even when it had the perfect motives, opportunities, and instruments to discriminate, it would not do so. Such decisions had a major impact on the structure and welfare of domestic producers.

---

[128]This opinion is also expressed by Charles Maier, "Preconditions for Corporatism," in John Goldthorpe, ed., *Order and Conflict in Contemporary Capitalism* (Oxford: Clarendon Press, 1984), pp. 39–41.

CHAPTER TWO

West German Prosperity
and British Poverty

During the 1970s and 1980s there was no shortage of attempts to explain the postwar decline of Britain's industrial economy. This literature generally identified the malaise as "the British disease."[1] West Germany was commonly adduced to contrast the unsuccessful British economy with a successful European producer—"Model Deutschland."[2] Various explanations have emphasized the nature of labor relations or of industrial organization and rely on interpretations of history that emphasize such factors as the timing of industrialization, or the nature of British industrial relations, or patterns of foreign investment.[3]

Yet what all these studies try to explain, economic success, is often ill-defined (if defined at all), and the causal relationship is incomplete if not oblique.[4]

In this book I focus on individual firms to understand national economic prosperity, accepting the classical micro-economic assumption of

[1]Relying on the work of Caves and Krause I define the constituent indicators of the British disease as declining terms of trade, low rates of growth in productivity, and ineffective macro-economic policies. See Robert Caves and Lawrence Krause, eds., *Britain's Economic Performance* (Washington, D.C.: Brookings, 1980), p. viii.

[2]See for example Wolfgang Streeck, *Industrial Relations in West Germany* (New York: St. Martin's, 1984).

[3]For industrial relations, see ibid. For the nature of industrial organization see Michael Piore and Charles Sabel, *The Second Industrial Divide: Possibilities for Prosperity* (New York: Basic, 1984). For foreign investment patterns see Robert Gilpin, *U.S. Power and the Multinational Corporations* (New York: Basic, 1975).

[4]An exception is Mancur Olson, who uses growth rates as his dependent variable. This is a very limited indicator of economic success, although it does provide a ready statistical measure for comparative purposes. See Mancur Olson, *The Rise and Decline of Nations* (New Haven: Yale University Press, 1982).

a relationship between the success of individual firms and the economy as a whole. I do not presume to provide a comprehensive explanation of both the British disease and the German economic miracle. I cannot generalize about national prosperity on the basis of data drawn from the automobile industry. However, I do attempt to explain the relative economic success of automotive firms from the early 1930s to the 1960s, making limited generalizations on that basis. In defining economic prosperity I compare firms within and across Britain and West Germany and use three indicators: amount of net profit, level of sales, and percentage share of market.[5] In attempting to explain why certain firms have been prosperous and others not I do two things: first, I causally link the form of political regime with the type of firm that has been successful in each market; second, I link the type of firm that has been successful with the sector's propensity toward sustained prosperity.

Individual firms reveal anomalies for many explanations for the British decline and German rise. The automobile sector has regularly been used to show both British failure and German success, yet it provides cases that contradict such assessments.[6] In postwar Britain, BMC and Ford (UK) Ltd. illustrate divergent degrees of economic success. Similarly, in the Federal Republic of Germany, Volkswagen provides the classic example of the economic miracle whereas, Ford-werke AG has been less successful.[7] Indeed, during the 1950s Ford-werke AG did not approach the levels of success of its British counter-part. In 1959 Ford (UK) Ltd., after a period of unrivaled growth, sold 405,100 vehicles, nearly three times as many as Fordwerke AG in West Germany.[8] Both countries provide examples of economic successes and failures in a strategic sector where during the 1950s one would expect to find *consistent* examples of the effects of the British disease and the German economic miracle. This counterintuitive finding needs an explanation.

[5]When comparing firms in different economies one must be alert to factors such as different tax laws and national ways of interpreting measures and formulating figures. However, by using three measures I hope to avoid that problem.

[6]For evidence that supports this conventional image see Daniel T. Jones, *Industrial Adjustment and Policy: Maturity and Crisis in the European Car Industry* (Lewes: Sussex European Research Center, 1981).

[7]Although this book examines the early 1930s until the early 1960s, it discusses implications for subsequent years. When I refer to British Leyland in this example, the units analyzed are actually the major subunits before BL existed—Austin until 1952, BMC after 1952 when Morris and Austin merged, and BL only when I reflect on implications for the 1970s and 1980s. Even successful companies have not enjoyed uninterrupted success in the 1970s and 1980s. For Volkswagen's subsequent problems see "End of the Wunder?" *The Economist*, 12 April 1975; and Krish Bhaskar, *The Future of the World Auto Industry* (London: Kegan, Paul, 1981), p. 165.

[8]Allan Nevins and Frank E. Hill, *Ford: Decline and Rebirth, 1933–62* (New York: Scribner, 1962), p. 405.

DOMESTIC STRUCTURE AS THE BASIS FOR EXPLANATION

Since Alexander Gerschenkron published his classic study of the advantages of backwardness, scholars concerned with the issue of economic success have developed a variety of political explanations of relative industrial prosperity.[9] These theories commonly share a set of assumptions that emphasize domestic structure and tend to generalize about national economies without distinguishing winners from losers. Yet they make claims about the attributes of political systems that accommodate inferences about the conditions for economic prosperity.[10] Such explanations have adopted increasingly sophisticated analytical tools, but the four auto companies I examine in this book, with examples of both winners and losers within one country, pose problems for general theories.

First Anomaly. Any explanation that emphasizes the British disease and the German economic miracle leads us to expect consistent British failure and German success. However, even superficial historical examination of the four auto firms (Austin, Ford, Fordwerke, and VW) reveals no such neat pattern. These outcomes cannot be explained by simply emphasizing variation between states.[11] To explain this variation between firms we must move beyond the conventional approach in the study of domestic structure.

Second Anomaly. One way to tackle the issue of variation among domestic producers is to focus on one justifiable, prudently selected explanatory factor.[12] For example, Michael Piore and Charles Sabel em-

---

[9]Alexander Gerschenkron, *Economic Backwardness in Historical Perspective* (Cambridge: Harvard University Press, Belknap Press, 1962).

[10]Examples of this approach include the pioneering work of Andrew Shonfield, *Modern Capitalism: The Changing Balance of Public and Private Power* (London: Oxford University Press, 1965); Peter J. Katzenstein, ed., *Between Power and Plenty* (Madison: University of Wisconsin Press, 1977); and John Zysman, *Governments, Markets, and Growth: Financial Systems and the Politics of Industrial Change* (Ithaca: Cornell University Press, 1983).

[11]Here I conceptualize the state as a set of institutional structures, more than the set of state bureaucrats Eric Nordlinger depicted in *On the Autonomy of the Democratic State* (Cambridge: Harvard University Press, 1981), or Graham Allison in *The Essence of Decision: Explaining the Cuban Missile Crisis* (Boston: Little, Brown, 1971). Rather, the *state* refers to an amalgam of institutions that collectively process political action within civil society. See, for example, Theda Skocpol, *States and Social Revolutions: A Comparative Analysis of France, Russia, and China* (Cambridge: Cambridge University Press, 1979); Stephen Skowronek, *Building a New American State: The Expansion of National Administrative Capacities, 1877–1920* (Cambridge: Cambridge University Press, 1982); or Ezra N. Suleiman, *Politics, Power, and Bureaucracy in France: The Administrative Elite* (Princeton: Princeton University Press, 1974).

[12]See Adam Przeworski and Henry Teune, *The Logic of Comparative Social Inquiry* (New York: Wiley, 1970), pp. 23–33. They suggest it is better to examine the most comparable cases first, where one can maximize the number of constants. A theory that fails in such cases has little value. However, should the theory fail where the greatest number of variations exist, there is no way of determining which variable is most significant for the purpose of reformulation.

phasize the dominant technology of the firm as the factor that promotes a nation's economic prosperity. They claim a causal relationship between the predominance of craft or mass production and the possibilities for economic success. Yet the four firms discussed here provide countervailing evidence. These firms all employ the same technology, as large-scale, mass-production firms, yet enjoy varying degrees of economic success. I compensate for the possibility that technology plays a crucial role in economic success by examining only mass producers in the case studies. I thus eliminate technology as the factor that explains economic prosperity and demonstrate that political variables are the critical determinants of success and failure.[13]

While relying on work by those who emphasize the role of domestic structure, I offer an explanation that can distinguish *within and between nations*. I hope at least partially to explain both variation in economic success among firms and aggregate development of the sector as a whole. Then I link firm-level and sectoral developments to national tendencies, making limited inferences about the basis for prosperity. Thus I use an approach that attempts to put various elements, such as the nature of state-firm relations, labor relations, and investment policy, in a broader political framework.

How Political Regimes Influence Economic Prosperity

My major argument is that the nature of political regimes in Britain and West Germany is important in explaining the relative economic prosperity of the countries' auto firms. I assume the historical evolution of different political regimes is comparable and that crucial variables serve to distinguish or cluster nations as cases.[14] Where Barrington Moore's seminal study ends, in explaining the discernable, comparable historical pattern of development of different types of political regime (communist, fascist, and liberal-democratic), I begin, in explaining the pattern of prosperity of each country's auto sector.[15] The industry's

[13]The significance of the predominant indigenous form of technology to economic success is considered in Piore and Sabel, *Second Industrial Divide*, p. 206. Piore and Sabel have a prior political explanation of how a particular form of technology comes to predominate. However, once that form predominates, there is a complex causal link in their argument between the form of technology, the nature of labor relations, and prospects for prosperity.

[14]I recognize the unique development of each nation. However, as Przeworski and Teune suggest, crucial similarities and differences in the evolution of nations provide the basis for comparison. Each nation's development is both unique and comparable. See Przeworski and Teune, *Comparative Social Inquiry*, pp. 4, 13. This view is most compellingly discussed by Barrington Moore, Jr., *The Social Origins of Dictatorship and Democracy: Lord and Peasant in the Making of the Modern World* (Boston: Beacon, 1966).

[15]Moore suggests that the form of the political regime is the outcome of a political

pattern of economic success I explain by the form of political regime derived from Moore's typology. Specifically, the existence of a liberal-democratic or fascist regime is crucial in explaining which firms were successful in each country and what the implications have been for both the sector and the national economy. The most important factor of the political regime for explaining domestic winners and losers is its dominant ideology and resultant interventionist limits of the coercive state apparatus.

The Argument Applied to Germany

The fascist German regime between 1933 and 1945 restructured the relationship among critical economic actors in the German automobile industry.[16] This book focuses on the change in the relationship between the state and individual firms.[17] The state contributed to the fragmenta-tion of capital by consciously discriminating between firms, using politi-cal criteria.[18] A great deal of attention has focused on the aggregate, macro-level effects of state policy on capital, but this book emphasizes the fragmenting effects of state policy and the resultant pattern of benefits. Specifically, it examines the state's capacity to form a new, exclusive coalition of firms based on the promise of extensive rewards. The German state's capacity to do so had significant implications for the development of the industry between 1933 and 1945. The discriminato-ry ideology and enlarged discretionary capacity of the Nazi state to implement policies gave cumulative advantages to selected firms and changed the distribution of wealth among producers. I therefore make three claims. First, power was redistributed between capital and the state

---

process in which the configuration of specific variables takes a particular form. In this book I look at the consequences of the formation of two of the three regime types—liberalism and fascism—on economic prosperity.

[16]*Structure* here is the dominant distribution of power among actors or institutions. *Power,* an explicitly political concept, indicates the economic significance attached to access by economic actors to the formulation or implementation of state policy and the resulting distribution of benefits.

[17]Controversy surrounds what constituted the state during the Third Reich because what had formerly been considered the state now had parallel institutions within the Nazi party. In this instance I consider the state to be represented by the Nazi party. While it is apparent that functions in the Third Reich were split between the party and the tradi-tional institutions of government, ultimate power rested with the SS. The SS thus had a monopoly on the means of coercion, all other institutions being subject to its dictates. I invoke Weber's definition of the state as having "a monopoly on the means of coercion within a given territory." See Max Weber, "Politics as a Vocation," in M. Gerth and C. Wright Mills, eds., *From Max Weber: Essays in Sociology* (New York: Oxford University Press, 1946).

[18]On state policy as applied to labor see Edward Homze, *Foreign Labor in Nazi Germany* (Princeton: Princeton University Press, 1967).

in this period—an uncontroversial claim.[19] Second, the state accelerated the tendency to fragment portions of capital by distinguishing between producers on the basis of indigenous ownership and cooperative attitude toward the Third Reich. This is a more controversial claim.[20] Third, and most controversially, I suggest that state policy during the Third Reich changed the structure of the German auto industry, providing elite firms with a cumulative advantage. Exclusive bilateral agreements and channels of communication were not dismantled during the Allied Occupation. These advantages provided a basis for these firms to compete successfully in world markets and were enhanced by vestiges of the Nazi state ideology that survived the transformation to the Bonn Republic. The success of specific auto firms in the early postwar period, and the uneven distribution of prosperity in the German auto industry in the 1950s, can therefore be traced to changes in state ideology and policy innovations in the Third Reich.

This argument has significant implications for Mancur Olson's explanation why some countries have been economically prosperous in the postwar period. Olson conflates systemic and subsystemic factors, failing to distinguish between the effects of indigenous fascism (subsystemic), war (systemic), and external occupation (systemic) in explaining the causes of economic prosperity. I suggest the subsystemic factor is the most important determinant because the changes wrought by Nazi policies in the auto industry predated the war and survived the Allies' inept and limited attempt at reformation.[21] In the auto sector three identifiable changes survived the Occupation: first, preferred firms retained the economic gains they had made through discriminatory state policy; second, the exclusive links forged by preferred firms with components of the state apparatus and banking community, and with one another, were sustained; and third, the new German state, though it discarded many of the characteristics of the Nazi period, retained a greater propensity than the Weimar governments for discriminatory intervention in the affairs of the auto industry. The result was a shift from private, nondiscriminatory control in the Weimar Republic to public, discriminatory control in the Third Reich and quasi-public discriminatory control in the Bonn Republic.

[19]As suggested in general terms by Karl Hardach, *The Political Economy of Germany in the Twentieth Century* (Berkeley: University of California Press, 1980).

[20]In suggesting that capital was increasingly fragmented I rely on Henry A. Turner's assessment that both big business and labor were already fragmented in the Weimar Republic. See Turner, *German Big Business and the Rise of Hitler* (New York: Oxford University Press, 1985).

[21]See Peter J. Katzenstein, *Policy and Politics in West Germany: The Growth of a Semi-Sovereign State* (Philadelphia: Temple University Press, 1987), p. 13, on failure to implement the 4 Ds of demilitarization, democratization, denazification, and decartelization.

In sum, the residual effects of Third Reich state policies coupled with discriminatory state intervention during both the Occupation and the Republican period helped determine the distribution of economic prosperity among German auto firms in the 1950s. If this claim is correct, some common assumptions about German political history may be misleading. Some political analyses of postwar West Germany have identified this pattern of institutional intermediation as societal corporatism; others have suggested that postwar German history can be divided into a liberal period of the 1950s and a corporatist period that begins in the 1960s.[22] Both analyses are gross oversimplifications when applied to the German auto industry. Rather, a discretionary state ideology with an extensive capacity for intervention violated both the noninterventionist principles of classical liberalism and the egalitarian characteristics of contemporary liberalism and societal corporatism. My findings dispute the description of the German state in the early postwar period as liberal. Germany favored liberal characteristics in Ludwig Erhard's open investment policy but was more statist in its discriminatory treatment of firms.

In the German context the decisive factor in explaining the pattern of economic prosperity among major auto producers during the 1950s is the policies of the Third Reich regarding state-firm relations. In brief, I argue that the new discriminatory ideology and enlarged discretionary powers of the German state of the 1930s and 1940s brought changes to the German auto industry, changes that provided impetus for variations in the degree of economic success of individual firms in the 1950s.[23]

State activity in the auto industry during the Nazi period contrasted with that in the Weimar period. The contrast was reflected in the struc-

[22]Unlike Philippe Schmitter, "Still the Century of Corporatism?" in Philippe Schmitter and Gerhard Lehmbruch, eds., *Trends toward Corporatist Intermediation* (Beverly Hills: Sage, 1979), pp. 7–52, I do not accept the generalization that the state in a corporatist system takes an indiscriminate view toward all producers and workers. Rather,the corporatist system distinguishes between producers in terms of both the strategic importance of the sector and the basis of ownership of the individual firm. This behavior by the state originated in the Third Reich, not between 1880 and 1910 as suggested by historians such as Werner Abelhauser, "The First Post-Liberal Nation: Stages in the Development of Modern Corporatism in Germany," *European History Quarterly* 14 (July 1984), p. 287. Heinrich A. Winkler asserts that the more repressive elements of corporatism in West Germany warrant description as the "more human face of Fascism." He therefore concludes that a link between fascism and corporatism exists. Winkler is quoted by Leo Panitch, "Recent Theorizations of Corporatism: Reflections on a Growth Industry," *British Journal of Sociology* 31 (June 1980), p. 165.

[23]Unlike many of the studies cited earlier, I am not making aggregate generalizations based on a limited number of cases. My choice of cases is justified on epistemological grounds. I have selected four firms with critical attributes in a strategically important industry, and neither the cases nor the context are therefore trivial. I have selected the industry in which my claims are most likely to apply. Should it sustain them, I can extend both the test and the generality of my theory's claims.

ture of the industry. The dominant characteristics of the Weimar auto industry resembled those found in liberal Britain. Conventionally, historians of German industry characterize the political arrangements of the Weimar Republic as corporatist.[24] I do not disagree with this description, but the use of an umbrella term serves to disguise tremendous differences between the Weimar and Bonn Republics. While in general terms the British regime may be characterized as liberal and the Weimar Republic as corporatist, I do contend that the characteristic institutions and distribution of power in their automotive sectors bore significant similarities before 1933. In this instance generalized claims about the characteristics of the regime may be enriched by examining sectorally specific factors.[25] Although the political institutions in the Weimar Republic can be described as a variant of corporatism, two factors allow me to reconcile my claim of similar political and economic structures in German and British auto industries with the dominant view that the British state was liberal and the German corporatist. First, the relevance of corporatist institutions to the infant automotive industry was minimal. Second, the importance of some of these institutions eroded in the face of the economic crisis that began in the late 1920s. Corporatist institutions were therefore essentially irrelevant to the German auto industry, and the effects of systemic crisis made them increasing irrelevant to the organization of the German economy.[26]

---

[24]The classic defense is Gerald Feldman, *Army, Industry, and Labor in Germany, 1914–1918* (Princeton: Princeton University Press, 1966).

[25]Michael Geyer claims that one of labor's major failings in the Weimar Republic was its inability to structure the organization of political and economic processes, which suggests that national agreements were ineffective. Geyer, "The State in National Socialist Germany," in Charles Bright and Susan Harding, *Statemaking and Social Movements* (Ann Arbor: University of Michigan Press, 1984), p. 196.

[26]Abelhauser suggests that although the 1920s were initially characterized by class collaboration and consensus, economic crisis led to a breakdown of these corporatist arrangements. By the end of the 1920s big business favored mass unemployment to regain from labor some of what it had lost in the early part of the decade. See Abelhauser, "The First Post-Liberal Nation," p. 300. He stresses that this corporatist institutional framework could not cope with the problems that confronted it, citing David Abraham's controversial work *The Collapse of the Weimar Republic* (Princeton: Princeton University Press, 1981). By the latter 1920s the Weimar institutional framework was converging with the British in important ways, a view seemingly supported by Abraham's chief critic, Henry Ashby Turner, *German Big Business and the Rise of Hitler.* See his comments referring to the fragmented nature of business representation on p. 4, the relative neutrality of central government to the political process on p. 13, and the intention of generating a mature, capitalist, market-oriented system on p. 18. There is rare accord between Abraham and Turner on this issue. However, Abelhauser's claim that the Bonn Republic is a return to the societal corporatist framework of the Weimar Republic is challenged by Geyer's claim that the end of the interwar period saw the disintegration of old class formations and identifications and the formulation of new ones. See "The First Post-Liberal Nation," p. 196. Geyer's historical work claims that the Third Reich resulted in an irreversible remaking of the German state. The old bureaucratic authoritarian state was replaced by a new state in which power was parceled out to new public actors who

This argument further suggests that fascism was not the ultimate stage of capitalism in crisis or the prelude to an infant form of socialism, as Marxists often claim, but a critical stage in the rejuvenation of capitalism, in a manner that found relatively undiluted expression in the 1950s.[27] The new Nazi political regime placed primary emphasis on cooperative class relations, commonly referred to as "organic harmony" in the literatures on totalitarian and corporatist regimes.[28] This form of relations bent the laws of the marketplace through state intervention and legitimated a state apparatus that discriminated among producers in Germany.[29] Certain firms in this strategic sector benefited from the coincidence of their interests with the state's.[30] These firms

---

exercised coercive sovereignty and autonomy over resources within a limited domain. The traditional essence of politics—the routine and institutionalized processes of negotiated access to resources—became meaningless as actors rarely met in a state apparatus composed of whole units. See Geyer, "National Socialist Germany," pp. 206–7. This is expressed in the Bonn Republic by continued reliance on peak associations. Geyer's analysis supports my claim that this irreversible change could not mean, as Abelhauser claims, that the Korean crisis brought an end to the *Sozialmarktwirtschaft* and a return to societal corporatism. See Abelhauser, "The Economic Policy of Ludwig Erhard," EUI Working Paper 80 (Florence, n.d.), p. 1. The Korean crisis may have prompted the United States to encourage the abandonment of the free market economy in the Federal Republic, but that did not signal a return to the business as usual of the Weimar Republic—societal corporatism. Abelhauser's claim supposes that no effective, meaningful change took place between 1933 and 1945 (what Abelhauser called a distorted form of authoritarian corporatism). Geyer, unwilling to accept that assessment, rather claims that the Bonn Republic had to reflect the changes in the nature of class formation and identification and in the nature of the state apparatus effected in the Third Reich. For a discussion of corresponding developments in Britain see Robert Skidelsky, *The Politicians and the Slump: The Labour Government of 1929–31* (London: Macmillan, 1967).

[27]The classic Marxist position is illustrated by Daniel Guerin, *Fascism and Big Business* (New York: Pathfinder, 1973); Jurgen Kuczynski, *Germany: Economic and Labor Conditions under Fascism* (New York: Greenwood, 1968); and Alfred Sohn-Rethel, *Economy and the Class Structure of German Fascism* (London: CSE, 1978). Olson calls this revolutionary process the abolition of "distributional coalitions," through the activities of the German "totalitarian government" that dismembered the institutions of the left and the Allied government of occupation that emasculated the institutions of the right. Olson, *Rise and Decline*, pp. 75–76.

[28]For examples see Carl Friedrich and Zbigniew Brzezinski, *Totalitarian Dictatorship and Autocracy* (Cambridge: Harvard University Press, 1956), p. 12, and Andrei Markovits and Christopher Allen, "Power and Dissent: The Trade Unions in the Federal Republic of Germany Re-examined," *West European Politics* 3 (January 1980), pp. 68–86.

[29]I refer to producers in Germany rather than German producers; one of the criteria by which the German state differentiated among producers was basis of ownership rather than location of production. "German producers" are specifically companies either privately or publicly owned by Germans; the term omits foreign multinationals located in Germany.

[30]Consider the case of Volkswagen in the 1950s. Beyond the fact that VW was publicly owned, both VW and the federal government wanted to maximize industrial exports and foreign capital imports. It was in the interest of the nation that the federal government assist VW in maximizing foreign sales. In contrast, the efforts of Fordwerke AG were aimed at maximizing sales within the Federal Republic—contributing to a possible drain on foreign currency.

benefited in the 1950s from changes initiated in the Nazi period and then, more mildly, from the sustained nature of their privileged relationship with the state in the fifteen years after the war.

These indigenous, strategically important firms, whose relationship with the state was established during the Third Reich, formed what Edwin Hartrich labels the "core of German industry" during both the Occupation period and the formative decade of the Bonn Republic. Other firms constituted the periphery.[31] According to Hartrich, this core defines the industrial "establishment" in the Bonn Republic, and, unlike subsidiaries of foreign multinational corporations, these companies enjoy a privileged relationship with the state apparatus. In this book I make two causal connections, first, substantively linking Hartrich's general argument to the auto industry, and second, explaining the origins of those core firms. I suggest the emergence of the core in the Bonn Republic's industrial establishment is predicated upon the formation of a relationship with the Nazi state. This relationship with the state was sustained in the 1950s when Bonn was keen to use the automotive sector to pursue policies that were clearly defined as national priorities. The characteristics of core and peripheral firms survived the Occupation period and were, ironically, often reinforced between 1945 and 1949. The characteristics of core and peripheral firms, and their relationship to successive Nazi, Allied, and Republican governing authorities, are summarized in Figure 2.1.

Core firms were favored because they shared interests with the state. The firms wanted to maximize profits; the state wanted them to remain competitive in order to earn foreign currency and, later, to maintain German technological development.[32] As a result, the firms and the state cooperated, benefiting from advantages denied to other firms such as sharing technical information. Core firms were protected by the state in that they were less subject than peripheral producers to the vagaries of the marketplace. The state has been prepared to underwrite the financial stability of core auto firms in postwar Germany.[33]

In contrast, peripheral firms in the auto industry were completely subject to the rigors of the marketplace. They were not supported in times of crisis, and some went bankrupt.[34] Peripheral firms had a diffi-

[31]See Edwin Hartrich, *The Fourth and Richest Reich* (New York: Macmillan, 1980), pp. 206–13.

[32]See James Womack and Daniel T. Jones, "The Competitive Significance of Government Technology Policy in the Auto Sector," paper prepared for International Automobile Program, International Policy Forum, Hakone, Japan, May 1982, pp. 1–10.

[33]Examples of short-term aid include the involvement of federal and Bavarian state governments in the purchase of Glas by BMW in 1967 and federal activities to aid Volkswagen during the mid-1970s. See Streeck, *Industrial Relations*.

[34]In the case of Borgward a seemingly secure company was allowed to go into bankruptcy as a result of a short-term cash-flow crisis in 1961 and then allowed to crash—at the cost of 23,000 jobs in Bremen, 25 percent of the local labor force.

	Core	Periphery
Membership characteristics	Public firms, Coopted partners	Multinationals, Paternal industrialists
Labor relations	Formal, Legalistic	Informal, Market-oriented
Relationship to state	Cordial, Cooperative	Aloof, Constrained
Relationship to state goals	Shared interest	Diverse but generally conflictual
Prospects for prosperity	Extensive	Limited

Figure 2.1. Characteristics of the core and periphery of the German automobile industry

cult time finding indigenous funding for long-term research and development (very costly in any industry) and were generally not the recipients of government research grants. Economic prospects for peripheral auto firms were therefore limited. They could not rely on governmental aid and sought alternative sources of funding. Among peripheral firms only the multinational producers whose home base lay in another country succeeded in securing extensive financing—through their parent companies. Peripheral firms had a distant, aloof neoclassical liberal relationship with the state, generally by the latter's choice though sometimes by mutual consent. In contrast, an intimate relationship provided core firms with the basis for a competitive advantage.

Two different labels have been used to describe the Bonn Republic—corporatist and liberal. I suggest that both labels may be partially correct about the characteristics of the German auto industry, depending on which part of the sector one examines and in which time period.

The core of the German automobile industry during the 1950s did indeed share an intimate, corporatist relationship with the state, as part of Erhard's "formed society,"[35] whereas the periphery of the German auto industry tended toward a relationship with the state more commonly associated with classical liberalism. This pattern was a product of Germany's fascist past. Only with the shift toward social democracy in the 1960s did the state's attitude toward major producers begin to involve a less discriminatory, indeed less interventionist, form of corporatism. By the late 1960s German societal corporatism bore the hallmarks associated with the analysis of Gerhard Lehmbruch, Philippe Schmitter, and Wolfgang Streeck.

The Argument Applied to Britain

Unlike the fascist experience that radically changed the development of the German state, the British regime retained basic liberal characteristics throughout the period studied in this book. The dominant characteristics of the liberal British state remained a relatively limited, unimposing state apparatus and, most important, a nondiscriminatory ideology. In practice, the state maintained an egalitarian set of criteria with significant implications. No firm could drive its rivals out of the marketplace completely, and gross disparities in the relative success of individual companies were narrowed. The state dispensed patronage broadly, preventing firms from suffering in a competitive market. Perversely, the state also intervened against firms that threatened to become dominant, just as successive American governments used antitrust legislation against General Motors, while simultaneously sheltering all firms from the excessive effects of international market forces. The component of fairness in this ideology, reflected in state policy, therefore narrowed the gap between winners and losers. The capacities of potential winners were shackled, and uncompetitive firms were subsidized. Cushioned by state policy, both potentially efficient and effectively inefficient British firms (and institutions) became increasingly incapable of achieving economic success in the postwar world.[36] The result was mediocrity. The state's reluctance to institute drastic changes

[35]See, for example, Katzenstein, *Policy and Politics*, pp. 107–9.

[36]Abelhauser describes this process in Britain as early economic success accompanied by the neglect of national economic development and the retardation of institutional development. Abelhauser contrasts this historical neglect with the case of Germany. Like many scholars, he depicts a linear relationship between 1750 and 1986. Such appraisals have their place but may weigh early developments with undue significance, ignoring intervening historical developments unfairly. See "The First Post-Liberal Nation," p. 311.

through coercive policies maintained traditional vestiges of political power, and these constrained the options available to the state in charting Britain's economic policy. In the Federal Republic of Germany, by contrast, such constraints were effectively swept away by the comprehensive changes instituted by the Nazi regime.[37] The nature of power relations between the British state and the various fragments of capital (and labor) remained intact throughout the 1950s and constrained the possibility of state innovation. Britain experienced no fundamental changes.[38]

These inflexible sets of relations, dominated by an egalitarian ideology and constrained forms of intervention, limited the likelihood of bankruptcy. Auto firms were guaranteed resources and, until the mid-1950s, access to markets that had inelastic demand. Conversely, nondiscriminatory ideology coupled with a constrained capacity for intervention artificially limited the possibilities for expansion. Individual British auto firms became incapable of adapting to competitive international pressures as flexibility became increasingly important.[39] Political decisions dictated both the effects of market forces and the capacity for expansion among British firms. At the same time core German firms were benefiting from the cumulative effects of fascist policies and their sustained, privileged access to the German state. There is little evidence to suggest that what remains of Britain's automobile producers has yet changed.

This explanation does not resolve how to explain the success of any automobile producer in Britain between the 1930s and the 1950s. Although the liberal British state did not encourage prosperity for particular firms through discriminatory behavior, it also did not create special barriers to the success of other firms. No firm suffered in Britain as the auto industry's periphery suffered in Germany. It is no surprise to

[37]In discussing Britain, Olson stresses that the lack of totalitarian government, revolution, or invasion by foreign forces has left Britain's distributional coalitions intact, and their number and complexity have continued to grow. Olson claims it is precisely this powerful network of special interest organizations that so adversely affects decision making and therefore the rate of growth: "In short, with age British society has acquired so many strong organizations and collusions that it suffers from an institutional sclerosis that slows its adaptation to changing circumstances and technologies" (*Rise and Decline*, pp. 77–78). However, unlike Olson, I do not assume that the Nazi state only dismantled *all* distributional coalitions but also (in Olson's terms) that it instituted new bases of association which survived the military government and the formation of the Bonn Republic. The FRG did not start with a clean slate but rather retained what Olson would call "distributional coalitions" instituted *after* 1933.

[38]For the significance of this point see Eric Hobsbawm, *Industry and Empire* (Harmondsworth: Penguin, 1969).

[39]A recent study that emphasizes this point is David B. Friedman, *The Misunderstood Miracle: Industrial Development and Political Change in Japan* (Ithaca: Cornell University Press, 1988).

find that the type of firms whose ambitions were frustrated in Germany from the beginning of the Third Reich should be successful in the postwar British automobile industry, including the subsidiaries of multinational corporations such as Ford and Vauxhall (the latter being General Motors' subsidiary in Britain).[40] In the absence of discriminatory barriers imposed by a politically powerful state, the economically successful firms had different characteristics. A less discriminatory political regime created a different distribution of rewards among competitors: in strong terms, the firms that failed in West Germany succeeded in Britain, and vice versa. To test this claim, in the following chapters I examine the development of two national subsidiaries of one company, Ford.

Stagnant British state policies in the auto sector often exacted a price from the overall health of the British economy. Multinationals within Britain succeeded at the expense of domestic producers. Unlike in Germany, the British state could not impose substantial rationalization or integration on domestic auto producers and would not discriminate against American multinational corporations in the 1930s or 1940s, so domestic producers remained uncompetitive relative to these multinationals in the early postwar period.[41] Later attempts by the state to rationalize the industry, consolidating British firms in the formation of British Leyland, proved purely cosmetic; that company was still comprised of 60 plants with 246 unions in 1968.[42] Ford's and General Motors' subsidiaries succeeded at the expense of British mass producers such as Austin, and their profits did not accrue in Dagenham, Luton, or the City of London.[43] Eric Hobsbawm claims that the economic decision to favor free trade was based on the fact that the preponderance of political power in Britain rested with an elite whose interests favored a liberal system that gave free license to the diffusion of capital. The absence of a discretionary state to arbitrate on important decisions favored the interests of finance capital at the expense of industrial capital.[44] My theory challenges this view. Hobsbawm's interpretation explains the decline of the British auto industry in terms

---

[40]This logic also applies to paternal industrialists who are craft producers, such as Borgward in Germany and Rolls Royce in Britain.

[41]Jones, *Industrial Adjustment and Policy*, p. 45. Jones asserts that this uncompetitiveness extended beyond the period of my study.

[42]David B. Friedman, "Government and Growth: Automobile Policy in America, Japan, and the U.K." unpublished paper, Department of Political Science, MIT, p. 48.

[43]On the effects of the diffusion of capital and technology on a hegemonic power as applied to liberal states, see Gilpin, *U.S. Power and the Multinational Corporations*, and Robert Gilpin, *War and Change in World Politics* (Cambridge: Cambridge University Press, 1981).

[44]See Hobsbawm, *Industry and Empire.*

of a segment of the capitalist class acting to the detriment of an advanced capitalist economy because of the absence of an autonomous state to limit the excessive effects of self-interest.[45] But I suggest it was not the state's lack of autonomy but its ideology that dictated its behavior. The British state had a clear consensus of values that favored the free flow of investment capital but not finished products. This bias encouraged foreign direct investment and egalitarian treatment of foreign firms. The two combined to produce a policy of national treatment.

The result was the neglect of auto producers at a time when they were potentially competitive and the subsequent diffusion of investment capital by foreign multinationals. These factors eventually combined to drain the industry of internally generated investment capital. The auto industry, neglected by state policy and rebuffed by dominant financial institutions, subsequently had to appeal to the state for funding. By that time funding earmarked for investment capital was generally being used to pay debts, putting British producers at a cumulative disadvantage. This is not to suggest domestic British producers bore no responsibility for their decline. Domestic producers, unbridled by the dictates of state policy, had diffused potential resources through high dividend payments motivated by fear of impending nationalization. Yet the British and German auto sectors had looked very similar in the early 1930s, with limited state intervention, dominant American multinationals, and fragmented domestic producers. And they would have looked very similar in the 1950s, I argue, had state policies not diverged in the interim.

Britain therefore provides an example of continuity for my general argument that the historical evolution of the political regime can plausibly explain which types of firm have been successful in the respective automobile industries and the relative success of each sector as a whole. Although events in Britain provide examples of continuity, they are neither insignificant nor dull. The reasons why the status quo was maintained in Britain, and its consequences, are just as interesting and significant to our understanding of economic success as the political decisions that provoked sweeping changes in Germany.

The German and British automobile markets before 1933 had crucial similarities. The nature of the relationship between the state and firms in the two sectors diverged during the 1930s as a result of con-

---

[45]See Stephen Krasner, *Defending the National Interest: Raw Materials Investments and U.S. Foreign Policy* (Princeton: Princeton University Press, 1978), pp. 20–26, or Theda Skocpol in Peter Evans, Dietrich Rueschemeyer, and Skocpol, *Bringing the State Back In* (New York: Cambridge University Press, 1985), pp. 3–43, for the theoretical possibilities and contextual limitations on the potential autonomy of the state.

trasting state policies. The Nazi state consciously pursued policies that contributed to the fragmentation of manufacturing capital in the German automobile industry. Different firms benefited or were handicapped by the introduction of a state system that discriminated against foreign producers and uncooperative paternal industrialists and in favor of a domestic elite. This discriminatory pattern was maintained in the Bonn Republic during the 1950s.

The liberal British political regime, in contrast, was incapable of reorganizing industry during the 1930s and 1940s, and the dominant ideology would not permit the state to discriminate among producers in the 1950s. The state therefore had to tolerate the excesses of capital (and labor), although its limited capacities meant that it generally chose to side with capital or with labor rather than stand (and therefore fall) alone.[46] During the 1940s and early 1950s elements of the state generally sided with labor. The state encouraged all auto firms to prosper, including foreign multinationals, even if the long-term effect of such policies was detrimental to the health of the British economy.

In the short term the type of successful auto firm in the two countries was starkly different, resulting in two very different postwar market structures. In the longer term this divergence had two related effects after 1945. The first was in the nature of state ideologies. The liberal British ideology emphasized egalitarian values and could conceive of only a limited range of interventionist policies. The German state had no such ideological limits. The Bonn Republic combined Erhard's classical liberal finance policies on exchange and investment with statist, discriminatory trade policies on issues of market access, pricing, and research and development. Second, during the Nazi period the state had instituted channels of access for an elite of auto firms and widened the scope and domain of state activity. This discriminatory ideology and these privileged channels were reinforced during the Allied Occupation, giving particular firms a cumulative advantage. In such a market discretionary access by select firms and wide scope for state

[46]The traditional image in pluralist societies of the state as umpire with politics as an arena is therefore replaced in this case by an image of the British state as weak but not neutral. See David Truman, *The Governmental Process: Political Interests and Public Opinion* (New York: Knopf, 1951). Even a relatively weak state is capable of both determining the boundaries of the political process and also being a political actor. The work of Steven Tolliday and Jonathan Zeitlin has placed this perspective on the British state in a historical context: see *Shopfloor Bargaining and the State: Historical and Comparative Perspectives* (Cambridge: Cambridge University Press, 1984). Note Andrew Gamble's consideration of the possibility that a revolution is taking place in Britain under the Thatcher government: the state is adopting an increasingly coercive stance, taking on many of the more authoritarian corporatist characteristics of the German state, and losing many liberal characteristics. See Gamble, "Introduction to the American Edition," *Britain in Decline: Economic Policy, Political Strategy, and the British State* (Boston: Beacon, 1981).

action seemed intuitively acceptable, even to the leaders of governments that professed classical liberal principles in their approach to policy making. The British regime therefore retained its liberal characteristics, whereas the German regime retained a greater tolerance toward, and capacity for, effective discriminatory intervention. These differences were reflected in the distribution of economic prosperity among auto producers in Britain and West Germany in the 1950s.[47] The coincidence of objectives between the German state and the core producers limited the diffusion of investment capital. On occasion the banking community mediated between government and producers to ensure that interests continued to coincide.[48] In contrast, British state policy was often confrontational rather than complementary to its own producers' interests.

Examining the two largest producers in the auto industry in each country provides a basis for generalization about the industry in each country in the period specified. Although the auto industry is an important, strategic sector, however, it is not the basis upon which to generalize about development of West German industry as a whole. My claims are confined to the auto industry, though there may be a broader line of enquiry to pursue—speculating on the applicability of this model to other industries in West Germany or Britain and to automobile producers in other countries. The divergence in market structures, accumulated economic advantages, and institutional remnants I describe may have had important implications in the 1950s not only for West Germany in relation to Britain but also for other advanced industrialized nations.

I stress the significance of the historical development of a political regime. The nature of the political regime serves to explain not only the variation in industrial prosperity between countries but also variations in the type of prosperity among auto producers within countries. Crucial historical processes explain the development pattern of each political regime. In turn, the nature of the political regime explains the distribution of economic prosperity among firms, both their uniformities and their variations.

Having established a theoretical relationship between historical developments and the modern form of the political regime, I examine

[47]The obvious example among German mass producers was Opel, whose share of the German auto market fell from its prewar dominance of over 50 percent of all sales to less than 20 percent in the early 1950s and as low as 11.7 percent in 1952. See "Organizational and Management Basic Data Book: Ford of Germany" (Cologne: Fordwerke AG, 1951–1952). File AR-75-63-430:93, Ford Industrial Archives, Redford, Mich.

[48]For historical perspective see Karl-Heinz Roth, "Der Weg zum guten Stern des Dritten Reichs," in Roth, ed., Das Daimler-Benz Buch: Ein Rüstungskonzern im Tausendjährigen Reich (Nördlingen: Delphi Politik, 1986).

four automobile firms. Each of the following four chapters therefore constitutes a case, describing the development of a particular firm from its origins to the early 1960s. Two focus on representative firms in Germany; I chose Ford because it is a foreign multinational and Volkswagen because it was the "child of the fascist state." I also examine British Ford and Austin, focusing on potentially the most coercive policies of the British state. I attempt to move beyond a simple correlation between form of political regime and type of successful firm. I look for a causal relationship by demonstrating the effect of contrasting state policies on the distribution of economic success, in terms of the individual firms and in terms of the structure of the industry as a whole.

CHAPTER THREE

At Home in a Foreign Land: Ford in Britain

Liberal states, I have suggested, employ egalitarian principles in their treatment of auto firms, disregarding the nationality of the owners. The classic case was Britain, where a nondiscriminatory ideology was complemented by weak institutions. Unlike the German state, successive liberal British governments limited intervention to the macro-level. Ideology, and the state's capacity for action, were reciprocally supportive. The British liberal state lacked the political tools to do more than incrementally adjust policies toward the auto industry.

Yet it would be misleading to suppose that British liberalism was noninterventionist. As Karl Polanyi effectively demonstrates, even when the British state reflected orthodox liberal values, and its interventionism was in a conventional sense minimal, the market was always framed in a context of political relationships.[1] Furthermore, the state has always intervened in the workings of the British automobile industry through the use of tariffs, quotas, regional policies, and financial aid. What distinguished liberal regimes was their unwillingness and their general inability to discriminate between firms. Even on those rare occasions when British political leaders conceived of discriminating against foreign multinationals, they were driven to reverse their policies by their dominant values and by the limits of the state apparatus. The British state traditionally emphasized the importance of short-term employment and balance of trade issues, reflecting the primacy of electoral considerations. These same generalizations apply today.

[1]Karl Polanyi, *The Great Transformation: The Political and Economic Origins of Our Time* (Boston: Beacon, 1957).

The British state's behavior concerning the auto industry demands a reappraisal of the meaning of liberalism. *Liberal* here means no open markets for goods but open markets for finance—liberal states encourage foreign investment once they have lost their comparative and competitive advantages. Once committed to invest in liberal Britain, foreign firms were eligible for all the rights and privileges of domestic producers. The larger size of American mass producers allowed them to take advantage of economies of scale in Britain's stable and expanding markets, while they had access to investment financing unavailable to British firms. So multinationals could dwarf the immature British mass producers who were never given the political context in which they could have made the transition from limited to global production.

In the following four chapters I examine two major producers in Germany and two in Britain. Austin was generally the largest British producer even prior to its merger with Morris in 1952 and would have been a strong candidate for a "national champion" like Volkswagen in the Federal Republic of Germany. Ford consistently dominated the British market after its introduction in the early twentieth century. The convivial relationship between firm and state convinced the company to build its "little River Rouge" at Dagenham on the banks of the River Thames. I also look at two German firms, Volkswagen and Fordwerke. This limited selection may confine generalization, but it does hold many variables constant.[2] By examining two subsidiaries of the same multinational company, I discard the possibility that differences in their success stem from the form of technology and the dominant priorities in company policy. Neither subsidiary, moreover, had been deprived of investment opportunities for expansion due to lack of finance because both could avail themselves of their parent company's resources.[3] Differences in outcome should be due purely to domestic influences rather than systemic variations.

Inevitably, the comparison of Austin and Volkswagen is not so neat. However, the major comparison is not between Austin and Volkswagen but rather between two relationships: that of Austin, Ford, and the British state and that of Volkswagen, Fordwerke, and the German state.

[2]See Adam Przeworski and Henry Teune, *The Logic of Comparative Social Enquiry* (New York: Wiley, 1970), p. 32.

[3]The constant nature of company policy is reflected in Thornhill Cooper's discussion of labor relations throughout Ford's European subsidiaries. Cooper notes that throughout his employment in the company an identical labor policy was adopted in all countries, beginning with the famous initial terms of contract—5-day, 40-hour week, and salary at a level 25 percent above the market rate—first adopted in the United States in 1926. Once recognition of unions was conceded in England in 1944, the company made this policy universal. Interview, Mira Wilkins with Thornhill Cooper 27 June 1960, Wilkins Personal File.

I try primarily to understand why different firms succeed in different contexts and, secondarily, what the aggregate effects are on the sector. This chapter examines Ford in Britain, and subsequent chapters examine Ford and Volkswagen in Germany, and then Austin. The logic of the sequence is simple; I compare Ford's relatively favorable treatment in Britain with that in Germany, and then I compare Volkswagen's favorable treatment in Germany with Austin's treatment in Britain.

THE FORD MOTOR COMPANY IN BRITAIN BEFORE 1939

The first three Ford Model Ts were imported in 1904, but the Ford Motor Company (England) Ltd. was not formally registered as a company until 1911. By then a plant had been purchased at Trafford Park in Manchester where imported American parts were assembled.[4] Ford sales were double those of Wolseley, the next largest producer.[5] The domestic content of Ford vehicles grew, encouraged by the threat of import duties.[6] By 1914 over two thousand people were employed at the plant, and its production included both the Fordson tractor and a delivery van.[7] During World War I Ford received government contracts to supply military vehicles and hospital vans and, subject to extensive government controls, mechanics for machinery and instruction in exchange for permission to export to neutral and allied European countries.[8] The company grew rapidly: 1,485 cars were sold in 1911, 17,782 in 1919, and by 1925 over 250,000 vehicle had been built.[9]

The company's growth warranted expanded facilities, and a site at Dagenham, just outside London, was purchased in 1924. Cheap land and immediate access to the River Thames were ideal attributes, though there were initial construction problems. In 1928 the company became the Ford Motor Company Ltd. under the chairmanship of Percival Perry, who remained its titular head until his retirement in

[4]See "Historical Data," File AR-75-63-430:65, Ford Industrial Archives, p. 2.

[5]Graham Turner, *The Car Makers* (London: Eyre & Spottiswoode, 1963), p. 20.

[6]The McKenna duties were introduced during World War I to limit imports by sea, increase domestic revenue, limit the shipment of luxury and bulky goods, and (most significantly) to protect British industry. The measures included a 33 percent import levy on motor vehicles and parts from outside the British Empire, 22.22 percent on those from within the Empire. This new duty "profoundly affected" the Ford operation in southern Ireland and resulted in the closure of the Cork plant when the new Irish state was formed in 1922. For a detailed discussion see Mira Wilkins and Frank E. Hill, *American Business Abroad: Ford on Six Continents* (Detroit: Wayne State University Press, 1964), p. 63.

[7]"Historical Data," Ford Industrial Archives.

[8]Wilkins and Hill, *American Business Abroad*, p. 62.

[9]"Historical Data," Ford Industrial Archives.

1948. Perry had been involved with the company in its early days but had left in 1919 in a conflict over the company's financial policies. This restructuring consolidated the American parent company's control and, in a rare admission, Henry Ford essentially conceded his earlier mistake by recalling Perry to head the new company.[10] Perry favored a new plant in Southampton, but 310 acres of land had already been purchased at Dagenham and, with new competitive pressures on Ford's traditional market leadership from Morris and Austin and the threat posed by General Motors' purchase of Vauxhall in 1925, Ford felt the need to act quickly.[11] The parent company realized that under Ford's bafflingly complicated global stock distribution system, in which every subsidiary seemed to own large blocs of another subsidiary, the British company had tremendous potential for growth: it had the exclusive right to export to the European, Near Eastern, and Far Eastern markets. In the absence of assertive behavior, however, new British competitors including Singer, Standard, Austin, and Morris would usurp these markets. The American company therefore developed a new stock arrangement that increased the English company's capitalization from £200,000 to more than £7 million.[12] Construction began in 1929 on the new, smaller "River Rouge," and by 1931 the plant was in production. This new plant gave Ford an immediate advantage. Its British counterparts lacked an efficient components industry, whereas the new plant at Dagenham could manufacture, at a cheaper rate, all the parts conventionally produced by components firms. Ford could thereby force down the prices charged by components firms.[13]

Although the company made a loss in the first two years of production at Dagenham (the only such time in its first half-century of production), statistics for the 1930s prove impressive, especially in view of the global depression's effects on the British economy (see Table 3.1). These numbers should be considered in the context of a deepening world recession, which made the company's expansion a tremendous risk.

The potential convinced management to enter the "baby car" market to compete with the smaller, more fuel-efficient English cars, rather than the shrinking section of the market that purchased larger,

---

[10]Wilkins and Hill, *American Business Abroad,* pp. 86, 189.

[11]From its inception in 1911 Ford was the British market leader until it fell behind Morris and Austin in 1924, partially because of bad management decisions (such as periodic switching of the steering wheel between the left- and right-hand side) and partially because of its incapacity to approach economies of scale because of the Manchester plant's limited capacity. Ibid., p. 145.

[12]Ibid., p. 193.

[13]D. G. Rhys, *The Motor Industry: An Economic Survey* (London: Butterworth, 1972), p. 8.

THE FRUITS OF FASCISM

Table 3.1. Profits of Ford U.K., 1931–1939

Year	Profits after tax (in £000's)	Dividend (%)
1931	−135	—
1932	−726	—
1933	742	—
1934	484	5
1935	597	5
1936	497	6
1937	375	5
1938	169	5
1939	625	6

SOURCES: Memo, "Attention Special Finance Projects," R. A. Winter, 19 September 1952, File AR-75-63-430:64, Ford Industrial Archives; Report, "Dividend for 1955: A Draft Study," Ford Industrial Archives, p. 14.

American-designed cars.[14] This decision was the foundation for the company's later decision to enter the fleet sales segment of the market—that is, sales of cars to companies that need to supply their labor force (usually salespeople) with reliable, cheap cars to conduct company business. Fleet sales subsequently became a cornerstone of Ford's market strategy and one of the bases of its extended success in postwar Britain.[15]

New demands required a larger labor force. By 1932 over 7,000 men were employed, and the prewar peak was 12,000 in 1937. Expansion of capacity coincided with a contraction in demand, and Ford's traditionally high wages were cut 10 percent in 1932, leading to the nonunionized labor force's only prewar strike at Dagenham. Comprehensive participation in the strike, which lasted three days, resulted in the company's agreeing to revert to former wage levels.[16]

Reduced demand in 1931 threatened Ford with bankruptcy because of high operating costs. Such pressures took the new baby Ford model from conception to exhibition hall as the Popular within six months—by February 1932—and into production within eleven months, with 8,260 being produced in 1932. The Popular was the first car designed by Ford to meet the specific requirements of foreign conditions.[17]

[14]See *Daily Express*, 26 August 1931.
[15]See Perry to Edsel Ford, 22 October 1931, Accession 38, Box 1, Edison Institute, Dearborn, Mich. The peculiarities of the British tax system meant that a company often provided its sales force and managers with company cars as "perks." Fleet sales were a lucrative market in postwar Britain. Under the Thatcher government reforms, this traditional tax loophole has been tightened.
[16]Notes, Norman St. John Stevas, "Ford in the United Kingdom," unpublished mimeograph, pp. 100–101, copy at Ford Industrial Archives.
[17]Wilkins and Hill, *American Business Abroad*, p. 241.

Despite an enthusiastic reception, sales fell further and Ford recorded its second year of losses in 1932, slipping into third place in sales in the British market behind Austin (28.8 percent) and Morris (27.2 percent) for the only time in its history. The company was restored to financial stability by 1933, and two years later Ford made a revolutionary move, comparable to the introduction of the Model T in the United States—the £100 car. This price created the possibility of ownership for a large new segment of the British population.[18]

Although sales had grown in 1933 and 1934, the company felt that sustained competitiveness lay in reducing costs rather than producing a new model. "Cost consciousness" was emphasized by management, with the objectives of reducing prices, raising the volume of sales, and so moving toward an optimal level of production. Suppliers of components were pressured to reduce their costs, and every component was examined. The Popular, which had been on the market for four years, underwent a drastic reduction in price which Mira Wilkins and Frank Hill claim "was achieved without effecting the design or manufacturing quality in any way," although Graham Turner argues that mass production techniques inevitably trade off quality and quantity—a view supported by the labor force at Ford. Sales of the new car soared, and in the small, eight-horsepower sector Ford's price advantage raised its market share between 1934 and 1935 from 22 percent to 41 percent.[19] The firm's market growth prompted plans for two future models, the Anglia and the Prefect.

British Ford became the leading subsidiary, though these financial gains carried their own costs in terms of industrial relations at Dagenham. Efforts at cost cutting created new demands on the labor force, increasing work place tensions and destroying the characteristically cordial relations that had existed before 1935.[20] During this prewar period Ford declared a universal industrial relations policy.[21] Perry disliked the original plant in Manchester, a city he considered a hotbed of union radicalism; his view was strengthened by strikes in 1912 and 1913 that sought union recognition and severely curtailed production.

[18]Ibid., p. 246. Ford did not suffer alone—Morris's share of the market declined from 51 percent in 1929 to 27.2 percent in 1933, a level maintained until 1939. In this period of turmoil large producers lacked the flexibility to adjust to rapidly changing market conditions. However, mass producers reasserted themselves as the market stabilized. For figures see Turner, *The Car Makers*, p. 26; "Historical Data," Ford Industrial Archives.

[19]See Wilkins and Hill, *American Business Abroad*, pp. 288, 290, and Turner, *The Car Makers*, p. 160.

[20]Wilkins and Hill, *American Business Abroad*, pp. 293, 303.

[21]Interview, Mira Wilkins with Thornhill Cooper, 27 June 1960, Wilkins Personal File. For a controversial but interesting consideration of the Ford Company's labor relations policies in this period see Stephen Meyer III, *The Five Dollar Day: Labor Management and Social Control in the Ford Motor Company, 1908–1921* (Albany: SUNY Press, 1981).

The strikes ceased when Charles Sorensen arrived from the United States and promised wage increases to strategically placed workers, but Perry feared a recurrence. Perry also found the Manchester plant repugnant and was enthusiastic about moving to the more civilized environment of Southampton where a better climate, cleaner working conditions, the availability of a port, and lack of union development were appealing. However, his temporary departure in the early 1920s killed that plan.[22]

All 2,000 workers were shipped to London when the Dagenham plant opened, and the move did improve working conditions. The company provided canteen services, medical services, and sports facilities, in addition to introducing a noncontributory benefit scheme in 1935 which gave each employee upon retirement the sum of £5 for each year he had been employed by the company.[23] These numerous welfare functions were designed to prove to the labor force that unions were not required to serve their best interests.

Prior to the war, unions were not recognized. High wages were paid, but the company hired and fired at will, prompting L. T. Blakeman to suggest later that the company earned "a bad reputation for its ruthless approach." The insecurity that developed in the labor force lasted long after the introduction of unionism according to Graham Turner, creating constant apprehension and alienation and high turnover. The company publicized its new pension scheme for workers, but only later did it become apparent that the scheme would apply only to salaried workers. Furthermore, conflict over unionization grew at Ford, fostered by the acceptance of unions by such domestic producers as Austin, Morris, and Standard. Resentment grew into militancy with the appointment of D. Marsden Jones as labor relations manager toward the end of the war—a man Blakeman, his successor, described as having an "authoritarian personality."[24]

With a reduced share of domestic market came a reduction in exports. The English company had exercised control over all European subsidiaries before 1934 and had used this power to export large quantities of cars. After 1934, however, control of the German, and then the French, subsidiaries slipped from its grasp. In Germany the Nazi regime demanded that Ford's German subsidiary produce domestically (not just assemble) and that it standardize production with German manufacturers—creating interchangeable components. American management also allowed European subsidiaries to import from either

[22]Wilkins and Hill, *American Business Abroad*, pp. 49, 59, 68.
[23]St. John Stevas, "Ford in the United Kingdom," pp. 101–2.
[24]Interview, Mira Wilkins with L. T. Blakeman, Labor Relations Manager, 2 September 1960, Wilkins Personal File; Turner, *The Car Makers*, p. 127.

Dagenham or Dearborn. The much lower cost of production at Dearborn outweighed the extra costs of freight to Europe, offering the product at a lower price than Dagenham.[25] In a rare show of "dog eat dog" within a multinational, Dagenham found itself competing not only with other British and European producers but with its own parent company.[26]

As the 1930s came to an end Ford found its traditional dominance of the British market threatened. Nevertheless, in the decade it had made a remarkable transition from small-scale to mass production and developed the most modern facilities in Europe. Ford's management had overcome discriminatory barriers by locating production in Britain and relying on exclusively British management. British managers had cultivated acceptance by government in leading efforts to export both within and outside the markets of the British Empire.

FIRM-STATE RELATIONS BEFORE 1939

Although Ford was a foreign multinational, it quickly integrated itself into the British economy. Initially an assembler of components manufactured abroad, the company was accepted as a domestic producer once it began to *produce and assemble* components within the United Kingdom. When World War I began, Ford, led by Perry, seized the opportunity to turn heightened demand to the company's advantage.

Perry initially sought access to lucrative government contracts, and Model Ts and vans were sold for war use while civilian production continued. By May 1916 government contracts had procured one thousand vehicles for military and medical purposes, and inflexible government demands prompted Wilkins and Hill to suggest that the Ford plant in Manchester had become "a government-controlled establishment." Perry became heavily involved in war production, leading to the accusation that he devoted too much time to government affairs and not enough to company business—criticism that presumed the two were not complementary. In contrast, Wilkins and Hill suggest that Perry's two pursuits were linked: "As to the government, he [Perry] had been able to protect Ford and the company by establishing relations

---

[25]In a letter to Sorensen dated 12 December 1930, Perry suggested that the loss of the German, Central European, French, and Italian markets had already so adversely affected economies of scale in England that it cost three times as much to produce in Britain as in Dearborn. I assume the construction of Dagenham reduced this differential, but the figures are still indicative of the cost difference between the two.

[26]See Allan Nevins and Frank E. Hill, *Ford: Decline and Rebirth: 1933–1962* (New York: Scribner, 1962), p. 84.

with members of the War Cabinet." Perry claimed these government posts had been "of material assistance in enabling me to carry on the company business," feeling that he "ought to receive commendation rather than criticism." However, American company officials accused him of pursuing his political aspirations in a "frank and undisguised" fashion among "a group of men who preferred each other, whose directorates interlock, and who help each other whenever possible." The whole issue came to a climax in 1919 when Perry was questioned about his financial dealings, not by the forerunners of C. Wright Mills but by William Knudsen, director at Dearborn.[27]

Whether Perry was pursuing his own interests or those of the company, the beneficiaries were both Perry (who was later knighted) *and* Ford. His prestige may have personally increased in Britain, but the company also benefited from lucrative government contracts that allowed it short-term profits and a reputation for reliable products. The company benefited from export rights to neutral and allied European states, and it responded to the British government's call for increased food production by developing and building the new Fordson tractor at their Irish plant at Cork. From this early date England became the basis for Ford's European operations, and cordial relations were established between the firm and successive British governments.[28]

FORD DURING WORLD WAR II

In 1939 Ford was as unprepared for conversion to wartime production as the rest of British industry. It had shown some foresight, suggesting to the government in 1937 that it buy 3,000 Fordson tractors with an agreed "buy-back" clause if there was no war.[29] But the suggestion was unusual. Even in the "phoney war" from September 1939 to March 1940 very few adjustments were made, and civilian production continued. However, in October 1939 Perry was approached by Air Vice Marshall Wilfred Freeman, assistant chief of air staff, about the possibility that Ford might manufacture Merlin aero engines, leading to further talks in November between Ford and Rolls-Royce, the original manufacturers. These talks accelerated with Churchill's accession to power. Ford introduced its latest model, the Anglia, on 1 January 1940 but was forced to suspend production for the duration under

[27]Wilkins and Hill, *American Business Abroad*, pp. 61–62, 83–84.
[28]Ibid., pp. 62, 69–72.
[29]St. John Stevas, "Ford in the United Kingdom," p. 120.

the Emergency Powers (Defence) Acquisition and Disposal of Motor Vehicles Order of 1940.[30]

Churchill was determined to use the Dagenham facilities to their full capacity in the war effort, despite misgivings about their strategic vulnerability.[31] The plant was located in the southeast, accessible to German bombing, and easily identifiable because of its location on the banks of the Thames. It was agreed that Ford would produce Merlin aero engines at a newly constructed "shadow factory" near the site of its old Manchester plant.

This decision had important repercussions. Henry Ford's initial hesitancy had brought a storm of protests from his own executives at British and Canadian subsidiaries and a tremendous amount of bad publicity. Even Ford could not resist the pressure and conceded, suggesting he had been referring only to the American company's policy and that his comments did not apply to subsidiaries—certainly a reversal, because subsidiaries were normally given little autonomy. Tremendous efforts were then made at Dagenham and Manchester to restore cordial relations with the British government.[32]

Ford's decision to build the Merlin has interesting implications for the distinction between mass and craft production techniques.[33] The engine was normally produced by Rolls-Royce, which employed craftsmen of the highest caliber in an exacting process. Under a new arrangement between the companies, employees from Dagenham moved into Rolls-Royce plants at Derby and Crewe, where Merlins were manufactured, and studied the process. Ford employees were supervised and advised by Rolls-Royce employees at every stage. The two sets of employees worked cooperatively, and Ford engineers left the premises determined to apply the principles of mass production to the construction of these engines.[34]

The new plant cost £6.6 million, paid for by the government.[35] Urgently needed machine tools were flown from the United States by the Royal Air Force. Close relations were established between the company and the newly formed Ministries of Supply and Aircraft Production, the latter headed by Lord Beaverbrook. Ford engineers were

---

[30]Notes, Mira Wilkins on Fawcett, *Wheel of Fortune*, Wilkins Personal File; A. Hall to Ford Dealers, Facsimile File 1939 and 1940, Wilkins Personal File.

[31]Nevins and Hill, *Ford: Decline and Rebirth*, p. 282.

[32]*Midland* [Mich.] *Daily News*, 27 June 1940; Nevins and Hill, *Ford: Decline and Rebirth*, p. 284.

[33]See, for example, Michael Piore and Charles Sabel, *The Second Industrial Divide: Possibilities for Prosperity* (New York: Basic, 1984).

[34]Interview, Mira Wilkins with Sir Rowland Smith, General Manager, 23 August 1960, Wilkins Personal File.

[35]See PEP, *Report on the Motor Industry* (London: HMSO, 1950).

appointed as civil servants to provide the government with the necessary expertise for the construction of both the factory and the new engine.[36] Despite his own initial resistance to cooptation as a civil servant, Patrick Hennessy (later knighted for his efforts) was added to the Advisory Council on Aircraft Production, and Perry became an adviser to the Ministry of Food. Construction of the plant started in February 1940 and was completed by June; production began immediately.[37]

The manufacturing process used in Manchester differed radically from Rolls-Royce in Derby. All tasks were simplified so that unskilled labor could be used. William Squire, a company executive, suggested that the difference was demonstrated in the construction of the crucial cylinder block, crank case, and cylinder head. He said that "for these Ford used a multiple-spindle and multiple way machine tool, where Rolls-Royce had employed a single-spindle radical arm drilling machine."[38] In effect a machine bored forty holes simultaneously instead of one person drilling forty holes individually. Squire stressed that Rolls-Royce adapted some of Ford's ideas and later applied them to their own practices at their Hillington plant near Glasgow.

For the duration of the war the plant employed 17,300 people, including 7,000 women, most of whom were totally unfamiliar with engineering skills. Yet the plant produced over 30,000 Merlin engines between June 1941 and November 1945 at a fraction of Rolls-Royce's costs while maintaining comparable quality. During the war the plant suffered one bad hit, in the polishing shop, halting production for two days. Sir Rowland Smith, who was in charge of production, described the plant as a "supreme achievement."[39] Certainly, the evidence casts doubt on assumptions that mass production necessitates a markedly inferior product.[40] And quality control was maintained even though the labor force included a large minority of women entering the job market for the first time.[41]

While Manchester captured much of the attention, Dagenham was receiving scrutiny of a different sort, as company officials sought to

[36]Hilary St. George Saunders, *Ford at War* (Dagenham: Ford Ltd., 1947), p. 18.

[37]Nevins and Hill, *Ford: Decline and Rebirth*, p. 282.

[38]Interview, Frank Hill with William Squire, 20 June 1961, Wilkins Personal File.

[39]Interview, Oliver Moore with Sir Rowland Smith, "Sir Rowland Smith: Man of the Month," October 1948, Wilkins Personal File.

[40]An example of this problem is the Manchester plant where company figures reveal that by 1941, of 17,000 workers employed only 14.2 percent of the labor force was skilled. Yet the process involved the construction of an engine composed of 2,128 different parts, with 10,349 individual pieces, made from 27 different types of alloy steel and 9 types of aluminum alloy, in which each part was individually inspected. See "The Merlin Engine," *Ford Times*, November–December 1945, pp. 564–65.

[41]William Squire suggests that in practice the women performed better than the men. They tended to perfect their tasks and displayed patience, whereas the men demanded more variety in their jobs and were less tolerant. Interview, Hill with William Squire.

camouflage this huge factory against aerial bombardment. The task tested the creative skills of company and government officials but was achieved through an effective blackout system coupled with some creative painting of the plant's roof, making it appear from the sky as if the plant was part of the Dagenham marsh. Shelters were constructed, siren and drill alarms initiated, and blast walls built along side production lines to cut the time lost through workers having to retire to air raid shelters. By June 1940 Dagenham was producing 130 war vehicles per day: vans, trucks, and infantry carriers, including new four-wheel drive vehicles.[42]

These innovative four-wheel drive vehicles radically improved Allied fighting capabilities in the deserts of North Africa, the jungles of Asia, and the mud of Europe. Erwin Rommel paid personal testimony to the quality of Dagenham products in a specific instruction to capture *any Ford vehicle* for use in the German war effort.[43] In the winter of 1940 production shifts were extended from eight to twelve hours a day, and additional production plants were constructed at Leamington, where 90 percent of tracks for the army's Bren gun carriers were made.[44] Cars and trucks were also produced at Cramlington and Wigan, in the north of England. Ford built every tracked light carrier in the British army during the war, and every wheeled light carrier in the British army was either built by Ford or contained a Ford V-8 engine.[45] The first contract, for 4,500 carrier vehicles, was not received until September 1941, but the first vehicle was produced six months later, in February 1942. Ford also assembled the first Jeep ever constructed in Britain at its Wigan plant in 1942, and within two years 10,000 Jeeps had been assembled there.[46]

Ford's manufacture of military vehicles is only half the story, because so much of Ford's efforts were directed toward the Fordson tractor. Between 1940 and 1944 the manufacture of tractors doubled at Dagenham, where Ford ran the only blast furnace of its kind in Britain at full capacity. In 1940 the number of tractors produced, at 20,000, exceeded the prewar record of 8,000 in a year (in 1937). In 1942 the figure had risen to 27,650, and by 10 November 1943, 100,000 tractors had been produced as part of Britain's "Dig for Victory" campaign.[47]

[42]Nevins and Hill, *Ford: Decline and Rebirth*, p. 282; St. George Saunders, *Ford at War*, p. 18.
[43]St. John Stevas, "Ford in the United Kingdom," p. 125.
[44]St. George Saunders, *Ford at War*, p. 30; interview, Sir Rowland Smith with St. John Stevas, 15 March 1953, Wilkins Personal File.
[45]Nevins and Hill, *Ford: Decline and Rebirth*, p. 283; St. George Saunders, *Ford at War*, p. 51.
[46]Wilkins and Hill, *American Business Abroad*, p. 334.
[47]St. George Saunders, *Ford at War*, pp. 19–20; St. John Stevas, "Ford in the United Kingdom," p. 123.

Table 3.2. Vehicle production at Ford, 1939–1945

Model	Total quantity produced
Anglia	5,136
Prefect	14,281
61 Model	212
5/7 cwt. Van	2,882
10 cwt. Van	15,516
15 cwt. Van	375
25 cwt. Van	2,375
2/5 Ton Normal Control Truck	4,525
2/5 Ton Forward Control Truck	29,188
Fordson Tractor	134,474
Major Tractor	786
WOA-1 Utility Car	1,623
WOA-2 Utility Car	9,059
WOC1 15 cwt. Truck	2,001
WOT-1 6 Wheeler Survey Truck	9,154
WOT-2 15 cwt. Truck	59,498
WOT-3 30 cwt. Truck	17,966
WOT-6 3 Ton Truck	29,693
WOT-8 30 cwt. Truck	2,516
AOP Carrier	4,576
Lyod Carrier	4,213
Universal Carrier	5,153

SOURCE: PEP, *Report on the Motor Industry* (London: HMSO, 1950).

All Ford Motor Company plants worked to full capacity throughout the war. The most impressive figures are those from Dagenham, listed by vehicle types in Table 3.2. The percentage share of types of vehicles produced between 1939 and 1945 are shown in Figure 3.1. Ford produced 93,810 separate V-8 engines in these years and 355,202 wheeled machines, of which 53,000 were cars and light vans, 13,942 were Bren gun carriers, and 75,000 were Fordsons. In addition, over 30,000 Merlin engines were produced in Manchester.[48]

The sophisticated camouflage techniques and warning systems employed at Dagenham meant that very little time was lost through enemy aerial attacks. The worst attacks occurred in September and October 1940, followed by a series of steady attacks until July 1941. Subsequent calm was followed by renewed but unsuccessful attacks in 1943. Although one fatal attack was recorded in 1940, the factory sustained no serious damage during the war.[49] The company's "alarm within the

[48]See Wilkins and Hill, *American Business Abroad*, p. 335; PEP, *Report on the Motor Industry;* and July–August 1944 and 1945 editions of the *Ford Times.*
[49]See Wilkins and Hill, *American Business Abroad*, p. 130; "ARP Air Raid Precautions Facts and Figures, 1939–45," Wilkins Personal File.

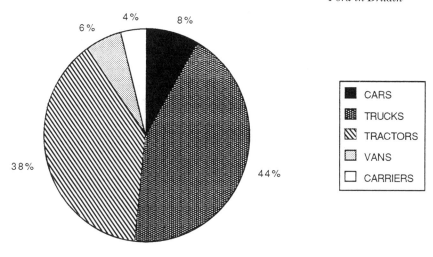

Figure 3.1. Ford's U.K. production by vehicle type, 1939–1945

alert" system, designed to keep workers at their posts until the last possible minute through the construction of on-site shelters and use of spotters to warn of impending attack, proved very successful, as indicated by total production hours lost to bombing attacks (see Table 3.3).

Table 3.3. Production hours per worker lost at Ford through factory closing, 1940–1945

Year	Hours Lost
1940	630.54
1941	88.5
1942	1.04
1943	15.07
1944	114.59
1945	1.49

SOURCE: "ARP Air Raid Precautions Facts and Figures, 1939–45," Wilkins Personal File.

In total, eight high-explosive bombs fell on the factory, three oil bombs, one parachute mine, and six anti-aircraft shells. Many incendiary bombs fell on the factory, but none caused serious damage. Bombing resulted in five fatalities at the plant (most in an attack in October 1940 that halted production for two days), and there were thirty fatalities to workers away from the plant. Twenty-three workers were injured at work, forty-three elsewhere. All these figures suggest that the Ford plant suffered astonishingly little damage to life or property, especially given initial concern about the strategic vulnerability of the plant and the fact that the German High Command had precise aerial photographs taken in October 1940.[50] In contrast, most of the rest of the British auto industry, located around Coventry, suffered considerable damage from regular aerial attacks.

Roland Smith was quick to claim that the Ford Motor Company never made a penny from its wartime production of Merlin aero engines at Manchester.[51] And Allan Nevins and Frank Hill suggest the government benefited a great deal more than the company did. Yet they suggest that new capital expenditure, new facilities, new methods, and an intangible, a new spirit, were sufficient to lift Ford to a position of supremacy among British producers that it could effectively exploit in the postwar period. Further, they suggest that the harmonious relations between the company and the government allowed Ford to profit from the Lend-Lease program through "suitable arrangements."[52]

As far as Ford was concerned, war was clearly good for business. The company evidently profited from its wartime activities, even though management claimed they acted only in the national interest. In the two years before the war the company's position in the market had dropped to a relatively lowly position among the Big Six producers, with 19.0 percent of the car market in 1938 and 14.7 percent in 1939.[53] Net profits had also fallen. However, the company was reinvigorated by government contracts, as reflected in Figure 3.2.

Profits during these years were unstable and subject to an excess profits tax of 100 percent after 1942.[54] Yet Ford managed to improve net profits and, in accordance with government policy, was restricted from paying out large dividends, providing the company with excess cash for reinvestment. Furthermore, the company benefited from the injection of valuable government-funded research not reflected in these net profit figures. Ford consistently repeated the refrain of 1941 that "it will be observed that the affairs of the company are in a strong and satisfactory position."[55]

There were interesting trends in industrial relations at Ford plants,

[50]St. George Saunders, *Ford at War*, p. 25; "ARP Air Raid Precautions"; Nevins and Hill, *Ford: Decline and Rebirth*, p. 283.

[51]Interview, Roland Smith with St. John Stevas.

[52]Nevins and Hill, *Ford: Decline and Rebirth*, p. 285.

[53]Wilkins and Hill, *American Business Abroad*, p. 303.

[54]Ford Motor Company Annual Report of 1942, reprinted in *Ford Times*, September–October 1942.

[55]Ford Motor Company Annual Report of 1940; Ford Motor Company Annual Report of 1941, reprinted in *Ford Times*, July–August 1941.

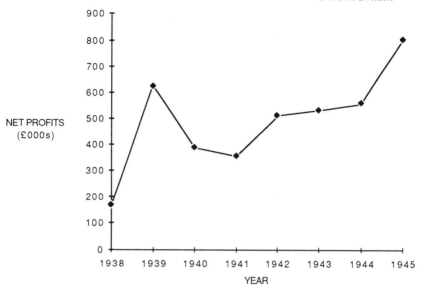

Figure 3.2. Net profits at Ford U.K., 1938–1945

SOURCE: "Accountants' Report of Mellors, Basden, and Mellors," File AR-75-63-430:63, Ford Industrial Archives.

notably at Dagenham, in this period. Ford had formerly been known for a ruthless employment policy, its labor force for general flexibility. There were a couple of exceptions to this pliancy, although the disputes concerned had been nonviolent and brief. The war left industrial relations in limbo as the national interest took precedence.

The labor force quickly made adjustments at the end of the phoney war, shifting to a twelve-hour day. The *Ford Times* noted that the company treated such extra work as unpaid overtime.[56] The composition of the labor force changed markedly due to conscription, prompting Perry to complain about a shortage of suitable labor as early as April 1940.[57] By the end of the war 3,695 Ford employees had left the company ranks to join the armed forces, and 138 had been killed.[58] Nevertheless, while the number of skilled workers dwindled, the total number of workers at Dagenham swelled. The Dagenham foundry reached full production for the first time in May 1940.[59] The govern-

[56]St. George Saunders, *Ford at War,* p. 30; *Ford Times,* September–October 1942.
[57]Perry to A. M. Wibel, 29 April 1940, Accession 507, Box 61, Edison Institute.
[58]St. John Stevas, "Ford in the United Kingdom," p. 128.
[59]The number of workers employed at Dagenham grew from a total of 12,000 in 1939 to 34,163 in 1945; see Wilkins and Hill, *American Business Abroad,* p. 328; Letter, Patrick Hennessy to A. M. Wibel, 10 May 1940, Accession 507, Box 61, Edison Institute.

ment recognized the value of the work carried out at Dagenham and sought to maintain the skilled labor force, but it became apparent after the military failure at Dunkirk that all eligible men would have to be called up to serve in the armed forces. As a result, women were employed at Dagenham for the first time in March 1941, their number peaking at 3,500.[60] They were engaged in a varied set of tasks. The company's annual reports suggested that throughout 1941 and 1942 there were low levels of absenteeism among a loyal work force.[61]

As recognition grew that the worst of the fighting was over, so did pressure from the Ministry of Labour (who had supposedly guaranteed Ford employees the right to organize and bargain with their employers) and the work force for the company to recognize and negotiate with trade unions as representatives of the labor force, as other large British producers had done.[62] Ford officials resisted this concerted pressure as they had effectively done since 1937.[63] Workers' attempts to deal with the head of the company's labor relations department, Marsden Jones, proved unsatisfactory, primarily because he refused to deal reasonably with their representatives.[64] Hennessy, a self-made man, evidently shared Perry's distrust of unions and labor representatives, feeling that as a fair employer the company had no need for union representatives in the plant and finding the whole desire for union representation inexplicable.[65]

Agreement was reached in 1944 between the company and representatives of the labor force, by then primarily composed of men returning from the war.[66] L. T. Blakeman suggests the 1944 agreement did not satisfy workers' demands for representation because the company did not keep to the spirit of the agreement. It signed but immediately refused to recognize elected shop stewards as representatives of the labor force. Marsden Jones's obstinacy provoked particular hostility among the workers, and this turned to resentment and then militancy.

[60]St. George Saunders, *Ford at War*, p. 21.
[61]For example, see the Ford Motor Company Annual Report reprinted in *Ford Times*, September–October 1942.
[62]See Wilkins and Hill, *American Business Abroad*, p. 332, and interview, Wilkins with L. T. Blakeman.
[63]Wilkins and Hill, *American Business Abroad*, p. 333.
[64]Again, this was the opinion expressed quite candidly by Blakeman, who succeeded Marsden Jones as Head of Labor Relations.
[65]Interview with Mira Wilkins, Miami, July 1986, drawing on her many interviews with Hennessy. Hennessy made no attempt to conceal his contempt for the trade unions, an injudicious and undiplomatic attitude for a man who was to become chairman of the board of the subsidiary.
[66]Company figures suggest that, of the men who joined the armed forces, 91.5 percent returned to the company. Of the remainder, 144 men had died in the war. See *Ford Times*, July–August 1946, p. 105.

Labor leaders, questioned later about the ill-feeling between management and labor at Ford, laid the blame for hostility on events in 1944–46, when the management thought they were running a wartime firm while labor renewed demands commonly made in a market-oriented economy with a tightening labor supply.[67]

The war thus began with a show of unity by management and labor and ended in disharmony and disaffection, with labor resolved to renegotiate its agreement or seek alternative, political action. By now the organization of Ford was described by Wilkins and Hill as a "ruling junta" led by Perry and supported by Patrick Hennessy, Sir Rowland Smith, and Sir Stanford Cooper.[68]

STATE-FIRM RELATIONS IN WORLD WAR II

Evidently Ford was heavily involved in government work during World War II. Three forms of evidence confirm a close relationship between Ford's management and government officials. First, Ford's highest managers served in elite government posts—notably Perry and Hennessy, though Hennessy's involvement was cut short by ill health. Ford managers received recognition, with Perry, Hennessy, Smith, and Cooper being honored for their efforts.[69]

Second, some managers had had a degree of influence with government officials in the prewar period, but now many Ford officials became simultaneously part of the state as, in Theodore Lowi's terms, sovereignty was parceled out.[70] A good example of this integration is the Ford engineers at the Merlin production plant who became government officials. The Ministry of Aircraft Production paid for the construction of plants run by Ford, paid for the machinery used by Ford, and awarded Ford government contracts that guaranteed minimum profit levels.[71] Ford's management legitimately denied profiteering, but the company's increased net profits, liquidity, and capitalization were all the direct result of government measures. Total wartime production amounted to a book value of $760,017,248—indicating the degree of increased capitalization.[72] According to Nevins and Hill,

[67]Wilkins and Hill, *American Business Abroad*, p. 333ff.

[68]Ibid., p. 339.

[69]Ibid., p. 333.

[70]For example, Perry to Russell Gnau on the influence of Sir John Davies, Ford director and former official at the Home Office, concerning U.S. immigrants working with the company, 16 December 1931, Accession 38, Box 5, Edison Institute.

[71]Company Secretary to E. Ford, 1 March 1943, in folder "Letter: Preliminary Financial Statement December 1943," AR-75-62-616:25, Ford Industrial Archives.

[72]"Historical Data—A," ID, CF, in folder "FMC—England WWII," England Dagenham FMC Ltd., Wilkins Personal File.

these measures provided the basis for a boom in Ford's postwar sales.[73] When government contracts ended after VE Day, the company reconverted to civilian vehicles by adapting sophisticated, multipurpose machinery. Other British firms had concentrated on aircraft production, which often required single-purpose machinery that was ill-suited to adaptation for car production. By the end of 1945, 10,412 of the new Fordson Major tractors had been built, as had 2,324 Anglia cars, 26,266 commercial vehicles, and 57,044 engines.[74] Although civilian cars still conformed to the specifications of prewar models, it was easier for Ford to reconvert to civilian production because the British taxpayer had replaced unsophisticated, single-purpose machinery with adaptive, multipurpose machinery.

The third form of evidence concerns the nature of state-firm relations. The company regularly exceeded the Ministry of Supply's quarterly production targets, producing record output at record value.[75] Such efforts received regular public recognition in public government announcements that commended both the volume and the quality of Ford's products.[76]

In sum, relations between Ford management and British government officials during the war were, to quote Nevins and Hill, "completely harmonious." The company conformed to every reasonable demand of the government, and the government responded by giving the company autonomy in decision making, providing generous terms under Lend-Lease arrangements, and honoring company managers personally and employees as a whole. While Ford on the continent of Europe was racked by dissension and sporadic damage, and approached financial ruin, its British subsidiary experienced rising confidence and achievement.[77]

FORD IN POSTWAR BRITAIN, 1945–1960

In the aftermath of war the pent-up demand for new cars expressed itself both inside and outside Britain. In a country still desperately

[73]Nevins and Hill, *Ford: Decline and Rebirth*, p. 285.

[74]Wilkins and Hill, *American Business Abroad*, pp. 339–40.

[75]For example, two letters from Hennessy to Wibel dated 18 May and 13 July 1942—both note that, as customary, the company completed 104 percent of the government's target for the first quarter and that both production and output were at the highest levels in the company's history. Hennessy to Wibel, Accession 390, Box 84, Wilkins Personal File.

[76]For example, see the letter to Edsel Ford from the British Company Secretary (name indecipherable) on 1 March 1943, Folder entitled "Letter: Preliminary Financial Statement December 1942," AR-75-62-616:25, Ford Industrial Archives.

[77]Nevins and Hill, *Ford: Decline and Rebirth*, p. 285.

short of basic raw materials, however, the government faced choices. A newly elected Labour government saw its major priority as securing foreign capital to address the balance of payments.[78] The government considered the automobile industry a strategic sector, to be used to secure maximum foreign capital, and instructed all auto firms to emphasize exports and indefinitely postpone the fulfillment of domestic orders. With Britain the only advanced industrialized country in a position to export cars abroad, it was important that all domestic producers realize the advantage while it lasted. The government set initial aggregate targets of 50 percent exports of cars for the industry as a whole. Later specific targets instructed each company to export at least 75 percent of car production and 66 percent of trucks and tractors.[79]

By now Henry Ford had retired and his son Edsel had died. The new head of the company was Edsel's younger brother, Henry Ford II, who concurred with the British government policy of emphasizing exports. While many industrialists complained about a new set of restrictions, the Ford Motor Company responded enthusiastically to this new government initiative. Henry Ford II favored free markets in which Ford products could compete. He favored the British initiative although, in truth, it did not involve a free market because imports were barred and the amount of exports was defined by government policy. Ford's view coincided with Perry's who had always insisted that Dagenham should export in large quantities. However, for the sake of fair competition, Dearborn now required the English company to divest itself of control of all the subsidiaries it had traditionally dominated.[80]

British firms held a virtual monopoly over potential buyers who held sterling, the only limitation on sales, according to Peter Dunnett, being domestic supplies of raw materials. They could sell all they produced despite poor quality or inappropriate designs.[81] Government policy on the issue of scarce resources was to allocate steel to each producer on the basis of percentage share of market *in the prewar era*—an egalitarian method. But this policy had the drawback that all firms could sell their products regardless of quality or price. The system therefore tended to support inefficient producers. Conversely, large producers could not exploit their potential superiority and increase their market share through expanded production.

[78]J. M. A. Smith, Assistant Managing Director at the time of the interview, expressed the opinion that the Labour government's export push at that time was what a Conservative government would have done. See interview, Wilkins with J. M. A. Smith, Assistant Managing Director, 30 August 1960, Wilkins Personal File.
[79]Wilkins and Hill, *American Business Abroad*, p. 364.
[80]Ibid., p. 365.
[81]Peter J. S. Dunnett, *The Decline of the British Motor Industry: The Effects of Government Policy, 1945–1979* (London: Croom Helm, 1979), pp. 33–34.

Dunnett describes the steel quota as "freezing" the industrial structure by underwriting losers and holding back winners. Although the
government sought to rationalize, standardize, and modernize British
industry, its policy had the opposite effect. The total number of models
in the auto industry remained too high to achieve economies of scale,
and without a free market or comprehensive government regulation
the quality of the product was generally low—which would haunt British producers when overseas markets became more competitive in the
1950s. This period was marked by two main factors: government intervention without regulation, and government targets without the means
to achieve them. Home prices were set by calculating what prices would
be in a free market, because the government feared a political backlash
if companies were allowed to profiteer as a result of government
intervention.[82]

Yet despite these problems, it was a time of tremendous expansion at
Ford. Relying on its prewar models while other producers tried to
develop new cars, Ford produced over 250,000 cars between May 1945
and February 1948. The company's two main export markets were the
United States, where the Prefect was sold, and the Commonwealth
"Sterling Bloc" market. Ford was the first subsidiary earning foreign
exchange, and mutual trust developed between the English and American companies.[83] By 1945 the value of exports had reached £1.75
million, and the following year *monthly* sales averaged around £1.5
million.[84] The new emphasis on exports is illustrated by a comparison
of the sale of company products for 1938 and 1947—both years when
the company was involved in "normal" production (see Table 3.4).

Lack of domestic supply was a product of government policy, and
Ford took advantage of this frustrated demand by increasing prices by
75 percent despite the government's concern about profiteering, blaming the price increase on a rise in production costs.[85] This policy

---

[82]Ibid., pp. 35–38. Langworth and Robson support this position in discussion of the
case of Triumph Motors. They suggest that in 1939 the company was crippled with debt,
due to falling demand and rising prices. In November 1940 the Triumph factory in
Coventry was destroyed in an air raid. However, in the postwar era, with stable, high
demand and a guaranteed quota of steel, the company was guaranteed market sales even
if its vehicles were expensive. See Richard Langworth and Graham Robson, *Triumph
Cars: The Complete Seventy-Five Year History* (London: Motor Racing Publications, 1979).

[83]See Wilkins and Hill, *American Business Abroad*, p. 364. The significance placed on
Commonwealth markets is clear from correspondence between company employees—
for example, Hennessy to Graeme Howard, Head of the new International Division in
New York, 31 March 1949, Folder entitled "England-Dagenham 1947–1949, Ford
Motor Company Exports," AR-75-63-616:768, Ford Industrial Archives; Nevins and
Hill, *Ford: Decline and Rebirth*, p. 395.

[84]*Ford Times*, January–February and November–December 1946.

[85]Perry in "1946 Report to Stockholders," 15 May 1946.

Table 3.4. Changes in Ford U.K. production between 1938 and 1947

	1938	1947	% Change
Cars			
Domestic	272,771	145,300	−46.73
Export	68,257	140,525	+105.88
Trucks			
Domestic	89,574	102,533	+14.47
Export	14,275	49,016	+243.37
Tractors			
Domestic	3,409	45,088	+1222.62
Export	7,993	17,806	+122.77

SOURCE: "Comparative Statistics of British Motor Vehicle Production, 1938–1947," Accession 713, Box 4, Edison Institute.

yielded Ford high profits between 1945 and 1951 while dividends were annually restrained at 10 percent, in line with a governmental guideline that sought to increase the capital available for investment by industry. The general trend of profits is illustrated in Figure 3.3. I include the year 1945 simply to illustrate how large were the level of company profits in this period.

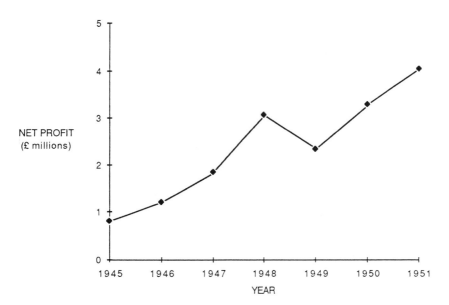

Figure 3.3. Net profits at Ford U.K., 1945–1951

SOURCE: Memo, "Attention Special Finance Projects," R. A. Winter, 19 September 1952, AR-75-63-430:62, Ford Industrial Archives.

To highlight the increase in profits between 1946 and 1950 relative to those between 1939 and 1945, consider the sum of net profits: in the first period net company profits totaled £3,156,000, and in the second £15,771,000.[86] Despite governmental guidelines, the company adapted to a new export policy and provided the resources for rapid capital expansion. The level of dividends was considerably lower than Ford's domestic competitors. The reasons for this difference are discussed more extensively in Chapter 6, but it should be noted that, unlike its counterparts, the American-owned multinational did not fear impending nationalization in the late 1940s and early 1950s and Ford's management, unlike its competitors, was disciplined by an external force, the board of the parent company. Meanwhile the directors of British firms felt their shareholders should get as much out of their companies as they could, while they could. Ford's management, however, could afford a long-term perspective.[87]

Perry announced his retirement in 1948, two decades after his return to the company as chairman. He was succeeded by Hennessy who had finally been elected to the board of directors only three years earlier. Hennessy wanted a new model to replace the Anglia and the Prefect, though a new model was not produced until 1951 because of internal disagreements over design and because the English subsidiary needed the agreement of the American parent company. Dearborn officials were slow to respond, mainly because Dagenham's prewar models were selling so well.[88] Competitors introduced their new models first, but Ford's four-cylinder Consul and six-cylinder Zephyr were more technically advanced when introduced in 1950.[89] The new, "stripped down" version of the Popular, known as the Anglia, was also intro-

[86]Memo, "Attention Special Finance Projects," R. A. Winter, 19 September 1952, AR-75-63-430:62, Ford Industrial Archives.

[87]For an illustration of how much more conservative Ford policy was in comparison to other producers see "Dividends for 1953—Preliminary Study," 30 November 1953, AR-75-63-430:64, Ford Industrial Archives. The most startling contrast is Rootes, which between 1951 and 1953 awarded a dividend of 32.5 percent each year. Between 1947 and 1956 Ford retained 79 percent of net earnings, compared to 68 percent by BMC, and 52 percent by Standard. The only comparable retention of net profits came from another American multinational, GM's Vauxhall, at 74 percent. See Nevins and Hill, *Ford: Decline and Rebirth*, p. 400. Meanwhile Austin awarded a 35 percent dividend in 1950 and proposed a dividend of 45 percent in 1951. See Memo, R. A. Winter to P. F. A. Prance, 19 November 1951, AR-75-63-430:64, Ford Industrial Archives.

[88]Interview, Wilkins with Harper and Beckett, 7 September 1960, Wilkins Personal File.

[89]These Ford models had new attributes for mass-produced cars, such as overhead valve engines, steel welded bodies, independent front suspension, and new hydraulic brakes, enhancing Ford's reputation for quality engineering. See Wilkins and Hill, *American Business Abroad*, p. 382.

duced, and it became a steady domestic seller though never the serious challenger to the VW Beetle that was initially expected.[90]

In the following years Ford expanded both its capacity and its sales. Between 1950 and 1953 Ford U.K. (as it was now known), flush with cash accumulated from paying low dividends, spent £15 million on both buildings and machinery. Capitalization through accumulated profits was uniquely successful.[91] Ford officials could pursue such a policy, using government guidelines on capital reinvestment to legitimate their actions. If other domestic automobile companies had limited dividend payments, they might also have prospered.

Ford led a boom in British industry between 1946 and 1955. The 1937 production record was soon broken, was doubled by 1950, and almost trebled by 1955, propelled by high demand. Demand did not approach supply until after 1955. Dunnett attempts to show how government involvement in the automobile industry served only to subvert the industry's development, but Ford generally found government involvement in this period helpful in providing scarce materials and tax reductions, such as on sales tax, and supportive in emphasizing the importance of an export drive.[92]

The helpful attitude of government officials was repeatedly demonstrated between 1950 and 1952 when the Ministry of Supply, faced with pressure on supplies created by British rearmament for the Korean War, allocated sheet steel and carbon alloys among firms in Britain. In an effort to maintain an explicitly egalitarian ideology, the Ministry of Supply extended Ford all the rights and privileges granted to any other firm based in Britain. If there was discrimination, it favored Ford. Under the explicit criteria outlined by the British government Ford was generally allocated as much steel as, and sometimes more than, its British competitors.[93] Hennessy's persistent claims that Ford had been discriminated against often netted him additional allocations of steel, as the British government sought to appear fair.[94] In a zero-sum context such additional allocations were a direct cost to other British firms.[95]

Ford was the leading firm in the British automobile industry from 1945 until 1952, when Austin and Morris merged to form the new BMC corporation. Their combined market share exceeded Ford's but,

[90]Interview, Wilkins with Harper and Beckett.
[91]Nevins and Hill, *Ford: Decline and Rebirth,* p. 397.
[92]Dunnett, *The Decline of the British Motor Industry,* p. 181; Nevins and Hill, *Ford: Decline and Rebirth,* pp. 396–97.
[93]W. M. Miller, "Steel Allocation—Period IV/1952, The Motor Industry," MinSupp 14/332, Public Record Office (henceforth PRO).
[94]See exchange of letters between Hennessy and Rowland, MinSupp 14/332, PRO.
[95]See Miller to DWVP, 7 April 1952, MinSupp 14/332, PRO.

unlike BMC, Ford had a sound basis for future growth with good, competent leadership, modern facilities, and sound engineering and design. Despite the BMC merger, bureaucrats still described Ford in the sentimental terms usually reserved for national champions.[96] With generous state policy and extra money available for capital investment, Ford developed a technological advantage over its competitors.

Not content with the capital investment and renovation undertaken between 1950 and 1954, management decided in 1954 to embark on the most ambitious modernization scheme in the history of the British automobile industry—a five-year plan costing £65 million.[97] Ford held only 30 percent of the British market in 1952, compared to BMC's 40 percent, but its sales were growing—at the expense not of BMC, whose market share stagnated, but of other, smaller British producers that ran into problems as demand began to tail off.[98] A 9 percent improvement on sales in 1955 was followed by a 20 percent improvement in 1956. Total dollar earnings in 1956 were $29.75 million and $50 million in 1957, with 23,000 Dagenham cars being shipped to the United States—a total of 25 percent of all British cars sold in the United States in 1957. The modernization scheme resulted in the opening of new machine shops at Woolwich and Basildon, the construction of a giant new foundry on the Thames, improvements and extensions to the Imperial foundry at the Leamington plant which (unlike the Manchester plant) had been retained after the war, and the opening of a spare parts depot at Aveley.[99] Ford also purchased two firms: the Briggs company, Ford's major supplier of steel components, prompted by the fear that Chrysler might buy it, and the Kelsey Hayes company, bought to ensure a regular supply of wheels.[100] The Briggs plant, near Dagenham, got a new tool room and a new press shop, in addition to a new assembly building.[101] When the government's regional policy finally limited development in the southeast of England, Ford opened a car plant at Halewood, near Liverpool, in 1959 designed to manufacture over 200,000 units per year.[102]

[96]Miller, Director Wheeled Production, "Steel Allocation—Period IV 1952," 28 July 1952, MinSupp 14/332, PRO.
[97]*Ford Bulletin* 21 (10 January 1958).
[98]Interview, Wilkins with J. M. A. Smith, Assistant Managing Director, 30 August 1960, Wilkins Personal File.
[99]*Ford Bulletin* 21 (10 January 1958).
[100]Wilkins and Hill, *American Business Abroad,* p. 386.
[101]Ford Motor Company Annual Report 1956.
[102]Wilkins and Hill, *American Business Abroad,* p. 411. Ford officials felt the Labour government's policy between 1945 and 1950, emphasizing exports and limited dividends, was dictated not by ideological considerations but by pragmatic ones. Events under the Conservative government between 1955 and 1960 seem to support that view. Although the Conservative government was ideologically committed to a free market economy, the

By 1956 Ford could announce an increased share of domestic market sales and exports (although sales actually declined). And this was despite government measures that created a credit squeeze, raised the purchase tax to 60 percent, and reintroduced an excess profits tax to encourage limited dividends. The decline was prompted by the Suez Crisis, which affected both the price of petroleum and the value of the pound.[103] Ford provided 25 percent of the industry's exports to the United States and 40 percent of vehicles exported to Europe by 1958, even though the Sterling Bloc accounted for 47 percent of the 184,669 cars it exported that year.[104] The company thus exceeded government export guidelines, although as early as 1952 these had been lowered from 75 percent to 50 percent.[105]

The company's 1958 annual report again announced the most successful year in the company's history. In the first million-car year for the industry, Ford management could claim an unprecedented year of success, despite a 30 percent levy on purchase tax that was curtailing home consumption and tighter demand due to increased competition.[106] Additional promise lay in the forthcoming introduction of new versions of the Consul and Zephyr and a luxury version of the Zephyr named the Zodiac.

In the following years Ford revolutionized British car production, again reducing the cost of a car one component at a time. These financial breakthroughs allowed Ford to make further technical innovations, such as the pioneering decision to put disc brakes on lower-priced cars. As Turner suggests, the philosophy of Ford was to spend 10 percent of the amount spent by Rolls-Royce on each model in order to provide 90 percent of the quality.[107]

By the end of the 1950s Ford (U.K.) Ltd. had enjoyed a period of unrivaled growth. In 1959 it sold a total of 405,100 vehicles, nearly three times as many as Fordwerke AG in West Germany, Ford's second-largest European subsidiary.[108] The expansion in production had gone

controls it introduced were just as exact as those introduced by Labour a decade earlier. See "Memorandum for the Board of Directors by the European Division," 7 December 1951, AR-75-62-616:70, Ford Industrial Archives.

[103]Interview, Wilkins with Mortimore, Ford Sales Manager, 26 August 1960, Wilkins Personal File.

[104]*Ford Bulletin* 21 (10 January) and 27 (4 April 1958).

[105]Interview, Wilkins with Mortimore.

[106]Note that in 1958 when the whole of British industry combined was producing one million cars, which is commonly considered the optimal level of production for just one company to achieve economies of scale, Volkswagen was itself producing 750,000 cars. See Turner, *The Car Makers*, p. 231.

[107]Turner, *The Car Makers*, pp. 184, 186, 188.

[108]Nevins and Hill, *Ford: Decline and Rebirth*, p. 405.

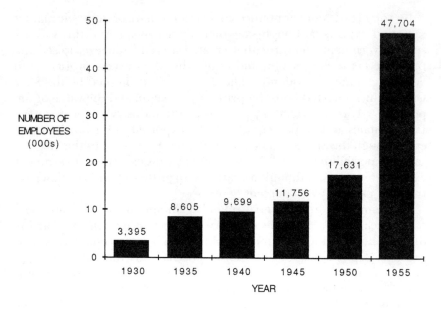

Figure 3.4. Employment at Ford's Dagenham plant, 1930–1955

SOURCE: Booklet, *Ford Motor Company*, Accession 225, Folder 1, Wilkins Personal File.

from 91,000 vehicles and tractors in 1946 to 417,000 in 1958, an increase of 358 percent. Employment had more than trebled, from 15,000 to 48,000.[109] The British company's overall growth in this period, in terms of employment, production, and exports, was impressive. The growth in employment is summarized in Figure 3.4. This growth in employment was matched by a growth in sales. Table 3.5 illustrates a similar pattern of growth. These numbers can be compared to the value of exports over this period, providing a picture of the company's pattern of development (see Table 3.6).

Scholars of the auto industry often argue that stable labor relations are a necessary condition for industrial prosperity. I avoid the issue of what constitutes stability by simply suggesting that stable labor relations usually limit conflict to well-defined parameters, are periodic and predictable, and are predicated on positive-sum rather than zero-sum assumptions. Yet Ford defies this generalization. Despite economic success, its industrial relations were far from stable.

Postwar industrial relations at Ford were initially racked by problems. These problems had developed toward the end of the war, when the labor force felt that having made significant sacrifices they had

[109]"Intercompany Communication: Area and District Managers," 16 July 1959, AR-75-63-430:65, Ford Industrial Archives.

Table 3.5. Unit sales of Ford
U.K., 1931–1951

Year	Units Sold (000s)
1931	26
1936	107
1941	55
1946	91
1951	165

SOURCE: Booklet, *Ford Motor Company*, Accession 225, Folder 1, Wilkins Personal File.

been cheated by the company. Pressure from both the Ministry of Labour and the labor force led to an agreement to grant union recognition but the company's unwillingness to abide by the spirit of the agreement created more problems than the pact had solved.

Fortunately the agreement was only for two years, and was revised in 1946, remedying many of the grievances of the 1944 agreement. It lasted until 1955, subject to some amendments in 1952. Yet a residual antagonism between labor and management persisted. On L. T. Blakeman's arrival in 1952 he encountered a great deal of hostility among company employees and "thought the bad atmosphere was a 'relic' of the unsatisfactory 1944–1946 period," suggesting that much of the problem may have been due to D. Marsden Jones's insensitive attitude to union demands.[110] Certainly other members of management were not so insensitive to union demands. Management discussions of stockholders' dividends always stressed that too high an award might prompt union demands for a pay increase. After all, union rep-

Table 3.6. Exports by Ford U.K.,
1931–1950

Year	Exports (£ millions)
1931–35	9
1936–40	13
1941–45	3
1946–50	109

SOURCE: Booklet, *Ford Motor Company*, Accession 225, Folder 1, Wilkins Personal File.

[110]Mira Wilkins, notes on interview with L. T. Blakeman, Labor Relations Manager, 2 September 1960, Wilkins Personal File.

resentatives argued, if the company could afford excessive rewards to stockholders, why not pay the workers more?[111]

Management's sensitivity to worker demands was heightened in March 1946 by the second strike in Dagenham's history, concerning the number of working hours. The prewar working week had been forty hours, composed of five eight-hour shifts, but it had been extended during the war to five or sometimes six shifts of twelve hours each. With a postwar labor shortage the company refused to return to a forty-hour week. An unofficial strike was called. After an eight-day suspension of production, workers returned to work under a new agreement that reduced the hours of a working week to forty-five.[112] This reduction should have reduced total number of hours worked, but in fact it had the opposite effect; workers had to do more overtime to compensate for the labor shortage. At least this raised their wages. More critically, to compensate for the increase in salary the assembly line was speeded up—both to ensure that demand was met and to increase the number of units sold. Instead of reducing the strain of work, the reduction in hours sustained the workers' hours of work, albeit at higher wages, and was more demanding. It created bad tempers, violence, and a generally hostile atmosphere at Dagenham. Shop stewards, initially excluded by the company, became the focus of the struggle and were among the most militant members of the labor force.[113]

The stewards headed the next major stoppage at Dagenham in 1951, a strike over the abandonment of the traditional "leaving benefit" (whereby employees upon retirement received £5 for every year they had been employed by the company) in favor of a new pension scheme. Workers were suspicious of the complex terms of the new scheme and went on strike to restore the old system. The management, fearful of losing production, agreed to restore the old system.[114]

In July 1952 another stoppage took place, this one an "all out" strike, over the organization of representation—specifically, how representation would be organized among the multiple unions at Ford. Both union leaders and company management agreed to union representation, but the membership defied the agreement because they wanted the established, departmental form of representation. This strike was a

[111]For example, see "Dividend for 1953, Preliminary Study," 30 November 1953, AR-75-63-430:64, Ford Industrial Archives; letter, Wieland to Smith and Hennessy, 15 January 1953, Wilkins Personal File.

[112]*Ford Times*, July–August 1946.

[113]Turner, *The Car Makers*, pp. 90, 129–30, 134.

[114]Interview, Mira Wilkins with Blakeman.

landmark; for the first time union leaders were unable to control their own membership. A new bitterness surfaced between the union leadership and its own labor force represented by the shop stewards.

Marsden Jones's sudden death in 1953 led to his replacement by Blakeman, who was more sensitive to union demands and more willing to deal in a cooperative manner with union shop stewards. However, the purchase of Briggs in 1953 did not help industrial relations. The Briggs work force had a history of militancy and resisted attempts to integrate their pay structure into Ford's. A procedural agreement in 1953 did nothing to resolve these problems, and by 1956 the Briggs plant was subject to five work stoppages per day. Further conflicts in 1957 brought the suspension of shop stewards at Dagenham, a source of further disputes, but fortunately the decision to refer the issue to a court of enquiry provided a safety valve.

The original apparatus set up to deal with all these industrial problems under the earliest agreement, the Joint Negotiating Committee, had atrophied. The committee was initially meant to include seven and later nine union representatives, but the issue of which unions should sit on the committee had provoked interunion conflict eventually resolved by the representation of all twenty-two unions. This inclusive solution rendered the committee so cumbersome as to be impotent.

While attempts to standardize arrangements at the Briggs plant dragged on, the Suez Crisis in 1956 brought a decline in demand, leading to cutbacks in the labor force that prompted an "all out" stoppage. This issue was resolved, but it took until 1960 before Briggs conditions were standardized, mainly because shop stewards at Briggs thought the changes threatened their own power base. By the time Ford management finally instituted standardized working conditions at Briggs however, it had been decided that local pay schemes were more advantageous to the company. The standardized wage system was based on both the supply of skilled labor and the cost of living in London. Labor costs in London were the highest in the country because of a regional labor shortage, and London had traditionally been the most expensive British city in which to live. Localized pay systems reduced Ford's wage bill.

This period closed as it had opened, with managers and labor representatives in dispute. The sense of intolerance and struggle initiated in the later years of the war was exacerbated by both sides. Yet throughout these years of strife the company was very prosperous. Disputes tempered neither the company's growth nor its capacity to produce profits. Perhaps good industrial relations are a prerequisite for prosperity only under conditions such as surplus capacity but not, apparently, where demand is effectively inelastic.

By the late 1950s the issue of company ownership had come full circle. The company had started out under American ownership in 1904, but it had undergone many changes. In 1960 it reverted to complete American ownership, with the justification that administration would be simplified and total purchase of the company represented a good investment for the American owners.

STATE-FIRM RELATIONS IN THE POSTWAR PERIOD

Between 1945 and 1960 the relationship between Ford and the state was more distant and contact more informal than in wartime. Officials of the company withdrew to carry on with their normal business, selling cars. Despite more limited contact between the firm and the state, relations remained cordial. Ford benefited from favorable treatment in the allocation of resources throughout periods of scarcity. Successive governments did not create a new, pluralist, free-market economy but indulged in selective intervention, generally regulating the automobile industry to achieve macro-level goals. These policies were equitably applied to all producers; the criterion for decision making was always publicly specified and defended, as in the case of steel quotas. Although the state did set some sectoral guidelines (such as in dividend payments) and sectoral targets (such as export levels as a total of production), it generally left firms with a great deal of autonomy.

Ford's management was not slow to sustain good relations with the government, regardless of which party held power. Hennessy, working for the day when controls would end, "cultivated good relations with the British Treasury, won its confidence, and at critical moments had its full support." "I make a point," he stated, "of trying to do more for the government than others in the industry."[115] Illustrations of this policy were Hennessy's involvement just after the war in the National Advisory Council for the Motor Manufacturing Industry (NACMMI), a corporatist body initially sponsored by the government, and his contribution to the writing of the PEP report on the future of the British auto industry, published in 1950.

All evidence suggests that Ford was treated as well as, if not better than, British producers, although Ford was not encouraged by the government to merge, as were Austin and Morris. However, BMC's merger was a response to a perceived European threat from Volkswagen, Renault, and FIAT, not from Ford. Ford was fortunate that policies pursued by successive British governments coincided with its

---

[115]Quoted in Nevins and Hill, *Ford: Decline and Rebirth*, p. 398.

own priorities and policies. This happy coincidence allowed Ford, both an American multinational and (for most of the time) the leading manufacturer in Britain, to prosper as never before.[116] The company was able to take advantage of economies of scale and to rely on a parent company for finance when it incurred debt, rather than the dominant financial system whose emphasis on short-term competitive prices plagued British industry.[117]

Fears expressed by Dearborn officials about the new Labour government proved groundless.[118] During the first fifteen years of the postwar period successive governments' policies created an environment that allowed firms periodically to exercise autonomy. Many British automobile firms used these periods as opportunities to drain themselves of resources through huge dividends payments; why did Ford not do the same?[119] Ford followed a rational strategy, pursuing high rates of investment through low dividend payments and avoiding the wrath of shareholders by blaming government guidelines ignored by the rest of the industry. The rest of the British automobile industry was quick to criticize government guidelines in the late 1940s and then ignore them in the early 1950s, but Ford chose to stay within those guidelines and avoid both high dividend payments and their inevitable result—labor demands for wage increases. British domestic producers such as Austin, Morris, Standard, and Rover, whose fiscal irresponsibility was stimulated by a fear of nationalization, would pay dearly for their decisions in the 1960s when capital shortage drove them to seek loans and public-sector aid, and then to become part of the public sector itself. Ford's distinct feature was its multinational status. Foreign ownership prevented Dagenham management from unduly rewarding shareholders and removed the specter of nationalization.

Like all domestic producers, Ford was protected by government measures designed to limit imports. The McKenna duties, levying a surcharge of 33.3 percent on all imported cars, remained intact. Two forms of taxation also helped domestic producers immediately after the war. The first emphasized a car's horsepower and acted as a barrier against cars designed for high-speed, long-distance travel—such as European ones designed for the autobahns. The second was a tax on shorter-stroke, small-car engines, that is, cars that were comparable in

---

[116]Nevins and Hill suggest that unlike Vauxhall, Ford raised absolutely no external capital. *Ford: Decline and Rebirth*, p. 400.

[117]See John Zysman, *Governments, Markets, and Growth: Financial Systems and the Politics of Industrial Change* (Ithaca: Cornell University Press, 1983), pp. 55–85.

[118]Wilkins and Hill, *American Business Abroad*, p. 358.

[119]These dividends often simply shifted profits from the corporation to private family members who owned the corporation itself, as with the Rootes family.

size to British models but were more efficient. Neither bigger nor more efficient competitors escaped this protective net.

As a producer within Britain, Ford was subject to the same benefits and market conditions as indigenous producers but not to the same obligations. As a subsidiary of a multinational, however, Ford was subject to exogenous constraints, unlike British firms primarily concerned about shareholders' interests. Only in a liberal framework, as in Britain, would multinational companies operate under identical market conditions and be allowed to pursue their choices whatever the long-term implications for domestic firms.

CHAPTER FOUR

The Wing and a Prayer:
Ford on the German Periphery

The Ford Motor Company's involvement began later in Germany than in Britain. The German market in the 1920s and early 1930s consisted of numerous small producers, one hundred fifty in all. Among German producers only Opel had successfully copied Ford's methods of mass production. Ford began in 1924 by importing tractors under license into Germany, with government approval, and the following January the Ford Motor Company AG was incorporated with the intention of assembling American-built cars in Germany. Ford was initially staffed by American executives, their intention being to provide a long-term challenge to Opel (still German-owned at the time).[1]

Ford was initially capitalized, by Dearborn's purchase of shares, at RM5 million, but Dearborn subsequently sold the shares to the Dagenham subsidiary, putting the German company under effective British control.[2] The company's assembly line was installed in its Berlin headquarters in January 1926, and the first car was assembled in April. Soon ten units a day were being assembled, and the company switched from the Model T to the Model A in 1928.[3] The technical demands of even this relatively simple task required increased capitalization, however, and by 1929 this was increased to RM15 million, actual assets rather than just promissory notes. The directorship of the company

[1]Mira Wilkins and Frank E. Hill, *American Business Abroad: Ford on Six Continents* (Detroit: Wayne State University Press, 1964), pp. 138–39.

[2]"Historical Data, Germany, Cologne, Fordwerke AG 1951–52, Organization and Management," AR-75-63-430:93, Ford Industrial Archives, p. 7.

[3]E. J. Palumbo, "Germany 1948: Economic and Political Review, Survey of German Vehicle Industry," Appendix Exhibit B, 15 April 1948, AR-75-63-430:86, Ford Industrial Archives.

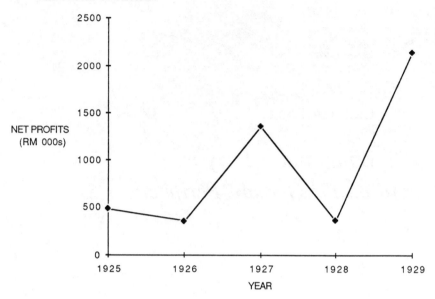

Figure 4.1. Net profits of Ford Germany, 1925–1929

SOURCE: E. J. Palumbo, "Germany 1948: Economic and Political Review, Survey of German Vehicle Industry," 15 April 1948, AR-75-63-430:86, Ford Industrial Archives.

reflected the distribution of power: chaired by Percival Perry, the board included Edsel Ford and Charles Sorensen from Dearborn and John Davies from Dagenham. The two symbolic German representatives were Carl Bosch, a notable engineer, and Alwin Schurig, whose credentials are less apparent.[4] The presence of the two Germans did nothing to mask the real center of decision making. Between 1925 and 1929 Ford's net profits increased at an erratic pace, as illustrated in Figure 4.1.

This pattern convinced officials in both Dearborn and Berlin that the company needed larger facilities to tap the potential growth in the German market. Against the objections of Perry, it was decided that company headquarters would be transferred from Berlin to Cologne, where a site on the Rhine would facilitate the construction of a factory suited to the manufacture of cars, components henceforth being produced in Germany. Henry Ford's optimistic view was that Ford could challenge Opel, whose dominance of the German market exceeded

[4]See "Manager's Report" in the "Annual Report of 1929," AR-75-63-430:90, Ford Industrial Archives; and "Fordwerke AG 1925–1933," Finance Reports Annual, Ford Industrial Archives.

that of Ford in England. He justified this policy by relying on an autarchic argument, that each national economy should be treated as an isolated entity and the development of each subsidiary should be maximized (a counterintuitive view for the leader of a multinational corporation to take). More practically, manufacturing was also switched to Cologne to avoid pricing the Model A out of the market, and components would be locally purchased to reduced costs.[5]

The total cost of the construction and furnishing of the new works, RM24,695,253, was paid for by the release of new capital stock and additional loans secured from both Dearborn and Dagenham. The new plant was finished in May 1931, and car production began immediately. The German company controlled none of its own shares, ownership being divided between Dearborn (which had repurchased its 52 percent share from Dagenham), Ford's Guernsey-based investment company which held 6.25 percent, and the German general public which altogether held 41.75 percent of the stock.[6] The timing of this expensive, ambitious new facility could not have been worse. Although the effects of the great economic depression were delayed—German Ford achieved a record profit of RM3,215,280[7] on increased turnover of 23 percent in 1930—1931 and 1932 proved disastrous as the company posted losses of RM1,696,427 and RM6,037,486 respectively.[8]

Nevertheless, Ford was part of an emerging German automobile industry in the late Weimar period. It introduced its first wholly German-produced car, the V-8, in 1932 as well as a new 4/21 horsepower Model Y car, despite the economic crisis.[9] The V-8 was well received by the public, and the introduction of both models was part of the company's plan to market "German products."

Company management was supervised by Edmund C. Heine, with Erhard Vitger as chief clerk, Robert H. Schmidt in charge of purchasing, and Roslof Sorensen as works manager. Schmidt was the only German citizen, although Heinrich Albert was also added to the board of directors, primarily to increase German representation. The fact that most Ford managers were foreign only fueled German nationalist claims that Ford products were not really German. These attacks on Ford cars increased after the Nazi seizure of power. They had a great effect on sales and, at one stage, the Cologne plant found itself running at only 13 percent of capacity. The company managed to break even in

[5]Wilkins and Hill, *American Business Abroad*, pp. 207, 226, 232.
[6]See "Annual Report for 1931," Ford Industrial Archives; Palumbo, "Germany 1948," Ford Industrial Archives, p. 39.
[7]Palumbo, "Germany 1948," Ford Industrial Archives.
[8]"Annual Report for 1930," Ford Industrial Archives.
[9]"Annual Report for 1932," Ford Industrial Archives.

1933 and recorded a nominal profit in 1934. It fared much worse between 1930 and 1934 than its competitors and fell to ninth place among German producers with a market share of between 1.3 and 1.9 percent.[10]

Paradoxically while Ford was coming under increased criticism, Opel prospered with a huge market share in both passenger cars and trucks.[11] Opel was just as much a foreign corporation as Ford, General Motors having purchased 76 percent of the company's stock from its German owners in 1929 for $28 million. In 1929 the Opel Baby was manufactured at a rate of one hundred cars a day, and the rate had grown to 150,000 units per year by 1938.[12]

Opel's acceptance in official circles appears to have been due to four factors. First, the company followed a good public relations policy, maintaining both its German name and its German management. Second, the company continued wholly domestic production, pleasing and placating German nationalists. Third, Opel's new ownership did everything in its power to maintain cordial relations with the new German leadership. Fourth, Opel accounted for half the output of the German auto industry and the government, to implement its *motorisierung* policy, needed Opel's full cooperation. Opel's and Ford's contrasting reactions to the issue of rationalization demonstrate these points.

In the first few months of Nazi rule, Hitler made it apparent that all domestic manufacturers would be required to standardize production so that parts would be interchangeable. This was inconvenient for all domestic producers but most complied immediately, intimidated by the new regime. Ford protested, pointing out that it had to remain standardized with other Ford firms to trade components whereas Opel did not. Opel was the largest German producer with a large percentage of sales in the domestic market, and General Motors owned no comparably large European subsidiary with which Opel might exchange parts. Opel's management therefore saw no reason not to standardize and, as the largest producer in Germany, was able to dictate many of the terms of standardization, imposing the cost of adjustment on smaller, more vulnerable, domestic producers. Furthermore, the Nazi authorities badly needed domestic producers to export, in order to maximize the influx of foreign currency. Opel could freely export, because no other

[10]Wilkins and Hill, *American Business Abroad*, pp. 234–35. The German company's position was so bad that Dearborn froze a debt of $4,157,857 owed to it by Cologne. Ibid., p. 247.

[11]By 1935 Opel held 42.8 percent of the market while Ford held only 4.5 percent, and Opel was still cutting the price of its car to increase market share. See "The Importance of German Passenger Car and Truck Factories, 1935," Accession 38, Box 33, Edison Institute. In 1935 Opel recorded a net profit of RM35 million. Letter, Diestel to Sorensen, 2 March 1936, Accession 38, Box 33, Edison Institute.

[12]Palumbo, "Germany 1948," Ford Industrial Archives.

major General Motors subsidiaries held rights to European markets (Vauxhall concentrated on British sales) but Dearborn had granted Dagenham rights of access to most European markets. Opel could export to Britain, France, and Eastern Europe, whereas company policy gave Ford no comparable markets. Finally, Opel's involvement in the development of the new Volkswagen was crucial. A committee of Germany's largest producers was formed to reduce production costs to the RM1,000 level specified by Hitler. Membership of this committee became important to car firms as it provided a channel for involvement in the affairs of the auto sector and gave industrialists a way to exercise influence with state bureaucrats. Opel's involvement was considered indispensable. Ford's was not as important, and Ford was the only major auto producer in Germany initially excluded from the Volkswagen project.[13] Not for the last time did an exclusive form of corporatism manifest itself.

Opel initially shared a good working relationship with the Nazi authorities, and in the mid-1930s it benefited from a wealth of government contracts—the main source of business in Germany in the early Nazi period. Opel became the benchmark against which Ford's activities were measured, prompting the claim that Ford resisted government demands not because of circumstances beyond its control but because of company policy.[14] It is apparent that Opel was a willing and active military supplier to the German army throughout the 1930s and 1940s.[15] Yet even Opel developed an antagonistic relationship with the Nazi authorities when it tried to resist government suggestions to site a new factory east of the Elbe in 1935. Relations worsened during the war when Opel was unable to fulfill all the contractual demands of the Third Reich. As Opel's share of national production declined, its relationship with the state worsened.

The new Nazi regime was keen to rejuvenate the automobile industry, which it considered an economically and militarily strategic sector.[16] One of the first measures of the new authorities was to exempt

---

[13]On the treatment of Ford see "Niederschrift über die Besichtigung der von Herrn Dr. Porsche gebauten 2 Probewagen am 24.2.1936 im Ausstellungsraum der Daimler-Benz AG, Berlin," Hamburger Stiftung Archive. For the belief that Ford should be excluded see the letter sent by Popp of BMW Abt. Flugmotoren to the Reichsverband der deutschen Automobilindustrie suggesting that the RDA should oppose Ford's involvement, 8 May 1934; or W. Kissel, chair of the board of Daimler-Benz, to Felix Lauscher, Chefredakteur der Deutschen Bergwerks-Zeitung, 19 March 1935, Hamburger Stiftung.

[14]For Opel's behavior and the problems it caused Ford see exchange of letters between Albert and Sorensen, notably Albert to Sorensen, 20 January 1936, Accession 38, Box 33, Edison Institute.

[15]For an example, see Wilkins and Hill, *American Business Abroad*, p. 331.

[16]For the role of the automobile industry in the Third Reich see Richard J. Overy, *The Nazi Economic Recovery, 1932–1938* (London: Macmillan, 1982).

the automobile industry from taxation to stimulate an increase in demand. Ford's sales increased by 75 percent in 1933, although because of increased production costs the company still only broke even. Ford made a modest recovery, recording a profit of RM3,824 in 1934 and RM62,779 in 1935.[17] After some struggle to gain acceptance, Ford joined the German Automobile Trustee Association in an attempt to integrate itself into the new power structure. The increasingly significant role of the government, biased both as legislator and as contractor in favor of firms considered "wholly German", convinced Ford management and some members of the directorate (notably Albert) that the company had to ingratiate itself with the authorities.

By 1935 Ford AG was given a choice between submission to the state's demands or closure, in effect between confiscation or loss of autonomy. The Reichsverband der deutschen Automobilindustrie, the governing body of the automobile industry, ordered that:

(1) All automobile parts must be made in Germany.
(2) All parts must be made of German raw materials.
(3) All parts must be standardized across firms and models.[18]

Ford pursued some curious tactics to secure government approval and gain recognition as a German company, because although Opel (in conforming to national tastes, laws, and standards) was still expanding rapidly, Ford was stagnating. Initially, company manager Edmund Heine replaced the normal meritocratic criterion for hiring staff with a racial criterion. A 1935 auditors' report suggested that Heine had dismissed capable executives without replacing them, had overemphasized distinctions of class and blood, and had given specific staff members contracts guaranteeing them lifetime employment. This policy of accommodation was sustained after Heine's replacement by Erich Diestel.[19]

The company also asked Dearborn for export rights to some European markets Dagenham was reluctant to give up. To placate the German authorities, Dearborn officials granted Ford AG the right to export to Denmark, Rumania, and Bulgaria, markets that had previously been Dagenham's exclusive preserve. In an agreement secret from Dearborn and Dagenham, the German company subsequently received an export subsidy from the German state, allowing it to reduce its

[17]"Annual Report of 1933," Ford Industrial Archives; Palumbo, "Germany 1948," Ford Industrial Archives.
[18]Allan Nevins and Frank E. Hill, *Ford: Decline and Rebirth, 1933–1962* (New York: Scribner, 1962), p. 95.
[19]Ibid., p. 96.

billing price on exports, and Ford's exports rose by 283.25 percent in 1936.[20]

Moreover, the company sought to reduce its reliance on foreign components and on domestic components bought from other firms by designing new models. This policy proved partially successful. By 1936 Ford's percentage of foreign components had fallen to about 0.5 percent.[21] Ford's management also felt a new car with a distinctly German appearance would reduce official prejudice—hence the construction of both the Eifel and a new V-8.

Some attempts to placate the government proved dramatic failures. One example was the decision to name one Ford model the Ford Y Volkswagen on the assumption that this would please Hitler. Ford's managers were curtly informed by the Fachgruppe Fahrzeugindustrie im Reichstand der deutschen Industrie that they would have to change the name immediately. Another notable example concerned the proposed purchase of the Stoewer Stettin works in 1935. The idea of purchasing the Stettin company came from the increasingly influential Albert, who suggested "that by taking over the Stoewer-Werke, the psychological basis is created for breaking down the resistance against the sale of Ford cars with the support of the dominating circles, especially the National Socialist Party."[22]

Albert thought the new company should be given the German name of Stoewer rather than Ford (following General Motors' example of calling its subsidiary Opel), hoping it would reduce government prejudice and the new company would receive official contracts. The government was fully in favor of this plan, promising contracts so lucrative they would ensure the new company would be profitable for at least three years.[23] As Albert stressed, "in view of the interest shown by the government, especially by the military forces in the Stoewer works . . . in my opinion the continuance of the Stoewer plant may be considered assured, except of course for an economic catastrophe which however would then not only involve the Stoewer Works but all of Germany."[24]

A quick Dearborn decision was imperative to Ford's German management because it was rumored that Opel was about to make an offer for the firm. The initial figures concerning the Stoewer-Werke sent to the Dearborn board seemed promising despite an ailing market posi-

[20]Ibid., pp. 97–100.

[21]Ibid., p. 97.

[22]"Verhandlungen über der Preis den Volkswagens," B115/3414, Bundesarchiv, Koblenz; memo, Albert to Sorensen, 1935, Accession 38, Box 33, Edison Institute.

[23]See Annual Report of 1936, Accession 38, Box 33, Edison Institute; letter from Diestel, Albert, Vitger, and Hoyler to Edsel Ford, Accession 38, Box 33, Edison Institute.

[24]Letter, Albert to Diestel, 28 October 1936, AR-75-62-616:43, Ford Industrial Archives.

tion. However, a second investigation, by the American management itself, suggested that Stoewer's ownership had not provided an accurate portrait of the company's financial and technical position.[25] Ford agreed to give Stoewer a six-month loan to stave off an Opel takeover while it carried out a further investigation of Stoewer's finances. This investigation revealed that Stoewer was encumbered with huge debts, had no working capital and zero liquidity, and had exhausted its credit. Technically, the company's tools were unsuited to Ford's mass production methods, relying heavily on craft production principles. Although the report conceded that purchase of the firm would improve relations with the authorities and that the opportunity to buy a German firm might not recur in the near future, it could not sanction the purchase, and Ford withdrew from the deal.[26] The Nazi authorities became more hostile to Ford than ever, and the company's efforts to gain favor had resulted only in a worsening of its position. While the rest of the automobile industry was producing at full capacity—business generated by government contracts—Ford was in a slump.[27]

Diestel continued to stall the Reichsverband, promising that Ford was moving toward standardization, and the company pursued other policies to earn favor, with equally disastrous results.[28] Albert attempted to get rid of Diestel because one of Diestel's ancestors was a Jew, thus classifying him as a Jew in the eyes of the authorities. Albert advised Edsel Ford to replace him with Schmidt (a "full blooded German") or find a new man acceptable to officials of the NSDAP and the government. A knowledge of the automobile industry was not a prerequisite.[29]

Albert was acting with increasing autonomy as the German company's activities became obscure to Dearborn, although he reassured U.S. headquarters that the company's best interest was always his priority. Albert, with the post facto support of Edsel Ford, Charles Sorensen, and Perry, sacked Diestel.[30] However, Henry Ford overcame the protests of both Sorensen and Albert and insisted on Diestel's reinstate-

---

[25]See unsigned letter to Wibel, 9 October 1936, AR-75-62-616:43, Ford Industrial Archives.

[26]See "Memo: Concerning the Stoewer Works, Stettin," Berlin, 15 May 1936, AR-75-62-616:43, Ford Industrial Archives, where the company is described as manufacturing a number of products in small quantities within separate buildings at a high labor cost.

[27]Memo, Albert to Edsel Ford, "Business Policy of the Ford Motor Company AG," 17 August 1936, Accession 6, Box 335, Edison Institute.

[28]See letter, Diestel to Reichsverband, 13 January 1936, Accession 38, Box 36, Edison Institute.

[29]Memo, Albert to Edsel Ford, "Business Policy of the Ford Motor Company AG."

[30]See letters from Albert to Edsel Ford, Accession 6, Box 346, Edison Institute.

ment, thereby providing evidence to nationalists that Ford was a haven for outsiders and should not be considered a German company.

The company's fortunes were at their lowest ebb when suddenly rejuvenated by Hitler's arbitrary, irrational behavior. At the International Automobile Exhibition in Berlin, held during February 1936, Ford was surprisingly allocated a prime location. Hitler insisted on visiting the Ford stand while at the show. Standing in front of the Ford exhibit to address the audience, Hitler, accompanied by Hermann Göring, stressed that Henry Ford was a pioneer whose methods should be imitated by all German producers. Göring then purchased an Eifel. These events, according to Diestel, significantly helped company business.[31] Later in the year, however, the company faced a new threat, a shortage of raw materials caused by the government's new quota system that favored producers of German origin. As a result, Dearborn had to supply Cologne with rubber tires to maintain sales, increasing Cologne's foreign materials content and thereby justifying further nationalist claims that it was a foreign company.[32]

The company was caught in a web of restrictions. During May 1936 the government issued more exacting standardization restrictions, making specific component designs and sizes compulsory.[33] Ford was unable to comply, but the government's threat of closure receded because the authorities' primary target was to maximize production. However, seizure of property by the state remained a constant threat, and company officials kept emphasizing their desire to conform to government demands. New regulations specifying acceptable profit margins at 8–9 percent were introduced, and Ford concentrated on the production of cars and spare parts, having ceased tractor production in 1934.[34]

Ford was finally certified in January 1937 and became eligible for government contracts when it received recognition from the Propaganda Office for German Economics.[35] The decision to grant certification was conditioned more by the state's need for greater productive capacity than anything Ford had done. The company hoped to maximize production by securing government contracts, just as all other major

[31]See letter from Diestel to Sorensen, 2 March 1936. Hitler's speech coincided with a period when Ford was personally receiving a great deal of publicity in the United States concerning his anti-Semitic attitudes and behavior.
[32]See letter from Perry to Sorensen, 11 September 1936, Accession 38, Box 33, Edison Institute.
[33]"Brief Outline of the German Norms for Passenger and Truck Engines," 13 May 1936, Accession 38, Box 28, Edison Institute.
[34]See Palumbo, "Germany 1948," Ford Industrial Archives.
[35]"Annual Report of 1937," Ford Industrial Archives.

producers had done for the previous three years.[36] However, shortages in late 1937 resulted in a maldistribution of materials that closed the plant. Even certification did not change quota arrangements that discriminated against Ford, even though Ford now used German parts exclusively and exported 25 percent of production.

Once the free flow of materials resumed, Ford's orders increased, and so did the number of its employees—by 47.28 percent, from 2,297 to 3,383. Secret negotiations over government contracts left Perry in an untenable position, and he resigned from his position as chair of the board to be replaced by Albert.[37] Diestel was appointed head of management, and Schmidt and Vitger were appointed joint managers in a managerial reshuffle. Ford then successfully negotiated its first exclusive contract with the government, for a truck with a three-ton payload.[38] Then, in perhaps Ford's greatest public relations coup in Germany, Hitler awarded Henry Ford the Grand Cross of the German Iron Eagle in celebration of Ford's seventy-fifth birthday. Ford, ignoring American and British criticism, visited Berlin to accept the award. The German company immediately received orders for 3,150 V-8 trucks from the state, and government contracts rose to consume 25 percent of production.[39]

In 1938 Ford revealed the new Taunus prototype.[40] Events were to overtake company strategy, however, with the government's decision to appoint a new plenipotentiary for cars, a colonel named Von Schell. His strident nationalism resulted in the final departure of Diestel (Vitger and Schmidt became joint managing directors) and signaled a greater demand that producers strictly adhere to state requirements. Yet despite these problems, Ford was still running at 94.3 percent of potential output.[41]

Regulations limiting dividend payments and barring the diffusion of profits generated abroad meant that Ford, like Opel, had to retain its profits and reinvest them in new capital. The government insisted the money be used for construction in Berlin of a new plant especially designed to manufacture military vehicles. The factory was built and

[36]Memo, "Business Policy of the Ford Motor Company AG."

[37]"Annual Report of 1937," Ford Industrial Archives.

[38]See Memo, "Covering the Plan to Execute Orders from the Government," 7 December 1937, Accession 6, Box 361, Edison Institute.

[39]See Wilkins and Hill, *American Business Abroad*, pp. 283–84.

[40]See letter from Diestel to Sorensen, 30 August 1938, Accession 6, Box 361, Edison Institute.

[41]Again it was Albert who instigated Diestel's removal, informing Sorensen that the government had approved this change; see letter from Albert to Sorensen, 12 December 1938, Edison Institute. See "Manager's Report to Directors," Fourth Quarter 1938, AR-75-62-616:2, Ford Industrial Archives.

Table 4.1. Net profits of Fordwerke
Germany, 1935–1939

Year	Net profit (RMs)
1935	62,779
1936	368,900
1937	414,304
1938	913,359
1939	1,287,877

SOURCE: Palumbo, "Germany 1948:
Economic and Political Review," Ford
Industrial Archives.

began production in 1939, being so secret that even Dearborn executives knew nothing of its activities. Postwar evidence reveals that the
plant was used to build the SPKW, an army vehicle designed for use in
rough terrain. The fleeting possibility of acceptance by the German
authorities convinced German managers to change the name of the
company to the Germanic-sounding Fordwerke AG in July 1939.[42]

Ford officials had now decided that active cooperation with Hitler
was the only way to achieve prosperity. It is astonishing that Fordwerke
managed to make a profit at all. Despite exporting at a loss (even with
an export subsidy) between 1935 and 1939, the company still managed
to record a net profit (see Table 4.1). An annual increase in profits was
an accomplishment, although much of the credit had to go to Diestel,
sacrificed for the sake of public relations, and to Albert, motivated by
burning personal ambition.

Company records and the secondary literature on Fordwerke in this
period devote remarkably little attention to labor relations, primarily
because the company was obsessed with its relationship with the state
after 1933. Constant constraints kept the Ford work force small. Nonetheless, the limited evidence available on labor relations at Ford in the
Weimar Republic suggests parallels to developments in Britain. A small
work force was uprooted from its initial location and shifted. The work
force worked on the same alienating mass production system as in
Britain and was equally well rewarded. Once the Nazi regime was consolidated, however, Ford found it increasingly difficult to secure labor—not just because of conscription or general scarcity of labor but
because of the social and psychological barriers attached to working for
a foreign firm. In a tight labor market, where skilled labor was in high
demand, these barriers were a major impediment. Cologne could mus-

[42]Nevins and Hill, *Ford: Decline and Rebirth*, pp. 99, 107; Wilkins and Hill, *American
Business Abroad*, pp. 284, 330.

ter only 4,200 employees in 1938, producing 37,000 units.[43] As in England in this period, strikes were rare. The work force was paid on a flat rate system and, in the Ford tradition, were provided benefits including healthcare, pensions, and sports facilities.

STATE-FIRM RELATIONS: FROM REPUBLICANISM TO FASCISM

Ford's prewar development can be divided into two periods, each with different characteristics and consequentially different implications for relations between firm and state. In the Weimar period, when Ford was a member of the competitive market and faced the usual market constraints, the company based decisions on economic considerations. Fordwerke was inaugurated fifteen years later than its British counterpart, but its pattern of development was identical to Ford in Britain: initial assembly of imported products, followed by the construction of an assembly plant, and then heavy investment in a manufacturing plant. The process was condensed in Germany, and construction at Cologne coincided with development at Dagenham. Cologne was not a second River Rouge plant for Europe, as Dagenham was to be. Like Dagenham, however, the Cologne plant's construction was motivated by the need to surmount local tariff barriers.

The Third Reich changed criteria for decision making and the objectives of the company. The objectives of the Nazi state were primarily political and military rather than economic, although these policies had extensive economic implications for individual firms. A company's standing now depended on exogenous variables, often beyond the management's control, such as the nature of ownership. Ford, as a subsidiary of a foreign firm, suffered. Instead of a welcome manufacturer in a relatively competitive market, Ford became an unwelcome intruder, to be used to supplement military production and gather foreign exchange. Unlike Opel, which often found it convenient to conform to Reich stipulations, Ford had a structure and economic objectives that were not conducive to state policy, and the company resisted state policies that resulted in a reduction of small vehicle models produced in Germany from 150 to 30 and of truck models from 113 to 19.[44] Although the long-term goal of the company remained maximizing profits, its more immediate concern was simple survival as a corporate entity. Ford was willing to adhere to state policy if that was the

---

[43]Nevins and Hill, *Ford: Decline and Rebirth,* p. 107.
[44]See Palumbo, "Germany 1948," Ford Industrial Archives, p. 4.

price of economic survival, thereby revealing much about corporate priorities in a capitalist system.

The Third Reich made no attempt to mask its inequitable treatment of firms. Discrimination was legitimated through the ideology of nationalism and administered through a bureaucratic process that was superficially meritocratic but essentially arbitrary. The authorities suggested that adherence to state policy was all that was required to gain acceptance, but despite Ford's attempts to gain legitimacy (and Hitler's personal admiration for Ford), the company could not overcome official prejudice.

The company returned profits between 1934 and 1939, but its development was stymied. It was constrained by limited access to raw materials and skilled labor, by diffusion of profits, and by limits on the design and development of new products. Even the composition of management was subject to government approval. Ford truly became, and remained, a stranger in a strange land.

Fordwerke AG during the War

The war brought a reorganization of Fordwerke. Although the Taunus and V-8 continued to be produced in 1939 (33,928 units), civilian automobile production ceased in 1941.[45] Thereafter the Cologne plant produced only V-8s, four-cylinder trucks, and service parts. With Alwin Schurig's sudden death new board members were needed to ensure a quorum in the absence of English members, and so Carl Krauch, an executive from IG Farben—which now owned 7 percent of the company—and Wilhelm Boetzkes of the German Industrial Credit Bank were added to the board. These additions relieved Albert who was conscious of public relations issues. Another German, Hans Huehnemeyer, was later added to give the board a more "satisfactory" composition.[46]

In 1940 Opel remained the cheapest producer, charging RM1,450 for their smallest model, but even they could not approach the RM1,000 mark set as a target by Hitler. Construction had begun on the new Volkswagen plant at Wolfsburg in May 1938 with the initial objective of 450,000 units a year, rising eventually to one million a year. Ford enjoyed neither public support, like VW, nor the advantages of the

[45]See "Report of the German Company" prepared by the office of Lord Perry in "Historical Data" (A), CF, ID, Germany Wartime, Wilkins Personal File.

[46]See letter from Albert to Edsel Ford, 18 September 1940, Accession 6, Box 361, Wilkins Personal File; letter, Albert to Edsel Ford, 1 April 1941, Accession 6, Box 376, Wilkins Personal File.

largest producer, like Opel, and as government restrictions increased the firm became wholly dependent on government contracts. Henry Ford's initial refusal to build Merlin aeroengines in Britain enhanced Fordwerke's popularity with the authorities,[47] but his change of mind enraged both the government and the general public.

Schmidt was by November 1940 the sole executive dealing with the government officials on issues of contracts and the control of Ford property.[48] When the German army invaded the Netherlands, Belgium, and then France, and threatened to confiscate Ford property in these territories, Schmidt successfully intervened to have these plants placed under his direct control. He took this opportunity to confiscate the best machinery from the French Ford plant at Asnières and transport it to Cologne.[49] The question is open as to whose interest Schmidt was trying to serve, the company's (as Albert claimed at the time or his own (as Maurice Dollfus, head of the Asnières plant claimed).[50] Nonetheless, it is surprising Ford was able to maintain as much plant autonomy as it did. Even Opel, like General Motors' plants in Belgium, Denmark, and France, had its major Russelheim and Brandenburg plants seized by the state, to integrate the company's efforts into the German war economy under military management.[51] Ford plants were under direct Nazi orders, but the orders were administered through Ford headquarters in Cologne, which Albert and Schmidt hoped would replace Dagenham at the dominant Ford firm in Europe. Ironically, the German High Command resisted Schmidt's plan for Europe-wide integration because they thought it might reduce output. By 1940, however, Fordwerke was engaged in secret work—manufacturing turbines for military equipment at Cologne, producing the SPKW heavy infantry-carrying vehicle at Berlin—while still, according to Albert, trying to avoid standardization.[52] Production continued despite political pressure and despite more practical shortages of raw material and labor.[53]

By December 1940 managerial changes at Cologne were confirming that Schmidt's contacts with the government had made him increasingly influential. Schmidt was made joint manager with Vitger. Vitger did

[47]See letter, Albert to Edsel Ford, 11 July 1940, Accession 6, Box 361, Edison Institute.

[48]See letter, Albert to Edsel Ford, 18 November 1940, Accession 6, Box 361, Wilkins Personal File.

[49]See letter, Dollfus to Edsel Ford, 27 November 1940, Accession 6, Box 361, Edison Institute.

[50]See letter, Albert to Edsel Ford, 18 November 1940, Wilkins Personal File; Nevins and Hill, Ford: Decline and Rebirth, p. 277.

[51]Wilkins and Hill, American Business Abroad, p. 331.

[52]See Nevins and Hill, Ford: Decline and Rebirth, pp. 278–79, and Albert to Edsel Ford, 11 July 1940, Accession 6, Box 361, Edison Institute.

[53]Albert to Edsel Ford, 18 September 1940, Accession 6, Box 361, Edison Institute.

not get sole managership, as seemed merited, because he was a foreigner.[54]

At the beginning of 1941 the company was more reliant than ever on the goodwill of the government for materials and contracts. Ford had to conform to the requirements of a war economy, reducing both the volume and the value of its turnover. The company was also compelled to establish a special transport fleet for processing production material; it was kept in Haus Neuerburg.[55]

The promise of future government contracts prompted the board of directors to increase Fordwerke's capital stock by offering 12,000 shares at a cost of RM1,000 each. The directors maintained that despite the war, the primary order of business was profit rather than the political and military aims of the Third Reich, although if the two coincided, all the better. This strategy had some success because the Third Reich's need for vehicles coincided with Fordwerke's need to manufacture. Between 1939 and 1943 the company paid a gross dividend of 15 percent, indicating healthy profits.[56] Total production for 1940 was 16,537 military vehicles, which kept the 3,869 employees moderately busy, but the following year only 14,330 vehicles were produced— mainly due to the loss of labor to the armed services.[57] The government noted this decline in production and announced on 15 May 1942 that Schmidt had been appointed custodian for the company. This appointment introduced the *Führerprinzip* to Ford: a "leadership principle" hierarchically centralized power, and the board of directors were dismissed. The last board meeting for almost a decade was held on 17 June 1941, although the more influential German members, Albert, Krauch, Boetzkes and Huehnemeyer, were retained as honorary advisers to the new custodian.[58]

During 1940, when a shortage in skilled labor diminished production levels, the authorities introduced compulsory foreign labor for the first time. In 1941 a barracks for the euphemistically termed "foreign workers" was built, and more land had to be rented from the city of Cologne to accommodate extra facilities.[59] French prisoners of war

---

[54]See letter, Albert to Edsel Ford, 12 February 1940, Accession 6, Box 361, Edison Institute.

[55]"Business Report for 1940," April 1941, FMC-Germany Wartime, Wilkins Personal File; "German War Recovery Study 1950," AR-83-69-891:2, Ford Industrial Archives, p. 34.

[56]"Business Report for 1940," Ford Industrial Archives; Palumbo, "Germany 1948," Ford Industrial Archives.

[57]Office of Lord Perry, "Report of the German Company."

[58]Memo, "Germany, Cologne, Fordwerke AG Directors 1939–51," CF, ID in FMC-Germany Wartime, Storage B-38, Box 97B, Wilkins Personal File.

[59]Memo, "Subject: Wage Index and Index of Cost of Living," 22 September 1948,

were initially used in the tool and machine shops, but 800 Russians were brought to Cologne in 1942, boosting the total number of employees to 3,888 and production to 14,762 units. In 1943 the government set Fordwerke the seemingly impossible production target of two thousand units per month and provided Fordwerke with an additional four hundred Italian prisoners of war.[60] The government's plan was partially successful; production increased to 19,005 units but still remained approximately five thousand short of the goal. The foreign workers' campsite expanded every year between 1941 and 1944. By 1942 Fordwerke was producing exclusively military equipment for the government, and Schmidt took pride in noting that Fordwerke fulfilled a government contract for 10,000 half-track vehicles on which Opel had failed. Schmidt also formed a secret subsidiary named Arendt (76 percent owned by Schmidt in cooperation with Albert). Arendt supplied equipment to produce a 15mm turbine used in the manufacture of flame throwers and the warm gears for the production machinery for Junkers aircraft. For this business Albert, Schmidt, and four hundred employees were arrested by the Allies after the war.[61]

Despite the plant's vulnerable position on the banks of the Rhine, the company suffered little damage in the early years of the war. The only damage incurred was to depots containing spare parts, such as in 1942 when a bombing raid destroyed a spare parts store at Rheinauhafen.[62] Under the German Law of Indemnification of 1939 Fordwerke was eligible for compensation due to loss of property or income resulting from war damage, and Fordwerke received a total of RM333,436.86 for losses sustained in 1939.

Yet events in 1942 demonstrated that despite all the company's efforts, it was still not accepted as a domestic producer. Under the new Third Regulation and Supplement to the Ordinance Concerning War Damages (Treatment of War Damages of Foreigners), issued by the Ministry of Internal Affairs in January 1942, all companies were required to apply for permission to seek indemnification for war damages. The regulation declared that companies considered under enemy ownership could not receive compensation, and, a ministry ruling shortly afterward denied indemnification to Fordwerke as its owner was a member of a state "not on mutual terms." The company was classified as "enemy property" because more than 25 percent of the

AR-75-62-616:78, Ford Industrial Archives; "German War Recovery Study 1950," Ford Industrial Archives, p. 25.

[60]Office of Lord Perry, "Report of the German Company."

[61]"German War Recovery Study 1950," pp. 31–33, 80.

[62]"Inventory of War Damages to Fordwerke AG," Cologne, Germany, December 1947, Accession 713, Box 20, Wilkins Personal File.

company was owned by foreigners (52 percent of the cor
owned by Dearborn). Fordwerke was therefore both c
treated as a foreign firm, an outsider in the German a
Fordwerke sustained direct war damages amounting to F
in 1942; RM1,728,817.48 in 1943; RM4,066,524.58 in 1944,
RM2,005,706.06 in 1945 but had to await an Allied military government to apply for compensation.[63] The issue remained unsettled for
over two decades. Ford claimed $7 million in damages, but the Ameri-
can government eventually awarded $1.7 million minus payments re-
ceived from the Nazis, yielding a net of $522,525.[64]

In 1942 dramatic changes took place in the organization of the German economy. Albert Speer was appointed new head of the *Wehr-*
wirtschaft (command economy), an economic dictator supposed to impose industrial mobilization. Speer's reforms sought increased efficiency—producing on the principles of mass production under a systematic plan—and signaled the Nazis' recognition that the Blitzkrieg
strategy had failed to win the war.[65] Industry had to contribute greater
production, and Schmidt thereafter ignored Dearborn. In making decisions concerning the company's capital structure, dividend payments,
and process of manufacture he ruthlessly implemented Speer's plans.
This iron rule increased production levels at Fordwerke plants in Cologne, Berlin, Amsterdam, and Antwerp in 1943, just as it did in other
production plants in Germany and Axis territories.[66] The value of
Fordwerke's wartime sales peaked in 1943, at RM181.5 million on a
profit margin of 11–12 percent. Despite these efforts, the shortage of
raw materials, pressures on the work force, and increased external
threats reduced Fordwerke's production in 1944.[67]

As invasion loomed larger in 1944, Schmidt attempted to gather all
machinery from occupied Ford plants closer to Germany. Budapest's
equipment was moved to Salzburg, in annexed Austria, only to be
captured later by the Allies. As defeat became increasingly likely, events
at Cologne took a new twist. First, Albert was arrested and jailed by the
government, charged with involvement in the July uprising plot that
sought to assassinate Hitler.[68] He was finally released in February

[63]"German War Recovery Study 1950," pp. 80–88, 148–51.

[64]"Before the Foreign Claims Settlement Commission of the United States in the
Matter of the Claim of the Ford Motor Company," Claim No. W17,536, Washington,
D.C., 16 January 1967, AR-83-69-891:3, Ford Industrial Archives.

[65]Berenice Carroll, *Design for Total War: Arms and Economics in the Third Reich* (The
Hague: Mouton, 1968), pp. 49, 223.

[66]Nevins and Hill, *Ford: Decline and Rebirth*, p. 285; Carroll, *Design for Total War*, p. 247.

[67]Palumbo, "Germany 1948," Ford Industrial Archives, p. 41; "German War Recovery
Study 1950," p. 80.

[68]Nevins and Hill, *Ford: Decline and Rebirth*, p. 289.

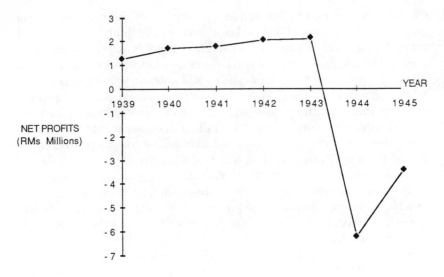

Figure 4.2. Net profits at Fordwerke, 1939–1945

SOURCE: Palumbo, "Germany 1948: Economic and Political Review," Ford Industrial Archives.

1945. Second, a new surplus export earnings tax was introduced which depleted Ford's earnings by over RM10 million for the year.[69] Finally, in September 1944, because of the increased intensity of air raids, the government ordered the dispersal of Ford's machinery and its 5,800 employees to six sites, at Bergisch-Gladbach, Osberghausen, Friedrichstal, Kloster, Dummlinghausen, and Derschlag, although the move was never completed.[70] Even under such difficult conditions the company produced 12,915 vehicles in 1944, although the figure fell to only 170 in the first three months of 1945. The Cologne plant was occupied by Allied forces on 6 March 1945, the Allies seizing control of the Fordwerke under Military Law 52.[71]

The war was financially a mixed blessing for the company. Early years of solvency were ruined by catastrophic subsequent years, illustrated in Figure 4.2. In terms of share of production, a sharp increase in market share in the early years of the war was followed by subsequent stagnation (see Table 4.2).

Fordwerke avoided major plant damage in air raids, and although

[69]Palumbo, "Germany 1948," Ford Industrial Archives, p. 42.

[70]Office of Lord Perry, "Report of the German Company"; and "German War Recovery Study 1950," p. 57.

[71]For figures see ibid. For details concerning the seizure of the plant see "Annual Business Report for 1944–1946," Ford Industrial Archives.

Table 4.2. Fordwerke production figures and market share, 1939–1945

Year	Total German production	Ford production	% of total
1939	352,533	25,745	7.30
1940	155,449	17,557	11.29
1941	121,312	16,200	13.35
1942	108,407	14,750	13.61
1943	127,437	17,000	13.34
1944	98,833	13,052	13.21

SOURCE: Palumbo, "Germany 1948: Economic and Political Review," Exhibit G, Appendix, Ford Industrial Archives.

the company's dispersal after September 1944 had been incomplete, the prudence of employees ensured that surprisingly little property was damaged before the Allies seized control. Fordwerke's limited losses are indicated in Table 4.3, which lists *direct* damages suffered by Fordwerke, although the firm claimed a much larger amount in compensation by including losses in trade due to war. According to Fordwerke's own figures, of these damages only RM785,000 was accounted for by lost factory machinery, RM687,875.42 in destroyed buildings, and RM1,306,792.35 in damaged buildings. The buildings badly damaged or destroyed were the receiving department, the recreation hall, a wooden office building, and fifteen wooden barracks in the foreign workers' camp—none essential to the running of the company. Greatest losses were in merchandise stored at depots; the firm's infrastructure remained intact.[72] This company report suggests that Fordwerke "did not suffer as much direct war damage as did other auto-

Table 4.3. Direct damages sustained by Fordwerke, 1942–1945

Year	Direct damages (in RMs)
1942	419,622.09
1943	1,728,817.48
1944	4,066,524.58
1945	2,005,706.06

SOURCE: "German War Recovery Study 1950," AR-83-69-891:2, p. 85, Ford Industrial Archives.

[72]"German War Recovery Study 1950," pp. 85–88. Ford claims on merchandise losses—RM9,313,659.92—exceeded combined losses on property and machinery.

motive producers and made a rapid recovery." It therefore appeared remarkably well placed to take advantage of increased demand in 1945.

Labor's experiences were just as turbulent as management's. Historians stress the traditional German shortage in wartime of both a skilled labor force and a *Lumpenproletariat*.[73] As in World War I, the longevity of World War II revealed the full effects of these shortages, as the German war economy became increasingly reliant on foreign labor. These foreign workers were in Germany for a variety of reasons. Some were attracted by the promise of high wages; some (generally those from the east) were forced to migrate by the desperate economic position in the Axis territories; some (notably "racial undesirables" such as German Jews and Slavs) were prisoners of war or slave laborers. These people were all euphemistically termed foreign workers.[74]

Foreign labor was imported only after all alternatives had been exhausted. The *Notdienstverordnung*, issued in 1938, was an Emergency Service Decree that permitted the state to conscript workers and the new Reich Labor Service made extra work compulsory for young men and women. However, these and other attempts to rationalize the work force, such as the *Dienstpflichtverordnung* (Compulsory Labor Decree) and Göring's Fifth Directive, only partially addressed the problem. Although Göring's Four Year Plan was so detailed that it specified employment levels for firms by industry, it could not solve this basic problem, and by 1939 Göring was planning to use foreign labor for the war economy. Foreign labor then constituted less than 1 percent of the work force, but the longer the war continued, the greater became the reliance on foreign labor.[75] Initially harsh treatment was somewhat modified after 1942 when Speer, less encumbered by ideological considerations, took control of labor allocation.[76] Better treatment made

---

[73]For a notable example see Gerald Feldman, *Army, Industry, and Labor in Germany, 1914–1918* (Princeton: Princeton University Press, 1966).

[74]See Edward L. Homze, *Foreign Labor in Nazi Germany* (Princeton: Princeton University Press, 1967).

[75]Ibid., pp. 12 and 17. There were two great periods of work force rationalization between 1939 and 1945. Göring's first attempt was only partially successful because it was constrained by ideological considerations—for example, it neglected use of women. Speer's rationalization came in 1942 when he gained control over labor issues. Speer, a pragmatist, had no qualms about using women and foreign workers. He extended the instrumental rationality epitomized in mass production principles to other realms of industrial production and labor allocation in serving the objectives of the Nazi war economy. See ibid., pp. 86–88.

[76]There was no humanitarian motive in Speer's actions. Speer merely recognized that the most effective way to maximize production was by feeding workers better and providing them with reasonable working conditions. Although Speer's general policy was not applied to all workers (notably Jews), many foreigners did benefit—most pointedly, workers from Eastern Europe.

the growing number of foreign workers easier to control, more productive, and less of an internal threat as German forces began to retreat.

Much of this general pattern applies to Fordwerke's work force during the war. Only German labor was employed in Cologne and Berlin in 1939; of approximately 3,000 workers, 500 were salaried staff. As the demand for workers to join the armed forces grew, so did the pressure to increase production. The two factors combined to create a serious labor shortage. Unlike at Ford plant's in Britain, where the work force was supplemented by female workers, longer hours, and more efficient forms of production, Fordwerke boosted its work force with foreign labor. Between 100 and 200 foreign workers were brought to Cologne in September 1940, and were located next to the factory in wooden houses that were equipped with their own kitchens. At this point employees numbered 3,869 and had a production target of 1,300 units per month.[77]

Conscription decreased production by over 2,000 units at Cologne in 1941, so newly arrived French prisoners were employed in tool and machine shops, in violation of the Geneva Convention. Production increased slightly the following year, by 432 units, as a result of a further 800 Russian prisoners of war, maintaining a work force of 3,886. In 1943, 400 more Italian prisoners of war raised the total work force to 5,711, and by autumn 1943 the work force included well over a thousand prisoners of different nationalities.[78] By 1944 the 4,500 employees included 2,000 foreign laborers—50 percent were Russians, 12.5 percent were prisoners of war, and the remainder were volunteers—living in 45 foreign workers' barracks.[79] At the end of the war only five workers chose to retain their positions, the rest scattering as soon as possible.[80]

Critical distinctions were made between workers by nationality, those from the west being treated considerably better, regardless of job capabilities. Western workers received pay comparable to their German counterparts, minus RM1.50 per day for living costs. French prisoners of war (not classified as western) were, under the regulations of the Stalag Bonn (*Kriegsgefangenenstammlager*), paid RM0.80 per hour, subject to a 60 percent deduction paid to the Stalag for living expenses.

---

[77]Memo, "Subject: Wage Index and Index of Living Cost," 22 September 1948, AR-75-62-616:78, Ford Industrial Archives; "Historical Data" report prepared by the office of Lord Perry, 19 September 1946, Cologne, Germany, Ford Industrial Archives; and "Fordwerke AG," AR-75-62-616:78, Ford Industrial Archives.
[78]"Historical Data" and Memo, "Subject: Wage Index and Index of Living Cost."
[79]See Memo, "Subject: Wage Index and Index of Living Cost" and "German War Recovery Study 1950," p. 31.
[80]Memo, "Subject: Wage Index and Index of Living Cost."

This system lasted until 1 September 1943 when French prisoners of war were reclassified as ordinary western workers and had their wages upgraded. Eastern workers (generally from Soviet Russia or the Ukraine) were paid the same amount whether they were voluntary workers, conscripted workers, or prisoners of war. The range of hourly pay for a man was RM0.32–0.78 according to age. While ideologically opposed to employing German women, Germans felt no such qualms about eastern women, who were paid RM0.24–0.59 per hour, also determined by age. These wages were subject to a 50 percent deduction for taxes and a charge of RM1.50 per day for living expenses, leaving eastern workers a pittance. Conforming to general developments in the German economy, wages improved considerably in autumn 1943, and the range for all workers was increased to between RM0.60 and RM1.20 per hour, with aggregate deductions amounting to a maximum of 50 percent of earnings.[81]

In contrast, Fordwerke's German workers were relatively well paid throughout the war, because of Ford's universal policy of paying above industry average. High wages tempted labor to move to Fordwerke's Cologne plant, and in 1942 Speer issued a directive that auto firms not steal scarce labor by offering high salaries. Local authorities told Fordwerke AG it had to conform to local conditions, and any changes that took wages or salaries over RM800 per month were subject to approval by the authorities. Between 1939 and 1942 the wages of Ford's German personnel were:

Nonproductive labor	RM1.00–1.20 per hour
Nonproductive departments	RM1.00–1.50 per hour
Productive departments	RM1.20–1.70 per hour[82]

Even the least skilled of German workers was paid almost 25 percent more than the most skilled foreigner and was not subject to the RM1.50 deduction for living expenses or so high a level of taxation. Between 1939 and 1944 German workers came to occupy fewer low-level positions and more supervisory jobs—increasing the wage gap between German workers and foreigners. Despite the war, this system therefore proved financially attractive for German workers employed at Fordwerke.[83]

[81]Ibid.

[82]Ibid. The ceiling was in fact flexible, and people could earn more in cases of exceptional efficiency.

[83]For a more general discussion of this point and how it may serve to reconstitute the ideas of the working class see T. W. Mason, "Labour in the Third Reich, 1933–1939," *Past and Present*, April 1966.

The conditions of salaried workers were even better, despite the multiple hierarchical distinctions common to Nazi Germany under the leadership principle. The monthly payroll range for salaried personnel was:

Nonskilled employees	RM125–325
Skilled employees (dependent)	RM130–475
Skilled employees (independent)	RM150–475
Assistant department heads	RM600–750
Department heads	RM800 and above[84]

Company employees benefited financially while foreign labor struggled. Yet this benefit proved to be limited, because there was very little to spend their money on (and most of their wartime savings were rendered irrelevant by inflation and the currency reform of 1948).

All wage employees worked the same hours, and the increased burden of war was most apparent. The prewar working week of forty hours lasted until May 1942, when Speer's appointment was confirmed. From June to December 1942 the minimum working week was raised to 44.5 hours, and then to 48 hours in 1943. From January to July 1944 the required minimum was 54 hours, and from August 1944 onward that figure was again raised, to 60 hours per week. Salaried workers followed a similar pattern: in January 1940 the figure was raised to 48 hours, then 54 in January 1943, 57.5 in January 1944, and 60 hours in August 1944. Some of Fordwerke's fringe benefits suffered, notably the private investment scheme, which was halted by state order after 1937, and the food provided in the canteen and the rations for foreign workers, which steadily declined in quantity between 1941 and 1945. The canteen had always been expensive before 1939 (averaging a loss of RM4,000 per month), but during this period the loss grew to RM25,000 per month as food became more expensive.

Labor force and firm shared an ambivalent relationship common throughout Germany. As a result of the economic division the state created within the working class, those who avoided conscription and remained in the work force held an elite status as part of the *Volk* and were financially well rewarded. The price they paid for those rewards was a lost of personal liberty and a greater isolation from the political process. They became subjects instead of citizens. This alienation from the democratic process made workers subject, arbitrarily and unmercifully, to the dictates of the state, resulting in a flexible laboring class that feared the coercive apparatus of the Third Reich and remained

[84]Memo, "Subject: Wage Index and Index of Living Cost."

pliant in the postwar period. However, German workers were no longer the *Lumpenproletariat* in the auto industry, that role being assigned to
foreign workers. These foreign workers were replaced by eastern refugees after 1945 and then by *Gastarbeiter* in the Bonn Republic. As Wolfgang Streeck's discussion of the treatment of "guest workers" in the
1970s suggests, these workers were not accorded the hospitality conventionally shown to guests.[85]

STATE-FIRM RELATIONS IN WORLD WAR II

The prewar conflicts between Fordwerke and the Third Reich stabilized to become, at best, a relationship characterized by the state's
indifference and the company's humility. Any illusions Fordwerke
might have had about a healthy working relationship with the state,
such as that created by Volkswagen and Daimler-Benz, or even about
achieving the status initially achieved by Opel, were rudely shattered.
The state treated the company as enemy property and reflected that
attitude in policy decisions such as compensation for war damage. This
barrier was not simply a matter of personnel relations. From the early
part of the war Fordwerke's management was headed by a German and
the directors were all German (foreigners such as Perry were not re-
elected at annual general meetings held between 1939 and 1941). Furthermore, those Germans who sat on the board were distinguished
men—members of the Creditbank and IG Farben, and most notably
Bosch himself. Schmidt developed a close relationship with the state,
which appointed him Fordwerke's custodian in 1942. Schmidt's loyalty
to the state's ideology was reflected in his willingness to implement the
principles of economic dictatorship (although self-interest could also be
used to explain his behavior). Fordwerke fulfilled every demand made
by government and, furthermore, volunteered to complete contracts
when other firms could not do so. Yet the firm's relationship with the
state was increasingly strained, and as a result of its political position,
Fordwerke stagnated while other firms developed both technically and
economically. The abandonment of free market competition in favor of
political criteria to allocate government contracts and raw materials

---

[85]Streeck's case study demonstrates that when crisis struck the automobile industry in
1973, the first action of the Federal Government in Bonn was to renege on promises
made to guest workers by throwing them out of the country. Many of these workers had
signed contracts with individual firms—in the case discussed by Streeck, Volkswagen.
However, the government relieved VW of the burden of these contracts by canceling the
visas of the workers. Wolfgang Streeck, *Industrial Relations in West Germany: A Case Study of
the Car Industry* (New York: St. Martin's Press, 1984).

froze the structure of the company. Belated recognition of this fact prompted Fordwerke to begin a program of expansion after 1945. As a later annual report suggests of the immediate postwar period, "we would have been in an untenable competitive position had we not adopted promptly a broad program of expansion and improvement of our manufacturing facilities. Since our main competitors were larger at the outset and were also at the same time expanding their facilities and manufacturing capacity, the program required necessarily was and still is of great size and complexity."[86]

This passage echoes the sentiments of aspiring British mass producers (with the exception of Ford U.K.). Fordwerke had been rendered as uncompetitive in Germany as a typical British mass producer was in the world market. Artificial limitations left the company unable to achieve economies of scale and unprepared to deal with a competitive postwar environment. This competitive disadvantage was not inherent in the firm's dominant technology of production, nor was it due to any fundamentally poor economic decisions. Rather, it was the result of political decisions that had handicapped Fordwerke in the Third Reich and would be reflected in the firm's aloof political relationship with the state in the postwar era. Only such an analysis can explain why a firm well prepared for economic prosperity in 1945 (its infrastructure was still intact, unlike some of its competitors') maintained its peripheral status in the Bonn Republic.

FROM MILITARY RULE TO REPUBLICAN FEDERALISM

To understand Fordwerke's immediate postwar development, one must bear in mind the national context. The ravages of war constrained economic development, and the effects of war were more severe because of the occupation and division of Germany, great shortages of raw materials, devaluation of the currency, and high rates of inflation. Companies such as Fordwerke often found that their dispersed plants were under the control of different authorities. Although the British and American sectors eventually unified into one economic sector, and the French practiced a policy of "parallelism" (which meant they retained the right of sovereignty over their sector while in practice generally following the same policies), the Soviet Union isolated its sector economically and politically.

Ford's Cologne plant was occupied by Allied forces on 6 March 1945 and immediately placed under the control of the new military govern-

---

[86]"Annual Report of 1956," Ford Industrial Archives.

ment. Schmidt, arrested in June 1945 because of his wartime activities, was released in September after cooperating with the military government but was forbidden from seeking reemployment at Ford.[87] Albert applied to be appointed custodian, but the British vetoed him as a result of his wartime record. A Dagenham official named Charles Thacker soon arrived in Cologne to reorganize and reconstruct the company. Cologne lay in the British sector, but the Berlin plant was in the American sector, and Albert took advantage of bureaucratic confusion to get the American authorities to appoint him custodian of Fordwerke's interests in Berlin. Altogether about forty of Fordwerke's employees were immediately arrested. Some were quickly released and reemployed by the company. By September the military government had decided to appoint Erhard Vitger as the new custodian; he worked closely with C. B. Lonsdale, the Dagenham official who had replaced Thacker. The Allied government instituted a special committee at Fordwerke to examine more systematically the wartime activities of all employees. This committee reported to the Central German Panel, which then reported to the military government. The military government decided which cases to act upon. Records are sketchy, but they suggest only a few important employees and directors were held for any length of time, among them A. Streit, who was works manager, and Carl Krauch, the deputy chairman. Again most of those arrested were soon released by authorities and reemployed by the company.[88]

The confusion that accompanied the seizure of the plant resulted in a stoppage in production from March to May 1945. The acute shortages of steel, tires, and wood—compounded by initial barriers to interzonal transportation—limited company activities to the production and reconditioning of trucks. There was also an an acute labor shortage and high rates of absenteeism among workers, due to illness and because people chose to forage in the countryside for food rather than work to earn money that had no purchasing power. One company official's comment described the company's average absentee rate of between 11 percent and 15 percent as "favorable." Workers returned to an official five-day week, although they were often required to work extra hours on Saturdays. Wages rose but did not approach the pace of inflation. Perhaps most problematic for management was a shortage of electricity that often halted production for lengthy spells.[89]

During Thacker's brief stay he organized the reassembly of machin-

[87]See letter, Erhard Vitger to R. I. Roberge, Accession 713, Box 2, Edison Institute.
[88]Office of Lord Perry, "Report of the German Company"; "Historical Data," Ford Industrial Archives; "German War Recovery Study," p. 134.
[89]Office of Lord Perry, "Report of the German Company"; "German War Recovery Study 1950," p. 134.

ery that had been dispersed after September 1944 and reactivated the factory. Production lines were initially exposed to the elements because the windows had been destroyed and the roof damaged during the seizure of Cologne. However, the plant suffered no major structural damage; the windows were quickly replaced and the roof effectively, if crudely, repaired.[90] The military government cooperated to locate crucial missing equipment, getting Soviet authorities to return some Fordwerke dies that had ended up in the Soviet sector. British officials helped install an engine line at the Cologne plant to manufacture and recondition British army trucks.[91] Fordwerke's good relationship with the military government got it machinery confiscated from a Krupp factory that had been dismantled under Military Law 52. However, Cologne officials had to return eighteen machines bought from French suppliers during the war, on the grounds Fordwerke had secured them under duress during the Vichy regime.[92]

Truck manufacture restarted in May under the scrutiny and sponsorship of the military government. The Strassenverkehrsaemter allocated production to essential public authorities such as the Reichsbahn and Reichspost. By December the company had produced 2,443 trucks (out of total German production of 5,512 units) that were used in the British sector.[93] The Control Commission for Germany (CCG), to whom the company was responsible under Control Council Law 5, set Fordwerke a monthly target of 3,000 trucks, but the continued steel shortage constrained production.[94] Additionally, new laws introduced by the CCG suspending the use of telephones, teletypes, telegraph, and radio services across sectors paralyzed Fordwerke by curtailing contact among company offices and between Fordwerke and its suppliers.

Some major manufacturers had suffered extensive wartime damage (Opel lost 50 percent of its productive capacity) and could not recommence production quickly, but Fordwerke was the first company to restart production in postwar Germany, just as it was in Britain. Under the initial Allied plan, the Level of Industry Plan, car and truck production in the British sector would be confined to Fordwerke and the

[90]Report by C. B. Lonsdale, "General Review January 1946–September 1947," Accession 713, Box 20, Wilkins Personal File; G. S. Hibberson to R. I. Roberge, 12 June 1946, Accession 713, Box 19, Wilkins Personal File.

[91]Lonsdale, "General Review."

[92]"German War Recovery Study 1950," p. 96.

[93]See the company's annual reports for 1944, 1945, and 1946, which were published as one report. For figures see Wilkins and Hill, *American Business Abroad,* p. 345; and "Manager's Report" in the "Ford Business-Report for the Years 1944, 1945, 1946," Agenda for the Ordinary General Meeting to be held 16 December 1947, Accession 713, Box 20, Wilkins Personal File.

[94]Report, "Fordwerke AG," Cologne, Accession 713, Box 19, Wilkins Personal File.

Volkswagen plant would be dismantled (for details see Chapter 5). At this time Dearborn officials rejected the idea of acquiring a controlling interest in VW because the company did not appear viable.[95] However, Volkswagen's later reprieve made it and Fordwerke direct competitors, each seeking to maximize political influence as a way to enlarge production. Immediate return to production gave each company a competitive advantage over other firms that should have provided both with a basis for economic expansion and development. However, only VW became a dominant market actor.

Nineteen forty-six proved to be more problematic than 1945 for Ford. The shortages of materials and food became if anything more acute, increasingly threatening production. Then, on 15 February, a fire broke out as a result of faulty plumbing, destroying over two-thirds of the main offices and their contents.[96] Although the damage was confined, it was greater than anything sustained during the war. Many company records were destroyed forever, although one fastidious accounts clerk had taken the company's ledger of accounts home for safe keeping.

Manufacturing nevertheless continued, and Fordwerke remained the only mass producer effectively operating in the British sector. Manufacture of the prewar Taunus resumed at Cologne, but production was hampered by the Soviets' continued refusal to return dies stored at the Ambi-Budd factory in East Berlin. Material problems were severe: truck cabs were still being made out of pressed board in 1946 (steel cabs were not reintroduced until March 1947), and wood, straw, and hay were used to pad upholstery. Production for 1946 was 4,650 trucks and vans, 148 staff cars, and 50 WOT 6s (four-wheel-drive trucks), out of the industry total of 13,916 vehicles. Fordwerke also dismantled and reconditioned four hundred Bren carriers. In sum, Fordwerke was briefly the dominant producer in Germany. Even under adverse conditions, company activities proved very profitable.[97]

[95]Opel never recovered from the destruction of its plants, other firms filling the vacuum. Most of this vacuum was filled by VW which, by the end of the 1950s, had cornered a 25 percent share of the market. Opel's prewar dominant share of the market (between 36 and 52 percent) fell to 19 percent—only 7 percent more than Daimler-Benz, a specialist producer! Many of Opel's failures during the war disgraced the company with government authorities. Opel's distant relationship with the government was sustained when the new Bonn Republic emphasized helping auto firms whose primary concern was to export—such as Volkswagen and Daimler-Benz—not those firms primarily intent on producing for the domestic market such as Opel. See "Organizational and Management Book: Ford of Germany," Cologne, Germany, Fordwerke AG 1951–1952, AR-75-63-430: 93, Ford Industrial Archives; Wilkins and Hill, *American Business Abroad*, p. 346. Nevins and Hill, *Ford: Decline and Rebirth*, p. 392.
[96]"German War Recovery Study 1950," p. 96.
[97]Office of Lord Perry, "Report of the German Company"; Lonsdale, "General Review." For Fordwerke's production figures see Lonsdale; for aggregate figures see Wilkins and Hill, *American Business Abroad*.

However, Fordwerke's management now had to face labor relations for the first time since the Weimar period. Workers had been accorded no effective representation throughout the Third Reich, but under Allied Control Authority Control Council Law 22, dated 10 April 1946, workers had the right to representation through a works council.[98] The company had struggled vainly to be included in representative organizations during the Third Reich; now it fought just as vehemently to remain autonomous of such representative organizations. The company refused to join the Employers' Association, set up to coordinate and represent the industry's owners after the war, and refused to recognize trade unions, noting its exclusion from representation in the Third Reich.[99] However, Fordwerke found its autonomy increasingly threatened by the military government. In a period of labor scarcity, the company could raise wages only with the consent of the new German Labour Ministry and despite its continued refusal to recognize labor unions was forced to accept the works council. In practice, members of the works council functioned as union representatives at Fordwerke because they were elected from the ranks and were all union members, but the company maintained the charade. Ironically, Fordwerke had unsuccessfully fought to be included in every representative organization in the Third Reich and unsuccessfully fought to be excluded from every one in the Bonn Republic.

The first works council election did not take place until 1947, and the result revealed how radically the workers opposed some aspects of company policy and how ignorant the company was about those feelings. Of the fourteen members elected to the works council, twelve were members of the Communist party (KPD). Management's response was effective, because the following year, at the next election, the Christian Democrats (CDU) triumphed and only one KPD member was elected. This political counterrevolution prompts Mira Wilkins and Frank Hill to claim "Communism as a problem now disappeared for the Fordwerke management. In fact the company's relations with labor were to be marked by a lack of friction and an absence of strikes."[100] This superficial description does not describe what prompted this change in attitude.

Throughout the very cold winter of 1946–47 and the very hot summer that followed, the company suffered continued strikes over food rations, forcing Vitger regularly to close the plant. Hunger fostered worker radicalism. Fordwerke's refusal to be involved in the historic

[98]The German Labor Front was an instrument for the suppression of labor. See Mason, "Labour in the Third Reich."
[99]See letter, Cooper to R. I. Roberge, 30 May 1947, Accession 713, Box 2, Edison Institute.
[100]Wilkins and Hill, *American Business Abroad*, p. 389.

agreement between the Employers' Association and IG Metall, the metalworkers' union that represented all unionized workers in the auto industry, caused increasing resentment.[101] Worker militancy initially resulted in recognition for the works council in exchange for compromise on its form.[102] Then the unions, through the works council, made demands to be involved in the decision-making process on wage levels, fringe benefits, and policies on hiring and firing.[103] Dissatisfaction with company policy, plus continued food shortages, raised the absentee rate to 22 percent by November 1947, and one company report described the employee situation as "hopeless."[104]

Management's response took two forms. First, the company increased the scope and depth of benefits, sending food parcels from the United States to improve the diet of its German employees and housing workers in the camps formerly occupied by foreign workers. These moves satisfied immediate needs.[105] Fordwerke's newfound wealth absorbed the additional costs. Second, a new board of directors was elected, the first in the postwar era, providing the company with new leadership even though formally under Allied control until April 1948.[106] The new board reflected traditional Ford policy in Germany. Although the titular head was C. W. Hauss, a German who had been the company's lawyer for two decades, the rest were Henry Ford II, Ernest Breech, R. I. Roberge, and Sir Stanford Cooper, all foreigners.[107] A third factor was the fear that radicalism would bring swift response from a military government concerned about events at Fordwerke. By January 1948 the food situation had reached a critical point, and strikes were a regular occurrence. Works council members called a meeting of the work force to decide whether to strike, and management questioned the legality of such a meeting with the British authorities in Düsseldorf. The British military authorities declared such meetings illegal, intimidating potential strikers with threats of imprisonment and effectively dispersing the work force.[108] This threat proved a turning

[101]Erhard Vitger to R. I. Roberge, 23 June 1947, and Cooper to Roberge, 30 May 1947, Accession 713, Box 2, Edison Institute.

[102]*Die Welt,* 8 May 1947; and memo, "Cologne Plant: Labor Relations," Accession 713, Box 2, Edison Institute.

[103]Departmental Communication to R. I. Roberge, 26 August 1947, Accession 713, Box 2, Edison Institute.

[104]Memo, "Subject: Social Help Program and Labor Conditions," 20 November 1947, Accession 713, Box 2, Edison Institute; "German War Recovery Study 1950," p. 164.

[105]G. S. Hibberson and A. T. Platt, "Fordwerke AG Cologne Audit Report August 1949," AR-83-69-891:4, Ford Industrial Archives.

[106]Memo, "Re: 1948 Income Tax Return War Loss Recovery," AR-83-69-891:4, Ford Industrial Archives.

[107]Memo, "Germany, Cologne, Fordwerke AG Directors 1939–1951."

[108]See Fourth Quarter Report by Erhard Vitger to R. I. Roberge, 19 January 1948, Accession 713, Box 19, Wilkins Personal File.

point, marking the end of the period of militant labor relations at Ford. A combination of carrot and stick engendered a new political conservatism, prompting one Cologne company official to claim that "the political change in our plant, however, was more complete and revolutionizing than in any other of the big industries of our district."[109] The effect was a return to a more traditional, conservative politics, although even after the 1948 election a relatively conservative works council contained nine members of trade unions.

Fordwerke production proceeded, rising by 20 percent in 1948 because of a general increase in steel quota. The effect of the German currency reform was stunning, however, cutting the value of the company's savings by 93.5 percent.[110] On the positive side, companies were for the first time able to pursue exports, although most contracts did not come into effect until January 1950 when an effective means of administrating exports was instituted.[111] Salaries and wages at Fordwerke were still below prewar levels; wages were not subject to terms agreed between the Employers' Association and IG Metall; and employees worked between 40 and 48 hours a week.[112] Fordwerke finally accepted the works council as the representative of labor and signed a new, comprehensive agreement with the work force that governed all aspects of wages, conditions, and behavior. The soothing effect of these moves is indicated by a company report that "we are informed that the works council is very advantageous to the well-being both of the company and its employees and is a decided asset to the smooth running of the company."[113]

By August 1949 Fordwerke had repaired all the damage done in the fire of 1946 and was adding a second floor. The firm was producing 1,000 Taunus cars per month, and 100 trucks per month; it planned further expansion. Yet Volkswagen, whose size and cost of production had been comparable to Fordwerke's four years earlier, produced 40,000 units in 1949, most being exported to Belgium, Switzerland, and Holland. Fordwerke officials thought this rapid growth was due to VW's low costs, an explanation that remains unproved. VW was certainly paying the same wages as other producers (and probably more

[109]"German War Recovery Study 1950," p. 140.
[110]Hibberson and Platt, "Fordwerke AG Cologne Audit Report," p. 2.
[111]"German War Recovery Study 1950"; "Annual Report of 1948–1949," Ford Industrial Archives.
[112]For work conditions see Hibberson and Platt, "Fordwerke AG Cologne Audit Report." Company profits for 1946 were RM396,520 and RM1,046,716 for 1947 according to Palumbo's "Germany 1948." Company profits were DM434,198.94 in 1948 according to the "Annual Report of 1948–1949, Germany Cologne Fordwerke AG," AR-75-63-430:90, Ford Industrial Archives.
[113]Hibberson and Platt, "Fordwerke AG Cologne Audit Report," p. 15.

than Fordwerke before the new agreement in 1946), but its total costs were undisclosed because it was classified as a private company. Fordwerke officials pointed out that VW received exceptional support from the new German government, noting the refusal to make VW responsible for debts the company had incurred during the Third Reich to subscribers in VW's savings schemes.[114]

Fordwerke, the largest producer in 1945 under the Allied government, had slipped in three years to fifth-largest producer in Germany—even worse than its position in the Weimar Republic or in the early years of the Third Reich. A similar fate befell the other U.S. multinational, Opel. Wilkins and Hill explain the decline of the multinationals relative to VW in economic terms, claiming that Volkswagen had the right product and leadership.[115] Yet Fordwerke trucks were highly regarded, and the Taunus car maintained a good reputation in the next decade. Certainly, the Beetle, though reliable, was both uncomfortable and ill-designed. In a market notable for excess demand, moreover, there was no shortage of potential consumers.

Purely economic factors therefore appear inadequate in explaining how Volkswagen, Opel, and Fordwerke could operate under the same market conditions, pay the same wages, and yet experience different results.[116] The most credible explanation contains three elements: First, Volkswagen could now systematically reap benefits it had accumulated during the Third Reich (studied in detail in Chapter 5). Second, VW was the recipient of some form of government export subsidy to secure foreign currency.[117] Third, VW benefited from extensive capital investment whereas Fordwerke was neglected by the British subsidiary, its owners until 1950. This third point prompts questions as to the source of Volkswagen's financing, but again the status of Volkswagen as a private firm despite public ownership (a paradoxical position) denies access to the information. The combined effect was that Fordwerke's production lead of 1945 rapidly disintegrated.[118] Events suggest a causal relationship between a company's political sponsorship and its economic success. Fordwerke had been the leading producer in the immediate postwar period, under the sponsorship of the military government, but market leadership declined as this sponsorship dissi-

[114]Ibid., p. 55.
[115]On Ford in the late 1940s see "Annual Report of 1948–1949"; Wilkins and Hill, *American Business Abroad*, p. 391.
[116]See Hibberson and Platt, "Fordwerke AG Cologne Audit Report."
[117]These sorts of company suspicions prompted Ford officials almost a decade later to seek assurances from Erhard that government policy did not systematically favor domestic producers over foreign firms. See Tom Lilley, "Executive Communication: Meeting with Minister Erhard," 31 March 1958, AR-75-63-430:86, Ford Industrial Archives.
[118]Wilkins and Hill, *American Business Abroad*.

pated. Instead, the Allies began to adjust their relative treatment of Fordwerke and Volkswagen in favor of the latter almost immediately after the war, and Fordwerke thereby lost the chance to redress the cumulative advantage built up by Volkswagen over the previous decade.

Ownership of Fordwerke shifted formally from Britain to the United States with the purchase of a controlling percentage of shares by Dearborn in 1950. The parent company provided resources for an enlargement of the Cologne plant to manufacture a new version of the Taunus. This model, finally marketed in 1952, proved very successful, and 50,000 had been produced by summer 1953. Still, this was nothing in comparison to Volkswagen's spectacular rates of growth, which Nevins and Hill accredit to state sponsorship and support. Fordwerke decided not to compete with Volkswagen at the lowest priced level of the market, that is, for political not economic or technological reasons. Fordwerke's management "concluded the state-owned Volkswagen did not live by profit alone, but that its taxes, depreciation, amortization and even operating deficits, could be covered up in government budgets." Both Fordwerke and Opel decided not to compete in VW's market segment.[119]

By 1952 former custodian Schmidt had returned to the company as technical director. His return completed the reassembly of Fordwerke's main actors in the Third Reich, indicating the superficial nature of denazification. New transmission and manufacturing facilities were acquired, then a new power plant was built, along with a transformer station, a medical building, garages, and apprentice shops—a total expenditure of $2.5 million. The new Taunus was not built to the specifications of foreign Ford cars but designed to conform to local tastes. Ironically, Hitler's demand that Fordwerke standardize according to national requirements had been realized. Still, although Ford's output rose between 1950 and 1954, from 24,443 to 42,631, its market share declined, falling from 11 percent to 8 percent.[120] Fordwerke therefore held about the same market share as Daimler-Benz, a specialist producer.

The parent company's response was a policy of capital injection in the Federal Republic, as in Britain, to enable Fordwerke to compete in a dynamic market. Between 1955 and 1962 the Cologne plant grew from 123 to 476 acres, and between 1950 and 1960 its productive capacity increased by 800 percent.[121] In 1950 the company produced 30,000

---

[119]Nevins and Hill, *Ford: Decline and Rebirth,* pp. 396, 402; Wilkins and Hill, *American Business Abroad,* p. 391.

[120]Wilkins and Hill, *American Business Abroad,* pp. 391–93.

[121]Ibid., p. 413.

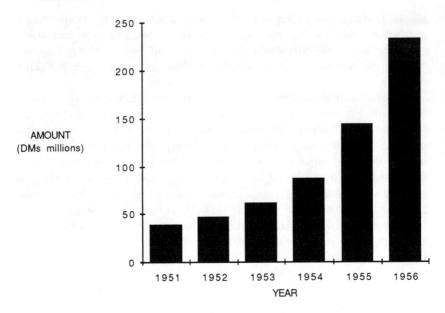

Figure 4.3. Gross investment by Fordwerke, 1951–1956

SOURCE: "Annual Report for 1956," Ford Industrial Archives.

cars with 4,715 employees; these figures rose to 35,160 cars produced by 5,000 employees in 1951. By 1957 the number of employees had risen to 10,746 waged and 2,603 salaried.[122] The growth in gross investment is shown in Figure 4.3.

Following on the heels of the original Taunus 12 and then the 12m came the more sophisticated 15m in 1955–58 and the radically new 17m in 1957–60. Yet Fordwerke remained only the fourth-largest producer. As the 1956 annual report clearly stated, Fordwerke's lack of facilities in the early postwar era made it heavily reliant on suppliers, a disadvantage relative to its biggest competitors "who commanded larger facilities and production capabilities, with greater integration."[123] Fordwerke's competitors, notably Volkswagen, had been integrated in the rationalization instituted by the state during the Third Reich. Fordwerke had been isolated and now paid the price for isolation. By 1956 Fordwerke officials recognized the importance of rationalization to remain competitive with both German and foreign manufactures. Market share therefore drove investment—but existing market forces were the result of state policies in the Third Reich.

In contrast, British Ford pursued simultaneous policies of capital

[122]"Annual Report of 1957," Ford Industrial Archives.
[123]"Annual Report for 1956," Ford Industrial Archives, p. 8.

investment and rationalization in the 1950s not to keep up with market leaders but to create market leadership for Ford. This policy, given the absence of wartime attempts to rationalize national auto producers, proved successful. The belated attempts of the British state to integrate domestic producers through the formation of BMC in 1952 tacitly recognized the failure of market forces to produce a large, competitive British firm.

Throughout this period Ford company policy worldwide was revolutionary, creating an international division to exercise direct control over all subsidiaries. As part of this policy, American executives were appointed to head foreign subsidiaries; Britain, with proven local leadership, was the only exception. Once again German nationalist sentiment turned against Fordwerke, comparing it to Opel (an inappropriate comparison, as 48 percent of Ford was German-owned whereas none of Opel was).[124] In a meeting with Ludwig Erhard, Fordwerke executives sought reassurances about how public attitudes might affect Ford's treatment by the government. In a company memo Tom Lilley said: "The Minister commented on German government and public attitudes towards U.S. investment in Germany and Ford of Germany in particular. The government's attitude and certainly Erhard's is for complete freedom of foreign investment and equal treatment for foreign and German investment." Yet Erhard said that the switch to American management and the "overrepresentation" of U.S. investment would inevitably lead to public resentment, but he would resist any temptation to discriminate against foreign firms.[125]

As the 1950s closed, the German economy resembled Britain's in two important macro-economic respects. In a decade of sustained growth the problems of unemployment had disappeared, and the government had tried to address the issue of balance of payments. The two Ford subsidiaries followed identical policies with markedly different degrees of success. Ford was a giant among British producers but merely mortal, if not a dwarf, among German firms. Critics might suggest the relative levels of investment in the two subsidiaries determined level of production and thus relative status, but such a view overlooks a crucial point: decisions about how and where to invest, and on what, were determined by management's perceptions of the political relationship between the firm and the state. Management's feeling that it was unfairly treated by the state was decisive in determining its pattern of investment. State policy certainly disadvantaged the firm in the Third Reich and during the occupation, although evidence is less definitive

[124]Ibid., p. 424.
[125]Lilley, "Executive Communication."

for the Bonn Republic in the 1950s. Nevertheless, management perceptions determined the company's economic investment policy.

More clearly, Fordwerke between 1945 and 1960 experienced two distinct periods of labor relations. The first has the characteristics of a class struggle between workers and employers over basic redistributive issues. The company's inadequate response to obvious welfare needs—food, medical care, clothes, and shelter—created a militant mood among traditionally placid workers. Radicalism expressed itself through high rates of absenteeism, election of radical representatives, and "sit down" strikes. Although radicalism was increased by the continued refusal of Fordwerke management to recognize labor unions within the factory, its superficial nature was demonstrated by the speed with which it was replaced by acquiescence, even though labor demands were not met.[126]

It would be a mistake to assume this process was simple. Management was clearly aware of, and very concerned about, the pervasive influence of Communist radicals. Unlike their British counterparts, Fordwerke managers decided that the company had the spirit and the means to employ both incentives and coercion. Policies took three different forms. The first set of incentives took the form of food, shelter, health care, and clothes, in addition to new sports facilities, libraries, and orchestras—a paternalistic supply of welfare functions to satisfy immediate material needs. Yet this policy was predicated on increased prosperity, which allowed the company to perform more welfare functions.

The second policy was the promise of access to the decision-making process, although in practical terms access was not accorded to the works council. As an auditors' report suggested in 1949, works councils were no longer required by law, but to reject them would lead to further unrest. The auditors stressed that works council members were allowed to see salary records, object to personnel decisions, provide one of three managers of the pension fund, and request information on planning, production, and the company's financial situation—but this did not mean they were included in the decision-making process. Seeing salary records achieved little purpose, few personnel decisions caused conflict, the workers' representative could always be outvoted on the pension fund committee, and questions about company dealings would be answered in only a very general way.[127] The works council appears to have become what Leo Panitch suggests is the epitome of

---

[126]For a discussion of how schedules were affected by these labor disputes see "Monthly Review—June 1947" in "Manager's Monthly Report, 1938–1948," Storage B-38, Box 2A, Accession 713, Box 19, Wilkins Personal File.

[127]Hibberson and Platt, "Fordwerke AG Cologne Audit Report," pp. 13–14.

corporatist institutions: a cooptive instrument for the control of workers rather than an instrument of workers' control.[128]

The third element of company policy was the use of force. Force was resorted to only when the first two policies failed. A limited use of force was enough to tip the balance to management's advantage. By the middle of 1948 a return to conservative forms of industrial relations was evident.[129] Yet an absence of strikes should not be mistaken for the agreeably stable labor relations commonly depicted in the corporatist literature. Fordwerke struggled to stay out of the employers' association until the early 1950s and refused to recognize labor unions, which excluded it from agreements made between IG Metall and the employers' association (Reichsverband). Fordwerke's opposition to the advance of labor was reflected in the company's attitude toward the institution of "codetermination." In an internal company memo in July 1951 the company stressed the need to defeat codetermination and suggested how it might be done: "One of the most effective ways in which American business could influence the efforts towards the defeat of further codetermination would be by indicating that American capital would obviously not be attracted to Germany if trades unions and labor had a share in the management of business enterprises. Also, of course, not only would American capital not be attracted to Germany but neither would other foreign capital or even private capital within Germany."[130] The report's author stressed that better labor relations would be another weapon in the fight against codetermination. A policy option of exit was rejected: subsequently, the principles of codetermination spread in Germany simultaneously with the growth of Fordwerke's investments.

During the 1950s the work force proved to be both flexible and submissive. Growth in the company's capacity, and therefore in the size of the work force, may have resulted in an alienation of the work force as in Dagenham, but it did not lead to the industrial militancy evident at Dagenham. Fordwerke was the epitome of a mass production firm, yet it lacked the industrial conflict of its counterpart in Britain. However, it did not bear the characteristics of a corporatist firm, refusing to recognize labor unions, continuing company paternalism, and maintaining its distance from the state and from other producers. It looked a lot more like a producer in a classical capitalist economy—trying to

[128]Leo Panitch, "Recent Theorizations of Corporatism: Reflections on a Growth Industry," *British Journal of Sociology* 31 (June 1980), pp. 159–87.
[129]"German War Recovery Study 1950," p. 140.
[130]Memo, J. C. Golden to P. Prance, "Subject: Germany and Codetermination," 27 July 1951, AR-75-63-430:86, Ford Industrial Archives.

operate as if in a free market and struggling to maintain its autonomy on labor relations and membership in the employers' association.

FORDWERKE AND THE NEW REPUBLICAN STATE

Fordwerke's relationship with the state between 1945 and 1960, like its relationship with labor, can be divided into two contrasting periods: before and after 1949.

Between March 1945 and April 1948 Fordwerke was under the direct control of the Allied government, which dictated the type and pace of production. The CCG decided, on 1 April 1948, that Erhard Vitger would be the sole agent and representative of Fordwerke AG.[131] Under CCG sponsorship, Fordwerke was the first firm to resume production after the war. Furthermore, the military government helped Fordwerke in three tangible ways. First, it provided a guaranteed market in a period when there was little money to buy the goods Fordwerke produced. The government ensured not only that all the trucks Fordwerke produced would be bought for use in public service but also that Fordwerke would be paid relatively quickly. Under the Third Reich (especially when it received its first government contracts) Fordwerke often had to wait a considerable time for payment, creating a liquidity problem.[132]

Second, under the sponsorship of the Allied government, Fordwerke was given scarce machinery, such as the Krupp machinery noted above. This machinery counterbalanced Fordwerke's payments to French firms and its losses to the Soviets in Eastern Europe.[133] Third, the Allied government helped Fordwerke in access to raw materials, notably steel. The shortage of raw materials after the war was a major impediment to production, and prices quickly jumped. To combat inflated prices and reduce the power of suppliers, the Allied government introduced a quota system for steel on 1 January 1946.[134] In the absence of a stable market, the British state assumed control of allocation for raw materials in the Western sectors of Germany, just it did at home. In Britain the allocative process involved an explicit set of criteria, but in Germany there was no publicized formula. The military government had a great degree of discretionary power, and Fordwerke

[131]Memo, "Re: 1948 Income Tax Return War Loss Recovery," AR-83-69-891:4, Ford Industrial Archives, p. 2.
[132]See Letters from Albert to Edsel Ford, 14 and 15 November 1938, Accession 6, Box 346, Edison Institute.
[133]"German War Recovery Study 1950," p. 105.
[134]Ibid., p. 136.

was a direct beneficiary.[135] Although the company suffered considerable shortages of raw materials, it was *relatively* better off than competitors for a brief period, thanks to state aid.[136] Not until 1949 were all restrictions on supplies, except gas and diesel oil, dropped, and then because currency reforms had created a new constraint on demand.[137]

For the first (and only) time in its history, Fordwerke shared a close working relationship with Germany's supreme authority. Of course issues inevitably separated Fordwerke from the authorities, notably the British order that the parent company should cease providing food parcels for employees on the grounds that such benefits were inequitable (illustrating the traditional liberal emphasis on equitability at home). Yet for a brief period, under the sovereignty of the Allied government, Fordwerke was part of the core of German industry. It briefly prospered under state sponsorship.

State support did not last long. With the decision to develop the VW plant to its maximum capacity rather than dismantle it, the Allied government stopped favoring Fordwerke and shifted toward Volkswagen.[138] The effect on Fordwerke's performance was immediate. A competitive imbalance between Volkswagen and Fordwerke had been instigated during the Third Reich. The decision of the British authorities essentially to sustain the relationship between the two thus reinforced the advantage Volkswagen had received from the policies of the Nazis.

Fordwerke's initial relationship with the military government contrasted with its relationship with the new Bonn Republic. Although not as belligerent as the Nazi state, the Bonn Republic in its first decade treated Fordwerke with negligent indifference. Erhard professed to support a classical liberal ideology that would treat all firms equitably, but Volkswagen could only benefit from state ownership. Successive Bonn governments acted to develop a select group of indigenous core producers, Volkswagen being the most publicized and most successful example. Between 1949 and 1959 Fordwerke found itself losing market share; a mass producer with a product designed for the mass mar-

[135]Relating this point of distribution of resources to the earlier discussion of the characteristics of liberal and corporatist regimes, note that the British, liberal regime attempts to use a formula that is both highly visible and essentially equitable. As discussed earlier, the purpose is not to achieve efficiency or to dictate winners and losers but to provide a system that underwrites all firms. In this example in Germany, however, there is obviously an attempt to distribute resources in the absence of a visible formula, leaving a greater space for arbitrary decisions.

[136]For a discussion of how the government aided Fordwerke on the issue of raw materials see Memo, C. B. Lonsdale, Cologne Plant, 28 May 1947, Accession 713, Box 20, Wilkins Personal File.

[137]"German War Recovery Study 1950," p. 142.

[138]For details, and a discussion of the Allies' motives, see the following chapter.

ket felt itself being forced into a market niche from which it was difficult to profit. Perception and reality may have differed—perhaps a paranoid Fordwerke management unjustifiably felt forced to pursue uneconomic policies. Fordwerke company memos suggest that Fordwerke was actively encouraged to limit the scope of production by Erhard on the promise that in time the German working class would graduate from the Volkswagen to the more expensive Taunus. Any attempt to compete at the lower end of the market would lead to resentment, and any further investment by American firms would cause public dissatisfaction (he was referring to Fordwerke's extensive investment program over the previous five years).[139] Company records do not indicate whether management accepted this explanation at face value or deemed it merely a ploy to thwart the further growth of American multinationals. Nor do the memos discuss whether Erhard was describing how Germans felt or trying to get Germans to feel that way. It is unlikely that Fordwerke managers could have believed Erhard's comments were made with their best interests in mind. Regardless, the outcome was the same—Fordwerke's high level of investment in its German subsidiary declined, and once again Volkswagen, and other indigenous producers, began to race ahead. The evidence presented in Chapter 5 on Bonn's relationship with indigenous firms does much to legitimate these suspicions.

Fordwerke's relationship with the German state had undergone a transition of sorts. An equal competitor in the Weimar Republic, Fordwerke had become an unwanted intruder in the Third Reich. The company initially became an "insider" under the Allied government, only for its position to be transformed—first by a new set of Allied policies that favored Volkswagen, then as a neglected outsider in the Bonn Republic, subject to unhelpful advice if not outright hostility. As the new German state outgrew Allied influence, from the late 1940s onward, Fordwerke's relative position among producers in Germany weakened. Attempts at dynamic growth by the company were originally tolerated and then tacitly discouraged.

[139]Lilley, "Executive Communication."

CHAPTER FIVE

The Core of German Industry: Volkswagen and the State

Classical liberal theorists often seize upon explanations that support the claim that history is driven by economic factors, whereas political scientists prefer to point at political factors. I could choose no better example to support the latter view than the development of the sedan that came to be known as the Volkswagen Beetle.

Evidence concerning Volkswagen is crucial in deciding if the theory presented in the opening two chapters can be sustained. I examine Volkswagen for two reasons. First, it was, for the period of my study, the German auto company most important to the welfare of the German political and economic system. The Volkswagen project was the focus of attention for bureaucrats and auto industrialists for most of the 1930s and in the 1950s, as the largest industrial concern, was the symbol of the German model in the Federal Republic.[1] Second, as the child of the state, Volkswagen is the best prospective case for sustaining my claims.

In this chapter I focus on the relationship between Volkswagen and elements of the state apparatus, members of the banking community, and industrialists who headed either core or peripheral German auto firms during the Third Reich, the Allied Occupation, and the first decade of the Bonn Republic. This chapter demonstrates three points. First, the motivation behind Volkswagen's creation was political rather than economic. Only political motives can explain the development of a project with such huge start-up costs. This political motivation is critical

---

[1]For figures see Woratz, "Besprechungsunterlagen für das Zusammentreffen der Automobilindustrie mit dem Herrn Minister," B102/5196, Bundesarchiv, Koblenz, Germany.

to the claim that the state in the Third Reich systematically favored core firms and that these benefits were sustained during the Allied Occupation, because it shows that the state consciously manipulated the market structure. Ideology played a significant role in state policy and, coupled with the extensive coercive powers of the fascist state, it ensured that even industrialists dubious about the Volkswagen Project cooperated with the NSDAP. Conversely, firms rejected by the Nazi state could not gain favor regardless of the magnitude of their efforts. The prosperity of domestic firms was critically affected by whether they were called upon to help develop the Volkswagen and how much influence each firm had in the process.

My second point is that Volkswagen directly benefited from a favored relationship with the powerful institutions of the state during the Third Reich. Neither powerful state institutions nor nationalist ideology were prevalent during the Weimar period. I press this argument further by suggesting that the discriminatory policies of the Nazi period were sustained by the policies of the military government between 1945 and 1949, providing a competitive advantage over rival producers during the 1950s. The British government was caught between discriminating against domestic producers because of past involvement in fascism (thereby undermining Germany's economic recovery and its capacity for self-reliance) and favoring those same mass producers to reduce the financial burden endured by the British exchequer. It chose pragmatism over ideology and reinforced the relations that had developed in the auto industry during the Third Reich. British policy differed from that of Allied partners. It was crucial to the auto industry because located in the British sector were the two largest firms, Volkswagen and Ford. Symptomatically, plans to use Volkswagen property to pay war reparations and to institute effective denazification were discarded. The military government favored domestic producers whose productive capacities had been either created or bolstered under fascism and discriminated against firms that had been disadvantaged under fascism.

Finally, I suggest that Volkswagen's institutional advantages, explicitly developed during the Third Reich and unwittingly sustained by the military government, were consciously sustained by the efforts of Ministry of Finance officials in the first decade of the Federal Republic. The fragmented nature of political power in the new Bonn Republic and the Finance Ministry's exclusive control over Volkswagen's affairs allowed officials to pursue discriminatory, statist policies despite Ludwig Erhard's efforts at neoliberal reforms. These discriminatory policies are not apparent in Erhard's liberal ideology or in the deliberations of tripartite corporatist institutions of government, business, and unions. They were sustained by the maintenance of exclusive channels of communication and action initially forged between Volkswagen, other core firms, and important fragments of the state in the Third Reich. Data indicate that from 1949 until privatization in 1962, and despite the constant claim that Volkswagen had no owner, the Finance Ministry of the federal government was de facto owner of the company. This unique relationship as a national concern in postwar Germany— between the federal government and the largest, most strategically important firm in the economy throughout the 1950s—resulted in a critical, exclusive, and secretive channel of communication. Bilateral discussions and agreements with other core firms, notably Daimler-Benz, NSU, and Auto-Union (the latter two were eventually purchased by Volkswagen) sustained the intimacy and exclusivity of the relationship.

Most of this chapter concerns itself with documenting the case of Volkswagen from its formation until the late 1950s. It is important to note, however, the significant role played by Daimler-Benz and BMW (other core firms) in Volkswagen's initial development and the relationship they shared with Volkswagen throughout the period. The relationship of Daimler-Benz and BMW to Volkswagen may help justify the conceptual framework that distinguishes core from peripheral producers, a theme that receives greater scrutiny in Chapter 7.

THE GENESIS OF VOLKSWAGEN

Robert Brady has extensively documented the growth of the rationalization movement in German industry during the 1920s.[2] His general description can be applied to the automobile industry, but it would not provide a good indication as to its health.[3] Auto production failed to expand in Germany despite the rationalization drive, auto registration reaching 600,000 in Germany compared to 1.4 million in Britain by 1929.[4] The German market was dominated by the subsidi-

---

[2]Robert Brady, *The Rationalization Movement in German Industry* (New York: Howard Fertig, 1974).

[3]See Franz Popp, "Die Automobilisierung Deutschlands, 1924," File 16 VW, Popp, Volkswagen Project, Bochum.

[4]See Richard J. Overy, *The Nazi Economic Recovery 1932–1938* (London: Macmillan, 1982); Ian Turner, "British Occupation Policy and Its Effects on the Town of Wolfsburg and the Volkswagenwerk, 1945–1949" (diss., University of Manchester Institute of Science and Technology, 1984), p. 51. For figures see Office of Military Government of the U.S. (OMGUS), Decartelization Branch, Economic Division, "The Automotive Industry of Germany," 31 December 1946, Box 479/775092, Automotive Industry Folder, Military Field Branch, National Archives and Records Administration, Washington, D.C., p. 2.

aries of foreign multinational corporations, and the remainder of sales was shared by small, uncompetitive domestic producers. The dominant actors were two American-owned firms: Opel, which was purchased by General Motors in 1929, and a smaller but aggressively growing Ford subsidiary. Domestic firms were divided between aspiring mass producers obsessed about copying American mass production techniques, such as Wanderer, Horch, Audiwerke, and Zschopauer (all eventually merged in 1932 as Auto-Union) and specialist producers that sought refuge from the rigors of the marketplace through diversified production. The primary specialist producers were BMW and Daimler-Benz, both supported through unprofitable years by the board of the Deutsche Bank. Emil Georg Von Stauß, chair of the Deutsche Bank, primarily supported these firms because of their potential as armaments producers and was later honored by the NSDAP for his efforts in sustaining the South German auto bloc.[5]

Although the auto industry had numerous producers and was organized through a trade organization, the Reichsverband der Deutschen Automobilindustrie (RDA), it lacked the powerful cartels found in the iron and steel and coal sectors during the Weimar period. With dominant foreign producers and multiple, small, uncompetitive domestic firms, the sector therefore more resembled the liberal, British model. The weakness of the employers' association was related to two factors. The first was the relative immaturity of the sector. Barely two decades old in the 1920s, the auto sector had not consolidated into a limited number of powerful producers that could negotiate to achieve stable market conditions. The second was that the automobile industry was exceptional in Germany because the primary competitive challenge came from multinationals that imported finance to produce locally rather than import finished, manufactured products. The presence of foreign subsidiaries fragmented the unity of local capital. The world economic crisis of 1929 had a predictably debilitating effect on German auto producers. Many firms consolidated or merged in privately

[5]As early as 1925 Daimler-Benz officials had contacted government officials inquiring as to when the German government would renew armament production. The economic health of their company was their dominant motive. See letter, Wilhelm Kissel to Von Schleicher, 1925, Hamburger Stiftung Archive. For the fiscal relationship between BMW, Daimler-Benz, and the Deutsche Bank see Hans Pohl, Stephanie Habeth, and Beate Brüninghaus, *Die Daimler-Benz AG in den Jahren 1933 bis 1945* (Stuttgart: Zeitschrift für Unternehmensgeschichte, Franz Steiner Verlag, 1986). For its political implications see Karl Heinz Roth, "Der Weg zum guten Stern des Dritten Reichs: Schlaglichter auf die Geschichte der Daimler-Benz AG und ihrer Vorläufer (1890–1945)," in *Das Daimler-Benz Buch: Ein Rüstungskonzern im Tausendjährigen Reich* (Nördlingen: Delphi Politik, 1986), pp. 28–40. The Deutsche Bank is also heavily emphasized in OMGUS reports on Germany. For example, see OMGUS Decartelization Branch, Economic Division, "The Automotive Industry of Germany," p. 1.

funded schemes; for example, the four firms that merged to become Auto-Union in 1932 used loans secured from the Sächsische Staatsbank and the Dresdner Bank. Daimler-Benz relied on the Bank der Deutschen Luftfahrt to subsidize the mass production of Messerschmidt engines.[6] The general condition of the German auto industry in the latter stages of the Weimar Republic is indicated by one report that suggested "prior to the Nazi regime Germany was slow in developing its automotive industry and therefore represented a political export market for the American manufacturers. The dominant position in Germany of American producers was achieved however only after the lifting of the tariff restrictions and import quotas commenced in 1926. The inability to compete, even domestically, with American output resulted in the ultimate loss of control of a major part of the German industry."[7]

The NSDAP's ascension to power, and its institution of the *Motorisierung* policy, marked the turning point in the fortunes of domestically owned auto producers. Expansion of production between 1934 and 1939 was highly dynamic—truck production increased by 263 percent, private cars by 74 percent, motorcycles by 176 percent—and the total number of vehicles produced was 556,648 in 1939.[8] By then motor vehicle production had displaced coal mining as the industry with the largest turnover, at RM2,017.2 million.[9] The Nazi authorities ensured that cash generated by this rapid growth was allocated, unlike before 1933, markedly changing the distribution of wealth.

The central objective of the NSDAP's dynamic *Motorisierung* policy was to legitimate the Nazi regime by raising the population's standard of living. Hitler himself considered the extension of popular systems of transport a key component in that process, regardless of cost. The *Motorisierung* policy involved the extension of the highway system, which had the added advantage of creating employment, and the popularization of automotive transport through the mass production of cheap cars. From this policy emerged the idea of the "people's car"—the Volkswagen project. Volkswagen, motivated by political considerations, was a public utility company whose objective was not to make a profit but to produce as many cars as possible.

Two alternative explanations for Volkswagen have gained currency.

[6]OMGUS, "The Automotive Industry of Germany," p. 3.
[7]Ibid., p. 1.
[8]Maurice Olley, "The Motor Car Industry in Germany during the Period 1939–1945," British Intelligence Objectives Sub-committee (BIOS), Report 21, Imperial War Museum (IWM), p. 7.
[9]United States Statistical Bombing Survey (USSBS), Munitions Division, "German Motor Vehicle Industry Report," 3 November 1945, p. 5.

The first is a security explanation; Volkswagen was developed as part of a grand military strategy for an armaments buildup. However, Richard Overy demonstrates that Volkswagenwerk was completely unprepared for war in 1939, closed down for most of 1940, and never functioned at more than half of its capacity during the war.[10] A second, economic explanation suggests that the motivating force behind the Volkswagenwerk was an unsophisticated form of deficit spending. Again, this interpretation has its flaws. The huge costs were so great that if the primary motives had been economic, the Nazi government could have found countless more fruitful ways to stimulate the economy.[11] Furthermore, spending on the project extended into wartime, when funds and resources were scarce and the problems prompting deficit spending had long since disappeared.

Hitler initially discussed the concept of a cheap car in 1934, declaring that the cost of the car should not exceed RM998 plus insurance. U.S. Ford was his recurring organizational example.[12] Operating principles were outlined by the government; the project would be turned over to private manufacturers under the leadership of the noted car producer Ferdinand Porsche. Auto manufacturers would design both the car and the construction plant in concertation, and the trade association, the RDA, would fund the project.[13] Germany would then mass produce a car primarily to serve the needs of its own populace and secondarily to bolster foreign currency earnings through exports.

Tensions developed among the German auto producers. Hitler's initial demand that 100,000 cars be produced annually by 1940, which would make Volkswagen the largest company in Germany, seemed impossible in a country where the largest firm, Opel, produced at only half that rate in 1934.[14] Even the most cooperative of domestic producers could not foresee a German car manufactured and sold for less than RM1,000. Even if costs were cut and mass production techniques were used, the car would still have to be priced around RM1,400–1,500.[15]

[10]Overy, *The Nazi Economic Recovery.*

[11]For the motives of the Nazi government see letter from Franz Popp, Head of the Supervisory Board of BMW, 24 June 1936, Archiv des Dokumentationzentrums der Staatlichen Archivverwaltung der DDR, Berlin, DK 713.

[12]See "Niederschrift über die Besichtigung der von Herrn Dr. Porsche gebauten 2. Probewagen am 24.2.1936 im Ausstellungsraum der Daimler-Benz AG, Berlin," Hamburger Stiftung Archive.

[13]See BMW AG, "Reichsdeutsche Automobilindustrie/Besprechung über das Problem 'Volkswagen' am 28.5.34," Hamburger Stiftung Archive.

[14]"Vortrag: Beiratsitzung Deutsche Bank," 28 October 1938, File 16 Volkswagen Popp, VW Project, Bochum. For Opel production see BMW AG, "Reichsverband der Deutschen Automobilindustrie (RDA) Besprechung über das Problem 'Volkswagen' am 28.5.34," Hamburger Stiftung Archive.

[15]Letter, Franz Popp to Dr. Emil Georg Von Stauß, 11 June 1937, File 16 VW Popp, Hamburger Stiftung Archive.

All the producers wanted to please the new Nazi leadership, whom many had supported, but all recognized that the successful development of a cheap car would affect their own sales.[16] A car RM500–600 cheaper than the competition would drive out of the domestic market many firms not positioned to substitute exports for lost domestic sales. Their ambivalence is apparent in correspondence between the manufacturers. Everyone earnestly discussed how the Volkswagen problem could be overcome, and they all developed viable explanations of why the project would not work.[17]

A second source of tension was the recognition by German auto industrialists that Opel was the firm most likely to build the new car because it employed the principles of mass production more effectively than domestic firms. Opel's involvement gave other producers an opportunity to dissent by invoking nationalist sentiment—a notion appealing to the NSDAP government. In a letter written to Wilhelm Kissel of Daimler-Benz, Franz Popp of BMW suggested that while Opel was the firm most capable of dealing with the Volkswagen issue, it would be "grotesque" if Opel were the primary beneficiaries.[18] The producers appealed to Hitler that foreign (i.e., American) firms should not be involved, and Ford was immediately excluded from the project, although the question whether it should be admitted to discussions was occasionally raised.[19] Dr. Wilhelm von Opel, still titular head of the Opel company despite its purchase by General Motors, immediately responded to Ford's exclusion by declaring his loyalty to the Volkswagen project.[20] But nationalist appeals reportedly struck a chord with the Nazi elite.[21] Although Opel's representatives continued to attend

[16]For an example of the efforts of company officials to please the Nazi leadership see Roth on the support of Daimler-Benz for the NSDAP, "Der Weg zum guten Stern."

[17]For example, see letter, Wilhelm Kissel to Director Ernst Hagemeier, Leiter der Wirtschaftsgruppe Fahrzeugindustrie (director of the economic board on the transport industry), Berlin-Charlottenberg, 21 January 1937, Daimler-Benz file in Daimler-Benz Archive, entitled "VW Kissel, DB Archive Fremdfirmen in Land 35 VW," Hamburger Stiftung Archive.

[18]Letter, Franz Popp to Wilhelm Kissel, Archiv der Daimler-Benz AG, File No. Kissel VII/5, Hamburger Stiftung Archive (#56).

[19]For example of Ford's exclusion see "Niederschrift über die Besichtigung der von Herrn Dr. Porsche gebauten 2. Probewagen am 24.4.1936 im Ausstellungsraum der Daimler-Benz AG, Berlin," Hamburger Stiftung Archive. For the belief that Ford should be excluded see the letter sent by Popp of BMW Abt. Flugmotoren to the Reichsverband der Deutschen Automobilindustrie suggesting that the RDA should oppose Ford's involvement, 8 May 1934; or Wilhelm Kissel, chair of the board of the Daimler-Benz company, to Felix Lauscher, Chefredakteur der Deutsche Bergwerks-Zeitung (editor-in-chief of *Deutsche Bergwerks-Zeitung*), 19 March 1935, Hamburger Stiftung Archive.

[20]"Nachtrag: Zur Niederschrift der Fabrikantensitzung am 28 Mai 1934," in RDA Volkswagen.

[21]See Albert Pietzsch, Präsident der Industrie und Handelskammer, München (president of the chamber of industry and trade in Munich) and Leiter der Reichswirtschaftskammer (director of the Reichs economic chamber) to General Director Popp of BMW,

meetings, they assumed a peripheral role. Ironically, one ostracized Opel representative at many of these meetings was to play a significant role in Volkswagen's successful development—Heinrich Nordhoff, the postwar general director of Volkswagen GmbH. With the decision that Opel was not to play a major role in Volkswagen, the Nazi authorities became increasingly hostile toward Opel, evident in the government's insistence in 1935 that the new Opel plant be constructed at Brandenburg, east of the Elbe and over two hundred miles from Opel's main Russelheim plant. The government's strategy, dictated by the *Lebensraum* policy, proved costly to Opel. The plant was vulnerable to Allied bombing during the war, and its contents were later confiscated by the Soviets.[22]

By 1937 the state authorities realized they could not leave the Volkswagen project to private manufacturers if they were serious about its development. The enormous costs involved in designing the car and constructing the plant; the potential losses involved, at least in the first few years of production; and the state of the world economy all made the project economically unattractive to the private sector. The impediments to success were so great that only state actors with a political motivation would have embarked on the project. The implications of creating stiffer competition, and possibly strengthening a foreign firm's subsidiary confirmed private-sector apathy. Indeed, it could be claimed that the focus on Volkswagen between 1934 and 1936 generally served to deter rather than advance the aggregate development of the German auto industry. Rather than combine the strength of all private manufacturers, as state officials had hoped, state policy created cliques, retarded competition between firms, and made them technically inert. They were concerned that any breakthrough might enhance the prospects for Volkswagen.[23]

Some major private actors acknowledged early on that only the state could devise and fund such a project. The most vocal proponent of this view was Popp of BMW, who insisted that he originally proposed that the Volkswagen project be taken over and supervised by the Deutsche Arbeitsfront (DAF).[24] If the idea was his, it earned him the approval of

---

2 June 1937. Also the influential Jacob Werlin's comments to Hitler that, in national projects, it would be better to exclude firms with an American orientation; "Besprechung am 21.7.1936 in RDA in der Volkswagen Angelegenheit," Hamburger Stiftung Archive or Jacob Werlin to Popp, 31 May 1937, in File 16, Volkswagen Popp, Archive of the Volkswagen Project, Bochum.

[22]See USSBS, "German Motor Vehicle Industry Report," p. 6; and the memo written by Colonel Wilkinson, which suggested that the Opel dies the Soviets claimed had been lost had in fact been shipped to Moscow. See OMGUS 451, Box 326, Military Field Branch, National Archives and Records Administration, Washington, D.C.

[23]Olley, BIOS Report 21, "The Motor Car Industry in Germany," p. 5.

[24]The most supportive evidence for Popp's claim that he was the original proponent of

the state but the enmity of most other industrialists, because it provided the means for the realization of the project. Subsequently, the fortunes of Popp's BMW and Kissel's Daimler-Benz were to become inextricably intertwined with those of Volkswagen.

The Nazi authorities shifted responsibility for the development of the project from private manufacturers to the DAF. The Volkswagen became publicly funded and publicly implemented. The structure of investment financing, tax relief, method of sales, and financing of construction were all heavily weighted in favor of the company. With the decision to retrieve the project from the private sector, Volkswagen became part of the German state and hence a beneficiary of its aggressive ideology and coercive apparatus.

To understand the decision to incorporate the Volkswagenwerk into the DAF, a brief description of this organization is needed. In May 1933 the German trade unions had been abolished and replaced by the DAF. Unlike the politically and financially independent trade unions in the Weimar Republic, the DAF was an arm of the German state. Robert Ley, its head, had aspirations to use his position to control all of labor, both within Germany and later the annexed territories, although these ideas were quickly revised by other Nazi leaders. Ley then changed objectives, seeking to make the DAF the most powerful financial organization in the Third Reich.

Armed with funds the DAF had confiscated from German labor unions and wealthy cooperative societies, Ley created a financial empire based on two holding companies, the Vermögensverwaltung der Deutschen Arbeitsfront GmbH (VV) and the Treuhandgesellschaft für Wirtschaftliche Unternehmungen mbH (TWU). Between them they owned 97 companies with a total capital of RM500 million, a former cooperative society of some 50 factories, 137 job supply centers, a chain of retain shops (with a turnover of RM770 million in 1943), building societies valued at over RM100 million, and the Bank der Deutschen Arbeit with capital in excess of RM50 million.[25] Membership in the DAF was theoretically voluntary for German workers but in practice

---

this scheme is a letter written by Franz Popp to Jacob Werlin, a personal friend of Hitler, member of the Supervisory Board of Daimler-Benz, and later a member of Volkswagen's preparatory board. In the letter Popp claimed he had previously written to Kurt Frey, Reichstreuhänder der Arbeit (Reich trustee of labor), with his idea. Frey had then informed Robert Ley, leader of the DAF, and Heinrich Simon, Director at the Central Office for Economic Finance (later to become Chairman of the Volkswagenwerk Supervisory Board), and they approved his proposal. See Franz Popp to Jacob Werlin, 29 July 1936, Archiv des Dokumentationzentrums der Staatlichen Archivverwaltung der DDR, DK 713, Berlin.

[25]Foreign Office (FO) report, "The Heritage of the DAF," in file FO 371/46829 in the Public Record Office (PRO), London.

conscriptive. Over 15 million German workers contributed five marks each a month to the funds of the DAF, providing a constant monthly cash flow of approximately RM75 million.[26] Among prospective German owners, whether private or public, the DAF was uniquely placed to finance and implement the Volkswagen project.

Volkswagen as an Instrument of the State

By the late 1930s all parties agreed that if the Volkswagen project was to succeed it would require state ownership rather than just sponsorship (although many would have preferred the scheme be stillborn).[27] On 22 May 1937 the Gesellschaft zur Vorbereitung des Deutschen Volkswagens mbH (or Gezuvor) was formed, a preparatory company to organize construction of the Völkswagen plant.[28] It initially received a capital subscription of RM480,000 from the TWU to cover the costs of preparatory work on the design of the plant.[29] The selected site was near Fallersleben in Lower Saxony, and the new town to be built on the site was given the cumbersome name of Kraft durch Freude Stadt—later reverting to the traditional name Wolfsburg. Unlike most German companies, Gezuvor had no supervisory board, so that Ley himself could directly supervise the project.[30]

The following year Hitler personally laid the site's first foundation stone.[31] According to the terms of the company charter, "it is the task of the enterprise to carry out the order given to the Deutsche Arbeitsfront by the Führer and Reichskanzler in respect to manufacturing, developing and sale of the Volkswagen." It was a public utility company and was not established for the purpose of making a profit, according to the third section of its charter. Dividends of 4 percent

---

[26]H. A. Goff, "Subject: Wolfsburg Motor Works," FO 1046/193, PRO.

[27]By then it had become apparent to von Opel that his firm would not be involved in the Volkswagen's design; he ceased to support the project because it would provide competition. See Department of Justice interview with Fritz von Opel, 12 April 1943, in omgus 4330 Autos File 745015, Military Field Branch, National Archives and Records Administration, Washington, D.C.

[28]"Es begann 1934: Die Geschichte des Volkswagenwerks"—a short history of the Volkswagenwerk drawn from the archival material collected by Ian Turner for "British Occupation Policy." All references to data received from Dr. Turner are noted as "Turner Personal Files."

[29]"Subject: The Volkswagenwerk Complex in Control under Law 52," June 1947, Property Control Branch, Finance Division, FO 371/65114, PRO.

[30]See "Niederschrift über eine Aussage Strauchs," 9 December 1949, p. 2., Z 36 I/91, Anlage 20, Bundesarchiv, Koblenz.

[31]Chief Custodian, "Preliminary Report: Volkswagen Chief Custodian's Report 1946," FO 942/197, PRO.

would be paid to any future private shareholders out of profits, but any capital gains on the sale of Volkswagen shares would revert to the DAF "for social purposes." Gezuvor was replaced as a legal entity by Volkswagen GmbH, which created a board of directors on 6 October 1938.[32] The board was chaired by Heinrich Simon, and his deputy was Hans Strauch, both senior members of the DAF. Other board members included Jacob Werlin, close personal friend of Hitler and member of the Daimler-Benz board; Ferdinand Porsche, designer of the Volkswagen car that was then in prototype; and three minor DAF officials, Bodo Lafferentz, Adolf Geyrhalter, and Alexander Halder. Usually, the management board included two members of the board of directors—Lafferentz and Porsche—plus Otto Dyckhoff, Felix Schmidt, and Hans Scholz, another DAF dignitary.[33] A subsequent United States Strategic Bombing Survey report concluded that "no experienced or qualified men of the caliber required were put in charge of operations. It was chiefly a political plant."[34]

Ley's objectives were clearly defined if a little overwhelming. He wished to fulfil Hitler's dream by eventually constructing the largest automobile plant in the world, capable after three stages of construction of producing 1.5 million cars per year. Ley did eventually build the biggest plant in the world; the first of the proposed three stages, when completed, was not only the largest plant in the world but had 50 percent more floor space than the Ford plant at Willow Run. The plant's purpose was to supply Germans with a car for under RM1,000, by employing the methods of mass production and dispensing with the government's sales tax (that went as high as 50 percent).[35] Financing for plant construction was provided by the Bank der Deutschen Arbeit, which was owned by the DAF, and expensive single-purpose machine tools were imported from the United States, sacrificing valuable foreign currency. No wonder the huge start-up costs, the plant's construction, and the initial losses later prompted foreign analysts to describe (with a great restraint) the arrangements devised by the DAF as "financially unsound."[36]

The DAF developed the infamous savers' fund that, in keeping with

[32]"Es begann 1934," Turner Personal Files.
[33]"Auszugsweise Abschrift aus der undatierten DAF-Denkschrift: Die wirtschaftlichen Unternehmungen der Deutschen Arbeitsfront," p. 142, Z 36 I/91, VW Project, Bochum.
[34]USSBS Report 88, "Fallersleben Germany, Volkswagen," p. 3.
[35]Ley quoted in a statement by Franz Popp concerning the Deutsche Bank's position regarding the Volkswagen Project, 28 October 1938, Archiv des Dokumentationzentrums der Staatlichen Archivverwaltung der DDR, Berlin.
[36]For proposed financing see "Subject: The Volkswagenwerk Complex in Control." The assessment comes from H. A. R. Binney, "Minute Sheet," p. 7, 12 September 1946, Board of Trade (BT), 211/92, PRO.

the economic principles of fascism, sought to bypass the marketplace by selling direct to the consumer at a set price. Savers could contribute a minimum of RM25 a month toward the purchase of a Volkswagen and would receive their car when they had completed payments of RM1,200 (including insurance).[37] This superficial description obscures the brutal terms of the scheme. Cancellation of an order would result in a penalty of 100 percent of the amount already paid; failure to pay or even late payment of one installment would result in an order's cancellation with 100 percent forfeiture; the DAF had the unreserved right to cancel an order or to delay providing the promised car; the loss of an individual's stamped subscription card would result in forfeiture of all paid contributions. The limitations seemed endless.[38] Yet by the end of the war 336,000 people had faithfully subscribed RM267 million without one car being delivered. Subsequently savers incorrectly claimed the money had been used to finance the construction of the Volkswagenwerk; numerous independent sources show that in 1945 the full amount of savers' fund money lay untouched in an account in the Bank der Deutschen Arbeit.[39] However, the prospect of providing 267,000 cars at no further cost to the savers did provide the postwar company with the very real threat of bankruptcy.[40]

By late 1939 the first stage of construction was completed, with 80 percent of the plant built and the machinery installed. The cost of investment in this plant, machinery, and equipment was in excess of RM215 million, paid for through the DAF's holding companies and banks. Cars had not been produced in volume by the outbreak of war, but it was estimated that the plant, which covered over 770 acres of ground, had an annual capacity of 150,000 units.[41] Nazi plans were expressed in the most expensive, economically irrational plant in history. It was to be of minimal value to a government at war but of unlimited value to another at peace.

STATE-FIRM RELATIONS IN THE PREWAR ERA

A significant revolution took place in the nature of state policy toward the automobile industry when the Nazis assumed power. Not only was this new regime more interventionist, it also proved to be discrimi-

[37]See Goff, "Wolfsburg Motor Works."
[38]For a full description of terms see BIOS Final Report 998, Item 19, p. 2.
[39]"Es begann 1934," Turner Personal Files.
[40]Transcript, Control Council for Germany (CCG), Economics Division, "Memorandum for Meeting with Professor Erhard," 8 October 1949, VW Treuhänder Files, Minutes of Control Board Meeting, Turner Personal Files.
[41]All these figures come from USSBS Report 88, "Fallersleben Germany," p. 3.

natory. In initial discussions concerning the Volkswagen project, the Nazis assumed that Opel would be indispensable, so it was tolerated while Ford was excluded. Although U.S. Ford was symbolically important to the Nazi elite, Ford involvement in this "national" project was unthinkable. As it became evident that the private sector could not handle the project, the Nazi authorities became more receptive to appeals to exclude Opel. The exclusion of Opel and Ford from all national projects had a cost to national security: "the Panzer-Kommission admits in an interview that the two largest producers, Ford and Opel, were left out intentionally because of their foreign associations, and that this decision later cost the Germans heavily in man hours."[42] In contrast, figures at both BMW and Daimler-Benz took the opportunity to ingratiate themselves with the Nazi authorities. With their credibility established by a history of arms production, both companies saw an advantage in integrating themselves in the decision-making process by attacking Opel and Ford.

By 1938 Ford and Opel were still responsible for 52 percent of all vehicles produced and sold in Germany, but as their political influence declined and the state became more hostile, their economic prospects appeared bleak. Both were awarded military contracts after 1937, but these contracts kept them less than fully occupied, whereas BMW and Daimler-Benz operations expanded rapidly.

Richard Overy claims that the automobile industry was singled out for special concessions; nonetheless, the pattern of distribution was selective and was accompanied by increased regulation, effectively reducing the autonomy of all producers. This was not simply a businessman's regime performing the unacceptable tasks associated with capitalism in crisis, as some Marxists suggest.[43] The unsuccessful efforts of influential producers to assuage the state's aggressive tendencies concerning the Volkswagen project bear testimony to the regime's autonomy.[44] Marginal producers were amalgamated or eliminated, although the efforts of Von Schell, the new minister for transport, to consolidate production further through a policy of standardization, instituted in November 1938, were thwarted by the outbreak of war.[45]

[42]Olley, BIOS Report 21, "The Motor Car Industry in Germany," p. 7.
[43]See Overy, *The Nazi Economic Recovery*, pp. 36, 39, 51, 58. For the Marxist position see Alfred Sohn-Rethel, *Economy and the Class Structure of German Fascism* (London: CSE, 1978); Jurgen Kuczynski, *Germany: Economic and Labor Conditions under Fascism* (New York: Greenwood, 1968); Daniel Guerin, *Fascism and Big Business* (New York: Pathfinder, 1973).
[44]One eliminated producer was Hugo Junkers, whose refusal to produce warplanes for Göring resulted in the nationalization of his firm. Overy, *The Nazi Economic Recovery*, p. 40.
[45]Olley, BIOS Report 21, "The Motor Car Industry in Germany," p. 5.

In the midst lay the unborn Volkswagenwerk, which proved politically influential even in its embryonic stage. Not only was Volkswagen treated in a favored way, but it also provided the context for discriminating between other favored German firms and American multinationals. The Nazi authorities treated the Volkswagenwerk in a way no firm had been treated. Only a firm built with such nearly inexhaustible resources, with such little concern for economic rationale, and with no backlog of debts could have been as successful as Volkswagen GmbH was in the 1950s. In 1945 Volkswagen possessed the economic framework and the technology; all it needed was the political latitude to succeed.

THE VOLKSWAGENWERK BETWEEN 1939 AND 1945

Most histories of Volkswagen tail off at the end of their brief summary of the prewar period to spend a few pages on events during the war or to ignore that period completely and go straight into a description of Volkswagen's glorious rise from the ashes.[46] This pattern has been dictated by lack of data, but it is also indicative of assumptions that events at wartime Volkswagen were insignificant to its postwar development. My thesis contradicts that assumption, suggesting instead that the revolutionary policies initiated by the Nazi government between 1934 and 1939 were reinforced in wartime and were therefore significant to Volkswagen's postwar development.

The completion of the first stage of the plant left Volkswagen with the largest press shop in Europe, 2,700 of the finest specialized machine tools, and the right to use the best raw materials and labor available.[47] A work force of between 4,000 and 6,000 had been employed in the construction of the plant and the city through the DAF-owned Neuland AG construction company, which had built 3,200 dwelling units.[48] The architect responsible for construction was initially accountable directly to Generalbauinspektor Albert Speer and then Robert Ley, to insure the independence of the project from local authorities. The Volkswagenwerk was entered in the local register as the owners of the town, creating a new area in July 1938—"Stadt des KdF Wagens bei Fallersleben." The workers were redeployed at the out-

---

[46]The best example of the book that pays homage to the company rather than describes its history is Henry W. Nelson's *Small Wonder: The Amazing Story of Volkswagen* (Boston: Little, Brown, 1965).

[47]See Olley, BIOS Report 21, "The Motor Car Industry in Germany," p. 7; and USSBS Report 88, "Fallersleben Germany," p. 7.

[48]"Subject: The Volkswagenwerk Complex in Control," p. 3.

break of war, leaving many of the town's planned amenities incomplete.[49] However, all planned facilities for the plant's first stage had been finished at a cost of RM215 million, with production scheduled at an initial rate of 4,000 cars per week.[50]

At the outbreak of war the plant's workers numbered 2,732, all of whom were Germans.[51] The theory that the Volkswagenwerk was constructed explicitly for armament production is contradicted by events. In the expectation that the war would be brief, the authorities decided not to convert the Volkswagenwerk to military production, despite the relative ease of the process. But the lack of available raw materials precluded any mass production for civilians. As a result, the plant lay mostly idle for late 1939 and most of 1940, with only 751 sedans built. Its extensive power plant was mainly used to provide electricity for the area.[52]

The plant was seized by Hermann Göring at the outbreak of war, but not until late 1940, recognizing that the war would not be brief, did Göring and the Reichsluftfahrtministerium (RLM) decide it should be used for military production.[53] Production lines were converted to the manufacture of two types of jeep, the *Kübelwagen* for land use and the *Schwimmwagen* for amphibious use. By late December 1940 the first 1,000 Kübelwagens had been built.[54]

The claim that no civilian products were made at the Volkswagen plant during the war has had an enduring quality, but evidence suggests that 51,224 sedans were built. In addition, because of the relative ease of conversion to jeep production—only minor adjustments in body and chassis were needed—50,432 Kübelwagens and 12,283 Schwimmwagens were produced for the Wehrmacht between 1941 and 1945.[55] This production provided a testing ground for the postwar model.

Other wartime production was unrelated to automobiles. Göring

[49]Turner, "British Occupation Policy," pp. 58–59.
[50]For construction costs see USSBS Report 88, "Fallersleben Germany," p. 3. For production schedules see "Summary Report: Provisional Reparations and Disarmament Working Party," Ref 2753/5/Econ 11, January 1946, FO 371/65114, PRO.
[51]USSBS Report 88, "Fallersleben Germany," p. 7.
[52]See Chief Custodian, "Volkswagen Chief Custodian's Report 1946," and "The German Automobile Industry," BIOS Report 768, BIOS B, Box 20, IWM, p. 11.
[53]Chief Custodian, "Chief Custodian's Report 1946."
[54]"Es begann 1934," Turner Personal Files.
[55]For the technical aspects of this conversion and its relative simplicity see "Investigation into the Design and Performance of the Volkswagen or German People's Car," BIOS Final Report 998, Item 19, IWM, pp. 1–2. For production figures see "Subject: The Volkswagenwerk Complex in Control," p. 3; Goff, "Wolfsburg Motor Works"; memo from Property Control Branch, Finance Division, to Chief, Finance Division, "The Volkswagen Complex in Control under Law 52," p. 7, Ministry of Supply (MinSupp) 14/397, PRO.

Table 5.1. Military division of Volkswagen
production, 1940–1944 (percentage)

Year	Army (OKH)	Airforce (RLM)
1940	18	82
1941	31	69
1942	29	71
1943	41	59
1944	44	56

SOURCE: Chief Custodian, "Volkswagen Chief
Custodian's Report 1946," FO 942/197, PRO.

used it for the repair of Junker 88 aircraft, the construction of fuel
tanks for aircraft, and for armament production, most notably teller
mines, bazookas, and V1 missiles. (Incorrectly assuming the plant had
already been converted to wartime production, the Allies launched an
unsuccessful strategic bombing attack in May 1940.)[56] The division of
production between 1939 and 1944 is given in Table 5.1.

Interestingly, the percentages reveal a greater emphasis on the manufacture of products associated with automobiles as the war progressed, counterintuitively indicating that the difficulty of reconverting
to civilian production decreased rather than increased. Of course, wartime production required money, raw materials, and labor. The initial
lull in production was financially costly, because fixed costs, such as the
labor force, still had to be paid. Furthermore, the conversion to wartime production required financing to modify both the machinery and
the production process, and such costs of production as requisitioning
additional machinery and purchasing materials also had to be met. As a
new public utility company, Volkswagen had generated no profits for
these purposes. Funding was provided by two sources, the DAF's
Berlin-located Zentralstelle für Finanzwirtschaft (ZfF) and the Bank
der Deutschen Arbeitsfront (BDA) (see Table 5.2).

The RLM also paid for all costs of production. Volkswagen operated
on a cost-plus basis, working exclusively on RLM and OKH orders and
combining profits with the subsidies provided by the two banks. A third
source of wartime financing came from the formation of Volkswagenwerk GmbH as a limited company in 1941. This new DAF company was
capitalized at RM150 million, RM145 million from the VV and RM5
million from the TWU.

The Volkswagenwerk did not stagnate from wartime neglect. Even if

[56]For production figures and bombing attacks see USSBS Report 88, "Fallersleben
Germany," pp. 4–5, 10.

Table 5.2. Volkswagenwerk financing by the ZfF
and BDA, 1939–1944 (in marks)

Year	ZfF	BDA
1939	51,793,163.67	42,798,117.99
1940	40,000,000.00	82,590,716.83
1941	30,000,000.00	110,497,593.08
1942	80,000,000.00	40,416,122.00
1943	50,000,000.00	22,493,281.53
1944	50,000,000.00	47,322,764.89

SOURCE: Chief Custodian, "Volkswagen Chief
Custodian's Report 1946," FO 942/197, PRO.

no more than 50 percent of the plant's capacity was ever used in war,
the plant continued to grow and prosper until 1944, fed by an abundance of government contracts, subsidies, machines confiscated in the
occupied territories, and businesses confiscated from Jews in Germany.[57] New capital was not neglected, and additional finance was
reinvested. The company's development is reflected in the wartime
growth in turnover (see Table 5.3).

Volkswagen experienced a dynamic growth in turnover between
1940 and 1944 within a national context of declining availability of
both raw materials and labor. Yet despite the tightening labor market,
the Volkswagen work force grew by over 600 percent between 1939
and 1944, from 2,732 to 17,365. This paradox was generally ignored in

Table 5.3. Turnover figures for Volkswagen,
1940–1944 (in RMs)

Year	Turnover
1940	26,060,097.80
1941	67,209,077.86
1942	145,819,525.95
1943	224,786,959.22
1944	287,271,496.74

SOURCE: "Volkswagenwerk GmbH," Volkswagen
Financial Reports File, Turner Personal Files.

[57]This claim is made most forcefully by Olley, "The Motor Car Industry in Germany."
The most publicized example of confiscation was that of 300 machines from Peugeot's
French plant. See BIOS Report 768, "The German Automobile Industry," and Ivan Hirst,
"The Volkswagenwerk under the British Trusteeship," Turner Personal Files, p. 168.
The most publicized forced purchase was of the Luckenwalder Feintuch Fabrik near
Berlin. See "The Volkswagen Complex in Control under Law 52," Ministry of Supply
14/397, PRO.

Table 5.4. Number and distribution of Germans, foreign workers, and POWs at Volkswagen, 1939–1944

	Germans		Foreigners		POWs		
Year	N	%	N	%	N	%	Total (N)
1939	2,732	100	—	—	—	—	2,732
1940	5,287	84	997	16	—	—	6,284
1941	5,063	66	2,035	26	435	8	7,632
1942	4,643	39	5,583	46	1,835	15	12,061
1943	5,621	33	8,677	51	2,724	16	17,022
1944	6,031	34	8,841	51	2,493	15	17,365

SOURCE: USSBS Report 88, "Fallersleben Germany, Volkswagen," p. 8.

postwar investigations by Allied inspectors, the results of whose studies were published in the Combined Intelligence Objectives Sub-committee, British Intelligence Objectives Sub-committee, and Field Intelligence Agency Technical reports. The major concern in these reports was to discover if any technical aspects of production could be adapted for the war against Japan and a possible future war against the Soviet Union. However, subsequent research has explained this puzzling contradiction: Volkswagen used slave labor after 1940.

One report on Volkswagen published just after the war characteristically classified these slave laborers as "foreign workers" or "prisoners of war," just as at Fordwerke. The numbers and distribution of workers are listed in Table 5.4.

The same report reveals two interesting facts about Volkswagen's wartime production. The first is that in 1943 and 1944 slave laborers were approximately 66 percent of the total work force—an unskilled *Lumpenproletariat* supervised by SS guards.[58] The second is that even in years when labor was most scarce, the number of Volkswagen's German workers generally continued to increase. This can be explained by Speer's insistence that the efficient consolidation of production would achieve economies of scale.[59] The Volkswagenwerk was a direct and obvious beneficiary of this policy, at the expense of such peripheral auto producers as Fordwerke. Even when strategic bombing caused the dispersal of some of the plant and its machinery in mid-1944, Volkswagen GmbH retained all of its German workers.

Until recently few details were known about the origins and treat-

[58]Hirst, "The Volkswagenwerk under the British Trusteeship," Turner Personal Files, p. 168.

[59]For a discussion of this policy see Alan Milward, *The German Economy at War* (London: Athlone, 1965).

ment of these foreign workers by the Nazi authorities and company staff. The report stated only that about 33 percent of Russian civilian workers were classified as skilled after a rudimentary training period, and after the middle of 1943 about 12 percent of the total work force were women.[60] However, the emergent interest in the plight of *Zwangsarbeiter* during the Third Reich, focusing on armaments producers that became notably successful car producers in the Bonn Republic, has provided invaluable material for understanding the dynamics of the wartime labor policy pursued at the Volkswagenwerk.[61] An important recent contribution, by the chief archivist of the Wolfsburg city records, adds substance to the aggregate figures of the early report.[62]

Klaus-Jörg Siegfried's figures show that by 1938, 3,000 Italians worked at the Volkswagenwerk and in the city. In 1940, 1,500 additional Polish civil workers were shipped to the plant, followed by 850 Soviet prisoners in 1941. In 1942, 800 French and Belgian prisoners were sent to Wolfsburg, and that year also marked the beginning of the *Ostarbeiter* program, which shipped Eastern workers into Germany.[63] Siegfried claims that from 1942 onward between 4,000 and 5,000 workers, mainly of Russian and Ukrainian descent, were involuntarily shipped to Wolfsburg. In addition, 1,500 French, 300 Belgian, and 200 Dutch workers were transported to the Volkswagen plant in 1943.[64] A subunit of the Neuengamme concentration camp was established in Wolfsburg to facilitate the procurement, arrival, and housing of these workers. Many of the inmates were women who were employed in the most dangerous aspects of munitions production.[65] Like the Eastern men, Eastern women were almost exclusively of Jewish extraction and were supervised by members of the SS.[66]

The brutal, inhumane treatment accorded to inmates, with minimal subsistence rations and negligent medical treatment, had a catastrophic effect on the health of the adult work force. Plant authorities organized

[60]USSBS Report 88, "Fallersleben Germany," p. 8.
[61]One of the first articles on this issue is "Herren und Knechte," *Der Spiegel*, 25 November 1985.
[62]Klaus-Jörg Siegfried, *Rüstungsproduktion und Zwangsarbeit im Volkswagenwerk, 1939–1945: Eine Dokumentation* (Frankfurt: Campus, 1986). For an evaluation see "Porsche und der geheimsache 'Kirschkern': Historiker erforschen NS-Zwangsarbeit im Volkswagenwerk," *Der Spiegel*, 13 April 1987. For the debate on Daimler-Benz see Pohl et al., *Die Daimler-Benz AG;* Roth et al., "Der Weg zum guten Stern"; and Hans Mommsen's comments on both books in *Der Spiegel*, 13 April 1987.
[63]See Edward L. Homze, *Foreign Labor in Nazi Germany* (Princeton: Princeton University Press, 1967).
[64]Siegfried, *Rüstungsproduktion und Zwangsarbeit*, p. 13.
[65]Turner, "British Occupation Policy," p. 60n.
[66]See *Der Spiegel*, 13 April 1987, p. 91; Hirst, "The Volkswagenwerk under the British Trusteeship."

the mass extermination of Polish and Soviet infants and of hundreds of Soviet prisoners of war, Italian resistors, and Soviet and Polish forced laborers. Deaths were often the result of a combination of starvation and exhaustion.[67] Once they could no longer work, inmates were left to die. For his supervision of the willful neglect of the inmates by the plant's medical staff, Körbel, the camp doctor, was found guilty of war crimes and was hung in March 1947.[68] Henry Nelson's claim in his history of Volkswagen—that Porsche looked after the camp's slave laborers so well that Nazi officials complained they were being pampered—seems misplaced.[69]

The systematic policy of working slave laborers to death accounts for the numerical discrepancy between the number of foreign workers admitted to the camp according to Siegfried's records and the annual numbers listed in the USSBS report. The USSBS report mentions that company records proudly note that the rate of absenteeism had been reduced from 16 percent when it had a predominantly German workforce, to under 5 percent by 1944—success was evidently achieved through attrition.[70] Siegfried's account leaves little doubt that the Nazi hierarchy, the company's management, and its supervisory staff were all aware and active participants. The management board consisted of many who had played a major role in the company's prewar development, including Lafferentz, Werlin, Schmidt, Porsche, and Piech (Porsche's son-in-law). However, the authority of the board of directors expired on 13 October 1943, and any vestiges of corporate autonomy disappeared as the *Aufsichtsrat* (supervisory board) was succeeded by the head of the commercial division of the DAF.[71]

The company benefited from an inexhaustible supply of cash, the growing allocation of German workers, the discretionary allocation of raw materials, and a steady supply of expendable slave laborers. It is not surprising that the Volkswagenwerk, after massive initial losses, proved to be a profitable venture during the war (see Table 5.5). Two interesting tendencies should be noted. First, huge losses in the first two years of production are commonplace among new state-sponsored corporations in contemporary capitalist societies, but for the state to shoulder such a burden was revolutionary in the 1930s, especially in an economy that predated the modern form of managerial capitalism. In the 1920s and 1930s the Italian fascist regime had accepted similar

[67]Siegfried, *Rüstungsproduktion und Zwangsarbeit*, pp. 163–70.
[68]Turner, "British Occupation Policy," p. 60.
[69]Nelson, *Small Wonder*, p. 94.
[70]USSBS Report 88, "Fallersleben Germany," p. 16.
[71]"Volkswagenwerk GmbH," Volkswagen Financial Reports File, Turner Personal Files.

Table 5.5. Volkswagen profits,
1939–1943 (in RMs)

Year	Profit
1939	−5,281,734.60
1940	−12,670,291.69
1941	859,367.64
1942	1,290,574.16
1943	10,414,457.19

SOURCE: "Volkswagenwerk GmbH,"
Volkswagen Financial Reports File,
Turner Personal Files.

responsibilities through the formation of IRI, a state-sponsored public holding company designed to assume control of strategically important but economically unprofitable firms. In contrast, the Nazi government created the Volkswagenwerk from scratch on mass production principles, providing the company with the best possible framework for economic prosperity in a domestic or global economy based on unlimited demand.

Despite a lack of concern about generating profits, state partisanship ensured that the company would become increasingly viable. Volkswagen could create a surplus through mass production, and both turnover and rate of profits grew at an exponential rate—a pattern recurring after the war. Furthermore, the Allied strategic bombing at Wolfsburg was not as damaging as at some Daimler-Benz plants, and the Volkswagen plant was not overrun by the Red Army like the Opel plant at Brandenburg, where all materials and machinery were mysteriously "lost."[72]

Although the Allies launched three aerial attacks before 1944, the Volkswagenwerk sustained no heavy damage. Flaws in allied intelligence could have accounted for the failure to bomb the vulnerable Wolfsburg plant at an early date while some of the better fortified production plants were so effectively attacked.[73] The first serious attack took place in April 1944, when 500 high explosive and 450 incendiary bombs were dropped on the plant with limited effect.[74] By this time a dispersal plan had been activated by Speer's Ministry of Munitions, decentralizing production in well-hidden, well-protected, and

[72]On the destruction of Daimler-Benz's Sindelfingen and Gaggenau plants, see "Report on the Visit to Daimler-Benz AG at Stuttgart-Untertürkheim," p. 28, BIOS Final Report 35, BIOS B, Box 1.

[73]See USSBS Report, Munitions Division, "German Motor Vehicles Industry Report," 3 November 1945, p. 15.

[74]USSBS Report 88, "Fallersleben Germany," p. 10.

often underground locations. In Volkswagen's case the dispersal plants were located within 100 kilometers of the main factory, the most important in Ustron in Silesia, Luckenwalde near Berlin, Schönebeck near Magdeburg, Neudeck near Karlsbad, a partially underground plant near Ahlfeld, and at Longwy near the Belgian and Luxembourg borders and the Harz mountains.[75] The dispersal plan was implemented by October 1944. Dispersal plants totaled 104,000 square feet, only about 2 percent of the main plant, but this small area accounted for 827 machine tools—32 percent of what was located in the main works. Subsequent bombing occurred on 20 June, 29 June, and 5 August 1944, and 1,383 high explosive and 799 incendiary bombs actually fell in the plant area. Of these, 205 high explosive and 58 incendiary bombs actually fell on plant buildings. Allied analysts later recorded that of the total 4,441,897 square feet of floor area, 1,795,417 square feet, approximately 40 percent, became unusable. They also suggested that 642,682 square feet of roofing had been destroyed.[76]

However, the controlling officer of the Volkswagenwerk under British trusteeship suggested that Allied attacks were not as effective as these figures indicate. Ivan Hirst claims that the Germans deliberately collapsed the roof on parts of the plant immediately after major raids, hoping to convince the Allies that the attack had been successful and the plant put out of commission, thereby sparing it from serious damage. The plan was successful, and all raids ceased after August 1944. Production was nevertheless reduced, as a result of the dispersal of machinery and the inevitable bottlenecks caused by the lack of raw materials.[77] There was no roof on the press shop, but the plan successfully protected essential machinery and the plant suffered very little structural damage.[78]

The USSBS report failed to recognize the anomaly between heavy damage to the plant's roof and low rate of machine tool damage. It did note that little damage had been done to the interior or the structure of the buildings, as a result, the report claimed, of the roof's construction from noncombustible and fire-resistant materials and its angle.[79] (On the two heaviest attacks launched against the plant, see Table 5.6). In fact, all the air raids on the Volkswagenwerk and the subsequent looting destroyed only 9.8 percent of machine tools. Fifty-five employees

[75]For details see Combined Intelligence Objectives Sub-committee (CIOS) Report XXXII-122, IWM; Nelson, *Small Wonder*, p. 95; and Hirst, "Volkswagenwerk under the British Trusteeship," p. 168.
[76]USSBS Report 88, "Fallersleben Germany," pp. 10–11, 20.
[77]Ibid., p. 16; Turner, "British Occupation Policy," p. 66.
[78]Hirst, "Volkswagenwerk under the British Trusteeship."
[79]USSBS Report 88, "Fallersleben Germany," p. 11.

Table 5.6. Machines damaged at Volkswagen as a result of air raids, by number and distribution

Date	Machines in plant (N)	Destroyed		Heavily		Lightly		Undamaged	
		N	%	N	%	N	%	N	%
20 June 1944	2,776	73	2.6	33	1.19	37	1.34	2,633	94.87
29 June 1944	2,176	152	7.0	106	4.85	123	5.65	1,795	82.50

SOURCE: USSBS Report 88, "Fallersleben Germany, Volkswagen," p. 14.

died and 174 were wounded.[80] I suspect that most of these casualties were prisoners in the concentration camp who were unable to take cover in the basements beneath the solid concrete floors of the production halls.

At war's end, factory officials tried to implement the Third Reich's scorched earth policy by destroying the factory and its power station. However, the mayor of Wolfsburg, recognizing the plant's potential and the immediate significance of the power station in heating and lighting the area, called out the local militia (*Volkssturm*) on 5 April. The management burned incriminating documents and fled with the SS camp guards. The *Volkssturm* offered little resistance to the U.S. troops that arrived a week later, on 12 April 1945.[81]

STATE-FIRM RELATIONS AT VOLKSWAGEN, 1939–1945

The outbreak of war was a major juncture in Volkswagen's history. The plant could have remained idle, as some historians have suggested it did; the plant could have been effectively destroyed, as some historians have suggested it was; and Volkswagen's prewar history could have been essentially divorced from its postwar history, as many historians have suggested it is. However, important state officials in the Air Ministry and the Munitions Ministry, such as Göring and Speer, used the war to solidify the significance of the Volkswagenwerk for the German economy, in a way that outlasted the Third Reich.[82]

[80]Ibid., p. 14.
[81]Turner, "British Occupation Policy," pp. 68–69.
[82]In extending this claim, Eva Brumlop and Ulrich Jürgens suggest that VW's product and locational structure, public character, and special structure of industrial relations were all derived from the firm's Nazi origins. See "Rationalization and Industrial Relations in the West German Auto Industry: The Case of Volkswagen," Das Internationale Institut vergleichender Gesellschaftsforschung (International Institute for Comparative Social Research) Papers/DP 83-216, Berlin, September 1983.

The plant did not stagnate in war but expanded its capacity tremendously as a result of sustained state sponsorship. The state poured money in, to purchase machinery, construct housing, and enlarge the production halls. The last vestiges of autonomy were lost when the nominal independence of the *Aufsichtsrat* was replaced by direct control from the Munitions Ministry in 1943. The Volkswagenwerk shifted from indirect control by the state through a public holding company to direct control by state bureaucrats, and the company became an indisputable instrument of state policy.

The Volkswagenwerk was provided with all it needed for its sustained success. Construction was unmatched among auto plants, with reinforced basements and roof. The sustained supply of slave labor, even in a tightening labor market, was not uncommon among strategically important German firms, but the sustained supply of German labor was unique to the Volkswagenwerk. In no other ostensibly auto-producing company was a German work force kept intact.

Finally, an effective early dispersal plan and the ingenious collapsing of the factory roof protected the plant from heavy damage. To the largest auto plant in the world, the loss of a mere 9.8 percent of machinery to a combination of strategic bombing and confiscation by Soviet and French forces was hardly a mortal blow. The management's thwarted attempt to destroy the plant can best be explained by the anarchy and irrationality of the last throes of the Third Reich.[83] During the war Volkswagen evolved from child of the state to a mature instrument of state policy. It would maintain that role in the postwar world.

FROM A POLITICAL TO AN ECONOMIC INSTRUMENT: VOLKSWAGEN IN THE POSTWAR WORLD

The SS guards' departure terrified the local population with the specter of rampaging slave laborers. Indeed, many Eastern workers seized arms left by guards and looted shops and goods trains.[84] However, when they sought to destroy the plant and its machinery, they

---

[83]Wendy Carlin quotes USSBS reports claiming that no more than 6.5 percent of all machine tools were damaged or destroyed by the bombing and fighting. Even in the critical ball bearings industry, only 16 percent of all machine tools were destroyed. Indeed, Carlin claims that industrial capital stock was both quantitatively greater and qualitatively better in 1945 than in 1939. See "Economic Reconstruction in Western Germany, 1945–1955; The Displacement of 'Vegetative Control,'" in Ian Turner, ed., *Reconstruction in Postwar Germany: British Occupation Policy in the Western Zones, 1945–1955* (New York: Berg, 1989).

[84]Turner, "British Occupation Policy," p. 69.

encountered an unexpected barrier—French workers, who recognized the value of the plant and its machinery and presumably wanted to save the machines for use in reparations.[85] American troops had already overrun the area and then withdrawn, failing to recognize the significance of the plant. They were persuaded by local officials to return and occupy the town on 18 April in order to quell local disturbances.[86]

A heroic myth has gained currency of the resurrection of the decimated, paralyzed Volkswagen plant. In fact the U.S. Army initially supervised the assembly of cars at Volkswagen in early May. The work force then consisted of a mere 200 employees. Foreign workers had been freed and most of the German workers had fled, many because of their involvement in war crimes.[87]

Subsequently the town of Wolfsburg passed from American to British control, a shift crucial to Volkswagen's future welfare. For, as Ian Turner demonstrates, key factions of the British government and their personnel in Germany (CCG) had objectives that deterred them from pursuing denazification and reparations policies as zealously as the Americans and French.[88] Both British Treasury and CCG officials lacked the ideological zeal of the American and the French authorities. Seizure and control of the Volkswagen plant by the British saved it from dismantling. Furthermore, British policy toward Volkswagen effectively reinforced the relationships and institutions that had preceded Occupation. Reform fell victim to two factors: the pragmatic need to restore German economic power, and the ideologically motivated British propensity toward "fairness."[89] As an unintended consequence, the advantages accrued by the Volkswagenwerk were sustained by the policies of the British Occupation.

The debate over the future of the plant occurred initially within the CCG, and then among the CCG and those government departments and factional interests who proposed the plant be dismantled. The CCG's industrial officers were supported by Treasury officials. The opposing view was supported by leading officials in the Board of Trade

[85]This anecdote was told to me by Professor Hans Mommsen, director of the Volkswagen project at the Ruhr University, Bochum. French interest was increased by the proximity of the plant to the oncoming Soviet forces.

[86]Turner, "British Occupation Policy," p. 70.

[87]Ibid., pp. 71ff.

[88]Turner's comments relate exclusively to VW. For the general lack of ideological zeal in favor of a pragmatic concern with reducing the cost to Britain of Occupation, in contrast to Allied partners, see also Alan Kramer, "British Dismantling Politics, 1945–1949: A Reassessment," in Turner, *Reconstruction in Postwar Germany.*

[89]Turner argues that the traditional German claim that the British were "so beastly to the Germans" was a myth; the policies of the British government were rather more benevolent than the Germans have ever conceded. See Turner, "British Occupation Policy," pp. 184, 630, 673, 730, 759.

and Ministry of Supply, augmented by British manufacturers who recognized Volkswagen's future competitive potential.[90]

Under the terms of the Level of Industry Plan, published in March 1946, the German auto industry was in effect to be dismantled, production in the British zone under the plan being confined to 20,000 autos and 21,000 trucks.[91] The Ford plant at Cologne could fulfill this quota, rendering the Volkswagenwerk redundant.[92] Furthermore, the Volkswagenwerk had not contributed to German prewar aggregate production, so even if the industry was allowed to produce at prewar levels, the Volkswagenwerk would be surplus to requirements.[93] According to the CCG, the Wolfsburg plant would certainly be dismantled and the machinery be used for reparations payments.

Popular myth suggests that many British industrialists visited the Volkswagen plant and rejected both car and plant. This claim is not supported by the evidence. One BIOS report suggested that "compared with other automobile factories in Germany, and visualizing the originally intended factory layout, the Volkswagen effort is outstanding and is the nearest approach to production as we know it."[94] This early report also suggested that the condition of both plant and equipment was good and could be satisfactorily operated for many years. Another team of industrialists, on inspecting the plant, suggested the company had the most modern installation in the world and, had the war not intervened, would already have had a major impact on the world market.[95] Representatives of the British automobile industry expressed reservations about the quality of the car and whether they could use the machinery effectively, but they did recognize the competitive threat the Volkswagenwerk would pose if it survived reparations.[96] The Volkswagenwerk was therefore no phoenix that later arose from the ashes.[97]

Ministry of Supply and Board of Trade officials, encouraged by Brit-

---

[90]See "Extracts from the Thirteenth Meeting of the NACMMI" (National Advisory Council for the Motor Manufacturing Industry), 20 April 1948, Ministry of Aviation (AVIA) 49/65, PRO.

[91]Letter, Sir Percy Mills, CCG, to Mark Turner, Control Office for Germany and Austria, 22 May 1946, BT 211/92, PRO.

[92]H. A. R. Binney, "Minute Sheet," 12 September 1946, BT 211/92, PRO. A subsequent plan would have let Ford purchase the Volkswagenwerk and divide its production between trucks at Cologne and cars at Wolfsburg, but it never came to fruition. See "The Zoning of Commerce and Industry Group," Bipartite Control Office, BOAR, Frankfurt, 15 April 1948, FO 1046/193, PRO.

[93]Turner, "British Occupation Policy," p. 154.

[94]"The German Automobile Industry: Visit from 10 February to 3 April 1946," p. 11, BIOS Report 768, BIOS B, Box 20, IWM.

[95]Field Intelligence Agency Technical (FIAT) report 300, BIOS B, Box 7, IWM.

[96]Minutes from "The NACMMI Thirteenth Meeting," 20 April 1948, AVIA 49/65, XC/A59211.

[97]"The German Automobile Industry," p. 13.

ish motor producers, saw the dismantling of the Volkswagenwerk as crucial to Britain's future prosperity. First, they thought an operational plant would threaten British competitiveness in world markets.[98] Second, they considered an operating plant would be an immediate burden, requiring scarce steel they felt would be more usefully employed either in other German projects or by British auto manufacturers.[99] They felt it would be a crushing blow to the morale of British manufacturers, already constrained by domestic shortages, if their own government provided a major competitor with tools for success.[100] Third, British industry would also benefit from dismantling by receiving the plant's machinery, although experts concurred that the facilities were so extensive that the whole of the British auto industry could not use all the machinery.[101] Finally, if the plant's machinery were to become available, it was important to preempt its acquisition by others, notably the French who were known to be keen to acquire it.[102]

The Treasury, adopting a characteristically pragmatic line and exemplifying the fragmented nature of the liberal British state, opposed the Board of Trade and the Ministry of Supply. Treasury officials suggested that every effort should be made to maximize the foreign currency that could be generated by the production and export of Volkswagens, to the advantage of the British exchequer.[103] Volkswagen production would play a key role in helping the German economy achieve self-sufficiency, thus helping relieve the British exchequer of the burden of clothing and feeding the German population.[104] In simple terms, the Treasury placed a higher priority on the short-term problem of supporting the German population than on the long-term problem of British competitiveness. The need of the British Treasury for hard currency was immediate, and in the absence of a short-term threat officials there felt that the opposition's perspective was overly pessimistic.

In theory the CCG was the least influential of the four parties involved, but its power was substantially increased by being charged with

[98]Turner, "British Occupation Policy," pp. 170ff.
[99]Letter, John Schuy to G. M. Jennings (HM Treasury), 17 October 1946, BT 211/92, PRO.
[100]See letter, John Selwyn (BT) to Colonel Rowell, 17 November 1946, BT 211/92, PRO, outlining the Board of Trade's position on this issue; and "Notes on an Informal Meeting Held 11 October 1946 on the Subject of Production and Possible Export of the Volkswagen Car," BT 211/92, PRO.
[101]See Letter, R. H. Bright (Ministry of Supply) to Derek Wood (BT), 3 September 1946, BT 211/92, PRO, and exchange of letters in MinSupp 14/397, PRO.
[102]See for instance H. A. R. Binney, "Minute Sheet," 12 September 1946, BT 211/92, PRO.
[103]"Notes on an Informal Meeting," BT 211/92, PRO.
[104]"NACMMI Thirteenth Meeting."

the responsibility of implementing policy and enhanced by the geographical distance from Whitehall. CCG officials believed in the value of the Volkswagenwerk to Britain. They also believed that they represented the true national interest against the vested, sectional interests articulated at the Board of Trade.[105] Like Treasury officials, the CCG considered the Level of Industry Plan unrealistic. Confronted with the misery and poverty of the German population, CCG officials were also more sympathetic to ways to relieve their suffering. This alignment of Whitehall departments and the CCG was to recur frequently over the issue of the dismantling of German industry.[106]

The decision to restart production at the Volkswagenwerk in August 1945 was of major significance to the eventual decision to sustain the plant. An operating plant with a work force in place would not be so politically vulnerable to dismantling once it was generating profits, particularly in an isolated Wolfsburg where closure would require relocation of the work force. Board of Trade officials, recognizing this logic, tried to prevent any moves to restart production.[107] However, CCG officials, supported by the Treasury, placed an order for 21,200 vehicles, including 20,000 sedans, in August 1945 for use by Allied military personnel.[108]

The Volkswagenwerk, like all DAF property, had had its assets confiscated under SHAEF Law 52 and placed under the authority of the Property Control Branch of the Finance Division of the CCG. When production restarted, a property control staff was posted to the plant to run the company. As it had no cash to pay for materials, the Property Control Branch ordered the Braunschweigische Staatsbank to provide RM20 million in credit so that the renamed Wolfsburg Motor Works could purchase materials and manufacture products for the military government.[109] Part of the shop area of the plant and its machinery was repaired by British military engineers, who also retrieved the machinery from Volkswagen's dispersal sites.[110]

The decision to award and then extend the contract to the company provided a stay of execution. The length of the contract meant that the

[105]Turner, "British Occupation Policy," p. 169.

[106]Kramer's discussion suggests that on all reconstruction issues the Treasury and the CCG were clearly divided from the Board of Trade and Ministry of Supply, which sought to restrict German economic competition and exploit their capital and technical know-how for the benefit of the British economy. Policy resulted from a complex web of relations between Whitehall departments and the CCG. This claim is mirrored in the Volkswagen case. Kramer, "British Dismantling Politics."

[107]Binney, "Minute Sheet."

[108]Turner, "British Occupation Policy," p. 182.

[109]The company was renamed to sever associations with its Nazi origins. Ibid., p. 183.

[110]See "Subject: The VW Complex in Control," p. 3; Hirst, "Volkswagenwerk under the British Trusteeship," p. 168.

plant would outlast the reparations policy, as Board of Trade officials predicted it would.[111] Conversely, the new emphasis on maximizing production under the Level of Industry Plan made the Volkswagen-werk indispensable. Volkswagen production for the Allied forces was designated mandatory, and so its raw material requirements took priority over those of other auto producers, and the plant received its allocation of resources directly from the Industrial Division of Property Control at Minden rather than through the new trade association, the PADA, which determined the allocation of resources for the rest of the industry. Volkswagen was unique: it had a predetermined, plentiful raw material quota over which other resource-starved producers had no control.[112]

Governed by a pragmatic concern for the feeding of the German people, the military government contrived a policy that gave Volkswagen an advantage over the rest of the industry in terms of access to resources, a consumer market, and a guaranteed rate of profit. British officials considered the Volkswagenwerk a key instrument in the future prosperity of Germany and thus gave it a comparative advantage over its competitors. Despite the change in political regime, the Volkswagen-werk maintained an exclusive political relationship with the governing authorities.

These conditions gave the company an excellent opportunity to revive its fortunes. Under the Level of Industry Plan the Fordwerke had been promised the discretionary advantage, motivated by political considerations, that Volkswagen had traditionally enjoyed. However, a change in policy resurrected Volkswagen's advantage, and Fordwerke was once again banished to peripheral status. Fordwerke's opportunity to enter the core vanished as quickly as it had appeared. Constraints on Volkswagen's production were imposed by the limited availability of resources, not by the British, who did everything they could to stimulate production. Reparations payments were confined to the forty-five machines originally confiscated from occupied territory, and delay in their removal meant that restitution had no major damaging effects on the plant. In addition, 1,300 tons of armaments machinery were destroyed, which did not affect the plant's new production plans.[113]

The decision to sustain the plant brought another issue to the fore,

[111]Hirst, "Volkswagenwerk under the British Trusteeship," p. 184; and Turner, "British Occupation Policy," p. 497.

[112]The Produktionsausschuß der Automobilindustrie (PADA) briefly replaced the Reichsverband der Deutschen Automobilindustrie (RDA) before the Verband der Deutschen Automobilindustrie (VDA) was formed. For raw material allocations see Turner, "British Occupation Policy," p. 188.

[113]Ibid., pp. 189, 192, 199.

that of its ownership and control. Both the British and the Germans recognized that British occupation was temporary. They would eventually need to address the question who owned the Volkswagenwerk. All DAF property had been confiscated under Control Law 52. Control Council Law 2 dissolved the DAF and authorized the CCG to control its assets. All other DAF complexes had been dismantled and used for reparation payments, but the CCG was initially in no immediate hurry to settle the issue of ownership of the Volkswagen plant. Volkswagen owed creditors in excess of RM600 million, and settlement of ownership might lead to the company's liquidation. Finance Division officials therefore set up a trustee body under British military control to represent the German people, and various bodies staked their claim to ownership.[114]

The labor unions noted that the company had been owned by the DAF, which had come into existence by confiscating union assets. As the initial source of funding for the DAF and its heirs, the unions led by the formidable Hans Bockler of IG Metall claimed ownership of the plant.[115] However, CCG officials, using a crude form of arithmetic, had a different opinion. They claimed that union funds were seized by the DAF in 1933 and exhausted by 1937 as a result of DAF payment for other schemes, such as the construction of labor centers. The unions, they concluded, therefore had no legal rights to ownership of the DAF.[116]

The second claimants were Germans who had paid into the Volkswagen savers' fund but had never received a vehicle. By 1945 the 336,000 savers had invested RM267 million, but their contributions had never been used to build or equip the plant; all their money lay untouched in an account of the old Bank der Deutschen Arbeit. Nevertheless the savers, led by two private citizens, Rudolf Meichsner and Karl Stoltz, claimed they were the rightful heirs to the plant, if not owners then at least collectively entitled to receive 267,000 cars. They made clear their intention to bring litigation to achieve that goal, organizing into the Hilfsverein ehemaliger Volkswagensparer e.V. Niedermarsberg by 1948.[117] Company management, like the British military government and the future German federal government, recognized that an early court decision in favor of the savers would

[114]"Subject: The VW Complex in Control," pp. 11, 13.
[115]See Volkswagen Senior Control Officer (Dir. Kemmler), "Minutes of the Eleventh Board of Control Meeting of the VWW GmbH and DAF Properties," 6 December 1946, Turner Personal Files; and "Volkswagenwerk" FO 371/76723, PRO.
[116]H. A. Goff, "Wolfsburg Motor Works"; Property Control Section HQ, Land Niedersachsen, Hannover to R. H. Parker, Property Control Branch, Finance Division, CCG Minden, 14 May 1948, FO 1046/193, PRO.
[117]"Es begann 1934," Turner Personal Files.

bankrupt the company.[118] A preliminary court decided in 1951, however, that the company was not responsible to the savers for money they had paid into the fund.[119] But the Volkswagenwerk did have to return stolen machinery and pay compensation to individuals whose property had been confiscated or bought under duress. This decision was remarkable because precedent in German and international courts held that official bodies and companies were accountable for their acts in the Third Reich. This anomalous court decision was appealed. Temporarily the company's management, Ministry of Finance officials, and the German courts removed the threat of liquidation, although the issue would be a thorn in the company's side in the late 1950s.

The third claimant was the local *Land,* under the control of the state officials of Lower Saxony. Officials of the state in which the plant was located pointed to juridical factors—anomalies in the registration of the ownership of both town and plant—to justify their claim. The DAF had initially registered the town under the ownership of the company in the *Grundbuch* (land register) to minimize the tax burden on the company. While this move gave the town a weak claim to ownership of the plant, it also created the confusion that allowed *Land* authorities to claim the matter should be resolved by their assuming control of the Volkswagenwerk. Some elements in the Property Control office of the CCG supported giving the *Land* ownership, on the grounds that it would avoid excessive centralization. However, Hinrich Kopf, the ministerpräsident of Lower Saxony, was not keen to pursue ownership because he feared the new owners might have to assume the liabilities of the plant. Kopf preferred the *Land* become the trustee of the plant, and so gain control without risking liability for the prior owner's actions.[120] Again, Lower Saxony's claim was not acted on by the British, but it came back to haunt the federal government when the privatization of Volkswagen emerged as a major issue in the first decade of the Bonn Republic.

The final major claimant to the plant, whether as owner or trustee, was the future German government. Future officials of the federal government, notably future economics minister Ludwig Erhard, claimed that the new government would be the rightful guardian of the interests of the German people and because the German people had funded the plant in the Third Reich, they should now be awarded ownership. Erhard claimed that as economics minister, he would per-

---

[118]The CCG had suggested that on impartial assessment, the company would probably lose and face bankruptcy. See CCG Memo, "Meeting with Erhard," 8 October 1949, B115/3377, Bundesarchiv.

[119]*New York Times,* 26 January 1951.

[120]Turner, "British Occupation Policy," pp. 660–61.

sonally act as trustee for the company and then organize its sale to its rightful owners—the German people—as part of his *Volksaktien* (Peoples' Shares) scheme, designed as a response to advocates of socialism and nationalization.[121] The company, having no owners, would have to be nationalized so that it could have owners, in order to be privatized.[122] Both Erhard's logic and his political motive were received sympathetically by important British military officials, even though government control, albeit temporary, of one of the largest complexes in Germany seemed at odds with his professed orthodox liberalism.[123]

Undaunted, but perhaps influenced by the way they felt elements of their own government had been manipulated by special interests, some CCG officials felt that

> it is necessary to ensure that the control of the complex is not restricted to a single land government or single social interest. . . . The works in full production would command a control over passenger vehicle output for domestic requirement and export. The output could mean that the German motor industry might attain European influence that would be dangerous if the undertaking is not controlled by a trustee corporation not directly connected with the central government and therefore beyond the manipulation of any one interest.[124]

Only a future German central government could ensure the plant was used effectively to benefit all the German people.[125]

The announcement of the first federal government, in September 1949, made the issue of the control of Volkswagen unavoidable. The dominance of the CDU in the federal government and the SPD in the *Land* government of Lower Saxony added another dimension to the disputed ownership of the plant.[126] Word leaked out that the Allies had decided the federal government would assume the trusteeship of the works. This decision prompted a quick response by the *Land* government, which sent finance minister, Strickrodt, to Bad Homburg to challenge the legality of the decision. Strickrodt claimed that he and Fricke, the Lower Saxony economics minister, were competent to act as

[121]*The Economist,* 18 May 1957.
[122]See *Financial Times,* 23 December 1955.
[123]Goff, "Wolfsburg Motor Works."
[124]Letter, Mechanical Engineering Industry Branch, Minden, to the Chief, Industry Division, "The Volkswagenwerk Complex and Control Council Directive 50," p. 11, FO 371/65114, PRO. The CCG's statement was a direct response to what it felt was the undue influence of British industrialists on the decision making of the British government. Yet Kramer suggests that British industrialists had little direct influence on British decisions on dismantling despite extensive lobbying. Kramer, "British Dismantling Politics."
[125]Ibid., p. 12.
[126]Turner, "British Occupation Policy," p. 662.

trustees and would not let the decision pass unchallenged. They directly quizzed Erhard on the timetable for the privatization of the Volkswagenwerk, at which point Erhard became evasive. Challenged on the details of his plan, he said that circumstances were too complicated to be specific. Pressed further, he simply muttered that the Volkswagen savers issue made future plans uncertain—uncharacteristically hesitant behavior for a usually forthright man.[127] Erhard may have foreseen many conflicts over the ownership of Volkswagen, between federal and state governments, between political parties and within the CDU itself, and between the company and the Volkswagen savers, which may explain his hesitation.

By this time the British military authorities, frustrated with a four-year-old issue, were looking to rid themselves of the problem rather than settle it comprehensively among the claimants. They ignored what they saw as the contrived claims of the labor unions and the Volkswagen savers, but they felt that both the federal and the state government had reasonable claims to ownership. A vacillating military government finally decided in Ordinance 202, effective September 1949, that (in the words of Ian Turner) "under the terms of the ordinance *Land* Niedersachsen was made responsible for the control of the Volkswagenwerk, but on behalf of and under the direction of the Federal government, until such time as the 'responsible German authorities' issued other directions."[128]

The federal government was now in control, however ambiguously, and was presumably the "responsible German authority" that would henceforth issue directives on the matter. Authority over the plant was therefore transferred formally to the federal government on 13 October 1949 in an act Turner describes as a "masterpiece of equivocation"; control was ambiguous, ownership undecided, and the decision-making apparatus unspecified.[129] The indeterminacy of the British statement kept the issue of ownership a focus of conflict over the next decade.

---

[127]Volkswagenwerk, FO 371/76723, PRO.
[128]Turner, "British Occupation Policy," p. 663.
[129]Ibid., p. 664. This behavior was characteristic of British colonial policies on property control and ownership. Unresolved land issues were evident in the Middle East, Cyprus, Ireland, India, and Africa, often with disastrous results. Vacillation was not motivated by malicious intent on the part of British officials. Having historically pursued a policy of "divide and rule" the British now sought to be fair to all sides in final territorial settlement. Having created a "zero-sum" conflict among these sides, they now found it impossible to negotiate a solution. Unwilling to pursue a policy that was inequitable among feuding parties, the British abandoned the issue either to be ill-managed by the UN or violently settled between warring factions. The feeble response at the end of colonial rule left a legacy of conflict; the question of Volkswagen's ownership was a microcosm of that failing.

While conflict raged in various offices and courts throughout the British zone, harmony and prosperity were dominant within the plant. The postwar development that began with the provisions for mandatory construction was given greater impetus by the arrival of Heinrich Nordhoff, who was to become the central figure in Volkswagen's rise in the 1950s. Nordhoff had formerly been employed by Opel. He played a significant role in the early Volkswagen project discussions, when Opel was an active participant, and was in charge of Opel's Brandenburg plant during the war. This position had earned him the enmity of the authorities in the American zone, and they had assigned him to menial work, forbidding his future reemployment by Opel. The British had no qualms and engaged him as general director of Volkswagen in 1948.

Nordhoff had never joined the NSDAP, but the methods and hierarchical structure adopted at the Volkswagenwerk suggest he had learned from the Nazis. The conventional picture suggests that while the issue of ownership remained unsettled, as general director he was like a *Wirtschaftsführer*, able to exercise a great deal of autonomy at Volkswagen, answerable neither to shareholders nor to a board of directors.[130] The firm's hierarchy led to widespread accusations that little had changed since the Third Reich, especially as many former Nazis were employed.[131] Certainly, British denazification was ineffective at the plant, and the extreme right-wing Deutsche Reichspartei won local elections in 1948.[132]

Volkswagen's exponential growth and dominance of German auto production began in the late 1940s, and by 1948 it was manufacturing half the cars built in Germany.[133] High profits and no shareholders meant the company could reinvest an exceptionally large amount of surplus capital in new machinery.[134] Attempts to subdue Volkswagen to the collective discipline of German trade agreements, through membership in employers' or trade associations, were rejected by Nordhoff, who attacked the greed and narrowmindedness of reactionary industrialists as the infectious source of such anticapitalist sentiment.[135] He

---

[130]However, occasional details suggest that Nordhoff may have been more subject to officials of the Bundesfinanzministerium than commonly supposed. For instance, as late as 1957 Fritz Schäffer, the Bundesfinanzminister, claimed that the federal government used Volkswagen as an instrument to control auto prices in the industry—suggesting it was the government and not management that determined the company's pricing policy. See *Manchester Guardian*, 27 June 1957.

[131]Volkswagenwerk FO 371/76723, PRO; *Wall Street Journal*, 20 March 1956, p. 1.

[132]See Turner, "British Occupation Policy," pp. 290, 696.

[133]"VW Reden Dr. Nordhoff," Turner Personal Files.

[134]*New York Times*, 2 October 1955, VII, p. 15; *Wall Street Journal*, 20 March 1956.

[135]*New York Times*, 2 October 1955, VII, p. 15.

thus rejected the inclusive corporatism that might have subjected Volkswagen to the constraints imposed on other producers, preferring to keep the firm's exclusive negotiating channels with the state and a select network of firms. First the Allies and then the Bonn state were unwilling to impose constraints on the national champion.

Nordhoff's attitude toward his work force reflected some aspects of labor policy that could be traced to Wilhelmine Germany and some to Nazi Germany. The emergent policy combined the "benevolent paternalism" of Bismarck with the Nazis' coercive hierarchicalism that rejected both political and decision-making roles for the work force. Nordhoff emphasized an "organic harmony" between labor and management and (implicitly) the plant as a nationalist undertaking. He considered labor unions acceptable only as apolitical bodies, claiming the class struggle was now over and unions were impotent as instruments of class conflict. His benevolent paternalism was reflected in his treatment of company workers who, he claimed, encompassed the best Prussian traditions of hard work, discipline, selflessness, and modesty. In exchange, workers were given annual dividends of 4 percent by the company and higher wages than in other mass producers.[136] During the debate on privatization Nordhoff rejected the idea that workers should be allowed to purchase shares in Volkswagen, suggesting the average worker would be disconcerted by such things.[137] Nordhoff also decreed that workers who voluntarily left the company should never be rehired—a policy designed to subdue the workings of the free labor market—and, despite promises, he strongly resisted worker representation in positions of authority.[138]

The wartime work force at Volkswagen had been composed of slave laborers and skilled German workers, most of whom had fled at the end of the war. In the immediate postwar era the company experienced a labor shortage because the plant offered the promise of no more than temporary employment. However, the clarification of Volkswagen's future, plus the guaranteed provision of food and accommodation by the British trustees of the plant (a rarity in the hunger- and poverty-stricken Western zones of Germany in 1946 and 1947), brought workers flocking to Wolfsburg. Most of these highly disciplined workers were refugees from the Soviet zone, and, incredibly, they took no form of industrial action during the 1940s and 1950s.[139]

[136]Ibid.; *New York Times*, 14 May 1961.
[137]*Vereinigter Wissenschaftsdienst*, 15 May 1957.
[138]Report in (Toronto) *Globe and Mail*, 18 September 1956, in File Z 8/376, Bundesarchiv, Koblenz. *The Times* of London referred to Nordhoff's system as "cradle to grave paternalism," 15 April 1963.
[139]*The Times* of London, 15 April 1963.

Turner points to a combination of factors. First, he suggests that the deference of the work force was, in part, a hangover from the Third Reich.[140] The hierarchical control exercised in the Third Reich was effectively assimilated at the postwar plant, inspiring worker pliancy. Second, an exceptionally large number of former soldiers were now employed in the factory who by instinct and training responded to tight discipline. They were later supplemented or replaced by an over-whelming flood of refugees, whose responsiveness to plant discipline was based on fear.[141] The unemployed and refugees therefore re-placed the slaves as the *Lumpenproletariat*.[142] They, in turn, were later replaced by the *Gastarbeiter*. Third, the Reichmark had become val-ueless after the war and remained so until the currency reform of 1948. Workers leading the widespread strikes in 1946 and 1947 in most other plants in the British zone demanded food and accommodation. The plant's privileged position under British trusteeship meant that adequate food and shelter were generally not a problem. The major incentives for strike action were therefore removed—they had food and accommodation, and the money they earned was worthless. Fourth, Turner suggests, on the rare occasion when food shortages did occur, the work force's resolute attempts to avoid conflict were fortified by the ideological comfort they derived from working for a national enterprise.[143] Malnourishment was not considered the product of company policy or an obstacle to harmony; management was not held responsible for food shortages, and the work force preferred to em-phasize their common interests. Finally, the low level of trade union activity at the plant contributed toward minimal DGB membership in the early postwar period. Military government red tape and worker resistance to any activity that might endanger the works provided fur-ther disincentives. Nordhoff promised to make concessions to labor once Volkswagen's future had been secured, for instance, the appoint-ment of a union-based *Arbeitsdirektor* to the management board of Volkswagen and the creation of a *Beirat* equally composed of labor and management representatives, but not until 1951 were any reforms in-troduced. British attempts to introduce reforms during the Occupation failed to change the traditional pattern of relations in the plant. Turner ironically concludes that the failure to introduce the more democratic British industrial model secured for the Germans a more peaceful industrial future.[144]

[140]Turner, "British Occupation Policy," p. 396.
[141]*New York Times*, 2 October 1955, VII, p. 15.
[142]Turner, "British Occupation Policy," p. 586.
[143]See "Subject: The Volkswagenwerk Complex in Control," p. 7.
[144]Turner, "British Occupation Policy," pp. 396–99, 405–10.

Powerful leadership, industrial tranquility, high-quality capital, and preferred access to resources, coupled with subsequent unquenchable global demand, all contributed toward Volkswagen's competitiveness and prosperity. Yet it would not have worked without the key political ingredient. The foundations provided by the Nazis, coupled with the advantages extended by the Allies, meant that no company was better placed to profit from a postwar surge in demand. The subsequent decision to impose currency reform, and to shift Volkswagen's production from the public to the private sector, gave the company tremendous impetus.

After an initial liquidity crisis, the currency reform stimulated a rise in supplies, production, sales, and wages at the plant. The immediacy of its effects on the free flow of goods is indicated by deliveries of parts to Wolfsburg, which rose from DM3.7 million to DM9.3 million between June and July 1948—allowing production to increase and wages subsequently to rise to 17 percent above those of the average German manufacturing worker by the end of 1948. A virtuous circle developed in which demand and capacity grew; improved conditions attracted more workers to the plant and increased its capacity to produce. Between January 1948 and December 1949 the work force grew from 8,819 to 10,227, with a drastic reduction in absenteeism.[145] However, the British emphasis on exports proved a problem. Because of an unfavorable exchange rate, the company lost money on exported vehicles. Volkswagen's management suggested a different exchange rate be used exclusively for the sale of their products, to ensure exports were profitable. The response of the British-controlled Joint Export-Import Agency (JEIA) was to suggest that Volkswagen should subsidize foreign sales through higher domestic prices and improve efficiency through lower production costs, forcing the firm to rationalize its costs of production.[146] Volkswagen eventually benefited from increased economies of scale that made both domestic and foreign sales profitable.[147] Turner contrasts the policies of the British authorities toward Volkswagen with those of the British government toward its domestic pro-

[145]Ibid., pp. 595–600.

[146]Nordhoff always prided himself on the provision of good servicing and spare parts for the company's customers, repeatedly crediting the company's American success to this policy. However, Hirst suggests the original emphasis on service and spares came from the British engineering army officers located at the plant, who forced company officials not to repeat the mistakes of their British counterparts and to take a significant interest. Hirst says that "the insistence of the British Board on the service and spares aspect is no doubt reflected in the present-day VW service organization which, though it has the advantage of dealing with only one basic model so far, is probably the finest in the world." Hirst, "Volkswagenwerk under the British Trusteeship," p. 172.

[147]Turner, "British Occupation Policy," pp. 608–9.

THE FRUITS OF FASCISM

ducers. While the military government's policies discriminated in favor of Volkswagen and stimulated efficient production, the British government retarded innovation and efficient, high-quality mass production at home through a series of fiscal and allocative measures marked by a scrupulous refusal to discriminate among firms.[148]

Once the currency reform had stimulated greater exports, and forced rationalization of the plant had increased competitiveness, the British military authorities had neither the will nor the apparatus to limit Volkswagen as they had originally promised their own producers they would do. After flirting with enforcement, the military government quickly retreated toward the type of behavior dictated by the equitable principles and weak apparatus of domestic liberal governments—it avoided direct, coercive behavior. As a result it had "neither the will nor the means to suppress German exports."[149] This unwillingness to use coercion was a recurrent theme in British Occupation policy.[150]

Turner concludes that British private interests attempted three policies concerning Volkswagen. They sought to dismantle the plant, to suppress Volkswagen exports, and to prevent Volkswagen from pursuing a strategy that they described as "unfair competition" in world markets. All three aims collapsed because of the overriding pragmatic priorities of British policy in Germany, which were to create economic stability and reduce British expenditures as quickly as possible.[151]

In the successful pursuit of those priorities the military government effectively reinforced the advantages that the Third Reich had originally extended to the Volkswagenwerk. A discretionary political relationship with the dominant political power gave the company preferred access to raw materials and cheap labor and retained the machinery and structure employed under the fascist regime. The final act of the British military authorities in passing control of the company to the new German state only confirmed this continuity. Four years of supposed reform had changed nothing at Volkswagen. Privileged ac-

[148]Ibid., pp. 613ff. For support see Eric Hobsbawm, *Industry and Empire* (Harmondsworth: Penguin, 1978), pp. 257–58.

[149]Turner, "British Occupation Policy," p. 622.

[150]See, for instance, Mark Roseman's description of how the CCG tried to pursue a coercive mining policy in an uncoercive manner in the Ruhr—a notable failure that had to be replaced by an incentive package offered to both mineowners and labor. In more general terms Roseman says that by September 1949 Ernest Bevin was convinced that dismantling could no longer be carried out against the mounting tide of German opposition, despite French reluctance to abandon the policy. See Mark Roseman, "The Uncontrolled Economy: Ruhr Coal Production, 1945–48," in Turner, ed., *Reconstruction in Germany*.

[151]Turner, "British Occupation Policy," p. 737.

cess to the new state by virtue of ownership by the Finance Ministry and inexhaustible global demand gave the company enormous potential.

STATE-FIRM RELATIONS DURING THE ALLIED OCCUPATION

One popular myth treats Allied policy as monolithic, suggesting that a mixture of American idealism and French vengefulness ensured that fascism was dismantled. The myth forgets the role of the British authorities. The military authorities did not radically reform internal corporate structures; did nothing to reduce the competitive advantage in plant capital or machinery enjoyed as a result of the discretionary policies of the fascist state; and did nothing to disturb the discretionary relationships between firm and state that originated during the Third Reich. In many ways, in fact, the CCG reinforced these patterns.

Volkswagen was uniquely exempted from the terms of SHAEF Law 52 and so spared from dismantling. Furthermore, it enjoyed the same discretionary relationship with the state that it had before 1945—with privileged access to government orders, raw materials, and finance. CCG authorities even used their own resources to help restore the plant to working order and feed the working population, thereby increasing the attractiveness of working at the plant.

A hierarchical structure was retained at Volkswagen; Nordhoff enjoyed powers unique in a postwar capitalist economy. Although the composition of the work force differed in form from the Third Reich, the social origins and economic position of workers, coupled with an ideological affiliation, ensured compliance with Nordhoff's labor policy, which was identified as industrial feudalism, unenlightened despotism, or paternal authoritarianism.

The British began the occupation sympathetic to substantial reform; but their capacity to achieve comprehensive reform coincided with their practical need to foster self-sufficiency and pragmatism. Conversely, when they did finally seek to institute changes, they were frustrated by the power of Volkswagen and the embryonic government, and by the overwhelming limitations of liberal ideology. The only limits they could impose came in the form of passive restraints: for instance, refusing to adjust exchange rates and therefore forcing the company to rationalize production. Compared to the objectives specified at the end of the war, their achievement was minimal.

In the end a mixture of frustration over ownership and control, coupled with the desire to be fair to the major protagonists, led to an ambiguous decision that effectively gave immediate control of the firm and the power to decide its future ownership to the federal government. After four years, the CCG simply handed the power of decision to the new German state, and the company enjoyed the same structured advantage over its rivals as it had in the Third Reich.

THE CULMINATION OF NAZI POLICY:
VOLKSWAGEN BECOMES THE PEOPLE'S CAR

In this final section I examine the relationships between the company and the state, business, and labor in the first decade of the Bonn Republic. Did Volkswagen unduly benefit from discriminatory advantages whose origins can be traced back to the Nazi and Allied periods? I focus on four issues: the conflict over the ownership of Volkswagen, its implications, and the principles reflected in the struggle for control; the scope and breadth of government intervention in company affairs, notably in pricing policy; the nature of Volkswagen's restrictive practices, both in its sales practices and in its selective marketing, sales, research, and development agreements with other core firms; and, finally, the unique nature of Volkswagen's industrial relations agreements with the labor unions.

First, I examine the unresolved issue of Volkswagen's ownership. The terms of Ordinance 202 gave the Bundesfinanzministerium (Finance Ministry) of the federal government ultimate control over the affairs of the company. As senior minister in the Bundeswirtschaftsministerium (Economics Ministry), Ludwig Erhard emphasized exports in the resurgence of the German economy and assured West German businessmen of his liberal principles: unrestrained trade with no price controls, unfair competition, or quotas.[152]

Erhard sought to reflect these principles in his treatment of Volkswagen by starting its sale to the general public under his *Volksaktien* scheme. The company was to be completely privatized. The project complemented his vision of the *Sozialmarktwirtschaft* (social market economy), with its neoliberal emphasis on a widespread distribution of ownership.[153] Erhard repeatedly claimed that the federal government would nationalize the company so it could be sold to the private sector.[154] But, it was twelve years after assuming control of the company,

---

[152]*Wall Street Journal*, 14 February 1955.

[153]Erhard reiterated this theme on the issue of Volkswagen's privatization throughout the 1950s. For a succinct statement of his position see *Handelsblatt* (Düsseldorf), 17 and 18 May or 19 August 1957.

[154]*Financial Times*, 23 December 1955.

in September 1949, before the federal government effected even *partial* privatization.

This delay and ultimate compromise can be explained by the character of the new German state. The new, fragmented distribution of power in the Bonn Republic contrasted with the monolithic power of the Nazi state. The new liberal democratic state therefore found it difficult to alter the structural transformations instituted by the fascist regime. The way Volkswagen maintained its advantages as a core producer is a classic illustration of how, in the absence of a powerful state apparatus, even the most determined political leaders cannot undo the work of previous regimes. Certainly, Erhard was a formidable leader. Yet the opposition to Erhard's plans for Volkswagen that initially stalled change and subsequently compromised his primary goal of freeing the company from governmental ownership and control came from a variety of sources.

Erhard's various opponents on the future of Volkswagen challenged him and frustrated his intentions despite support for him among German industrialists.[155] His most prominent, and persistent opponents were located in the Bundesfinanzministerium (BfM).[156] At the heart of the matter was their resistance to Erhard's belief in a neoliberal relationship between state and economy. They preferred a closer relationship in which the state controlled strategic economic levers through such mechanisms as the ownership and control of major industrial concerns and the building of consultative forums designed to enhance collaboration between state and societal actors.[157] The leading BfM officials, all members of the CDU, made use of any appropriate instruments provided by the Nazis (although not conscious of them as such), in contrast to Erhard who saw one of his major tasks as being the systematic, revolutionary dislocation of the FRG's economy from its past organizational, state-interventionist form of development.[158] The statist BfM view was compatible with the forceful ideological position of the Christian Social Union (CSU), led by Franz Josef Strauss, who opposed Erhard and supported the proposition that the state should play

[155]*The Times* of London, 8 January 1955.

[156]Alfred Hartmann understated this point in suggesting that the Bundesfinanzministerium and Bundeswirtschaftsministerium had a sustained problem when it came to working together. See "Plenarsitzung des Deutschen Bundestages" (Plenary session of the German parliament) on 10 and 11 January 1957, B102/5196, Bundesarchiv.

[157]Interestingly, this dominant perspective in the BfM proved most compatible with the views of SPD and union leaders who, despite their differences with BfM officials, agreed on the importance of state ownership and control of strategic economic instruments as a means of instituting both macro- and micro-level policies. See, for example, *The Times* of London, 7 May 1962.

[158]See, for example, *Hamburger Abendblatt*, 10 June 1958.

a decisive role in the conservative "dirigist" tradition.[159] Central to the struggle between these two opposing views was the debate over Volkswagen.

Three BfM officials—minister Fritz Schäffer, Staatssekretär Alfred Hartmann, and bureaucrat Heinz Maria Oeftering, who was also chair of the supervisory board of Volkswagen—took a variety of positions designed to stall privatization. Initially the BfM responded passively to Erhard's urging, hoping the issue would simply be forgotten. As the ministry responsible for Volkswagen, the BfM managed to stifle any real debate until 1955. In the face of Erhard's persistence and his political support from a faction within the CDU/CSU coalition and the parliamentary leadership of small centrist and conservative parties, Hartmann adopted three new tactics to hinder his plans. The first tactic emphasized economic impediments to privatization, claiming that Volkswagen was not yet ready for such a change because the company was not yet competitive enough to survive unprotected by the federal government.[160] Hartmann's dubious claim was legitimated by the support of Nordhoff himself who, as late as 1957, publicly announced that any consideration of privatization was premature. Second, Hartmann emphasized the controversal nature of two issues, planning and representation. He claimed that the price for the public sale of Volkswagen would have to be studied and debated before any scheme could be implemented. Third, Hartmann made the juridical claim that the unresolved legal dispute over the ownership of Volkswagen had to be settled prior to sale to the public.[161]

Oeftering's role in opposing Erhard was less public than his colleagues', but he considered Volkswagen a key instrument of state policy and a symbol for prosperity in the FRG.[162] He played a critical role in linking the BfM's strategy with that of the company's management, whose public pronouncements indicated they wanted nothing to do with privatization. The link was evident in apparently coincidental yet simultaneously timed public pronouncements by BfM officials and

[159]See Aline Kuntz, "Conservatives in Crisis: The Bavarian Christian Social Union and the Ideology of Antimodernism" (diss., Cornell University, 1987), pp. 198–201. Kuntz argues that the CSU has always subsumed the role of the market to broader social goals and has shown little concern for individual rights in the face of state power. The CSU has emphasized the state as a decisive political and economic actor in maintaining political stability and protecting domestic industry.

[160]Hartmann continued to make this claim as late as 1957 when Volkswagen was the largest and most prosperous auto producer in the Federal Republic. For the various positions of the political parties see *Die Welt*, 12 January 1957.

[161]See *Vereinigter Wissenschaftsdienst*, 15 May 1957; *Industriekurier* (Düsseldorf), 3 May 1957; and "Zur Frage des Eigentums am Komplex VWW," pp. 9–11, File No. I-395 031-1, Adenauerstiftung, Bonn.

[162]See *Vereinigter Wissenschaftsdienst*, 5 August 1955.

Nordhoff himself—a tactic that eventually earned Nordhoff public criticism from Erhard's supporters.[163]

According to Oeftering, a policy of broader ownership might have benefits but, in the case of Volkswagen, would also have costs and, specifically, the loss of control of a strategic instrument. In one discussion with British government officials in 1953 Oeftering was outspoken about the company, suggesting the BfM was convinced that it controlled a "world-beater" in Volkswagen and intended to build up production to a thousand cars a day. Only problems at the cellulose plant had prevented this happening so far. Oeftering boasted that the car had the most advanced design in the world. The company had such a big profit margin and could cut its price to such an extent that it could corner the world market, although circumstances dictated it would not do so.[164] Oeftering thus recognized that the BfM had received from the Third Reich a gift that had survived Allied reforms. It was one the BfM was not about to reject.

However, the most pointed and influential opposition to Erhard's plan came from the BfM's senior minister, Fritz Schäffer. As a highly respected member of the CDU, his party credentials established over three decades, Schäffer could call for support on a significant faction of the CDU's parliamentary representatives and its national membership. At first Schäffer maintained a low profile on privatization, allowing Hartmann and Oeftering to subvert the process through economic and juridical claims and coalition building. However, the implication of Schäffer's passivity was evident; the *Financial Times* in December 1955 noted that he appeared in no hurry to speed privatization.[165] His passivity was to Volkswagen's economic advantage because a company under federal government control was not required to pay any dividends to shareholders. Volkswagen thus sustained a high level of reinvestment despite its slim profit margin; reinvestment totaled about $100 million between 1948 and 1956.[166] Rival firms, noting this advantage, hoped Volkswagen would become less competitive when it had to pay out dividends.[167]

Only when Hartmann's strategies began to falter did Schäffer take a more public position on the issue, creating a definite rift between the

---

[163]As evidence of Nordhoff's sympathies see, for instance, the report of Nordhoff's speech against privatization in the *Hamburger Echo*, 18 May 1957, three days after Schäffer's speech as reported in the *Financial Times*, 15 May 1957. For an example of Erhard's criticism see *Die Welt*, 24 July 1959.

[164]Letter, R. J. Jackling, U. K. High Commission in Germany, to Robbie Burns, Board of Trade, 20 November 1953, Ministry of Supply 14/397, PRO.

[165]See *Financial Times*, 23 December 1955.

[166]*New York Times*, 15 July 1956, III, p. 1.

[167]*The Economist*, 18 May 1957.

BfM and the Bundeswirtschaftsministerium (BwM).[168] Schäffer pursued two subversive strategies. On the one hand he sought, successfully, to delimit the conditions of sale. Emphasizing popular nationalist sentiment, he declared that if Volkswagen were to be sold, its shares should go neither to foreigners nor to other German car producers— thereby transgressing pure neoliberal principles of exchange.[169] Simultaneously, he began to agitate actively within the CDU against any privatization scheme, invoking Nordhoff's support.[170]

Erhard was sensitive to the criticisms of these officials, members of his party and his government, and he must have cursed the decision of the British authorities to leave the company under the authority of BfM. No doubt Erhard wondered why Chancellor Konrad Adenauer neither transferred authority for Volkswagen to the BwM nor made Erhard senior minister at the BfM. He responded by pushing the issue of privatization at the CDU congress in the spring of 1957. With a written document signed by both Adenauer and Erhard, and supported by Arnold, formerly prime minister of North Rhine–Westphalia and then leader of the important trade union wing of the CDU, Erhard announced to the congress the details of his privatization plan. His action sparked a public debate in which Schäffer claimed he would create a "blocking minority" to any policy proposal tabled for a vote.[171] A majority at the congress nevertheless supported Erhard's proposal. Interestingly, Erhard was criticized for his tactics by Volkswagen officials who felt he was being too dogmatic and that a compromise would better serve the company.[172] Seeking to administer the final blow to his opponents in the BfM, Erhard portrayed the general election in the following fall as a referendum over his, rather than the government's, policies. The ploy worked. The CDU/CSU coalition won the election in a landslide and returned a third Adenauer cabinet to power. The victory was seen as a triumph for Erhard and a defeat for Schäffer, who had "historically resisted" Erhard on pivotal economic issues.[173]

Revitalized, Erhard appealed to Adenauer to form an elite "economic cabinet" within the larger cabinet and to shift Schäffer from his position as head of the BfM. Adenauer, ever the pragmatist, had to concede and appointed Schäffer to the position of Bundesjustizminis-

[168]*Handelsblatt*, 23 February 1955.
[169]See *Manchester Guardian*, 27 June 1957.
[170]For Schäffer's party activities see *Financial Times*, 15 May 1957; *Handelsblatt*, 17 and 18 May 1957; *Hamburger Abendblatt*, 21 October 1957. See Nordhoff's reported speech in *Die Welt*, 17 May 1957.
[171]*Financial Times*, 15 May 1957.
[172]See Novotny memo, "Volkswagenwerk, Aktiengesellschaft und Stiftung," 4 October 1957, B115/3395, Bundesarchiv.
[173]*The Economist*, 5 October 1957.

ter, where he could not exercise influence on economic issues. In the subsequent cabinet reshuffle Erhard's supporters were appointed to influential positions to facilitate privatization. Oeftering was replaced as chair of Volkswagen's supervisory board, and although Hartmann was retained as Staatssekretär until 1959, his reassigned duties diminished his influence.[174] Lindrath was appointed the new head of the Ministry of State Property, which was specifically designed to oversee the privatization of Volkswagen.[175] None of the members of Erhard's elite economic cabinet sought a compromise on the issue of privatization.

However, any illusions that privatization would now proceed smoothly were quickly dispelled by the reemergence of ownership claims the CCG had dismissed.[176] Although the newly constituted Bonn Supreme Court had dismissed the Volkswagen savers' claim against Volkswagen as early as 1954 and did so again in 1958, the savers refused to drop the case and continued to be a thorn in the company's side.[177] But their claim no longer threatened the company's very existence. Similarly, the claim of the labor unions resurfaced, demanding now that the company be turned over to public ownership, but it did not pose a serious threat to Erhard's plans.[178]

More significant was the claim made by the state government of Lower Saxony, which rejected privatization under any circumstances. At first the conflict between federal and state governments took on an added dimension with a division between a cdu/csu federal government and an SPD state government. But even when SPD authorities in Hannover were replaced by a CDU government, they still refused to drop the claim.[179] Interestingly, the CDU government of Lower Saxony found a coalition partner in the national leaders of the SPD, who were sharply critical of what they saw as the denationalization of Volkswagen.[180] Although neither wielded the power of the federal government, in tandem they provided stubborn, effective resistance. The scope of their influence best demonstrates the limited capacity of the new Bonn Republic to counteract the revolutionary changes instituted

[174]See *Der Volkwirt* (Frankfurt), 27 June 1959.
[175]For the merits of a national foundation, see letter from Lindrath to Birnbaum, 13 August 1957, B115/3395, Bundesarchiv.
[176]For example, see *Braunschweigische Zeitung*, 6 February 1958.
[177]*Manchester Guardian*, 22 December 1954; *Financial Times*, 10 November 1958.
[178]*The Times* of London, 8 January 1955.
[179]See *Hamburger Echo*, 17 May 1957; and letter from Alfred Hartmann to Birnbaum about the attitude of Höcherl, party official of the local CDU, 2 September 1957, B115/3395, Bundesarchiv.
[180]See *Hamburger Anzeiger*, 11 January 1957; and "Plenarsitzung des deutschen Bundestages" on 10 and 11 January 1957.

by the previous fascist state. For under the Allied government's original Ordinance 202, the *Land* indeed had a legal claim, giving some substance to their threat of a court injunction if Erhard tried to push through with his privatization scheme.[181] Relatively early in the debate Nordhoff expressed his opposition to the *Land*'s claim, emphasizing that the company should be owned by the federal government.[182] However, the dispute here was constitutional rather than purely political, so Nordhoff's comments had little effect. According to the government of Lower Saxony, the federal government had to negotiate with them over Volkswagen's future.[183]

The conflict between federal and state government remained essentially dormant while the conflict within the CDU and among government ministries was unresolved, although BfM and BwM officials demonstrated a rare unity in discounting Lower Saxony's claim.[184] It reemerged after 1957, involving hard bargaining for two years between Bonn and Lower Saxony officials. In the absence of their outright ownership, the government of Lower Saxony wanted a *Stiftung*— a public trust or foundation in which the ownership of the company would be equally divided between state and federal government—and the SPD agreed, considering it a way of maintaining the company as part of the public sector.[185] This proposal contradicted the principles of *Sozialmarktwirtschaft*, and Erhard refused to consider it. By 1959 Lindrath announced no possibility of compromise, and the parliament of Lower Saxony responded by enacting its own legislation making Volkswagen a public trust—essentially a symbolic gesture for which it was reprimanded by federal government.[186] But the action seemed to stimulate a meaningful response from the federal government. For the first time Adenauer directly intervened, suggesting that a compromise settlement would be appropriate.[187] Within two months the hitherto unbending Lindrath presented the federal cabinet with terms for a compromise solution, a *Stiftung* that would satisfy the SPD desire for public ownership, Erhard's needs for private ownership and a public distribution of shares, the state of Lower Saxony's insistence on an equal division of federal and regional ownership, and the defeated CDU minority's concerns for domestic ownership and a continued dominant voice for the federal government in the company's affairs.

[181]*Frankfurter Allgemeine Zeitung*, 2 July 1959.
[182]See *Die Welt*, 4 July 1953; *Industriekurier* (Düsseldorf), 7 July 1953.
[183]*Die Welt*, 30 May 1957.
[184]See Groeben, finance minister of Lower Saxony, "Abschlussprüfer für das VW," 23 January 1951, B115/3416, Bundesarchiv.
[185]*Vereinigter Wissenschaftsdienst*, 22 January 1957; *Financial Times*, 23 January 1958.
[186]See *Hamburger Abendblatt*, 2 July 1959.
[187]*Hamburger Abendblatt*, 5 August 1959.

The plan finally implemented in 1961 did not even remotely resemble the guidelines discussed by Erhard with the CCG in 1949. In the final plan 60 percent of the company's shares were to be sold to the public, subdivided into maximum lots of five per person, their cost dependent on the earning capacity of proposed purchasers with applicants eligible to a discount of up to 25 percent.[188] Furthermore, shareholders could not resell their stock without the consent of the company.[189] The expressed intent of the sales plan was to defy market logic and placate the CDU caucus, ensuring that neither large domestic institutions nor, more important, foreign auto firms could gain control over the company—a goal shared by the SPD.[190] The importance of consensus between government, opposition parties, banks, and capital on domestic control of core German automobile companies would be a recurrent theme in the Bonn Republic, as later attempted purchases of BMW by GEC in 1960, NSU by FIAT in 1968, and Daimler-Benz by Iranian investors in the mid-1970s demonstrate. This informal consensus was formalized in 1975 by legislation explicitly protecting these companies from foreign takeover.[191] Ernst Horn expands the argument to suggest that:

> The regulation of mergers has been used, in effect, to discriminate against foreign investment (e.g., when GKN tried to take over Fichtel and Sachs or BP tried to acquire a major share in Preussag) and the Deutsche Bank was applauded for taking over 25 per cent of the equity capital of Daimler Benz to prevent the shares falling into the hands of newly oil-rich countries. In public procurement (civilian and military hardware, the railways, the post office, state-owned public utilities) there is a strong preference for the domestic product, particularly in cases where technology policy wishes to demonstrate its success in the market-place.[192]

In Volkswagen's case, the remaining 40 percent of stock was to be divided equally between the state and federal governments, with mon-

---

[188]The concept of a "social rebate" that related cost to income was promulgated by the SPD and the union movement as a way of ensuring an equitable distribution of shares. The CDU considered the social rebate the price it would have to pay for privatization but, ironically, invocation of this principle also served Erhard's interests by extending the basis of property ownership. See *Deutsche Zeitung* (Cologne), 18 August 1960; *Die Welt*, 28 January 1961.

[189]*New York Times*, 17 January 1961.

[190]See for example, *New York Times*, 15 May 1957, 25 June 1956, 6 July 1956.

[191]For details see *New York Times*, 21 February 1960, 3 June 1960, 22 February 1968, 15 and 16 January 1975.

[192]See Ernst Horn, "Germany: A Market-Led Process," in François Duchêne and Geoffrey Shepherd, eds., *Managing Industrial Change in Western Europe* (New York: Pinter, 1987), p. 70.

ey from the sale to be loaned to the federal government at a low rate of interest and money from the divided payments to be paid by those governments to the *Stiftung* for scientific research and foreign aid. These terms seemed to satisfy all the major participants, and so began the laborious constitutional process of implementing the arrangement, first through the nationalization of the company by the Bundestag, which made Volkswagen the property of the federal government retroactive to 1949, followed by the signing of an agreement between federal and state government to form a *Stiftung*.[193] The following year the detailed plan to sell shares was implemented.

After the plan was announced, the German press constantly wondered whether the new arrangement would change Volkswagen's role as an instrument of state policy.[194] On reflection, according to Eva Brumlop and Ulrich Jürgens, this partial privatization should not mislead us into believing that the federal government was any less influential in Volkswagen's affairs than hitherto. Rather, they suggest, the company retained its essential character as a state enterprise.[195] As the company's joint largest shareholder, securing the most important positions on the new *Aufsichtsrat*, the federal government retained over company policy a considerable influence evident in matters of economic and regional policy and in industrial relations, as well as at such important times as the deliberation over Volkswagen's financial crisis in the mid-1970s.[196]

We have already examined the conflict over Volkswagen in the first decade of the Bonn Republic, but we would be remiss to ignore how Volkswagen was treated by various factions of Adenauer's successive governments and important social groups. The relationship between company, various ministries, and representatives of domestic capital and labor can give us insight into whether the company received a discriminatory advantage and whether it was treated as an instrument of state policy.

The compromise solution to the company's ownership did not fulfill Erhard's ambitions under the *Sozialmarktwirtschaft*. Moreover, the relationship between Volkswagen's new owners and the company itself often seemed to reflect the company's special status, derived from the

[193]*International Financial News Survey* (Washington, D.C.), 25 March 1960; *Wall Street Journal*, 6 December 1960.
[194]For example, see *Industriekurier*, 29 March 1960; *Die Welt*, 10 December 1959.
[195]Brumlop and Jürgens, "Rationalization and Industrial Relations," p. 5.
[196]For an example of the federal government's continued influence at Volkswagen consider the reappointment of Hans Busch, member of the federal government's Ministry for Federal Property, as chairman of the Supervisory Board under the new arrangement. See *New York Times*, 2 July 1961. More broadly see Alfred Thimm, "Decisionmaking at Volkswagen 1972–1975," *Columbia Journal of World Business*, Spring 1976.

Third Reich, rather than any dislocation of the company from the state. Paradoxically, Erhard's behavior often, perhaps unwittingly, reflected a belief that Volkswagen retained a special status, encouraging greater state activism than under a neoliberal vision. This was demonstrated in Volkswagen's pricing policy and epitomized by a clash between Erhard and the firm's management in the early 1960s.

Increased economies of scale allowed Volkswagen to reduce the price of its cars, in both domestic and export markets, throughout the 1950s.[197] BfM officials felt that by reducing price, Volkswagen could ensure export competitiveness.[198] Yet, by the beginning of the 1960s, Volkswagen could no longer afford to reduce prices as it had done for over a decade. Instead the company decided to raise prices by between $60 and $97, depending on model, only ten days after Erhard had appealed to German labor and management to refrain from wage and price increases.[199] Other German auto manufacturers immediately followed Volkswagen's example. Erhard publicly appealed to the auto manufacturers to review these price increases, and in private talks with Volkswagen' management he used "political and economic arguments."[200] However, Volkswagen officials resisted Erhard, claiming they had to raise prices because of their new responsibilities to the company's shareholders and staff, as well as to the West German economy in general. Erhard then threatened to reduce duties on imported French and Italian cars by 50 percent.[201] Duties on imported cars before the proposed cut ranged between 10 and 12.5 percent. The *Financial Times* suggested that Erhard was trying the same aggressive strategy on Volkswagen's price rises as John F. Kennedy had used in dealing with the U.S. steel strike. However, the paper added, Erhard's tactics foundered on Nordhoff's resistance.[202] The strategy failed because it was so trivial a threat to Volkswagen, whose market dominance was so complete and price advantage so great that such a reduction in duty would have minimal effects.[203] At this point Adenauer returned from vacation and personally intervened, chiding both Erhard and Nordhoff for publicizing the dispute. Adenauer's intervention resulted in a compromise: the price increases remained in effect, but the company agreed to include a built-in radio in the price.[204]

---

[197]See, for example, *New York Times*, 6 August 1955.
[198]*New York Times*, 25 June 1956.
[199]*New York Times*, 15 April 1962, III, p. 11.
[200]See *Bonner Rundschau*, 15 February 1962; *New York Times*, 27 April 1962.
[201]*New York Times*, 1 May 1962.
[202]See *Financial Times*, 3 May 1962; *Bonner Rundschau*, 5 May 1962.
[203]*New York Times*, 17 May 1962, p. 12.
[204]See *Bonner Rundschau*, 5 May 1962; *New York Times*, 10 May 1962; *Neue Rheinische Zeitung*, 15 May 1962; *New York Times*, 15 May 1962.

The government nevertheless instituted tariff reductions, which adversely affected American multinational producers in Germany, such as Fordwerke, subject to direct price competition from foreign firms. But Volkswagen's market share was sustained.[205] Indeed, Nordhoff had always welcomed the prospect of the Federal Republic's lowering trade barriers as a way of increasing pressure on the French and Italian governments to reciprocate. Volkswagen's superior product brought him to favor free trade as a means of enlarging sales.[206]

This episode highlights several major points. First, it demonstrates that the federal government and Volkswagen did not share an organic relationship—that Volkswagen was not part of the state apparatus. The two could disagree on policy. Even when they strongly disagreed on a policy, however, they could still compromise in a positive-sum rather than zero-sum settlement. Complementary interests encouraged Volkswagen's management to cooperate with the state, exchanging a loss of autonomy for increased profits.

Further, the federal government was unwilling to let market forces decide company policy. It is difficult to imagine a British government intervening in the affairs of a firm, in a healthy economy, to determine whether a 3 percent price increase in the cost of one product was permissible. But the pattern of negotiation and compromise with central government over trivial price increases has recurred at Volkswagen. Certainly the government's response lends credence to the view that it inherited a propensity toward aggressive, micro-level, interventionist behavior. Government officials demanded a role in company decisions about prospective price rises—generally not a neoliberal characteristic.[207] Erhard's demands regarding Volkswagen's prices received widespread support, indicating that a broad consensus existed among political parties.[208] However, the government took advantage of an opportunity to institute tariff changes that, it was then evident, would damage peripheral firms but not Volkswagen.

The concept of unrestricted trade was central to Erhard's economic principles. He believed that competition would have to be sustained to avoid the distorting effects commonly associated with a concentration of power.[209] The application of these principles to German auto pro-

[205]*New York Times*, 17 May 1962.

[206]For example, see *Manchester Guardian*, 14 May 1959. This competition between Volkswagen and FIAT reemerged as the focus of a debate on the institution of a free market in Europe in 1992. See *The Economist*, 9 July 1988.

[207]For instance, the $60 price increase negotiated between Nordhoff and Economics Minister Kurt Schmucker, *New York Times*, 14 December 1965.

[208]*New York Times*, 17 May 1962.

[209]For a discussion of Erhard's general opposition to cartels in the auto industry see *The Times* of London, 23 January 1958.

ducers would have required the maintenance of competitive markets free of cartels both at home and abroad. Yet in two areas Volkswagen management sought a policy that would restrict free market competition. The first concerned Volkswagen exports to its largest market, the United States. The company founded Volkswagen of America Inc. as a subsidiary in January 1956, after abandoning a proposal to become the first foreign car assembler in the United States (it was decided that adverse exchange rates and the possibility of low-quality production might hurt Volkswagen sales).[210] High demand and low supply in the United States strengthened Volkswagen's bargaining position with its fourteen distributors and the local dealers.

On 5 December 1957, focusing on the relationship between the parent company, subsidiary, distributors, and dealers, the office of the U.S. attorney general filed an antitrust suit against Volkswagen of America and its distributors, claiming illegal restraint of trade by fixing wholesale and retail prices and imposing restrictive practices upon the dealers. Substantively, it claimed that Volkswagen dealers had to agree not to sell new cars or parts manufactured by other companies and were strictly limited in terms of the prices they could charge. Dealers refusing to adhere to company guidelines were explicitly threatened with cuts in their allocations of cars and parts or with termination. Such behavior clearly violated the antitrust laws. The attorney general maintained the subsidiary had to have known it was breaking the law and claimed to have evidence showing that the parent company was a coconspirator. The only reason the parent company was not named a defendant in the civil suit was that it lay outside the jurisdiction of the U.S. courts. The Volkswagen subsidiary and parent company tersely responded that they had observed all laws. The subsidiary later changed that claim to the suggestion that all infractions, when noted, had been immediately corrected. The suit prompted legal action by Volkswagen dealers who claimed discrimination by the company. Then a $5 million antitrust suit was filed against Volkswagen of America and its distributors by the National Importer Car Dealers Association, which charged conspiracy to restrain trade in interstate commerce in violation of the Sherman and Clayton acts. The suit sought restitution for dealers who had been discriminated against, reinstatement of dealers who had lost their franchises, and protection for dealers against future conspiracies.[211] The issue brings a certain symmetry to this book. Just as Volkswagen was part of the core at home, so in its own American distribution network it developed a core that ignored market principles.

[210]*New York Times*, 25 September 1955, III, p. 1.
[211]For details see *New York Times*, 5 December 1957, 15 March 1958, 18 June 1958, 9 October 1958.

The problem kept growing for the company, which saw its best solution as denying all charges and sitting out the storm while demand for its product grew. This strategy proved relatively effective with a change in American administration. In 1962 the Department of Justice announced that it had filed a consent judgment which allowed Volkswagen of America to agree to avoid future antitrust actions without admitting current guilt. Some American producers were so incensed by the agreement that they unsuccessfully appealed in the federal district court of New Jersey, where the attorney general's office had bought the original suit.[212]

Volkswagen's discriminatory behavior toward its dealers merely mirrored the pattern of development from which it benefited at home. Coercive behavior that violated market principles was a part of the company's culture despite a domestic transition to a market-oriented economy. What the company's management considered perfectly acceptable forms of behavior in Germany violated sacred principles in liberal America.

A second form of restrictive behavior was to be found in the exclusive relationship shared by Volkswagen and other core auto companies. Nordhoff used the company's status as a public enterprise to stay aloof from the industry's trade association and the employers' federation.[213] Unlike Fordwerke, Volkswagen was permitted by law to be isolated. This isolation from tripartite institutions freed the company to negotiate mutually beneficial bilateral agreements with other core firms, and Nordhoff took advantage of this opportunity.

Volkswagen initially had little to gain from a web of bilateral relationships and so remained relatively isolated from those firms which had played an important role in its formation. When the company did seek to participate in this exclusive network, the machinery was available for it to do so.[214] When Volkswagen sales growth first slowed down in the 1960s, the company sought to cut expenses by signing agreements to offset the cost of research and development, which the firm had neglected while benefiting from the innovative capacities of others. Even the federal government offered a grant of DM 500 million to help Volkswagen pay for research and development.[215] The renewed competitiveness of American firms also convinced the federal government to intervene, in an attempt to preserve Volkswagen's lucrative monopoly on a popular market segment and stimulate core

---

[212]*New York Times*, 10 March 1962 and 3 April 1962.
[213]Brumlop and Jürgens, "Rationalization and Industrial Relations," p. 7.
[214]*New York Times*, 23 August 1966. This network of bilateral relationships did not come to fruition until the 1960s. See Chapter 7.
[215]*Hamburger Abendblatt*, 16 July 1960.

German firms to combine forces. The momentum toward mergers involving Volkswagen, NSU, Auto-Union, and Daimler-Benz was tempered only by legal barriers preventing the merger of Daimler-Benz and Volkswagen.[216] Nevertheless, the attempt to form a limited, all-German cartel in the face of renewed competition from Ford and Opel was evidence of the special relationship that had developed among these firms in the Third Reich. Volkswagen even entertained the prospect of an all-European cartel but rejected the idea when it discovered that the scheme proposed to include American-owned subsidiaries. Other core producers entered mutually beneficial research, development, and marketing agreements specifically designed to improve Volkswagen's competitiveness in relation to other mass producers with the consent, if not support, of the German government.

Did Volkswagen benefit from an advantageous relationship with labor? Here, according to Brumlop and Jürgens, the evidence clearly supports the proposition that the Bonn Republic sustained discriminatory patterns established during the Third Reich. Historically, Volkswagen management has been uniquely positioned in that the company has been allowed to negotiate with IG Metall its own firm-level agreement, the terms of which have remained distinct from regionally negotiated collective bargaining agreements. As representatives of plant workers, leaders of IG Metall have made allowances in these negotiations that they have been unwilling to make elsewhere. In contrast, when Opel or Fordwerke has tried to negotiate separate agreements it has encountered systematic hostility from other auto producers, labor, and the German government. Whereas Opel and Fordwerke have therefore been subject to the same terms as Daimler-Benz and BMW— both makers of high-quality products that can afford high labor costs— Volkswagen has not, providing it with a competitive cost advantage. The strongest evidence lies in the terms of the Volkswagen agreements, which often pay the work force the same or higher wages but provide fewer constraints on productivity. No wonder Volkswagen, as it entered the decade of the 1960s, had never experienced an official strike. IG Metall has historically justified this flagrant discrimination by suggesting that Volkswagen owes its special status to its exceptional works council rules—more a rationalization than a claim with any basis in logic, particularly since the firm's Beirat was considered a consultative organ of government rather than an instrument of labor representation.[217] In addition, the historically convivial working relationship that

---

[216]See, for instance, *Frankfurter Allgemeine Zeitung,* 26 October 1964.

[217]Brumlop and Jürgens, "Rationalization and Industrial Relations," pp. 7–10; letter, Dienst to Heinz Maria Oeftering, 23 March 1953, B115/3414, Bundesarchiv.

Schäffer had shared with the labor movement over such questions as taxation levels adds weight to the claim that the BfM and the labor movement worked in a complementary fashion to sustain Volkswagen as a state enterprise with a special status.[218]

STATE-FIRM RELATIONS IN THE EARLY BONN REPUBLIC

In the 1950s and early 1960s, it would appear, Volkswagen was favored by discriminatory patterns that originated during the fascist period and survived the occupation. Even influential elements of the new, fragmented German state, specifically officials of the BwM, could do little to alter the patterns of systematic discrimination instituted under fascism. Furthermore, it was often those very officials who most aggressively espoused the view that Volkswagen should be stripped of special status who then instigated behavior reflective of interventionist assumptions. On policy issues relating to prices and wages, restrictive sales, research and development practices, and industrial relations, neoliberals often encouraged interventionist policies that found broad support among mainstream political parties. Government ownership without control would not contradict a pattern identified in Britain. However, British governments relied on fiscal controls and allocative methods designed to be scrupulously fair to firms they did not own, whereas Erhard's neoliberal government intervened in the affairs of individual firms on issues traditionally reserved for boardroom decision making. This is convincing evidence in support of the claim that the structure of relationships created under fascism was embedded in the fabric of a postfascist, liberal-democratic society. Even those who held principles about the relationship between government and economy antithetical to fascism still behaved in a way congruent with the Nazis' discriminatory policies. Erhard's neoliberalism could not avoid discrimination resulting from a relatively weak state's incapacity to alter structural patterns instituted by a powerful predecessor.

Not all factions of government and societal actors had so unwitting a role in sustaining Volkswagen's advantage. BfM officials made little attempt to conceal their attitude. They wanted to preserve Volkswagen's comparative advantage over peripheral firms. So did other core producers, which saw Volkswagen's prosperity as intimately related to their own; and so did the German labor movement, whose concerns about Volkswagen were guided by self-interest and symbolic at-

[218]For example see *Time*, 15 February 1954; "VWW GmbH, Hier: Besprechung mit Herrn Generaldirektor Dr. Nordhoff am 3.3.53," B115/3416, Bundesarchiv.

tachments. The evidence supports the proposition that the structure of the relationship between the firm and the state had survived the transition from national socialism through enlightened despotism on to a rudimentary form of democracy.

Finally, this case study challenges Mancur Olson's claim, discussed in Chapter 2, that German growth rates can be explained by the fact that fascism, war, and foreign occupation combined to sweep away institutional barriers to entrepreneurial capitalism. The largest and most important enterprise in the opening two decades of the Federal Republic had survived the Third Reich and occupation intact. It was the cumulative advantage Volkswagen had gained during these periods, and the relationships that advantage had created, which provided the opportunity for economic prosperity.

CHAPTER SIX

In the Absence of a Core:
The Austin Motor Company

Austin provides an example of the continuity of the liberal British state's policies and principles, and the withering effects of a sustained egalitarian state ideology and limited state apparatus on a potential national champion. Under such circumstances, the opportunities to create the framework for economic prosperity generally go unrecognized, and when problems become too great to ignore, the common solution is to try to push the cost of adjustment on to external actors.[1] Having exhausted this avenue, liberal regimes face their central dilemma: how a limited state can distribute burdens among societal actors when the process is a "zero-sum" game—that is, when the politics of productivity are replaced by the politics of decline.

This dilemma suggests that in contemporary managerial capitalism the state is a central agent of change in sustaining prosperity—a function that liberal states are ill-equipped to perform. Liberal states rarely have tools for distributing the burden of adjustment in such a way as to benefit the "national interest." Their attempts to arbitrate reveal their ideological proclivities and limited capacities. These proclivities constrain both the breadth and the depth of intervention beyond the scope of sustaining a "fair market." Even if discretionary policies were thought of, the liberal state's capacity to implement them would be extremely limited, and when the situation actually arises the state rejects their use. Faced with the need to administrate the distribution of burdens, governments ineffectively attempt to push unwilling societal

[1]See Peter J. Katzenstein, *Small States in World Markets: Industrial Policy in Europe* (Ithaca: Cornell University Press, 1985), p. 23.

actors toward an ill-defined objective. The result characteristically is a chaotic process and an unsuccessful outcome.

The case of Austin incorporates all these themes. A liberal state effectively refused to support a prospective national champion; preferred to rely on macro-level fiscal policy as its primary means of intervention; and predicated its policies upon nondiscretionary principles consistent with a scenario of sustained growth even when growth was no longer feasible. The liberal state could remain relatively passive regarding the distribution of burdens between capital and labor when the pie was growing, but it could not avert or manage the politics of decline.

I chose Austin for examination for several reasons. First, Austin was suitably comparable to both Volkswagen and Ford because of Herbert Austin's avowed intent to "motorize the masses"—extending car ownership to the working man through use of the principles of mass production. Second, unlike the more flamboyant and enterpreneurial Lord Nuffield who owned Morris, Austin was primarily an engineer who sought to limit his use of "bought out" components (parts of the car purchased from outside contractors) as much as possible, in common with Ford and Volkswagen.

Third, throughout my period of study Austin was always one of the two largest indigenous British producers and, at the end of World War II, was the British firm best positioned to prosper. As the most efficient and profitable firm, and therefore the most likely candidate for the mantle of national champion, Austin potentially suffered most from the shortcomings in state policies that gave no thought to the welfare of indigenous companies. Those same government policies essentially ensured that the foreign firms with manufacturing subsidiaries would, in the long term, repatriate profits rather than sustain domestic investment—as was eventually the case with Ford and Vauxhall (the British subsidiary of General Motors).

Fourth, the Austin company did more than any other firm to support national policy as an armaments producer in both world wars and the Korean War and then as an exporter in the 1940s and 1950s.[2] If any firm's contribution qualified it for special status it was Austin, yet it received no advantage from government policy. Austin is thus a good case for my theory; if a firm can be this cooperative and still receive no discretionary help from the liberal state, then no firm can do so. Fifth, Austin for the period of this study defied all the stereotypical attributes

[2]Austin's policy contrasted starkly with that of Morris, especially before 1939 when Herbert Austin acted as chair of the committee for the construction of aeroengines at shadow factories. Lord Nuffield, owner of Morris, refused to involve himself in such efforts.

that have been used to explain the decline of British firms in the post-war era. It did not suffer historically from poor labor relations, nor did a chronically trained management give all the company's resources away to shareholders and neglect capital investment, despite periods of high dividends. Austin seemed to follow all the rules of good business practice. Common explanations are inadequate to account for its decline.

Finally, pragmatically, Austin was chosen because primary material still exists. Lord Stokes irrationally decided to destroy historical materials as each company was incorporated into BLMC in the 1960s and 1970s. Austin's materials survived, providing the data to examine my propositions.

In his polemical study of the auto industry since 1945, Peter Dunnett sets out to demonstrate that the intervention of the British state is axiomatic to the decline of the British automobile industry. Dunnett concludes that British governments have retarded the development of auto companies by using them as instruments or regulators of macro-economic policy.[3] Although he specifies no alternative path of development, his work suggests that if successive British governments had simply left these firms alone, and allowed them to act subject to market forces, both the companies and the British economy would be much healthier today. Neither Labour nor Conservative governments escape criticism for their interventionism.[4] Dunnett's criticisms of the Conservatives are reminiscent of those consistently made by Margaret Thatcher about the "Butskellite" 1950s, when Labour and Conservative parties, led by Hugh Gaitskell and R. A. B. Butler respectively, moved toward consensus on economic policies.

I dispute Dunnett's neoclassical position. The problems that beset British auto firms in the 1950s cannot be traced to *whether* the state intervened but rather to *how* the state intervened. British government intervention was predicated on the principle of "national treatment." I do not prescribe *more* intervention but, if I did, it would be a *different form* of intervention that recognizes the state's pivotal role as an agent of change in managerial capitalism. However, I concur with Dunnett on another important aspect. Like him, I suggest that many of the other factors used to explain Britain's industrial problems in this period are symptoms, rather than causes, of economic decline.[5] Specifically, undercapitalization, high strike rates, and poor management result from the form government policy has taken. For example, none of

---

[3]See Peter J. S. Dunnett, *The Decline of the British Motor Industry: The Effects of Government Policy, 1945–1979* (London: Croom Helm, 1979), pp. 15, 29.
[4]Ibid., p. 121.
[5]Ibid., p. 15.

these factors appeared to be significant at Austin until after state policies had encouraged their emergence or until the company had begun to experience decline. Various scholars have reached the same conclusion.[6] These factors subsequently became significant; once economic shrinkage has gathered momentum, the politics of decline becomes extremely important. Strikes, undercapitalization, and poor management become engaged in a vicious circle.

AUSTIN'S EARLY YEARS: SETTING THE PATTERN

The Austin Motor Company was formed in 1905 as a private company under the ownership of Herbert Austin with an initial capitalization of £11,000.[7] Austin first displayed his cars in public in 1912 at the motor show, where he criticized the authorities for their lack of discrimination in favor of British manufacturers. (Austin had been allocated a poor display site in the balloting process.)[8] The company initially produced unprofitable cars in small numbers but for the first time registered a profit, of £41,130 on turnover of more than £400,000, in 1913.[9] Herbert Austin then turned it into the Austin Motor Company (1914) Ltd., a public company, dividing the shares between Harvey Du Cros, Jr., Frank Kayser, and himself. The company was located at Longbridge outside Birmingham where in 1914 it employed 2,000 people, on 118 acres of land, with output approaching a thousand cars per annum and a prospective turnover of £550,000. Over £99,000 had been invested in the company in 1913 but the company's bright prospects demanded further capitalization. Austin sold Du Cros 186,663 shares and Kayser 26,667 while retaining 186,663 himself, for a total purchase price of £399,993.[10] Austin would remain as chair of the board and managing director for five years.[11]

The onset of war had an enormous effect at Longbridge, both on the company's immediate economic welfare and in the lessons learned about production techniques that were applied subsequently. Austin had the typical characteristics of an auto producer of the time, produc-

---

[6]See Karel Williams, John Williams, and Dennis Thomas, *Why Are the British Bad at Manufacturing?* (London: Routledge & Kegan Paul, 1983), pp. 210, 257; D. G. Rhys, *The Motor Industry: An Economic Survey* (London: Butterworth, 1972), p. 549.

[7]Roy Church, *Herbert Austin: The British Motor Car Industry to 1941* (London: Europa, 1979), p. 17.

[8]Ibid., p. 28.

[9]Ibid., p. 18.

[10]Richard J. Wyatt, *The Austin: 1905–1952* (Newton Abbot: David & Charles, 1981), p. 27.

[11]Church, *Herbert Austin*, p. 33.

ing a staggering variety of models but only 882 cars per annum and employing 2,638 people at Longbridge in the spring of 1914.[12] By 1918 it was one of the largest munitions producers in the country, employing in excess of 20,000 workers at Longbridge.[13] This expansion was due to Herbert Austin's inexhaustible willingness to accept military orders. Longbridge produced airplanes, aero-engines, armored cars, trucks, and electric lighting sets. However, the major product was shells, over eight million being produced during the war.[14] To accommodate this growth, the plant had to be expanded, the north and west works being financed by a Ministry of Munitions mortgage while the firm itself paid for the extension of the south works.[15] These new production facilities were augmented by the construction of a power station and an airfield. The value of the company's output rose to over £9 million by 1918.[16] The capacity of the plant was indicated by Austin's greatest wartime feat—signing and then completing a contract worth £500,000 for the Russian government in three months in 1918, then the largest military contract ever successfully fulfilled.[17]

Although car production practically ceased after 1915, Herbert Austin learned some valuable lessons from the mass production of shells. Most important, he learned about the advantages of flow techniques in volume production. Before 1914 the techniques used in arms production in Britain had been as antiquated as those used in auto production. However, the new Ministry of Munitions, formed in 1915 and headed by Lloyd George, advocated new production methods. Austin learned about mass production from ministry officials who virtually took over the company's facilities. Work was streamlined with press shops and various assembly bays introduced to the plant. The fragmentation of production allowed the use of unskilled workers, and piece-rate payment offered the incentive of high wages. As a result, 15,000 women worked at the plant during the war.[18] Austin personally received public recognition, a knighthood, for his work in 1917.[19]

Labor relations at the plant remained peaceful during the war. This tranquility was sustained despite the concerns of the larger engineering

[12]Ibid., p. 32.

[13]Wyatt, *The Austin: 1905–1952*, p. 29.

[14]Church, *Herbert Austin*, p. 43.

[15]The ministry gave the company an option to buy these new sites at the end of the war.

[16]Church, *Herbert Austin*, pp. 34, 43; "Austin Minute Book," 21 January 1920, MSS 226, Modern Records Center (MRC), Coventry, England, p. 31.

[17]Church, *Herbert Austin*, pp. 32–33.

[18]Wyatt, *The Austin: 1905–1952*, pp. 36–38.

[19]Coincidentally, at the same investiture the government bestowed the identical honor upon Perry, managing director of Ford, for his contribution to the war effort.

unions about the effects of mass production techniques and Austin's contempt for organized labor's attempts to institute formal representation and closed shop arrangements. The only exception to this docility was a strike in 1918 over the alleged victimization of a union member named Arthur Peacock. Ten thousand workers participated in a strike that lasted four days. Industrial action ended when the company agreed to lead an open inquiry into the matter.[20]

The war ended, and so did the contracts. Herbert Austin had always been very casual in his financial arrangements with the government, considering armaments production to be in the national interest and not an appropriate context for excessive profits. He took so puritanical a position on the issue of profiteering that wartime officials at the Ministry of Munitions described the firm as the most helpful in Britain. Austin had deliberately kept prices very low in order to break up what he considered an unethical arms cartel that existed among established producers. He gained a maximum 10 percent profit on government contracts but often asked for no profit at all. Furthermore, Austin let his company rather than the government pay for some of the plant's expansion. Subsequent memos written by Treasury officials described Austin's behavior as nothing short of "virtuous." Yet government officials saw no need to reciprocate when negotiating a price for the Longbridge facilities they had funded and constructed. Their duty, in the interest of fairness, was to get as high a price as possible. Austin Chamberlain defended the government's behavior by claiming that Austin had benefited from the war.[21]

Automobile manufacturers expected a heavy demand for cars in the postwar period. The McKenna duties, introduced in 1915, required a tariff of 33.3 percent on imported cars and was designed to limit foreign competition. Furthermore, the public had not been able to purchase cars for four years. As a result, Austin agreed to pay the government's boom prices for the north and west works, £240,000 for the buildings and £75,000 for the housing estate the government had constructed for workers.[22] Payment was made through the issuance of two mortgages to the company by the Treasury, to be repaid annually.

Austin immediately laid out the west works for the manufacture of car bodies, requiring the removal of one thousand machines that the government had insisted be included in the purchase price even though they were unsuited to auto production.[23] The company in-

[20]Church, *Herbert Austin*, p. 45.
[21]Ibid., p. 57.
[22]See "Austin Minute Book," 3 December 1919, p. 7; Wyatt, *The Austin: 1905–1952*, p. 51; Church, *Herbert Austin*, p. 56.
[23]Church, *Herbert Austin*, p. 56.

stalled new kilns, sheds, mills, and a boiler house. Similarly, the north works were rebuilt and nine hundred new machines installed. The forge was converted into a steel foundry and, rapidly, Austin had the largest and most integrated automobile plant in Britain.[24]

Genuine postwar prosperity was brief for the auto industry, for three reasons. First, surplus capacity was generated as numerous firms over-extended their capacity, just like Austin, and new firms entered the market. Second, analysts had exaggerated the pent-up demand. In the first year demand did exceed supply by 250,000 cars, but then new capacity, coupled with a steep rise in prices induced by the McKenna duties quickly ate into surplus demand. Many potential buyers reconsidered when faced with higher prices. Third, reconversion was hampered in 1918 and 1919 by shortages of raw materials and aggravated by industrial disputes, notably in the coal and iron industries. As a result, American producers, which had not closed down during the war, could still export to Britain at competitive prices, despite the McKenna duties, because of their efficient use of economies of scale. Ford and General Motors stole a march on British producers, and their sales accounted for much of the surplus demand. Imports from the United States grew from 5,000 units in 1919 to 29,000 in 1920.[25]

Recognizing early the need for protection from possible market downturns, Herbert Austin supported an offer from General Motors to amalgamate in 1919. GM management was looking to increase its competitiveness in the British market by circumventing the McKenna duties through local assembly. Mass production techniques made Austin a perfect candidate for merger.[26] However, Herbert Austin's board refused to sanction the plan's presentation to the shareholders.[27] General Motors was again rebuffed in the mid-1920s before settling for the purchase of Vauxhall instead. Next, Herbert Austin turned to the banking community for help, only to be rebuffed. By this time the firm's debts exceeded £200,000, in addition to the mortgages held by the Treasury on the north and west works and the housing estate. Furthermore, the company needed new capital to fund operating expenses. In desperation Austin turned to the government for help, recalling how cooperative the company had been during the war. Austin sought to exchange £315,000 of a proposed £1 million, five-year, 7 percent note for the outstanding mortgages. Treasury officials recalled the company's wartime help but rejected Austin's plea for special treatment, claiming (questionably) that government contracts had saved

[24]Wyatt, *The Austin: 1905–1952*, p. 42.
[25]Church, *Herbert Austin*, pp. 47, 53–54.
[26]Wyatt, *The Austin: 1905–1952*, p. 59.
[27]See "Austin Minute Book," 7 January 1920, p. 17, and 9 March 1920, p. 77.

Austin during the war and rejecting any notion that the government had contributed to the company's troubles.[28] Later attempts by board members to convince Ministry of Health officials that they should help finance the housing estate at Longbridge met with no success.[29]

The company issued more debentures, and in the first half of 1920 demand finally began to expand. Then the Finance Act of 1920, with its infamous horsepower tax that charged £1 for each horse power in an engine, pushed consumers to favor small-bore, long-stroke engines. It was designed to hurt long-bore, short-stroke American imports and protect domestic producers, but it also hurt sales of Austin's largest model—the Twenty. Company sales in the second half of 1920 plummeted, wiping out the profits of the first half of the year.[30] These problems were enhanced by continued global recession and the introduction of deflationary governmental policies designed to reduce demand. This time there was no escaping the impending crisis, and Sir Arthur Whitney was appointed official receiver to oversee the company's affairs.

Whitney had complete control over company activities, including production decisions.[31] Herbert Austin's personal powers were reduced by Whitney's appointment of C. R. F. Englebach as works director and Ernest Payton as secretarial director. The company then returned to the Treasury and, attempting to reduce its indebtedness, Payton offered Treasury officials the sum of £115,000 raised from the issuance of a further debenture to clear all outstanding debts to the government. The government offered to accept £200,000 in cash. Treasury officials, who had praised the company a few years earlier, suggested to Payton that the public interest might best be served by sending the company into liquidation. Despite Payton's inadequate response, Treasury officials agreed to accept £100,000 in cash with the rest to be paid off at an annual rate of £10,000 plus 10 percent interest.[32] The government's relatively uncharitable response proved characteristic. It sought to enforce its own priorities while bailing the firm out of bankruptcy, ignoring both the company's wholehearted contribution to the national interest and the fact that the government's initial policy might itself have partially caused the company's problem.

Between 1921 and 1924 Austin had a torrid time, often having to choose which creditor to pay—banks, suppliers, or government.[33] One

[28]Church, *Herbert Austin,* p. 62.
[29]See "Austin Minute Book," 13 July 1920, p. 117.
[30]Wyatt, *The Austin: 1905–1952,* p. 60.
[31]"Austin Minute Book," 7 October 1921, p. 295.
[32]Church, *Herbert Austin,* pp. 65, 67.
[33]For an example see "Austin Minute Book," 1 May 1924, p. 575.

impending threat of bankruptcy was so great that the organizers of the Olympia Motor Show refused Austin permission to display their models. Yet Herbert Austin's engineering capabilities overcame the company's economic difficulties and the government's indifference. Encouraged by the Board of Trade's exhortation to British producers to mass produce small, low-priced cars, he first designed the Austin Twelve in 1921 and then the Austin Seven in 1922, the latter a low-priced utility car to encourage motorization for the masses. The Seven's design was dictated by the tax laws of 1920 and 1921 that encouraged the development of a long-stroke, small-bore engine and was competitively priced to challenge the small car segment of the market hitherto dominated by Ford and Morris. The new tax laws conversely discouraged sales of the Model T in Britain because they raised its price by £23.[34]

The Seven immediately sold very well, despite a board so unenthusiastic about its design that it would not support development. Herbert Austin financed the Seven's development and the company had to pay him two guineas royalty on every Seven it sold.[35] This model's success expanded Austin sales tenfold in four years, inspiring confidence despite financial difficulties, and Austin cars became synonymous with reliability, performance, and low operating costs. The Seven itself attracted the sort of idiosyncratic, incredulous, romantic, and mythical loyalty later associated with the Volkswagen.[36] The company earned a gross trading profit of £198,835 in 1922, which doubled the following year.[37]

The general expansion of the industry after the slump was briefly threatened by the Labour chancellor Philip Snowden's decision to revoke the McKenna duties in 1924 because of the cost of the system to the Treasury.[38] The effect of the tariff's removal was so immediate and dramatic, with imports rising from 18,000 in 1924 to 41,000 in the first half of 1925, that the duties were immediately reimposed, convincing American multinationals that it was time to produce inside Britain.[39]

The price of the Seven continued to drop in 1924 and 1925, and the move away from financial difficulties led Sir Herbert to contemplate growth rather than survival. Despite his and Morris's mutual dislike, Austin proposed a merger of Austin, Morris, and Wolseley, the last an

[34]Church, *Herbert Austin*, pp. 72–80.
[35]Wyatt, *The Austin: 1905–1952*, p. 83.
[36]Church, *Herbert Austin*, pp. 83, 90.
[37]Wyatt, *The Austin: 1905–1952*, p. 75.
[38]Ibid., p. 92. Snowden relied on figures from the Treasury which showed projected losses in taxes as a result of lower sales of £2.5 million.
[39]Ibid., p. 93.

ailing company that, despite its losses, had the most modern facilities in Britain. This new company would have swamped domestic competitors, creating what would have amounted to the very first national champion, and it could have mounted an effective challenge in the United States. However, Morris resisted an innovative scheme conceived by others, despite Austin's willingness to give Morris almost complete control over the new complex. Morris claimed that he did not like to handle other people's money, and government indifference assured the failure of the scheme. Morris subsequently outbid Austin for Wolseley, purchasing it for £730,000.[40]

General Motors, supported by Sir Herbert, again offered to buy Austin in 1926 and was again refused by Austin's board.[41] Sir Herbert Austin then concentrated on developing the company.[42] As domestic sales expanded in the mid-1920s so did Sir Herbert's vision, and he entered into licensing agreements with firms in France, the United States, and Germany.[43] The German case is the most interesting because it involved the licensing of the Seven to the Gothauer Wagenfabrik, which was based in Eisenach.[44] The initial success of this scheme encouraged BMW to purchase the company and thereby assume the licensing rights. BMW spent two years producing Austin cars—the sort of fact overlooked when analysts insist there has been a historic emphasis on quality among German producers and negligence of quality among British firms.[45]

Austin's success in competition with Morris pushed it to a leading domestic position, orders rising by 40 percent at Olympia in 1925 and dealers complaining of a shortage.[46] Austin continued to register healthy profits despite the effects of a national coal strike and a flood at the company; company officials modestly attributed much of their success to the protection provided by the McKenna duties.[47] The company announced a further cut in prices by 1929, resulting in a 60 percent reduction between 1922 and 1929.[48] Impressive productivity increases were reflected in the fact that in 1922 it took 55 employees to build a car a week, in 1927 it took ten. Sales grew by 500 percent and the size of the work force by 300 percent, leading to profit increases of over 400

[40]Ibid., pp. 97–98.
[41]See "Austin Minute Book," 2 September 1925, p. 664.
[42]Wyatt, *The Austin: 1905–1952*, p. 104.
[43]See "Austin Minute Book," 27 February 1929, p. 887; Wyatt, *The Austin: 1905–1952*, p. 121.
[44]See "Austin Minute Book," 5 January 1927, p. 768.
[45]Ibid., 28 January 1931, p. 989.
[46]Ibid., 25 October 1926, p. 762.
[47]Thirteenth Ordinary General Meeting, "Austin Minute Book," 21 December 1927.
[48]Fourteenth Ordinary General Meeting, "Austin Minute Book," 11 June 1929.

Table 6.1. Austin profits and value of sales, 1922–1929

Year	Gross profit (£)	Sales (cars)
1922	198,835	2,559
1923	381,640	6,417
1924	470,902	9,673
1925	748,890	16,429
1926	648,415	24,900
1927	962,477	37,520
1928	861,299	44,654
1929	1,297,446	45,849

SOURCE: Richard J. Wyatt, *The Austin: 1905–1952* (Newton Abbott: David & Charles, 1981), pp. 286–90.

percent. A piece-rates wage system was introduced, and inefficient workers were weeded out. New production methods were introduced in a related move toward both greater automation and an increasingly unskilled labor force. The firm even awarded a cash dividend of 20 percent in 1930, its first to shareholders since December 1918.[49] By the end of the 1920s Austin and Morris accounted for 60 percent of the cars sold in Britain (for Austin's financial and sales development in this decade see Table 6.1).[50]

This period of extended growth was curtailed by the slump of 1930 and 1931, although the government's 1930 decision not to repeal protective tariffs spared the industry even greater ill effects.[51] Ironically, the 1930 budget improved Austin's position in the market. New taxes encouraged the purchase of smaller cars. This fact, and the tendency of the recession to encourage the purchase of cheaper cars, explains Austin's relative improvement, although profits per unit of output fell. However, the British share of the world market rose, led by Austin, from 7 percent in 1929 to 28 percent in 1932, due to low operating costs and substantial discounts offered on exported models. The cheaper British car became more attractive as the global economic situation worsened but, conversely, less desirable when the economic situation improved. Austin resumed its expansion (although at a slower rate than foreign competitors) as the effects of the slump eased in 1932, with sales moving from 42,520 in 1932 to 83,990 in 1937. The company was the largest producer of private cars in Britain for the time in

[49]Church, *Herbert Austin*, pp. 100–102, 109.
[50]Rhys, *The Motor Industry*, p. 308; Graham Turner, *The Leyland Papers* (London: Eyre & Spottiswoode, 1971), p. 88.
[51]Wyatt, *The Austin: 1905–1952*, p. 130.

1933 and 1934, even if partially because of temporary problems experienced by competitors. Ford was reorganizing with the continued construction of Dagenham. Morris suffered from sustained neglect by its owner (who had become Lord Nuffield in 1934); his eventual recognition of this negligence convinced him to hire Leonard Lord to reorganize operations at Cowley.[52]

However, the major auto companies felt content enough in 1933 to sign the only cartel agreement in the history of the British auto industry. In it the signatories agreed not to reduce prices for the forthcoming season.[53] However, the agreement proved difficult to sustain because of the proliferation of models on the market.[54] Significantly, at exactly the time Ford was being ostracized by other manufacturers in Germany, it was a central participant in this major agreement in Britain. Sir Herbert Austin's support of this agreement and other protectionist measures was inconsistent with his attacks on the arms cartel before the 1914–1918 war and his later, successful efforts to break the steel cartel. The new auto cartel did not last long, and Ford (with its new eight-horsepower car), Morris, and Standard soon returned to competitive strategies based on lower pricing. Longbridge's success, built around the Seven, did not encourage an innovative strategy at the company. In 1935 Austin announced that the company was taking a stand against the fetishism of annual model changes. As Austin stagnated, Ford grew with the completion of its plant at Dagenham. By 1935 Ford had surpassed Morris with 48,000 sales and announced the offering of the first £100 sedan.[55] Both Ford and Vauxhall had become significant actors in the British automobile industry by 1939. The "Big Two" dominant actors of 1929, with the remainder of the industry a multitude of small companies, had become the "Big Six" by 1939; many of these smaller firms declined due to market pressures.[56] Neither Austin nor Morris, intently watching each other, recognized Ford's growing threat until the postwar period.[57] However, Austin and Morris lost market share between 1929 and 1939, and it went directly to Ford and Vauxhall. Just as the two American subsidiaries were being forcefully and effectively constrained in Germany, they were expanding in Britain.[58]

The Longbridge labor force consisted of more than 25,000 people by

[52]Church, *Herbert Austin,* pp. 115, 117–19.
[53]See "Austin Minute Book," 26 July 1933, p. 1124. The firms that signed the agreement included Austin, Morris, Ford, Standard, Hillman, and Humber.
[54]Church, *Herbert Austin,* p. 116.
[55]Wyatt, *The Austin: 1905–1952,* pp. 201–3.
[56]Ibid., p. 214.
[57]Turner, *The Leyland Papers,* p. 92.
[58]Turner, *The Car Makers,* p. 26.

1936 but, despite rapid growth and increased automation, there was a history of industrial tranquility. This peace was broken by a strike by nonunion employees over piece-rates for the production of new bodies at the plant, resulting in the closure of the west works for four days and the layoff of 5,000 people. Company managers, in what was to become a characteristic response, said they were not willing to negotiate until the strikers returned to work. The workers complied, and the affair was seen as a victory for management. This loss encouraged higher enrollment in the Transport and General Workers Union and the National Union of General and Municipal Workers.[59]

That year Austin became a major armaments producer for the second time in its history. The growing threat of war convinced the government of the need to supplement the small, withering British aircraft industry.[60] Air Ministry officials sought to use the engineering facilities of allied industries to develop a skeleton support industry and decided that the experience and principles applied in auto production could be adapted relatively easily to aircraft. They contacted major auto producers to form a committee to organize a shadow factory scheme. Austin's noted engineering skills and pronounced nationalist leanings made him a perfect candidate to lead the group. Lord Nuffield was also approached as potential coleader of the group but refused to become involved. Lord Austin therefore assumed sole chairmanship of the Shadow Aero-Engine Committee, his first task being to coordinate organization of the construction of six shadow factory plants; each of the major producers except Morris was provisionally made responsible for one of these plants. In May 1936 Austin, once again leading the national effort, became the first firm to enter a contract with the Air Ministry, to build a shadow factory and produce nine hundred Fairey Battle airframes and Mercury engines over the next three years.[61]

However, Lord Austin did not adopt the casual approach to contracts that had cost him so dear in World War I. Indeed, as Roy Church notes, the "disastrous experience of government contracts during World War I helps explain why Lord Austin took such pains in discussing precise details of enumeration to avoid a repetition."[62] Austin's efforts annoyed civil servants at the Air Ministry who found his style unorthodox. In fact, "senior civil servant Swinton observed that Sir Herbert behaved in negotiation like a managing-director and seemed to assume that Neville Chamberlain possessed similar powers of deci-

[59]Wyatt, The Austin: 1905–1952, p. 212.
[60]Ibid., p. 232.
[61]Church, Herbert Austin, pp. 136–38.
[62]Ibid., and, for examples, see "Austin Minute Book," 25 March 1936, p. 1283, and 22 April 1936, p. 1288.

sion to those which he commanded. Chamberlain objected so much to
the notion of contracts being set as personal bargains that he refused to
attend a meeting of contractors, describing it as a 'poker party.'"
Eventually a deal was agreed that awarded Austin £50,000 in the first
year to cover research and development costs; £50,000 in the second
year toward payments for machines; £200 per subsequent machine;
and a bonus for cost savings. Austin's company was to manage the plant
for the government and receive a management fee; the government
was to pay for construction and manufacture and assume ownership of
all property and machinery.[63] To ensure that all firms got the same
deal, a break clause allowed the contract to be broken in the case of
inequitable benefits.[64] Between 1936 and 1945 this emphasis on equal
allocation and equal reward was a recurrent theme.[65]

Despite the annoyance over Herbert Austin's negotiating tactics and
his criticism of imports of American planes, government officials recognized his devotion to the scheme. Leonard Lord joined the Austin
company in 1938 and began a massive plant reorganization, allowing
Austin to devote his time to the new aircraft plant at Cofton Hackett.[66]
The costs, in addition to Austin's personal absence, included the transfer
of essential skilled workers to the new plant. Austin devoted both himself and his resources to the national rearmament effort, as he had done
two decades earlier.[67] Only ill health, in 1939, forced his retirement
from the chair of the shadow committee. He had devoted every working
moment to the welfare of the scheme for three years.[68]

The new Cofton Hackett plant required an agreement with labor
representatives about how their payment would be organized—a process not free from dispute. In December 1937 engine assembly began
at the plant, and Amalgamated Engineering Union employees who
worked in the tool room went on strike in protest against the new piece-
rates. Characteristically, the management made a negotiated settlement
conditional upon a return to work. A quick resolution did not allay
board members' concerns about future trouble at the plant.[69] During
the next three years the plant's production grew as the Battle airframe
and the Mercury VIII engine were replaced by the Mercury XV; re-

[63]See for examples "Austin Minute Book," 9 June 1936, p. 1295, and 28 July 1936, p. 1308.
[64]Church, *Herbert Austin*, p. 139.
[65]See, for example, "Austin Minute Book," 10 October 1938, p. 1434, and 14 December 1938, p. 1446.
[66]Lord was himself later coopted by Lord Beaverbrook to act as government controller of Boulton & Paul Aircraft Ltd.
[67]Wyatt, *The Austin: 1905–1952*, p. 219.
[68]Church, *Herbert Austin*, p. 140.
[69]"Austin Minute Book," 15 December 1937, p. 1393.

placement tooling was paid for by the Air Ministry, whose officials expressed complete satisfaction with the company's efforts.[70] The terms of government contracts were occasionally renegotiated to the satisfaction of both sides.[71]

As the company devoted more time and resources to the shadow factory, its main Longbridge plant suffered from neglect. The lack of resources, the disjointed effects of the reconstruction being undertaken by Lord, the general recession, and the new inroads into British markets by German cars all hurt Austin's sales. The company reduced prices and introduced a new, eight-horsepower model.[72] Then the firm's management, along with other major British producers, appealed to the government to stop the influx of German autos, which they felt were being dumped at subsidized prices to gain foreign currency. The architect of this joint appeal to government by the management of Austin, Morris, Ford, Vauxhall, and Humber was Percival Perry, chairman of Ford. The head of a foreign multinational therefore played a leading role.[73] Austin's innovations and responsive government policy coupled to produce a brief surge in growth that lasted until the outbreak of war.[74]

As the threat of war grew, Lord appealed that the Longbridge plant should be spared from obligations to manufacture only to Air Ministry requirements in the event of war. He implored ministry officials to leave car production facilities intact, asking that the Longbridge plant be allowed to manufacture only cars and trucks. Lord suggested that the only viable alternative was to compensate the company for changes made to the Longbridge plant as a result of ministerial requirements.[75] Some discussion followed among ministry officials about the strategic costs of producing in vulnerable parent plants rather than the more isolated dispersal plants. However, the requests of Austin management were ignored.[76]

STATE-FIRM RELATIONS BEFORE 1939

The relationship between Austin and various fractions of the state before 1939 reveals a pattern established early in the company's history.

[70]Ibid., 21 September 1938, p. 1430, and 26 October 1938, p. 1439. The government also paid for the construction of a new runway.

[71]For instance, in December 1938 the government agreed to pay Austin £20,000 for architectural and engineering services rendered in the construction of the aircraft engine and the flight shed. See "Austin Minute Book," 14 December 1938, p. 1446.

[72]Church, *Herbert Austin*, p. 140.

[73]"Austin Minute Book," 11 October 1937, p. 1378.

[74]Church, *Herbert Austin*.

[75]"Austin Minute Book," 25 January 1939, p. 1450.

[76]Ibid., 22 March 1939, p. 1463.

Herbert Austin consistently attempted to conform to the needs of government. He willingly subjugated his own interests and those of his company to the national interest, in breaking what Austin and government officials judged to be a conspiracy by the armament manufacturers' cartel to maintain artificially high prices in 1914. Austin then sustained unprofitable prices to maximize production. Skepticism suggests that he should not be depicted as too saintly, but government officials themselves described Austin's behavior as virtuous and altruistic.

Herbert Austin expanded his plant capacity in the immediate postwar era when encouraged to do so by officials of the Board of Trade, although the action was soon to prove a terrible drawback. Throughout the 1920s the company was the largest exporter from Britain, securing valuable foreign capital. Undaunted, but educated, by his previous experiences, Austin devoted himself and his company's resources to the defense of the realm despite his failing health in the mid-1930s. But he was also an outspoken critic of governments that contemplated lifting protectionist barriers, considering such changes a threat to profits, employment, and economies of scale. Such outbursts, however, were spasmodic and civilized in tone.

Government officials expressed gratitude and honored Austin for his personal efforts. Nevertheless, they were unwilling to act toward Austin in any way that could be construed as favoritism, perhaps considering the honors system a substitute for discriminatory behavior. Austin floundered in the immediate postwar period and almost went bankrupt as a direct result of the government's refusal to help it.

Both macro-level and sectoral government policies reflected egalitarian principles, which had a profound effect on technological development, consumer tastes, and protectionist practices in the automobile industry. Macro-level policies were exemplified by the McKenna duties, introduced in 1915, and the Finance Act of 1920. In addition to this legislation, and successive budgets that adjusted the rates of income and purchase tax paid by firms on sales, was significant sectoral legislation. Between 1930 and 1935 alone three major acts, and 70 orders and regulations containing over 455 individual regulations relating to motoring, were passed. Austin officials could reasonably claim, like everybody else, that these activities hurt their sales. Indeed, successive Ministers of Transport, notably Ernest Marples and Hore-Belisha, suffered a storm of criticism from manufacturers and public alike.[77]

Successive governments of diverse political persuasions established a tradition in this formative period of avoiding involvement in any discriminatory practices. At the same time as subsidiaries of General

[77]Wyatt, *The Austin: 1905–1952*, pp. 198–99.

Motors and Ford were being severely repressed in Germany, they were expressing themselves with increased confidence in Britain—treated as peers of domestic manufacturers by British governments.

What about alternative explanations so confidently used to describe the nature of British industrialization in the twentieth century? How do they relate to Austin in this period? Before 1939 industrial relations at the Longbridge plant suffered from occasional and limited conflicts between labor and management. A strike called by tinplate sheet metal workers and braziers in 1921 petered out. In 1923 a conflict over methods of payment relating to piece-rates resulted in the company's capitulation, reversing a 1922 company victory after an engineering lock-out. A strike in 1924 was called by skilled workers who feared their jobs were being reclassified as semiskilled. All these strikes concerned the effects of automation, were short in duration, and were settled between management, unions, and workers. Church suggests that despite a low level of union membership that might have encouraged wildcat strikes, and Herbert Austin's generally unenlightened views, there was an absence of friction within the company.[78]

The next strike, the most serious in the company's history to date, did not occur until 1929 and was over the introduction of a new grading system that threatened existing agreements over wage levels. A "sit-in" of five thousand workers and the management's customary refusal to discuss the issue until strikers returned to work stopped production for five days. Eventually the workers got the old system reinstated.[79] The next strike did not occur until 1936—a wildcat strike that lasted two days, the first to reveal any interunion rivalry at the plant, in this case between the National Union of Vehicle Builders (NUVB), the AEW, and the Transport and General Workers Union (TGWU). The intervention of union leaders brought an end to the strike. Finally, there was a strike at the shadow factory already discussed. Although that was a wildcat and unofficial strike, it did receive union and Labour party support. Faced with unanimity, the company was content to settle it quickly.

Strikes at Austin were occasional, limited in scope, and brief in duration. Conflict was orderly, set within strictly defined parameters. The company always demanded a return to work, pending negotiation, and the strikers always complied. The company consistently tried to play shopfloor workers against their union representatives, with varying degrees of success. Despite a consistently weak union and a strong company, there is no evidence the company victimized strikers.[80]

[78]Church, *Herbert Austin*, p. 149.
[79]Ibid., p. 152.
[80]Ibid., pp. 154–55.

On the second issue, capitalization, the data suggest that problems stemmed from over- rather than undercapitalization. Herbert Austin's profound belief in the value of mass production and automation, learned during World War I and from subsequent visits to the United States, pushed him to invest constantly in newer and better machinery. Though not an entrepreneur in the same terms as Morris, Austin was consistently willing to speculate on future market developments and risk overextending his capacity. Unlike Volkswagen in Germany, however, Austin received support from neither the government nor the banking community and had to build his integrated plant purely on the basis of reinvested profits. Only Payton's conservative fiscal management after 1923 allowed the company to accomplish this goal. This pattern of behavior—faith in the importance of automation and emphasis on capital investment—was to recur in the postwar period.

The industry was still afflicted by a propensity toward fragmentation, producing too many models to achieve economies of scale. The huge number of firms had been reduced, from 88 in 1922 to 31 in 1931 and was concentrated around the "Big Six" by 1939, but they still produced an abundance of models. At the 1929 motor show the ten largest producers had offered 46 models, and this figure increased to 64 by 1932.[81] However, Leonard Lord reduced the number of car models produced at Austin after 1938 and concentrated on a line of trucks and commercial vehicles, possibly in the hope they could be manufactured in wartime.[82]

AUSTIN AND THE WARTIME PERIOD

The company's position at the outbreak of World War II bore remarkable similarities to that in 1914. After a period of uneven growth the company was about to reassert itself, albeit under new leadership. Lord Austin had begun to play a reduced role in company affairs. Leonard Lord, the new and determined power behind the company, was deeply committed to sustaining car production in the event of war despite government opposition to his plans and had, in a relatively brief period, reorganized the administrative and productive capacities of the company at great financial cost. His objective was to reassert the firm's position in the market and shed its conservative image, devel-

---

[81]Andrew L. Friedman, *Industry and Labor: Class Struggle at Work and Monopoly Capitalism* (London: Macmillan, 1977), p. 206.
[82]Wyatt, *The Austin: 1905–1952*, p. 226.

Table 6.2. Austin's automobile production, 1939–1945

Year (to July)	Cars produced
1939	31,461
1940	39,097
1941	17,108
1942	4,485
1943	5,953
1944	6,885
1945	3,549
	TOTAL 108,538

Source: Wyatt, *The Austin: 1905–1952*, p. 229.

oped as a result of Austin's reliance on the Seven and supplemented by smaller production runs of a mid-sized and a large model.

Lord's success in sustaining auto production at Longbridge during the war, despite global events, is indicated by car production figures given in Table 6.2. Civilian production continued at Longbridge until 1940 when the acquisition of new cars was banned throughout the United Kingdom. The company continued to export, mainly to Commonwealth markets, although that stopped soon after. From 1941 onward cars built at Longbridge were for use by military and government officials, some traditional models being converted for use as a form of jeep. The company's truck production was expanded to offer a whole range of commercial vehicles that included both a one-and-a-half ton and a two-ton truck, two versions of a three-ton truck, and a five-ton truck, plus production of the Bedford troop carried designed by Vauxhall. During the war the company built 92,542 trucks for the armed services, a figure fairly evenly distributed across models.[83]

However, despite Lord's protests to the government, the firm concentrated on the production of armaments and aircraft. Once again Austin became of pivotal importance to the nation's war effort. Output was divided between planes, produced at the Cofton Hackett and later the Elmdon plants, and armaments production at Longbridge.

The Cofton Hackett plant was extended to cover over twenty acres of the twenty-three-acre site, including five separate factories, and was one of the two largest factories in the shadow production scheme. (The other was run by Rootes.) Lord Nuffield refused to become involved in any scheme that involved government supervision, preferring to produce aero-engines independently. Nuffield's strategy concerned Austin officials who feared that Morris might negotiate a more lucrative con-

[83]Ibid., p. 227.

tract. But Nuffield did eventually settle his differences with the newly appointed minister of air production, Lord Beaverbrook, at least long enough to build a shadow factory at Castle Bromwich near Birmingham.

Production of the Battle airframes and engines at Cofton Hackett was not as smooth as hoped. Company officials blamed many production problems on the haste with which the original design had been done in 1937. Initial design flaws meant constant alterations. However, Austin had laid out the plant on the principles of mass production, and so changes were carried out at a huge cost in time and money.[84] Nevertheless, the firm and the government signed new production contracts that incorporated bonuses designed to encourage cost savings and the maximizing of production.[85] By December 1940 the contractual order for production of Battle aircraft was fulfilled, 1,031 having been built; the Battle was discarded in favor of the superior Stirling aircraft.[86] It was also decided that Pegasus XVIII engines would be produced.[87] By May 1943, 700 Stirlings had been completed; then production switched to both the Avro Lancaster and the Hurricane MK II bomber.[88] Production at Cofton Hackett suffered from conventional problems of raw material and skilled labor shortages, plus the disruption caused by constant negotiation of new contracts.[89] In January 1941 Austin officials had to negotiate with the newly named Ministry of Aircraft Production. Ford's Patrick Hennessy was the intermediate in charge of negotiation over Hurricane production—officials of Austin, a domestic firm, found themselves negotiating with the representative of a foreign multinational firm who was acting with authority from, and on behalf of, the British government. The shadow factory scheme initiated by Lord Austin had passed from his control with his illness, and some of the most influential figures from the automobile industry were Percival Perry and Hennessy of Ford and C. J. Bartlett of Vauxhall. Whether through choice, as in the case of Nuffield, or circumstance, as in the case of Austin, many British manufacturers played secondary roles in the scheme. Yet the scheme itself paid testimony to Lord Austin's perseverance. The shadow factory scheme was responsible for the production of 12 percent of the wartime output of aircraft and over 45 percent of bombers delivered to the Royal Air Force.[90]

[84]Letter, Payton to Director of Contracts, Air Ministry, 5 December 1939, Ministry of Aviation (AVIA) 15/320, Public Record Office (PRO).

[85]Notes on meeting of Scott and Cotton (Director of Aircraft Contracts) with MacDonald of Austin Shadow Factory, 21 May 1940, AVIA 15/320, PRO.

[86]"Austin Minute Book," 27 November 1940, p. 1548.

[87]Ibid., 27 June 1939, p. 1475.

[88]Wyatt, *The Austin: 1905–1952*, p. 235.

[89]See, for example, "Austin Minute Book," 27 September 1939, p. 1485.

[90]Ibid., 29 January 1941, p. 1557.

On Lord Austin's death in 1941 Payton succeeded him as chairman of the board and Lord became managing director. The combative, ruthless Lord was a formidable negotiator with the government, but even he had to admit that, however unsatisfactory the terms, there was little the company could do given the government's monopoly over purchases.[91] Board members suggested that tax levels on profits were so high that there was little incentive to push for better deals, circumscribing the company's capacity to create reserves for postwar investment.[92]

Mutual frustration was increased by government accusations of inappropriate financial procedures by management.[93] A later study exonerated the company of any improper, informal, or illegal activities.[94] Yet maintaining wartime accounts at Austin was a problem. The disorganized state of the stores made stocktaking inconceivable, and accurate production figures were never available. Dividend payments were consequently delayed, and no payment was made between 1940 and 1943.[95]

In this generally unhealthy financial climate the original contract for management fees, negotiated between the auto firms' representatives and the government in 1937, expired and had to be renegotiated in 1940—by which time government had extended Austin's management to a second plant at Elmdon, complicating the new negotiations.[96] William Rootes, part owner of Rootes, and Payton tried to renegotiate a new agreement with ministry officials who described the proceedings as "acrimonious." The officials suggested a rise in the management fee from £20,000 a year to £26,000, but Payton noted that the capital involved in the Austin shadow factory project was now over £5.5 million. He could not accept the government's offer in view of the nominal rate of return it offered. Payton stressed that he would acquiesce if directed by the government but preferred to wait until after the war to settle the issue through the courts. Amazingly, the ministry's internal memos reveal that officials chose to accept Payton's offer of a deferred settlement, suggesting that they lacked statutory powers to enforce an agreement, even though Payton had volunteered to acquiesce! These

[91]See ibid., 10 September 1941, p. 1585, and 22 October 1941, p. 1586.
[92]See ibid., 22 October 1941, p. 1586. For the effects of Excess Profits Tax on manufacturers see Richard J. Overy, *The Air War, 1939–1945* (New York: Stein & Day, 1980), p. 181.
[93]Secret Air Supply Board, "Austin Motor Company, Cofton Hackett Shadow Factory, Longbridge, Birmingham—Capital Expenditure," SBM 733/41, AVIA 15/320, PRO.
[94]SB 34067, Secret Draft, AVIA 15/320, PRO.
[95]Wyatt, *The Austin: 1905–1952*, p. 237.
[96]See PS 7, Memo, W. Stevens, 1 June 1945, and PA 10, Minute Sheet, 1 May 1941, AVIA 15/320, PRO.

Table 6.3. Austin gross profits and income taxes,
1938–1945 (in £s)

Year	Gross profit	Income tax
1938	1,282,828	147,000
1939	1,609,580	270,000
1940	1,530,787	360,000
1941	1,760,993	380,000
1942	2,342,795	570,000
1943	2,164,530	500,000
1944	2,137,505	515,000
1945	2,077,400	500,000

SOURCE: Austin Company Report, 1946.

memos reveal that the British state, even in wartime, felt too weak to enforce a settlement despite knowing that the company would acquiesce, a stark contrast with the German situation.[97] At the end of the war the ministry offered an acceptable settlement before the issue reached the courts: a management fee of £155,000 for four years' service between 1941 and 1944, plus a further £40,000 in fees for 1945.[98] Settlement could not disguise the contempt each party felt for the other's behavior, providing the basis for hostile postwar relations between the firm and the state.

Despite Lord's efforts, armament production at the Longbridge plant included armor-piercing shells, ammunition boxes, steel helmets, jerry cans, Churchill tank suspension units, mine pressings, and a variety of gun magazines.[99] This production required the dismantling of a large part of the factory, although it generated limited profits, as indicated in Table 6.3. Wartime production therefore did not prove particularly lucrative for Austin, especially after the Excess Profits Tax of 1940 curtailed profiteering. Unlike Volkswagen, the company did not get new machinery that could later be adapted to the auto industry. Moreover, the machinery was owned by the government and, at the end of the war, was repossessed, so there was no lasting benefit to Austin.

Significant changes took place in the nature of industrial relations at Austin plants during the war, in a period marked by greater militancy at both the main and the shadow plants. Jonathan Zeitlin suggests that

[97]S. Robinson, SB 14260, 9 October 1942, AVIA 15/320, PRO.
[98]For settlement of fees for 1941–1944 see letter from A. F. Forbes to Payton, "Personal and Confidential Notes," 26 May 1944, AVIA 15/320, PRO; and for agreed fees for 1945 see letter from Payton to Neden of the Ministry of Aircraft Production, 1 November 1944, AVIA 15/320.
[99]For a complete list see Wyatt, The Austin: 1905–1952, p. 231.

the state, under pressure from labor representatives, played a key role in eroding managerial prerogatives at the work place throughout British industry.[100] Alistair Tough claims that during the war Austin management was under ministerial pressure to avoid disputes and production losses.[101] As a consequence, two contradictory government policies were applied to Austin, one emphasizing the importance of uninterrupted production and the other encouraging potential labor militancy. Both the Ministry of Supply and the Ministry of Aircraft Production encouraged the company to maintain high production levels, while the Ministry of Labour encouraged labor to make demands and management to concede. The Ministry of Labour's policy of placating workers created its own momentum, encouraging further claims. As a result conflicts became more hostile, widespread, and increasingly focused on trivial issues. The German state systematically destroyed auto workers' political and economic rights, but the British state asserted them and effectively encouraged industrial militancy. The Ministry of Labour's wartime policy gave unions in the auto industry a chance to assert their power—encouraging growth in union membership among workers and demands for greater financial rewards and worker control over production. Steven Tolliday refers to the consequences as "management by abdication," although he suggests that this development was more widespread at Standard and Rootes than at Austin. Nevertheless, Austin workers remained ill-organized until the late 1950s when unions finally began to build substantial membership, in contrast to firms in Coventry, especially Standard and Rootes, where militancy and worker control of production were typical.[102] At Austin, however, the war did bring a new militancy.

Morris's Cowley plant and Standard's Coventry plant were the first sites of industrial conflict after the outbreak of war.[103] It did not take long for the new pattern of industrial conflict to be replicated at Austin. Just one month after the well-publicized strike at Standard, seventy woodpattern makers in the motor department at Longbridge went on strike for four days over a dispute concerning piece-rate payments on new armaments production.[104] In the following months employers in

[100]Jonathan Zeitlin, "Shopfloor Bargaining: A Contradictory Relationship," in Steven Tolliday and Jonathan Zeitlin, *Shopfloor Bargaining and the State: Historical and Comparative Perspectives* (New York: Cambridge University Press, 1985), p. 2.

[101]Alistair Tough, "Richard (Dick) Etheridge," unpublished paper, MRC, p. 3.

[102]Steven Tolliday, "High Tide and After," in Bill Lancaster and Tony Mason, eds., *The Life of Labour in a Twentieth Century City: The Experience of Coventry* (Coventry: Cryfield, 1986).

[103]See Papers of the Ministry of Labor (Lab), "Reports of the Industrial Relations Officer, Midland Regional Area #9," 6 January 1940 and 5 October 1940, Lab 10, File 350, PRO.

[104]Ibid., 23 November 1940, Lab 10, File 351, PRO.

Coventry faced mounting pressure to increase wages, and they sought help from the Ministry of Labour to ensure that workers complied with existing contracts. Claims for higher wages in Coventry, union recognition at the Ford plant in Leamington, and strikes at Rover all served as catalysts to heighten tensions at Austin. Only a traditionally good record of industrial relations at Austin explains why it took until the middle of 1941 for conflicts to start there.[105] In July 1941 an employee at Austin was fired from a post to which he had just been promoted because he refused to discontinue activities on behalf of the Clerical and Administrative Workers Union. What was perceived as management's crude attempt at cooptation through promotion to high office was a source of strain between unions and management. After negotiations, a compromise was reached whereby the worker was reinstated to his position in exchange for modifying his union activities.[106]

The number of women working at Austin grew tremendously between 1939 and 1941. Their discontent at the lack of benefits from a national agreement concluded late in 1941 led to a strike at Austin that closed the north works. These womens' wages fell within the new statutory limits of the national agreement, so the firm refused to award any further increases. The women, who worked on a basic wage plus piece-rates, demanded a flat five shillings a week pay increase, but a TGWU official got them to return to work pending consideration of their claim at a works conference.[107]

At the start of the following year the company attempted to reclassify some skilled workers as semiskilled, claiming that improved automation had changed job requirements, reducing the wages of some sheet metal workers.[108] Management reconsidered when faced with widespread opposition from both the labor force and Ministry of Labour officials. Ministry officials successfully encouraged the company to withdraw its proposals, but the incident increased friction within the plants and the labor force escalated its demands.

In August 1942 the biggest wartime dispute to date erupted, as 250 Amalgamated Engineering Union (AEU) foundry workers went on strike over company stalling in the application of a new basic rate of wages and bonus system due under a nationally negotiated settlement.[109] The company demanded that strikers return to work and promised a speedy solution to an issue that had already dragged on for eight months. However, the traditional formula of enforcing a return

[105]Ibid., 15 March, 22 March, 12 April, and 26 April 1941, Lab 10, File 351, PRO.
[106]Ibid., 12 and 16 July 1941.
[107]Ibid., 13 December 1941.
[108]Ibid., 24 January 1942.
[109]Ibid., 29 August 1942.

to work pending a settlement was unsuccessful for the first time in the company's history. Workers stayed out on strike, returning to work only after negotiations between union representatives and management officials had commenced. This was a landmark change in customary behavior at Austin.

After a brief stoppage over wages by inspectors at the Cofton Hackett plant in September, and by unskilled workers over bonus payments in October, the next major conflict at Austin occurred in November—a dispute at Cofton Hackett involving the dismissal of three workers accused of participating in irregular booking procedures. The company alleged that two workers had performed a shop steward's assigned work while he conducted union activities. Stewards at Austin were generally considered moderate and conciliatory, so when these stewards accused the company of victimization against union members and called for industrial action, over seven thousand members of the AEU, the TGWU, and the NUVB went on strike. The rare militancy of the stewards gave them legitimacy among the work force. This case had been previously referred to the local appeals board, run by the Ministry of Labour, which had ordered the workers be reinstated. The company's refusal to abide by this decision had precipitated the strike. In the face of worker militancy and government pressure, the company reinstated the three workers.[110]

The decision was a watershed in industrial relations at Austin, marking an assertion of power by both unionized and nonunionized workers. Stoppages continued throughout 1943 and 1944, the reasons sometimes unclear to management and to ministry officials.[111] On other occasions the reasons were clear and trivial, such as a major stoppage at Cofton Hackett over the quality of the caterers who worked in the canteen. In this case a strike by six hundred people resulted in a secret ballot that overwhelmingly favored retaining the caterers.[112] Most conflicts concerned adjustments in fixed wages and piece-rates due to the changing nature of work. The most militant workers were the new female, unskilled staff whose attitude proved infectious.[113] As the war progressed the strikes lasted longer; if the number of workers involved did not increase, the strikes were increasingly disruptive to production. Even relatively small strikes could cause major bottlenecks

[110]Ibid., 12 September, 17 October, 21 November, and 28 November 1942.
[111]Letter, G. A. Durant, Ministry of Aircraft Production, to DAP/LO, 29 May 1943, AVIA 15/2548, PRO.
[112]See G. F. Wilkinson, AP 8, 25 February 1944; DAP Circular Letter No. 18 from G. A. Durant to D. Wilkinson, 28 February 1944, AVIA 15/2548, PRO.
[113]See memo, G. F. Wilkinson, AP 8, 25 May 1944, Ministry of Aircraft Production; also memo, R. G. Booth to DAP/LO, MAP 2 June 1944; and memo, G. F. Wilkinson, AP 8, "Austin Motors Ltd (Aircraft Section) Longbridge, Birmingham," all in AVIA 15/2548.

as resources grew scarce and alternative sources of supply disappeared. For example, one four-day strike at Elmdon by thirty-four electricians reduced production at the plant by 50 percent.[114]

The implications of this pattern of sustained, disorderly conflict at Austin's plants after 1941 extended beyond the immediate disruption of production. It added a new factor in the formulation of company policy—a vital, potentially disruptive labor force that would not tolerate management's traditional demand of an immediate return to work followed by a leisurely compromise.

In early 1945 the government began to wind down aircraft and armaments production. R. J. Overy correctly suggests that, with the government's close supervision of contracts and rigid application of the Excess Profits Tax, the auto companies' biggest gain from the war was the purchase of capital assets, effectively subsidized by the British government, at the end of the war.[115] But this generalization does not apply to Austin. The machinery the company had paid for could not be applied to automobile production and had to be removed. The government did give Austin first option on leasing the Cofton Hackett plant— a provision of the original agreement—but the asking price, an annual rent of £31,000, was beyond the company's means. Ministry of Aircraft Production officials were unwilling to compromise over price or to include any materials, equipment, or machinery in a deal, refusing to negotiate in order to be fair to all companies involved in the shadow factory scheme.[116] Lord, perhaps recalling Austin's deal with the government in 1918, decided to forgo the proposed offer.[117]

STATE-FIRM RELATIONS DURING THE WAR

In Britain's "darkest hour," it might be assumed, the relationship between Austin and the officials of the ministries of Labour, Supply, and Aircraft Production should have been at their most informal, cooperative, and sensitive. But such was not the case. On the contrary, relations became increasingly formal and juridical as the firm's objectives diverged from those of the ministries. The Labour Ministry want-

[114]See letter, Birchill to Wilkinson, 4 May 1945, AVIA 15/2548.

[115]Overy, *The Air War.*

[116]Letter, W. G. Stevens, Ministry of Aircraft Production, to R. W. Speed, 29 May 1945, AVIA 15/320, PRO; "Austin Minute Book," 26 September 1945, p. 1697. For those involved in shadow factory purchases see "Motor Companies Taking Over War Factories" in *The Motor,* 28 March 1945, p. 121.

[117]"Note of a Meeting with Lord, Vice-Chairman of Austin, regarding the Future of the Aero-Works, Cofton Hackett," 30 October 1945, AVIA 15/320, PRO.

ed to expand workers' wages and control over production, whereas management sought to suppress both; the Ministry of Supply and the Ministry of Aircraft Production wanted to maximize production at minimal cost, whereas management wanted to maximize profits; and all three ministries wanted an informal, speedy settlement of contracts, whereas company management, recalling its experiences of the previous war, placed a higher premium on precise settlement of contract terms than on the time involved.

Despite these differences, by 1945 no one could doubt the company had again made a significant contribution to the war effort. Prior to his death Austin had contributed to the shadow factory scheme an intangible asset, inspirational leadership, whose symbolic worth extended beyond production figures. Nevertheless, the company had no notable material gains to show for this significant involvement in arms production and their founder's deep commitment to the nation's survival. It neither retained any government machinery nor purchased any government facilities at a subsidized price. Although state officials recognized the important contribution of Austin to the war effort, and Austin's significant role in the forthcoming export drive, they refused to cooperate with Austin in any way that might show favoritism. Furthermore, the Excess Profits Tax had limited Austin's amassing of profits to finance its postwar recapitalization scheme; what money was available resulted from Payton's noted fiscal conservatism rather than the government's generosity.[118] The only major change at the company during the war was a new pattern of industrial relations detrimental to its prosperity. Neither Lord nor Payton was suited for diplomatic negotiations with an increasingly militant labor force. At the end of the war, ill health caused Payton's retirement from the board and Lord assumed the chairmanship, to lead Austin into what he saw as a bright new future.[119]

BENIGN INTENT, MALIGN EFFECT: AUSTIN IN THE POSTWAR PERIOD

At the end of the war Lord, convinced of high auto demand, thought it imperative to preempt competitors by being the first to supply consumer demand. The board authorized the spending of £1 million from company reserves on equipment, machinery, and plant improvements.

---

[118]The company did eventually receive a refund on part of the amount it had paid in Excess Profits Tax, in 1947—two years after the money would have been most beneficial. See "Austin Minute Book," 9 July 1947, p. 1761.

[119]Ibid., 28 December 1945, p. 1709.

Armament production was gradually phased out, and the factory was reorganized for civilian production. Fortunately, the Austin Ten's assembly line had remained intact throughout the war and it needed only minor adjustments for civilian production, but over five thousand machines had to be moved out of Longbridge before other lines could be built. Lord promised the government that two thousand of each model of the company's Eight, Ten, Twelve, and Sixteen cars, and its one- and five-ton trucks, would be produced by the end of the year, and they were.[120]

Lord envisaged a postwar market rid of internal and international restrictions, where his company could maximize production and profits.[121] However, the caretaker British government before the election of 1945 and the subsequent Labour government had other, intrusive priorities. Their policies led to descriptions in the trade press of government officials as "belligerent opponents" of auto producers.[122] While manufacturers sought freedom from government control, government objectives involved intervention in industry affairs.[123]

The priorities of the government were twofold. The first was to earn foreign currency in order to pay for imports of scarce materials. This objective required an emphasis on exporting to hard-currency markets, such as the United States. The second was to preserve hard currency and raw materials at home, requiring that consumer demand in Britain be curtailed. The government felt that steel shortages in the United States and reconstruction in France and the western zones of Germany prevented Britain's major competitors from supplying the global auto market. Britain should maximize exports while it still held a monopoly in some of these important markets.

Representatives of the car industry felt that government attempts to dictate policy or to control the supply of raw materials were simply the work of self-interested bureaucratic officials, and they said so in public. One representative of the Society of the Motor Manufacturers and Traders (SMMT) suggested that "those in charge of the control of the motor fighting vehicles at the Ministry of Supply will wish to prolong their jobs by controlling private motor car production."[124] Government officials sought to soften these attacks with two responses: first, they outlined general policy guidelines for the industry as a whole rather

[120]Wyatt, *The Austin: 1905–1952*, p. 239.
[121]See his comments in *Autocar*, 9 November 1945.
[122]See "Politics and Nationalization," *The Motor*, 27 June 1945, p. 411.
[123]See letter from the Secretary of the British Society of Motor Manufacturers and Traders (SMMT) to Hugh Dalton, President of the Board of Trade, 29 March 1945, Board of Trade (BT) 64/2898, PRO.
[124]See Sir William Palmer, "Motor Industry," 6 April 1945, BT 96/211, PRO.

than strict rules for each firm; second, they emphasized regular, informal, personal meetings with industry representatives to discuss future government policy rather than use more formal lines of communication.[125] Board of Trade officials asked industry representatives to produce 200,000 cars during 1945, at least 50 percent for export, and stressed they had no intention of supervising the distribution or sales of cars.[126] Government officials recognized that some firms would exceed the target, others would fall below it, and they hoped the average would meet the government's goal.

The election of 1945 resulted in a Labour party victory, and Sir Stafford Cripps succeeded Hugh Dalton as president of the Board of Trade. An informal agreement between Cripps and the president of the SMMT ensured that at least 50 percent of cars and 33.3 percent of commercial vehicles would be exported under a self-governing scheme for the auto industry. To enhance prospects for a cooperative exchange of information, the Labour government created a new peak association on which members of industry and civil service bureaucrats would sit— the National Advisory Council for the Motor Manufacturing Industry (NACMMI). This new body met for the first time in early 1946, with the government represented by members of the Board of Trade and the Ministry of Supply.[127] The manufacturers, including Lord, were openly suspicious of the Labour government. In the proposed nationalization of road and rail transport, which later materialized as the 1947 Transport Act, the industrialists saw a harbinger of the nationalization of car firms. They repeatedly stated these suspicions over the next six years despite the categorical denials of government ministers and civil servants, and their views were popularized in the trade press, driving a wedge between the industry's leaders and the government.[128]

Lord, despite his fear of nationalization and outspoken criticism of the government, continued to vigorously pursue the guidelines laid down by the government and the SMMT.[129] A combination of factors

[125]War Cabinet, Reconstruction Committee, R(I)(45), Sixth Meeting, BT 96/211, PRO.

[126]See letter, Preston to William Palmer, 19 April 1945; "Note of a Meeting with the British Manufacturers' Section of the Committee of the SMMT," BT 96/211, PRO.

[127]"Extract from the Minutes of the First Meeting of the National Advisory Council for the Motor Manufacturing Industry," 30 April 1946, BT 64/2898, PRO.

[128]For examples of governmental denials see Sir George Turner to the Second Secretary, Ministry of Supply, 29 May 1947, Ministry of Supply (MinSupp) 14/330, PRO; "Swaying the Balance," *The Motor*, 31 July 1946, p. 562. For accusations by industrialists see, for instance, "Auto-Austerity in Parliament," *The Motor*, 28 November 1945, p. 322.

[129]See, for instance, *The Motor*, 31 October 1945, p. 248; Wyatt, *The Austin: 1905–1952*, p. 243.

limited Austin exports to only 2,000 cars and trucks in 1945, but Austin exports expanded to 25,578 cars and 5,456 commercial vehicles in 1946 in a drive that emphasized "hard-currency" (i.e., dollar) markets.[130] With a total production of 42,500 cars of prewar design, mainly Sevens, Eights, and Tens, Austin's exports exceeded the government's requirement. This reliance on old models rather than new designs stemmed from a government policy that placed a premium on fulfilling current demand rather than concentrating on better-quality products. This policy encouraged companies to emphasize volume production and adopt piece-rates. Civil servants also encouraged the industry's management to placate worker demands, in order to avoid disruptions to production targets, persuading management to abandon control of production to the workers. Labor was often subdivided into self-governing "gangs" that were stimulated to produce by this incentive structure. The system placed little emphasis on quality, but most companies neglected quality control because they knew they could sell every car they manufactured. The long-term effect was to give British cars a lasting reputation for poor quality.[131] But redesign in 1945 would have taken time and would have cost the industry, and the country, hard currency in the short term through lost exports.[132]

With state policy built around maximizing exports, the government also encouraged the production of larger cars and increased standardization among domestic producers. The Labour government recognized that the horsepower tax enacted in 1920 was an impediment to exports because it encouraged the production of short-bore, long-stroke engines unsuited to foreign markets. Such engines were perfectly suited to small English roads and constant stopping and starting but ill-equipped to deal with the demands of a German autobahn or an American highway, which required an engine suited to cruising at high speed for long distances. These short-bore engines lacked power, encouraging the production of smaller cars that were ill-suited to long-distance driving because they did not provide the comfort of larger, foreign counterparts. The Labour government rescinded this duty to encourage the production of larger cars, introduced a new flat-rate license, and raised purchase tax levels on domestic sales to 66.6 percent to curtail domestic consumption. Despite its small size, the Austin Seven continued to be the most popular British export in Western

[130]Wyatt, *The Austin: 1905–1952*, p. 240.
[131]Tolliday, "High Tide and After."
[132]Extract from the Minutes of the First Meeting of the National Advisory Council for the Motor Manufacturing Industry, 30 April 1946, BT 64/2898, PRO. See also Dunnett, *Decline of the British Motor Industry*, p. 46.

Europe and North America.[133] Government attempts to influence producers to build larger cars failed, because British producers foresaw continued inelastic global demand.

Government officials, especially at the Treasury, also sought to standardize British production, because they realized that future competitors (like the American firms) would be more price-competitive than British firms that manufactured a multitude of models in small numbers. Standardization and rationalization were seen as two related methods of achieving greater exports.[134] Discussion of possible mergers abounded. Smaller firms felt threatened by the discussion of consolidation, and manufacturers also saw government support for this policy as an insidious step toward nationalization. Executives such as Lord, the Rootes brothers, Patrick Hennessy, and C. J. Bartlett (chair of Vauxhall) responded that the best thing politicians could do to encourage competitiveness was to repair Britain's roads, provide fiscal policies that encouraged growth, and remove such barriers to home sales as the rationing of petrol and the maintenance of purchase taxes. They felt that increased economies of scale would be achieved through enlarged domestic sales. Cheaper costs through increased production for the home market would reduce prices—thereby stimulating the international competitiveness of British firms. Foreign sales would allow them to increase volume and further reduce domestic prices. However, in what amounted to a contradiction of this position, other manufacturers said they could never compete with American firms in terms of price and thought that British firms should concentrate on production of high-quality, highly specialized vehicles of great technical merit.[135]

Government activity was again confined to discussion, fiscal measures, and some gentle prodding, and even these mild activities led to accusations of "totalitarian-style intervention" by the manufacturers. The industrialists' fear of the new Labour government was so great that the slightest sign of direct intervention led to hysterical claims about the Soviet model being assimilated in Britain. Nevertheless, both sides remained passive. Contrary to specified goals, government policy ensured neither rationalization of the number of models nor consolidation of the number of producers. No voluntary changes could take

[133]Dunnett, *Decline of the British Motor Industry*, p. 48. Early sales of Austins to the United States actually lost money for the company but earned valuable currency. See Turner, *The Leyland Papers*, p. 94.

[134]See letter, E. B. Bowyer to Sir B. Gilbert, HM Treasury, 18 April 1946, Ministry of Supply 14/357, PRO; and memo, Porgent to H. A. R. Binney, "The Motor Vehicle Industry; Note by the Board of Trade," 10 November 1945, BT 64/2898, PRO.

[135]See "Automobile Exports and Sir Stafford Cripps," *The Motor*, 28 November 1945, p. 322.

place as long as the government's policy emphasizing exports guaranteed that every firm could sell every car it produced, regardless of quality. Furthermore, limits on the availability of raw materials discouraged firms from pursuing takeovers, which in the absence of a discriminatory allocation of resources would not facilitate significant growth.[136] Mergers would neither guarantee greater efficiency nor improve collective profits; the combined aggregate would be no greater than the sum of its parts. In the absence of coercion or discrimination, then, all government policies relating to rationalization, standardization, consolidation, nationalization, and product design therefore failed to achieve their objectives.

Never was the disparity between the objectives of the first postwar government and its refusal to implement policies to achieve its goals more apparent than in the behavior of government officials concerning the Politics and Economic Planning (PEP) report on the automobile industry. The manufacturers feared that the report, conducted by an independent body but sponsored by the government, would recommend nationalization and they insisted that the objectives of the PEP group were sinister.[137] In an effort to subdue growing hysteria, Ministry of Supply officials said the government would dissociate itself from the report if manufacturers did not like the advanced copy of the report's recommendations.[138] The manufacturers were still not pacified, and so, before reading even a draft of the report, Ministry of Supply officials said they would withdraw all further government grants from the PEP group. Furthermore, the civil servants stated that their support or rejection of the report would depend upon manufacturers' responses.[139] These concessions quelled immediate objections, and when the manufacturers finally read a draft of the report and identified problems, the government delayed publication.[140] The government invited the manufacturers to rewrite the report themselves.[141] Disgruntled members of the PEP group were forced to accede to the demand that substantial revisions be made to the final draft.[142] The most influential industry representative in the redrafting

[136]For supporting evidence see Dunnett, *Decline of the British Motor Industry,* p. 49.
[137]Letter, Sir George Turner to Second Secretary (Ministry of Supply), 29 May 1947, Ministry of Supply 14/330, PRO.
[138]Memo, "PEP Engineering Enquiry," 31 May 1948, Ministry of Supply 14/330, PRO.
[139]PS/Secondary Secretary, "PEP Engineering Enquiry: Preliminary Draft on Motor Vehicle Industry," Ministry of Supply 14/330, PRO.
[140]"Notes on the Eighteenth Meeting of the PEP Engineering Group," 31 May 1948, Ministry of Supply 14/330, PRO.
[141]Letter, Turner, Deputy Secretary, to Second Secretary (Ministry of Supply), 1 June 1948, Ministry of Supply 14/330, PRO.
[142]Letter, A. K. Cairncross (chairman of the PEP Engineering Group) to Gresham

was Hennessy, managing director of Ford.[143] And so the managing director of a foreign multinational became the most influential figure in redesigning a landmark report about the future of the British automobile industry.

Many of the themes of government policy influenced developments at Austin between 1945 and 1948. Lord was attentive to the needs voiced by government despite his public disagreements, an attitude different from some of his contemporaries who chose to ignore the government's most urgent requests.

Austin embarked on a massive recapitalization. Some Longbridge workers, fearing for their jobs, resisted increased automation. The most resolute resistance came in 1948, when Lord's attempt to introduce new spindle cutters, which would improve production by 140 percent, led to a widespread strike.[144] The company's primary goal was to maximize dollar exports, and in 1947, to enhance sales in North America, the company formed subsidiaries in both the United States and Canada.[145] Policies emphasizing expansion, automation, and exports proved fruitful. Austin profits were far greater than those of its traditional rival, Morris, in 1947 and 1948, and the company was the leading British seller of cars by 1948.[146] Austin even overcame the debilitating effects of steel and coal shortages that had shut the Longbridge plant in February 1947. Lord, in what had now become a typical response, provocatively blamed shortages on shop stewards, the Labour government, and fears about impending nationalization. The firm enjoyed a sales boom in the North American market as the new A40 replaced three earlier models in a move toward greater rationalization. Production expanded to 62,544 cars in 1947, with a slight majority being exported. By June 1948 Austin had exported over 100,000 autos in the postwar period and, that year, exported 60 percent of production. As the firm's sales grew, so did profits and dividends. The shareholders, whose welfare had been neglected between 1939 and 1945, were now handsomely rewarded. Company dividends reached 20 percent in 1946 and were increased to 40 percent in 1948.[147] Lord then agreed to a request by the board of the Federation of British Industry (FBI) that dividends not be raised further in the short term.[148]

Cooke (secretary of SMMT), 8 June 1948, Ministry of Supply 14/330, PRO.

[143]"Notes on the Eighteenth Meeting of the PEP Engineering Group," 31 May 1948, Ministry of Supply 14/330, PRO.

[144]Dunnett, *Decline of the British Motor Industry*, p. 54.

[145]See "Austin Minute Book," 9 October 1947, p. 1761.

[146]Turner, *The Leyland Papers*, p. 94.

[147]Wyatt, *The Austin: 1905–1952*, pp. 243, 246.

[148]"Austin Minute Book," 28 April 1948, p. 1785.

Why did British automobile companies award such large dividends in the postwar period? The 40 percent awarded by Austin was relatively small; Morris dividends peaked at 64 percent. The answer lies in three contributory factors. The first was the belief that nationalization was impending. The directors rationally felt that, if companies were to be nationalized, the shareholders should get as much as possible before the government seized control. They were certain the government would not pay shareholders a market price for their shares. A second, related factor was that the larger British-owned producers—Austin, Morris, Standard, and Rootes—were all managed either by people who held a substantial number of shares in the company for which they worked or by people who owned the company outright. This generalization certainly applied at Austin, where Lord owned at least 80,000 ordinary shares. If the company was about to be nationalized, it was in their personal interest, as well as in that of their shareholders, to maximize dividend payments. Yet American-owned subsidiaries paid relatively modest dividends, partially because Ford and Vauxhall did not face the prospect of nationalization.[149] Relatively small dividend payments gave the American multinational firms more cash to finance recapitalization in the mid-1950s.

A third factor that explains high dividend payments was the need to attract new investment. The characteristics of the capital market in liberal states, John Zysman indicates, require companies to attract long-term financing through shareholder investment in company stock rather than borrow from financial institutions.[150] It was easier for Austin directors to offer high dividends as an incentive and regularly to issue new shares for public purchase to finance their investment program than to seek financing from capital markets. This process, once instituted, created a vicious circle: higher costs required more financing, which required more shares be sold; the sale of shares necessitated higher dividend payments, which raised costs. Dividend rates could not be dropped because that would deter new investors, leaving the company short of investment capital. But in 1950, as the threat of nationalization receded with the prospective electoral defeat of the Labour government, so coincidentally did the level of dividend payments at Austin.[151]

Between 1948 and 1950 Austin continued to be the leading, and most profitable, British-owned auto producer. The possibility of a merger between Austin and Morris was broached for the first time in

---

[149]Ibid., p. 521.

[150]John Zysman, *Governments, Markets, and Growth: Financial Systems and the Politics of Industrial Change* (Ithaca: Cornell University Press, 1983), pp. 70–71.

[151]Wyatt, *The Austin: 1905–1952*, p. 253.

1948.[152] Lord overcame his antipathy to his former boss at Morris primarily because he saw merger as a way to satisfy the Labour government's desire for greater rationalization and consolidation—while avoiding nationalization. The first stage of the merger was to pool technical and marketing information and encourage joint research and development. However, the scheme was abruptly terminated when Morris refused to accept these terms. The government's primary response was to supply an annual grant for a new research association, to provide the industry with research and testing facilities. Use of this facility was extended to all producers in Britain, including the American multinationals.[153]

The end of postwar austerity failed to provide British industry with the greater availability of raw materials it, and the public, anticipated. By 1950 the war in Korea was emphasizing a national rearmament program, increasing the scarcity of steel and carbon alloys.[154] As early as 1948 the government had raised the industry's aggregate target for exports to 75 percent, and Ministry of Supply officials had indicated for the first time that steel allocation might be influenced by export record. George Strauss, a Ministry of Supply official, said it was only fair to reward those who vigorously pursued government policy but added that firms not primarily structured for exports would be given special consideration.[155] The addendum stifled the emergence of a potentially discretionary policy and proved just the first among many, removing the threat that might have forced these smaller companies to adjust. The government thus subsidized inefficient firms, as Peter Dunnett points out, because their overriding concern was to be fair to smaller producers.[156] In a way characteristic of a liberal state, multiple exemptions ensured that losers were protected. However, by 1950 arms production became the government's major priority, and by statutory authorization the allocation of steel was cut to all auto producers by between 15 and 20 percent in 1951.[157] The state thereby avoided claims of discretionary behavior.[158]

The period between 1948 and 1952 marked the most direct form of

---

[152]See *Autocar*, 15 October 1948.

[153]See "OEEC Integration Study of the Motor Vehicle Industry: Reply from the UK to the Machinery Committee Questionnaire (Draft)," Ministry of Supply 14/340, PRO.

[154]Letter, H. Bailey, Engineering Division, to S. A. Davies, Regional Controller, Ministry of Supply, Ministry of Supply 10/326, PRO; and from McGregor, BT, to Robinson, Ministry of Supply, 16 August 1950, Ministry of Supply 14/332, PRO.

[155]See *Autocar*, 20 February 1948, p. 173.

[156]Dunnett, *Decline of the British Motor Industry*, p. 35.

[157]See "Iron and Steel Distribution Control," EID (51) 35, Ministry of Supply 14/331, PRO.

[158]Wyatt, *The Austin: 1905–1952*, pp. 255–56.

state intervention in the peacetime auto industry. Ministry of Supply officials became directly involved in the allocation of steel during those years. (Interestingly, the period bridges a change of governing party from Labour to Conservative.) The criteria for distribution were clearly specified to the manufacturers, and a fair and equal distribution of resources was emphasized at all times. The basis of allocation was:

1. Average production of each firm in the preceding year;
2. Export performance over that period;
3. Foreign currency earnings;
4. Distribution between home and foreign sales;
5. Future export contracts;
6. Contractual commitments to the defense program; and
7. Special consideration for smaller firms.[159]

Despite the initial fear that smaller firms would be squeezed out or some firms would be favored over others, ministerial officials handled allocations with a scrupulous concern to avoid maldistribution. The most significant factors in determining a firm's allocation were percentage of production exported to hard-currency markets and involvement in defense contracts. Perhaps the fairness of the civil servants is best indicated by the fact that everyone complained of unfair treatment.

Ministry officials, to avoid accusations of coercion, approached the auto companies' chief executives individually in an attempt to secure personal promises not to exceed home quotas. Such assurances were anticipated and considered a guarantee against excessive home sales, but no one was willing to make such a promise.[160]

Control over resources gave government officials potentially the most effective instrument by which to discriminate among producers. Such control would allow the government to achieve any specified goal—rationalization, standardization, consolidation, nationalization, even some form of discrimination against foreign multinationals—but officials made absolutely no attempt to enforce an allocative policy to achieve these goals. Despite warnings that companies transgressing the guidelines would be punished, no firm suffered from discriminatory distribution of resources.[161] Periodically, ministry officials reviewed the

[159]For two of many examples see "Period II—Steel Allocation," DGFV from W. M. Miller, Director Wheeled Vehicle Production (DWVP), 15 February 1952, Ministry of Supply 14/332, PRO; and "Minutes of the NACMMI Meeting," Twenty-third Meeting, 31 January 1951, Ministry of Supply 10/326, PRO.

[160]AS/E3, Ministry of Supply 14/332, PRO.

[161]See for example W. M. Miller, DWVP Adelphi, 13 December 1951. A major exception concerned Standard, which suffered one major cut in resources when it reneged on an agreement to export 9,000 Vanguards. See letter, Sir Eric Bowyer, Ministry of Supply, to Sir John Black, 5 August 1952; and Sir Eric Bowyer, Memo, "Note of Discussion with Sir John Black of Standard on 23 July," Ministry of Supply 14/332, PRO.

performance of each firm and, having done so, generally agreed to maintain the same allocation of sheet steel and alloys.[162] When more steel became available it was equally distributed, to avoid controversy, as in 1952 when Austin, Ford, and Vauxhall each received an additional 5,000 tons.[163]

One interesting exchange provides an insight into government priorities. Hennessy of Ford wrote to Archibald Rowlands, head of the Ministry of Supply, complaining that Ford had not received a full allocation of steel according to the government's stated formula and inquiring whether Austin had been allocated extra materials at Ford's expense.[164] Rowlands immediately responded, claiming that none of Ford's allocation had been given to anyone else.[165] The following year Hennessy again wrote to Rowlands complaining of an unfair allocation.[166] This time Rowlands, in an effort to appear fair, increased both Vauxhall's and Ford's allocation at the expense of domestic British producers.[167] Ministerial officials apologized to Ford's management and claimed a calculating error had been made.[168] Meanwhile Austin, the premier British exporter, had its allocation cut, which the government justified on the grounds that Austin had transgressed official guidelines by overselling in the domestic market.[169] However, the cut's purpose was to provide Ford with extra steel, and the government was indifferent to Ford's inferior export record.[170] This inferiority did not stop one Ministry of Supply official from claiming that "they have fought a good battle, and are still fighting one and it is not only on their own behalf but on behalf of the whole motor industry. The export performance of Ford has been so good so consistently that we look upon them as the 'old faithful.'"[171] (One might assume that any firm referred to as the "old faithful" was the national champion, not a foreign multinational.) This attitude toward Ford subsequently earned it the largest increase during the next allocation round.[172] On the rare

[162]See "Period II—Steel Allocation," DGFV from W. M. Miller, DWVP, Ministry of Supply 14/332, PRO.
[163]US (E), "Steel Allocation—Period 4/1952, The Motor Industry," Ministry of Supply 14/332, PRO.
[164]Letter, Hennessy to Rowlands, 28 May 1951, Ministry of Supply 14/332, PRO.
[165]Letter, Rowlands to Hennessy, n.d., Ministry of Supply 14/332, PRO.
[166]Letter, Hennessy to Rowlands, 31 March 1952, Ministry of Supply 14/332, PRO.
[167]Letter, Miller to Vauxhall and Ford (draft), n.d., Ministry of Supply 14/332, PRO.
[168]"Note of a Meeting Held in the Permanent Secretary's Room," 3:30 PM, 8 April 1952, Ministry of Supply 14/332, PRO.
[169]Miller, DWVP, 7 April 1952, Ministry of Supply 14/332, PRO.
[170]Letter, Rowlands to Hennessy (draft), 10 July 1952, Ministry of Supply 14/332, PRO.
[171]Miller, DWVP, "Steel Allocation—Period IV 1952," 28 July 1952, Ministry of Supply 14/332, PRO.
[172]Ibid.

occasion when government did favor one firm over its competitors, the firm it chose was a foreign multinational.

Throughout this period government officials were less sympathetic to Austin, which again produced record figures. With the manufacture of 142,723 cars and 23,000 commercial vehicles in 1950, Austin was the leading car producer in Britain, although Ford now produced the most vehicles. In the rearmament program Austin won a £1 million contract to supply a new field car, the FV 1800, and a contract to build a Rolls-Royce engine. In order to produce both, Austin leased back the Cofton Hackett plant from the government. Austin was once again a leading force in armaments, although military contracts were widely distributed to avoid accusations of government subsidization of any one company. Lord's pungent criticism of successive governments meant he was recognized for his efforts only belatedly, in 1954, despite his outstanding efforts to help the rearmament program.[173] The Austin chairman repeatedly claimed that his company had not received steel deliveries promised by the government, that official policies hindered freedom of competition and therefore the maximizing of production and sales.[174] At one point he even claimed that he had proof the Labour government had been selling scarce sheet steel to Renault to aid a French socialist company rather than supply British firms.[175]

The poor relationship between Lord and the officials of successive governments should not detract from the magnitude of Austin's efforts. Those same officials stressed that Austin was the company most willing to help fulfill defense orders, "showing a real zeal in helping," but these efforts did not affect allocation decisions.[176] For example, Austin applied to the Ministry of Supply for an extra 2,000 tons of steel so that it could produce the new A40 models for 1952. With the extra steel the company would not have to cease production of the old Seven model until reorganization of the new assembly process for the A40s was completed.[177] Ministry officials decided to allocate Austin an additional 1,000 tons to be used exclusively on the new project.[178] However, they later reneged on this promise and informed Austin it could not have the additional tonnage even though work on the scheme was

[173]Wyatt, *The Austin: 1905–1952*, pp. 253–54.
[174]See *Autocar*, 24 April 1950.
[175]See *Autocar*, "Fresh Air Doctor," 25 November 1949.
[176]Memo, W. M. Miller, DWVP, to DGFV, 3 September 1951, Ministry of Supply 10/326, PRO.
[177]See letter, Harriman, Deputy Managing Director, to L. Robinson, Undersecretary, Engineering Industry Division, Ministry of Supply, 16 August 1951, Ministry of Supply, 14/331, PRO.
[178]Minute Sheet E 109, F. F. D. Ward, 18 August 1951, Ministry of Supply 14/331, PRO.

well advanced. Austin officials, pointing to the success of the Seven and the good record of the company, were emphatic that the introduction of the new A40 was contingent on receiving the extra steel.[179] W. M. Miller, a Ministry of Supply official, responded that the request was hopeless and suggested that Austin adjust to the new situation.[180] A new version of the most popular model produced by the most successful indigenous British firm was therefore delayed for one year until more steel became available and ministerial officials felt they had a surplus of steel and carbon. By that time the project had expanded to include the marketing of the new model by Nash in North America—but a lucrative opportunity had been missed.[181]

In 1951, encouraged by the government, discussions returned to a possible merger between Austin and Morris, and a provisional agreement was reached in December to form the British Motor Corporation (BMC) in 1952. Under a complicated settlement, shareholders exchanged their preferred or ordinary stocks in Austin or Morris for corresponding stocks in the new company. Lord felt this new company would increase standardization and therefore achieve significant economies of scale. The merger looked impressive on paper as BMC instantly became the fourth-largest producer in the world with 42,000 employees. However, BMC effectively became only a holding company in a set-up described by Richard Wyatt as suited to please accountants more than engineers.[182] The decision by both managements to form BMC as a public company was heavily influenced by the common feeling that this consolidation would subvert further attempts at government intervention.

The government considered the deal a defensive merger designed to protect the British market from a further growth in imports. That is all the merger achieved, as BMC's share of the British market stagnated at approximately 40 percent for the rest of the decade. Although the new company was the largest producer in Britain, the merger had no positive effects on rationalization, standardization, or consolidation. The total capacity of BMC in 1952 was 300,000 units, but both Austin and Morris continued to compete directly, offering rival models in each class.[183] Their model ranges had discernibly different characteristics, Austin cars being designed to be more technically advanced than Mor-

[179]DGVF Minute Sheet, E 105, Ministry of Supply 14/331, PRO.
[180]W. M. Miller, DWVP, to DGFV, 3 September 1951, Ministry of Supply 10/326, PRO.
[181]"Note of a Meeting Held in the Permanent Secretary's Room," 31 July 1952, Ministry of Supply 14/332, PRO.
[182]Wyatt, *The Austin: 1905–1952*, p. 260. For details of the deal see Turner, *The Leyland Papers*, p. 98.
[183]Williams, Williams, and Thomas, *Why Are the British Bad at Manufacturing?* p. 54.

ris products.[184] Both firms retained their distributor and dealer networks, and so BMC had a total of 400 distributorships and 4,500 dealers.[185] The company could initially afford this inefficient structure in a seller's market, but the merger had a disappointing effect on long-term productivity and profits.[186] BMC's profit per vehicle averaged out at £40 a car in financial year 1952/53 but remained the same in 1959/60, and by the early 1960s the profit per car had halved.[187]

Each company retained the same structure and kept its own company records, although they paid a joint dividend. It took until 1958 before the financial structure of the holding company was simplified so that all preferred debenture holders had their assets converted into ordinary shares.[188] In this federal structure each company kept separate control over foreign subsidiaries. One key to BMC's problems concerning efficiency was that the company took as its model General Motors, with its decentralized power structure, dealership networks, and production locations. However, BMC sold only a small fraction of the vehicles sold by even one General Motors division.[189]

Between 1952 and 1956 Lord spend £25 million on expanding and modernizing the Longbridge plant, revolutionizing the production process. New models were introduced, the most notable success being the Mini in 1959. After a brief period Lord replaced the retiring Nuffield as chair of BMC. Lord strove to make improvements at both Austin and Morris, but the lack of consolidation of the two firms, and the many problems caused at Longbridge by the merger, frustrated his efforts. This pattern has prompted Peter Dunnett to suggest that the result of BMC was that Austin was injected with the inefficiency from which Morris suffered.[190] BMC production expanded, but a multiplicity of models made the company no more efficient. Profits fluctuated wildly as the new company's expansion was heavily influenced by the Conservative government's "stop-go" economic policies of the 1950s. The company was persuaded by the Conservative government, as part of its regional policy, to locate new plants at uneconomic sites in traditionally militant areas.[191] The lack of economic rationality in the selection of sites led to a proliferation of plants performing similar

[184]Turner, *The Leyland Papers*, p. 191.

[185]Rhys, *Motor Industry: An Economic Survey*, p. 339.

[186]See Turner, *The Leyland Papers*, p. 97; and Williams, Williams, and Thomas, *Why Are the British Bad at Manufacturing?* p. 219.

[187]Williams, Williams, and Thomas, *Why Are the British Bad at Manufacturing?* p. 225.

[188]"Austin Minute Book," 16 December 1958, p. 2151.

[189]Jeff Daniels, *British Leyland: The Truth about the Cars* (London: Osprey, 1980), p. 19.

[190]Dunnett, *Decline of the British Motor Industry*, p. 101.

[191]Ibid., pp. 62–65, 81–85. For the best example see "BMC Expansion," *The Motor*, 27 January 1960, p. 895.

functions and further contributed to BMC's poor productivity figures.[192] The adverse influence of this economically irrational regional
policy can be demonstrated by two examples. The first was a plant built
in South Wales next to a steel plant, for the purpose of producing Land
Rovers that were made out of aluminum. Meanwhile, in the second
instance, a car plant that needed steel was built next to an aluminum
plant in the West Midlands.[193] Even this proliferation of plants did not
reduce the percentage of "bought-out" components; indeed, the rep-
lication across plants was so great that the proportion of bought-out
components rose to 70 percent.[194] By the mid-1960s the capacity of the
company exceeded one million cars a year, but the largest plant still
could produce not more than 100,000. The largest run for any model
produced by BMC was for the Mini—whose production of 100,000 was
divided among four plants, thus negating any chance of approaching
optimum economies of scale.

The aggregate problems of the holding company had their effects on
Longbridge. Fluctuating profits meant that the recapitalization of
Longbridge in the 1950s had to be financed by external borrowing.[195]
The company's attempt to increase automation served only to bring it
into conflict with labor over the resulting redundancies and the dis-
tribution of benefits.[196]

Unlike workers at Standard and Rootes, Austin workers remained
poorly organized until the late 1950s, when unions finally began to
make inroads.[197] An indicator of fragmentation was the presence of
over forty unions at Longbridge during the 1950s, causing numerous
disruptive strikes over such issues as relative pay scales in different
parts of BMC.[198] Lord's autocratic style in dealing with union representatives, and his unceasingly critical comments about them in public,
exacerbated the problem. In the early 1950s three major redundancy
disputes pitted shop stewards against management and resulted in the
establishment of a shop stewards' committee at Longbridge. Of numerous conflicts one of the most embittering occurred in 1953 over the
sacking of a senior shop steward, John McHugh, which led to a strike
by NUVB workers that lasted eleven weeks. Labor conclusively lost, and
most of the NUVB shop stewards were fired for their involvement. The
strike heightened tension not only between labor and management but

[192]See "Microscope for Americans," *Autocar*, 23 January 1957, p. 996.
[193]Rhys, *Motor Industry: An Economic Survey*, p. 48.
[194]Ibid., p. 60.
[195]ibid., p. 369.
[196]*The Clarion*, January–February 1957.
[197]Tolliday, "High Tide and After."
[198]For figures on unions see Tough, "Richard (Dick) Etheridge." For examples see *The Clarion*, March–April 1957.

also between the NUVB and other unions which, NUVB officials felt, had not provided wholehearted support during the conflict.[199]

The BMC Joint Shop Stewards Committee was formed in 1956. The first major conflict it faced was a BMC management decision in June to immediately dismiss 6,000 people (including 3,000 from Longbridge), 12.5 percent of the labor force, because of falling demand. The fifteen major unions at BMC healed their rifts and, after unsuccessfully appealing to the company to reconsider, decided to strike. By the third day of the strike production at Longbridge had ceased. After one week the annual holiday fortnight intervened, although a picket of the plant continued. The strike ended on the last day of the holiday, with an agreement that secured compensation for those made redundant and a management promise that labor leaders would be consulted over future employment decisions.[200]

By the end of the 1950s the fabric of hitherto stable labor relations at Longbridge had been torn apart. The propensity toward militancy of a virtually 100 percent unionized labor force was encouraged by Lord's high-handedness. Unofficial strikes, led by shop stewards, became endemic.[201] The end of the decade was marked by a succession of lockouts and walkouts that culminated in a strike by 13,000 workers that brought the company to a standstill in January 1960.[202]

Many of these conflicts were precipitated by external factors that threatened the prosperity of the labor force, particularly the new financial and organizational constraints imposed on Longbridge as part of a larger complex. Additionally, seemingly inexhaustible home demand was finally satiated, and formerly secure foreign markets were being overrun by renewed German, Italian, French, and even American competition—worsening BMC's financial position and increasing tensions at BMC. These conflicts prompted many analysts to blame events at Longbridge and Cowley, and the subsequent decline of BMC, on the labor force. However, conflicts at Longbridge seem to have been stimulated by external factors—such as new financial constraints, disparities in payments between workers across plants, and attempts to reduce the size of the Longbridge labor force—designed to pay for BMC's expansion into new plants. One careful analysis concludes that workers and their union representatives were not really villains; rather, they were used as scapegoats.[203]

[199]Tough, "Richard (Dick) Etheridge," pp. 7–8.
[200]Ibid., pp. 15–16.
[201]Ibid, p. 17.
[202]See BMC Joint Shop Stewards Committee Minutes of the Meeting of 17 April 1959, File 2, MSS 228, "Misc," MRC. For the January 1960 strike see "Minutes of the Standing Orders Committee," 30 January 1960, File 2, MSS 228, "Misc," MRC.
[203]Williams, Williams, and Thomas, *Why Are the British Bad at Manufacturing?* p. 110.

POSTWAR STATE-FIRM RELATIONS AT AUSTIN

The postwar relationship between company executives and representatives of the Ministry of Labour, the Ministry of Supply, and the Board of Trade became increasingly hostile. Leonard Lord's criticism of government policy on exports, resource allocation, and rearmament was as outspoken as it was unrelenting. The formal response of officials was detachment and indifference; their informal response was reflected in the time Lord had to wait to receive formal honors.

The ambivalent relationship between Austin and the government was reflected in Lord's zealous adherence to government policies even where no statutory limits existed. Austin surpassed government export targets long before the "carrot and stick" incentive system for steel allocation became an issue in the late 1940s. Austin again accepted the role of a major armaments producer during the Korean War, and responded positively to government encouragement to merge with Morris despite his dislike of Nuffield, who was to be his boss, and his suspicions about the economic rationality of the scheme. Once Lord became chair of BMC he strove to make the company a success, and indeed, the company enjoyed its most successful years before his retirement in 1961.

While recognizing Austin's contribution to national objectives, British governments did nothing to help Austin achieve its economic goals. Successive governments relied heavily on macro-level policies that helped them avoid even the possibility of discriminating between firms. When two successive British governments, of opposing political persuasions, were finally given the perfect discriminatory instrument—to secure the future of Austin or any other domestically owned firm— they chose consciously to avoid discriminating against the American multinationals. Austin's resource allocation was even cut to placate the demands of Ford's management.

The government's final contribution to Austin's decline encompasses both actively and passively "violent" aspects of liberal state policies. First, one government coaxed and cajoled Austin into a marriage with Morris. Then, successive governments throughout the 1950s did nothing to help the new company. Instead, they contributed to its decline by insisting that expansion be confined to those areas prescribed under a new regional policy. Not until the 1960s would a Labour government take a more benevolent, active interest in BMC's welfare, by which time its decline was too advanced to be easily reversed.

In the postwar period industrial relations, which had worsened considerably during the war, took on many of the characteristics familiar in stereotypical depictions of British industrial relations. Strikes became more regular, more fragmented, and therefore more disorderly. Nevertheless, one cannot trace a causal relationship between the worsening of industrial relations and the company's decline. The company's decline clearly predated the development of more hostile and disjointed forms of industrial militancy. The extensive disruptions of production that originated during the war developed into outright hostility only during the 1950s. If the case of Austin does point to a causal relationship, then it may support claims that the economic decline of the company was *partially* responsible for the onset of greater militancy. But both the company's decline and its labor militancy can be explained by a third factor—state policies dating from the beginning of the war. State policies contributed to an environment where the politics of decline could fester. Furthermore, state politics designed to placate labor during the war had encouraged labor to make demands and management to accede to them. Similar patterns are discernible in the postwar period. Both the government's policy of maximizing car exports to bolster foreign earnings and the importance attached by government officials to rearmament encouraged similar responses from labor and management. Labor militancy was therefore, in large part, attributable to an opportunity framework developed by successive government policies.

CHAPTER SEVEN

Fascism's Critical Divide

So far I have focused on four specific firms in the British and German auto industries. In this chapter I broaden the scope of analysis. I first expand my argument to generalize about all major auto producers in Germany and Britain. I then examine three countries ruled by fascist regimes to see if their states' policies toward the automobile industry between the 1930s and 1960s reflect a pattern comparable to that found in Germany.

GERMANY

Between the 1930s and the 1960s there were six major producers in Germany: Bavarian Motor Works (BMW), Borgward, Daimler-Benz, Fordwerke, Opel, and Volkswagen–Auto Union–NSU. These firms exemplify different forms of ownership, technological production processes, and, most important, relations with the German state. Together they accounted for an overwhelming percentage of production and therefore provide a reasonable basis for generalization about the industry's development.

In the prewar period the German automobile industry was dominated by Opel. General Motors purchased a controlling interest in the firm in 1928. After 1933, in an insulated internal market protected by tariffs and quotas, Opel repeatedly accounted for over 50 percent of car sales.[1] With the exception of Ford, the remainder of the German

---

[1]See "Organizational and Management Basic Data Book: Ford of Germany," Cologne, Germany, Fordwerke AG 1951–1952, AR-75-63-430:93, Ford Industrial Archives. In the late 1920s Ford and General Motors occupied positions in the German market opposite to those they held in the English market where Ford was a more significant producer and GM's subsidiary was of lesser importance.

auto industry was divided between small German producers such as Wanderer, Horch, Audiwerke, and Zschopauer (which all merged in 1932 to form Auto-Union) that were trying to institute mass production principles and specialist producers such as Daimler-Benz and BMW, which were struggling to survive as they sought to create market niches and gain lucrative armaments contracts. By 1933, therefore, the structure of the market resembled Britain's. In each country there was one large American-owned subsidiary, one small but dynamic American-owned subsidiary, and many relatively small, domestically owned firms—although in 1933, British Ford had yet to realize its full potential as its Dagenham plant was then only recently completed.

Opel sustained its market dominance despite the onset of the Depression in the early 1930s. The new Nazi regime's recognition of Opel's significance as a manufacturer was reflected in its initially tolerant treatment of the company. Market strength allowed Opel to dictate the terms of standardization as the Nazis sought a pragmatic means of rapidly rationalizing the industry.[2] Opel offered the cheapest German car on the market, at between RM1,450 and RM1,650, and sold about 150,000 units per annum in this price range. It therefore seemed the most likely firm to achieve Hitler's public goal of producing a car that could be sold for RM1,000. Opel's yearly capacity exceeded 295,000 units (the Russelheim plant alone produced 140,577 units in 1938) and the company's capitalization exceeded RM60 million compared, for instance, to Ford's RM32 million.[3]

By 1935 Opel was the major trade supplier to the government, commanding over 42 percent of the domestic market for all vehicles.[4] Despite government-ordered price cuts, the company earned net profits in excess of RM35 million.[5] As a result of new legislation, Opel could not send its newly generated surplus capital abroad, and so profits from government contracts were reinvested at its German plants. This recapitalization achieved the Nazi authorities' goal of further increasing Opel's capacity.[6] Opel, unlike Ford, had no problems being certified as a German undertaking, even though German ownership of Opel's shares was negligible compared to Ford's.[7] Subsidized by state

[2]See E. J. Palumbo, "Germany 1948: Economic and Political Review, Survey of German Vehicle Industry," Appendix Exhibit B, 15 April 1948, AR-75-63-430:86, Ford Industrial Archives, pp. 4–12.

[3]See ibid., p. 39.

[4]See "The Importance of German Passenger Cars and Truck Factories, 1935," Accession 38, Box 33, Edison Institute, Dearborn, Mich.

[5]Letter, Diestel to Sorensen, 2 March 1936, Accession 38, Box 33, Edison Institute.

[6]Allan Nevins and Frank E. Hill, *Ford: Decline and Rebirth, 1933–1962* (New York: Scribner, 1962), p. 99.

[7]See Albert to Reichsverband der Automobilindustrie, 13 January 1936, Accession 38, Box 28, Edison Institute; Mira Wilkins and Frank E. Hill, *American Business Abroad* (Detroit: Wayne State University Press, 1964), p. 270.

aid, Opel was willing to undertake relatively risky and unrewarding ventures to maintain cordial relations. One example was an agreement signed between Opel and the government in 1938 to export cars to Britain at below German prices in order to secure valuable foreign currency.[8] As a result, Opel was responsible for over 50 percent of car exports and 24 percent of commercial vehicle exports.[9]

Yet this cordial relationship between Opel and Nazi officials depended on a coincidence of interests. Opel's involvement in the Volkswagen project was initially considered pivotal. But once Daimler-Benz and BMW executives convinced state officials that the project should be handled by the public rather than the private sector,[10] Opel lost influence and the firm began to be ostracized by competitors and ignored by the Nazis.[11] Nevertheless, Opel's management saw its best interest in maintaining as good a relationship with the Nazi government as possible and was eager to design and manufacture both military and nonmilitary orders for the state.[12] This superficially cooperative relationship was sustained until 1935 when Opel quarreled with the government over its demand that it site a new plant at Brandenburg, east of the Elbe. Opel's managers feared losing the plant in the event of war. They considered the site strategically vulnerable, with few geographical barriers to thwart invasion from the east; and it was isolated from large resource centers and from Opel's main Russelheim plant, two hundred miles away. Nevertheless, the Nazi authorities insisted the plant be built in Brandenburg at Opel's expense, consistent with their *Lebensraum* policy. Opel's fears were realized with the destruction of the plant and the loss of its contents to invading Soviet forces a decade later.[13]

[8]*Business Week,* 25 June 1938.

[9]Ministry of Economic Warfare, "Germany Motor Industry: A Summary," from 745015 RG 165, Regional File, 1933–44, Germany 4330, Box 1255, 14 October 1940, Bipartite Control Office (BICO) 45.I, Office of Military Government of the U.S. (OMGUS), Military Field Branch, National Archives and Records Administration, Washington, D.C.

[10]Letter, Franz Popp to Wilhelm Kissel, Archiv der Daimler-Benz AG, Bestand Kissel VII/5, Hamburger Stiftung Archive.

[11]See Albert Pietzsch, Präsident der Industrie und Handelskammer, München, Leiter der Reichswirtschaftskammer (president of the chamber of industry and trade in Munich and director of the Reich's chamber of economics) to Generaldirektor Popp of BMW, 2 June 1937. A second source is comments attributed by the influential Jacob Werlin to Hitler, that for a national works it would be better to exclude firms with an American orientation; "Besprechung am 21.7.1936 in RDA in der Volkswagen Angelegenheit," Hamburger Stiftung Archive. A letter written by Werlin to Popp on 31 May 1937 with the same theme is to be found in File 16, Volkswagen Popp, Archive of the Volkswagen Project, Bochum.

[12]Wilkins and Hill, *American Business Abroad,* p. 283.

[13]USSBS, Munitions Division, "German Motor Vehicle Industry Report," 3 November 1945, p. 6; OMGUS 451, Box 326, Military Field Branch, National Archives and Records Administration, Washington, D.C.

This issue proved contentious, but relations between firm and state worsened when Opel could no longer supply military trucks at the government's rapidly increasing rate of demand. They broke into open hostility when Opel failed to fulfill a government contract for 10,000 half-track vehicles and were aggravated by Fordwerke's subsequent successful completion of Opel's contract.[14] The firm that, for so long, had been compared unfavorably to Opel had proved more "cooperative" than Opel—a damning indictment in the eyes of the Nazi authorities. Opel's two largest plants, at Russelheim and Brandenburg, were seized by the state and integrated into the German war economy under the new management of Heinrich Nordhoff.[15] Although the treatment accorded to Opel in the opening years of the Third Reich differed drastically from Ford's, relationships with the state converged during the course of the war. At both firms indigenous management was replaced by political cadres, the hierarchical "leadership principle" was instituted, and the firms were reclassified as foreign property, making them subject to discriminatory measures. Neither was to get compensation from the Nazi authorities for war damages, even though Opel, unlike Fordwerke, had major plants destroyed.[16] As a result, Opel encountered numerous problems getting production restarted after the war, giving Fordwerke and Volkswagen a crucial advantage in those early years.[17] When Opel's production did recommence, the Allied government insisted that the firm concentrate exclusively on unsubsidized, loss-generating foreign sales, which denied Opel the capital for crucial reinvestment in a period of surplus demand.[18] The ravages of war combined with Nazi and Allied policies to leave Opel floundering behind its rivals. The situation grew worse. The company that had held 40–52 percent of the German market in the immediate prewar period had 19 percent in the late 1940s (Volkswagen's share then was 25 percent) and bottomed out at 11.7 percent in 1952.[19] When the Allied and embryonic Bonn governments refused to provide financial support comparable to that accorded Volkswagen, General Motors provided the funding to begin the reconstruction of Opel.[20] However, the vacuum created in the market by Opel's lost output had been filled by Volkswagen, and Opel never again approached its prewar market

[14]See "Report of the German Company" prepared by the Office of Lord Perry in "Historical Data" (A), CF, ID, Germany Wartime, Wilkins Personal File.
[15]Wilkins and Hill, *American Business Abroad,* p. 331.
[16]Ibid., p. 345; Palumbo, "Germany 1948," Ford Industrial Archives, p. 12.
[17]Wilkins and Hill, *American Business Abroad,* p. 346.
[18]G. S. Hibberson and A. T. Platt, "Fordwerke AG Cologne Audit Report August 1949," AR-83-69-891:4, Ford Industrial Archives, p. 55.
[19]"Organizational and Management Book."
[20]Wilkins and Hill, *American Business Abroad,* p. 391.

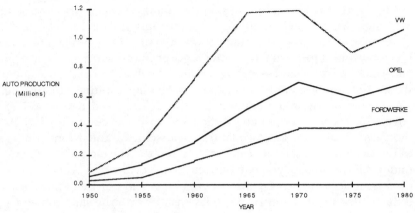

Figure 7.1. German auto production by company, 1945–1980

SOURCE: Motor Vehicles Manufacturers Association (MVMA), *World Motor Vehicle Data* (Detroit: MVMA, various years).

share—even trailing the formerly much smaller Fordwerke in the 1950s (see Figure 7.1).[21]

Opel's decline is also clarified by comparing Opel in Germany and Ford in Britain. On the eve of the Nazi seizure of power Opel dominated the German market, whereas Ford, with the completion of its huge Dagenham plant, was poised to assert such a position in the British. If anything, Opel was in a more powerful position than Ford. But by the early 1960s Ford in Britain had drawn far ahead of Opel in Germany in terms of profits, market share, and capitalization.[22]

Even this superficial description of events at Opel between 1933 and the late 1950s is indicative of the firm's precipitous decline. Opel's relationship with the Third Reich was contingent on a mutuality of interest that inevitably ended because of insatiable Nazi demands for military vehicles. Opel's inability to expand capacity signaled its shift from the core to the periphery among producers and, with it, the onset of discriminatory state policies that started its swift economic decline. For Opel, just like Ford, the nature of state-firm relations had a crucial effect on the company's prosperity in the postwar period.

Daimler-Benz, which is considered the oldest automobile company in the world and claims to have produced the first car ever built, is an

[21]Nevins and Hill, *Ford: Decline and Rebirth*, p. 402.
[22]Ibid., p. 412.

interesting contrast to Opel. Daimler-Benz has always specialized in large, expensive sedans that were ideal for the broad highways of Europe. But the company's postwar success has not always been indicative of its welfare. In the aftermath of World War I Daimler-Benz struggled in a market where there was little demand for luxury sedans and outdated designs. The struggling company was reliant on the financial assistance of the Deutsche Bank throughout the 1920s and early 1930s.[23] The bank was chaired by Emil Georg Von Stauß, who considered Daimler-Benz's capacity for military production critical to the eventual rejuvenation of Germany's armaments industry. Daimler-Benz's management approached government officials in the 1920s, suggesting defiance of the terms of the Versailles Treaty and recommencement of arms production, but these approaches were rejected.[24]

Daimler-Benz's senior managers, led by Wilhelm Kissel, were active supporters of the NSDAP in the early 1930s.[25] And with the Nazi accession, Daimler-Benz became influential in formulating state policy, as epitomized by their fomentation of the idea that Ford and Opel be excluded from the Volkswagen project.[26] The company became an able and willing military producer, which provided Daimler-Benz with a lucrative source of revenue when the Bank der Deutschen Luftfahrt subsidized the mass production of Messerschmidt engines.[27] Max Kruk and Gerold Lingnau's (company-sponsored) history of Daimler-Benz emphasizes state coercion—that the company was an unwilling partner to the state's demands.[28] Yet their own figures demonstrated how profitable were government contracts, which peaked in 1943, and alternative sources suggest that the company may have been a willing part-

---

[23]For the fiscal relationship between Daimler-Benz and the Deutsche Bank see Hans Pohl, Stephanie Habeth, and Beate Brüninghaus, *Die Daimler-Benz AG in den Jahren 1933 bis 1945* (Stuttgart: Zeitschrift für Unternehmensgeschichte, Franz Steiner Verlag, 1986). For the political implications of this relationship see Karl Heinz Roth, "Der Weg zum guten Stern des 'Dritten Reichs': Schlaglichter auf die Geschichte der Daimler-Benz AG und ihrer Vorläufer (1890–1945)," in *Das Daimler-Benz Buch: Ein Rüstungskonzern im Tausendjährigen Reich* (Nördlingen: Delphi Politik, 1986), pp. 28–40.
[24]Daimler-Benz officials explained that the economic health of their company was their dominant motive. See Kissel to Von Schleicher, 1925, Hamburger Stiftung Archives.
[25]See Karl Heinz Roth, "Der Weg zum guten Stern," pp. 71–103.
[26]See the exchange of letters between Popp of BMW and Kissel, Archiv der Daimler-Benz AG, Bestand Kissel VII/5, Hamburger Stiftung Archives.
[27]On Daimler-Benz's military aero-engines see OMGUS, Decartelization Branch, Economic Division, "The Automotive Industry of Germany," 31 December 1946, Box 479/775092, Automotive Industry Folder, Military Field Branch, National Archives and Records Administration, Washington, D.C., p. 3.
[28]Max Kruk and Gerold Lingnau, *100 Jahre Daimler-Benz: Das Unternehmen* (Mainz: Hase & Koehler Verlag, 1986), pp. 133–59.

ner.[29] Kruk and Lingnau explain the record growth in the size of the labor force to meet heightened demand by focusing on the employment of female workers as replacements.[30] However, Jorg Mettke offers substantial historical data to corroborate his claim that Daimler-Benz managers were keen to use slave labor.[31] Furthermore, he suggests that employment figures reached record levels while increasing numbers of Germans were being conscripted because voluntary labor was replaced not by female labor but by the systematic use of forced labor. His analysis explains how the company generated record employment levels and record production levels in a period of scarce labor and scarce raw materials. Daimler-Benz plants had two major types of slave laborers. Jews were worked to exhaustion and then shipped to concentration camps. Foreign workers were confined to the plant and paid less than Germans, their rate determined by whether they came from eastern or western Europe.[32]

Karl Heinz Roth's detailed, systematic study includes hundreds of pages of indictments leveled against Daimler-Benz regarding the use of slave labor.[33] He suggests that Daimler-Benz may have used as many as 50,000 slave laborers, in both the main and the dispersal plants—ten times as many as the company's sponsored historical study by Pohl, Habeth, and Brüninghaus concedes.[34] Data concerning the behavior of company officials toward slave laborers at Operation Goldfish, Daimler-Benz's largest dispersal plant, certainly provide incriminating evidence.[35] Company officials there recommended to Nazi officials toward the end of the war that workers should be killed when dispensible.[36]

Specific claims made by Mettke and Roth, such as those concerning the cooperative relationship in working laborers to death between Daimler-Benz's management and officials at concentration camps, have met with conspicuous silence from German company officials.[37] Mettke's and Roth's evidence suggests that Daimler-Benz fostered a close working relationship with the state, reflected in the company's

[29]Ibid., p. 324.

[30]For growth in employment see ibid. For the claim that so many replacements were women see, for example, p. 155.

[31]Jorg R. Mettke, "Die Herren nahmen nur die Kräftigsten," Der Spiegel, 7 April 1986, pp. 79–104.

[32]Ibid., p. 80. For recent corroboration, see Bernard Bellon, Mercedes in Peace and War (New York: Columbia University Press, 1990).

[33]Roth, "Der Weg zum guten Stern."

[34]Pohl et al., Die Daimler-Benz AG.

[35]See Rainer Fröbe, "Wie bei den alten Ägyptern: Die Verlegung des Daimler-Benz-Flugmotorenwerks Genshagen nach Obrigheim am Neckar 1944/45," in Roth, ed., Das Daimler-Benz Buch, pp. 452–53.

[36]Mettke, "Die Herren nahmen nur die Kräftigsten."

[37]Ibid., p. 80.

influence over the treatment of other firms, willingness to pursue state goals in the armaments industry, and treatment of foreign labor. Claims that company policies were pursued as a result of state coercion appear unlikely in the face of extensive evidence to the contrary.

At the end of the war Daimler-Benz was not as fortunate as Volkswagen. Much of its property was destroyed by strategic bombing.[38] The company received a further blow when its owner, Friedrich Flick, was convicted as a war criminal in 1947 for having been a member of Hitler's elite as owner of the huge Flick armaments combine. An avid proponent of fascism, Flick was convicted on two counts. First, he was held responsible for plundering large sections of the industrial wealth of Eastern European and domestic Jewry, backed by the Nazi state, and then destroying that property when the regime's downfall became inevitable. He was also convicted of enthusiastically using slave labor at his plants.[39] His combine was seized under Allied law and dismantled. Flick himself was stripped of all his property and sentenced to seven years' imprisonment. The new Bonn government, however, rehabilitated Flick at the first opportunity. The War Crimes Court's sentence was flagrantly ignored: he served only three years in prison, and on his release in 1950 the government returned much of his property to him, including his 39 percent holding in Daimler-Benz—which restored him to his position as the firm's dominant shareholder.[40]

With his renewed position and wealth Flick sought to rebuild Daimler-Benz in the Bonn Republic, primarily on the basis of production at the large Stuttgart plant. The firm relied on the company's traditional lines—expensive, luxury sedans—and a strategy of export-led growth. As a core firm, Daimler-Benz had privileged access to state officials. Indeed, apart from Volkswagen, Daimler-Benz appears to have been the only auto firm whose executives had regular, formal contact with government officials to discuss company policies, making a collusive relationship more plausible.[41] Similarly, Daimler-Benz officials enjoyed an intimate relationship with leaders of the CDU, who were influential policy makers as the dominant partners in the governing coalition.[42] The company entered a variety of patent, research, marketing, and

[38]See "Report on the Visit to Daimler-Benz AG at Stuttgart-Untertürkheim," p. 28, BIOS Final Report 35, BIOS B, Box 1.
[39]See Klaus Drobisch, "Flick und die Nazis," in *Zeitschrift für Geschichtswissenschaft,* 14 (1966), pp. 378–97; *New York Times,* 12 April 1958.
[40]See *New York Times,* 15 January 1975.
[41]The minutes of these meetings are extensive. Formal records are in the Bundesarchiv, Koblenz. For just one example see Pollak, "Besuch des Herrn Dr. Könecke beim Herrn Minister," 28 May 1957, B102/5196, Bundesarchiv.
[42]Aline Kuntz, " Conservatives in Crisis: The Bavarian Christian Social Union and the Ideology of Antimodernism" (diss., Cornell University, 1987), pp. 198ff.

selling agreements with other core firms, encouraged by the new German government, in order to protect itself and its partners from competitive American subsidiaries. What followed, beginning in the 1950s, was a systematic attempt to tie together core German firms in a network of agreements and mergers that would guarantee their corporate independence from economic interests abroad and their economic supremacy over foreign subsidiaries at home. Daimler-Benz and Volkswagen, supported by both government and the large German banks, were the two pivotal firms in this strategy.

The integrated network of core German producers began with Daimler-Benz's merger with the ailing Auto-Union in 1958. The move was justified on the grounds that the enlarged company would be better prepared for the heightened competition stimulated by the European Economic Community, even though Daimler-Benz was a niche producer with no direct competitor.[43] Unfortunately for Daimler-Benz the merger was followed by media exposure that members of the company's management, including managing director Fritz Könecke, were bribing high-ranking government officials, among them Konrad Adenauer's personal secretary Hans Kilb, who received company cars in exchange for government assistance in increasing foreign orders. Because of the publicity surrounding the case charges had to be brought against Daimler-Benz directors, and the subsequent investigation revealed the extent of the company's illicit involvement with government officials.[44] It appears that government involvement had two dimensions that gave the firm privileged access—a formal channel of communication through the ministries, and an informal one through the illicit payment of political appointees.

In the year following these revelations it became evident that BMW, because of incompetent postwar management and capital shortages, faced impending bankruptcy. Faced with liquidation or a foreign takeover, BMW's directors turned to Daimler-Benz in the hope the two companies could merge. BMW proposed a deal whereby a planned reduction in its basic capital, by writing off the company's losses at the expense of the shareholders, would allow Daimler-Benz to buy the new cheaper company with the assistance of the three major banks, forming an ownership consortium.[45] Daimler-Benz responded with a lower counteroffer that BMW rejected, and domestic ownership was threatened when the General Electric Company (GEC) of Britain made a takeover offer for BMW.[46] Daimler-Benz could not match GEC's offer,

[43]*New York Times,* 12 April 1958.
[44]*New York Times,* 15 November 1958.
[45]*New York Times,* 10 November 1959.
[46]*New York Times,* 12 December 1959.

but the CSU Bavarian state government temporarily purchased the company, justifying the action "out of local pride and concern for the company's 15,000 employees" although no evidence indicated that GEC would threaten local employment.[47] The Bavarian state government then orchestrated the purchase of BMW by the Augsburg-Nuremburg Machine Company (MAN), which made an offer identical to GEC's. Patriotic reasons supposedly tipped the balance in MAN's favor, with Bavarian CSU leader and federal defense minister Franz Josef Strauss exercising his influence as the chief negotiator with BMW on behalf of MAN.[48] After fifteen years of failures that had seen its market share slide to well below 2 percent, BMW started its rehabilitation with this purchase. Within two decades the company's position as a prosperous producer was established, its former difficulties forgotten in its boasts about a tradition of high-quality engineering.

Failing to secure BMW, Daimler-Benz then turned to trying to increase foreign sales and secure domestic market share through network agreements. Temporary agreements with Curtis-Wright to build jet engines and Studebaker to market Mercedes cars in the United States were complemented by a strategy designed to deny American firms a market share at home, where Daimler-Benz sold a controlling interest in Auto-Union to Volkswagen in 1963—giving the two companies a formal link.[49] The German government encouraged Volkswagen to assume full ownership of Auto-Union two years later.[50] However, to maintain the active cooperation between Daimler-Benz and Volkswagen, the government suggested that they pool patents and cooperate on basic research and development.[51] The integration of Auto-Union into the prosperous German core by merger was replicated in Volkswagen's purchase of NSU, to prevent FIAT or Honda from buying it and acquiring the revolutionary Wankel engine technology. Volkswagen subsequently merged its NSU subsidiary with Auto-Union to form Audi-NSU.

[47]*New York Times,* 21 February 1960.

[48]*New York Times,* 3 June 1960. Strauss repeatedly expressed dissatisfaction with Erhard's neoliberal economic policies. Strauss explicitly favored an activist state policy designed to mold industrial adjustment—a view that found support among factions of the CDU. For example, he later criticized the lack of decisive federal action in assisting the steel and coal industry and, with the backing of the CSU, argued for an enlarged state role during the recession of the 1960s. See Kuntz, "Conservatives in Crisis," p. 200.

[49]See, for instance, *New York Times,* 30 December 1964, when this agreement between Daimler-Benz and American firms finally ended.

[50]George Heaton, "Government Structural Policies and the Automobile Industry," paper prepared for the International Automobile Program, International Policy Forum, Hakone, Japan, May 1982, p. 10.

[51]James Womack and Daniel Jones, "The Competitive Significance of Government Technology Policy in the Auto Sector," paper prepared for the International Automobile Program, International Policy Forum, Hakone, Japan, May 1982, p. 8.

As the network of relationships tightened between core firms, Volkswagen became more involved in bilateral agreements. Heinrich Nordhoff, general director at Volkswagen, was initially attracted to greater cooperation with other companies because he wanted to increase the competitive capacity of Volkswagen against the European subsidiaries of American firms. He hoped to pursue this goal by negotiating an agreement with other European mass producers to divide production between them, by class or size, in order to avoid their producing cars of similar designs. Each company would concentrate on one model and thereby increase competitiveness against the American subsidiaries. The proposed agreement fell apart when FIAT suggested that American subsidiaries should be *included* in any European cartel.[52] Unable to reach an agreement directed against American subsidiaries on a European-wide basis, Nordhoff turned to domestic core producers to organize a more modest, national response.

As Daimler-Benz's and Volkswagen's relationship grew stronger, it stimulated discussion concerning a possible merger, but the law that privatized Volkswagen in 1961 did not permit private institutions or organizations to hold stock in the firm—an impenetrable barrier. The two companies did, however, create a joint-stock company to fund the coordination of their research, development, and safety projects, in April 1966.[53] The agreement made provisions for the joint company to buy, sell, or manufacture parts for both companies in either firm's foreign plants or dealer agencies.[54] Nordhoff pointedly suggested that this agreement "was designed to counter the 'overpowering economic weight' of the big American car manufacturers"—leaving no doubt as to motivation.[55] This arrangement gave Volkswagen, Auto-Union, and Daimler-Benz the chance to compete head on against American subsidiaries in separate market segments free from substantial indigenous competition. Subsequent agreements between Volkswagen and Porsche (recall that Porsche's owner had designed the Volkswagen), and the merger of BMW and Glas, further tightened the binding relationship among core firms.[56]

The state's behavior toward two comparable auto firms, BMW and Borgward, in periods of crisis reveals much about the treatment accorded to core and peripheral firms. Historically, BMW's prefascist development shares many parallels with Daimler-Benz. The firm was considered a specialist producer (of luxury sedans and motor bikes), and like Daimler-Benz it suffered from the terms of the Versailles

[52]*New York Times*, 28 July 1964.
[53]*Wall Street Journal*, 11 and 25 April 1966.
[54]*Wall Street Journal*, 30 June 1966.
[55]*New York Times*, 30 June 1966.
[56]*New York Times*, 23 August 1966 and 10 January 1967.

Treaty that forbade armaments production in Germany. Like Daimler-Benz, BMW was financially supported by Von Stauß and the Deutsche Bank in the 1920s because it too was considered a crucial component of the "South German auto bloc" that had to be sustained to guarantee capacity for future military production. Like those at Daimler-Benz, BMW's officials also proved influential with government officials in deciding the terms of the Volkswagen project, managing director Franz Popp repeatedly claiming credit for the exclusion of American subsidiaries and as the originator of the idea that control should be shifted from a private consortium to the public sector through the DAF's assumption of ownership.[57] During the 1930s and 1940s BMW was an influential arms producer, and its plants were seized at the end of the war when they fell under American control. However, because the firm was under private ownership, the plants and their contents were returned to the owners and BMW renewed civilian production.

Unlike the success stories generally associated with the *Wirtschaftswunder* (economic miracle), the first fifteen postwar years of BMW were disastrous. A Daimler-Benz study of BMW suggested that the basis of BMW's problems lay in a combination of incompetent management decisions and a poor product line. As a result, by 1961 BMW held less than 2 percent of the market and faced liquidation before being rescued by the Bavarian state government. The company's postwar development was reversed from that point onward. By 1967 BMW's share of the domestic market had doubled. Motorcycle exports as a share of production totaled 79.9 percent, securing foreign capital under the company's new management strategy. In 1967, while the German auto industry was experiencing its first postwar recession, BMW proved highly profitable. Success provided the basis for expansion, and BMW purchased Glas GmbH that year to extend its range of products. BMW was helped in its purchase of Glas by both the federal government and the Bavarian state government; the latter provided DM50 million to finance BMW with the blessing of both IG Metall and the banks.[58] At a time of widespread accusations against German auto producers of price inflation, inefficient management, and lack of foresight, BMW took a major step to secure a prosperous future by acquiring abilities to expand into new market niches.[59]

[57]See letter, Franz Popp to Wilhelm Kissel, Archiv der Daimler-Benz AG, Bestand Kissel VII/5; Popp to the Reichsverband der deutschen Automobilindustrie, suggesting the RDA should oppose Ford's involvement, 8 May 1934, both in the Hamburger Stiftung Archives.
[58]*The Times* of London, 5 October 1967. In 1967 the company awarded shareholders a 12 percent dividend as registration of new BMW cars in Germany rose by 27 percent. Worker productivity and new dealerships rose, as did export turnover, which increased by DM30 million.
[59]*Hannoversche Presse* article quoted in bound volume of *German Tribune*, 1966, p. 12.

A contrasting example is Borgward, a Bremen-based company that shared important attributes with BMW and Daimler-Benz as a low-volume, specialist producer of quality vehicles. Borgward had three production plants—the Goliath, Lloyd, and Hansa works—under the personal ownership of Karl Borgward. It was founded in 1905, but Borgward purchased what was then known as the Hansa-Lloyd company in 1929. Borgward then grew from a components producer to an auto manufacturer that specialized in high-quality (if not high-priced) sedans and commercial vehicles. The company was noted for its innovative designs and engineering, reflected in models such as the Isabela.[60] Borgward himself was generally described as a benevolent autocrat, reminiscent of the *"Herr im Haus"* syndrome, a loner who maintained personal control of his firm but had limited contacts with other producers in the industry.

As the largest automobile producer in the industrial town of Bremen, Borgward was a principal local target for armaments production by the new Nazi regime in 1933. Before 1938 the company concentrated on large military vehicles such as the three-ton LKW, initially developed in 1937.[61] Karl Borgward was given the title of *Wehrwirtschaftsführer,* redundant because he was the sole owner of a firm with a traditionally hierarchical structure that employed approximately eight thousand people at the start of the war. This level of employment was maintained throughout the war, during which the firm produced over 9,000 heavy goods vehicles, and 16,000 armored cars and LKWs. Throughout the war Borgward employed one of the highest percentages of foreign laborers, forced laborers, and prisoners of war among any auto producer in Germany, peaking at a combined total of 65 percent.[62] Borgward appears to have been a pillar of the state armaments program during the Third Reich, and the company's subsequent liquidation appears anomalous to my theory.[63] In fact, however, Karl Borgward disdained involvement with the Nazi state and maintained only a peripheral role in the peak associations.

Toward the end of the war, Borgward's plants were largely destroyed by strategic bombing. Indeed, the case of Borgward could have supported the popular claim that German postwar prosperity could be

---

[60]Borgward produced fifty models in forty years—an engineering accomplishment but a sign of economic ineptitude. *The Times* of London, 7 February 1961.

[61]See Ministry of Economic Warfare, "German Motor Industry," p. 28.

[62]See Ulrich Kubisch and Volker Janssen, *Die Männer von Borgward—Ein Blick zurück auf Wirtschaftswunder: Werksalltag und einen Automythos* (Berlin: Elefanten, 1984), pp. 30–31.

[63]Ibid., p. 27. Unlike other industrialists, who used a lower percentage of forced laborers, Borgward was not imprisoned because the Allies considered his use of them involuntary and their treatment acceptable.

explained by the introduction of new capital.[64] By 1961 Borgward was the fifth-largest German auto company, commanding about 5 percent of production (about 100,000 cars per year) and employing 20,000 people—23 percent of the city of Bremen's total labor force.[65] Yet its incapacity to fully establish itself in a market niche or become a mass producer left it in a precarious position, with neither a stable market nor economies of scale.[66] Borgward ran into inevitable financial problems, but with surprising rapidity. In the space of a few months in 1961 the firm went from financially stable producer to bankruptcy, with debts of $27.5 million, as an industry-wide market downturn caught the company in a cash-flow crisis. Like BMW, Borgward faced the threat of imminent liquidation during the 1961 recession. Yet Borgward held over double the market share of BMW and, unlike BMW, had excellent production facilities. Its main flaw according to analysts was its poor management—a problem easily rectified under new ownership. Like BMW, the company could have been purchased and its management structure adjusted; unlike BMW, it already had technically sound products and could be restored to profitability sooner.

However, Borgward personally shared a different relationship with banks, federal government, and other auto producers, and his personal appeal for help was made in vain. His failure to sell the company intact to a private producer resulted in its purchase by the state of Bremen, just as the Bavarian state government had bought BMW, and Borgward was removed as the company's chief. The state reorganized the company at a cost of $15 million in public funds but wanted to relinquish ownership as soon as possible, either by selling it to new owners or by returning control to Borgward if he could find the capital.[67] However, no industry member, bank, or federal department was willing to assist Karl Borgward. The Bremen state government then appealed unsuccessfully to bankers, industrialists, and politicians to purchase the company because, as the smallest German state, Bremen did not have the resources to finance the company indefinitely. It had to let Borgward lapse into liquidation. Attempts to revive it by an association of customers, dealers, and employees failed, and the company was declared bankrupt. Some plants (such as the Lloyd plant) were sold off to save jobs, but thousands of workers were left unemployed and local debts to over one hundred fifty creditors amounted to over DM200 million, devastating the local economy.[68]

[64]*New York Times*, 29 July 1961.
[65]*The Times* of London, 14 June 1960 and 31 January 1961.
[66]Kubisch and Janssen, *Die Männer von Borgward*, p. 114.
[67]*The Times* of London, 18 February 1961. See also *New York Times*, 29 July 1961.
[68]*The Times* of London, 31 July 1961. For the company's decline see Kubisch and Janssen, *Die Männer von Borgward*, especially pp. 112–25.

If we examine the Borgward case in isolation, it seems simple enough to explain the decision of bankers, industrialists, and the federal government in purely economic terms. Borgward was a mismanaged company with outstanding debts and an ill-defined position in the market. It had a reasonable product but a limited market share and limited potential for growth. In social terms the demise of Borgward has been treated simply as an example of the failings of the *Sozialmarktwirtschaft* or, interpretatively, as an illustration of the preeminence of liberal principles.[69] Yet considered in comparative terms, an economic explanation is unable to explain why the federal government went to such great lengths to save BMW not only from liquidation but from foreign ownership and ignored Borgward, which was in a much better economic situation and whose closure would have dramatic local effects. A political explanation works better.

Borgward had served the German state as an armaments producer, but its owner, an authoritarian conservative, had refused to be integrated into the Nazi state apparatus and so had remained on the political periphery. Like many conservatives, Karl Borgward endured the Nazis but did not support them. He therefore never benefited, as part of the network of industrialists, bankers, and government officials, from the safety net for core producers. Edwin Hartrich develops this theme in his wider discussion of the postwar German banks' lack of support for maverick entrepreneurial capitalists. Borgward needed short-term loans to deal with a temporary cash shortage but was refused aid by the banks despite owning a company that was financially viable.[70] The federal government's considered neglect led to the downfall of Borgward despite the efforts of the state government of Bremen.[71] BMW was in a worse economic situation with inferior products and a smaller market share, and it posed employment problems that were not so pressing. But it had one crucial advantage: its officials had been part of the core of the German auto industry from the early days of the Third Reich and had cultivated a close relationship with politicians, bureaucrats, bankers, and industrialists. At its hour of greatest need BMW could rely on this network; Borgward could not.

This evidence leads me to conclude that in the early postwar period

[69]For these conflicting interpretations see Wilhelm Eberwein and Jochen Tholen, "Der Borgward-Konkurs im Jahre 1961," in *Arbeitsmarkt Bremen* (Bremen: Kooperation Universität, Arbeitskammer, n.d.), p. 10.

[70]Edwin Hartrich, *The Fourth and Richest Reich* (New York: Macmillan, 1980), pp. 206–13.

[71]An additional factor in the Borgward case may have been that the Bremen state government had an SPD majority and the federal government was led by the CDU. The CDU leadership may have hoped that the demise of Borgward in Bremen would increase the local unpopularity of the SPD and provide the CDU with a political advantage in the next state elections. But partisan politics was not a factor in any of the other cases examined, weakening this claim.

CORPORATE—STATE RELATIONS

Core   Periphery

	Core	Periphery
Mass	VW NSU-Audi *Child of the State*	Ford Opel *Multinational firm*
Craft	Daimler-Benz BMW Porsche MAN *Coopted Partner*	Borgward *Paternal Industrialist*

(left label: TECHNOLOGY)

Figure 7.2. The core and periphery of the German automobile industry

there was indeed a corporatist structure *within* the Federal Republic of Germany, but it pertained only to specific firms. A corporatist core existed where economic forces were not the guiding principles of action, but also there was a periphery where members were not helped by the state and traditional market principles dominated. We can now employ more companies in our systematic distinction between core and peripheral firms in the German auto industry (outlined in Chapter 2). When we distinguish firms by core and periphery and by mass and specialist producers, it is apparent that economic success correlates more with political than with technological factors (see Figure 7.2). Chapter 8 addresses the durability of this arrangement in the 1970s and 1980s, and its implications.

BRITAIN

A contrasting pattern emerged in liberal postwar Britain. Unlike in Germany, state policies in Britain did not differentiate between domestic and foreign firms. The cases of Ford and Austin emphasize my argument that in a liberal regime, such as Britain, the state does not distinguish between auto firms on the basis of location or nature of ownership. As Chalmers Johnson suggests, the liberal state is characteristically a regulatory state that focuses on the rules of economic competition rather than more substantive policies.[72] Liberal states set up impartial rules based on egalitarian principles, and the unintended consequences of these rules may benefit some actors more than others.

Liberal governments, like those of Britain and the United States, are

[72]Chalmers Johnson, *MITI and the Japanese Miracle: The Growth of Industrial Policy, 1925–1975* (Stanford: Stanford University Press, 1982), p. 19.

therefore at least as tolerant of multinational corporations and paternal industrialists as they are of state-owned firms. In practice, for instance, because they have a more realistic prospect of "exit," foreign firms tend to benefit from the rights and privileges of domestic production without sharing the obligations imposed on domestic firms. Foreign firms are in that sense advantaged, suggesting the term "national treatment" is a misnomer. The emphasis on egalitarian principles may mean that there is such a thing as state ownership but it is not the same as state sponsorship in any meaningful political sense, because firms that are not state-owned qualify for the same benefits as state-owned firms— such as financial assistance in times of crisis. The British automobile industry has historically had state ownership but not state sponsorship. Indeed, state ownership has often proved disadvantageous in constraining a firm's behavior. As Stephen Wilks has observed, "the British State is most competent when dealing with industrial regulation and the administration of non-discriminatory schemes of industrial support."[73] In Germany, by contrast, state sponsorship has existed but has been unrelated to state ownership. Both public and private firms in Germany have benefited from state discrimination, only private firms have suffered from it.

The absence of discriminatory practices in Britain permitted multinational corporations in the auto industry to take advantage of economies of scale. Indeed, the tendency to provide foreign multinational corporations with the rights of citizenship without the corresponding obligations—what Wilks describes as the "minimalist position"—often served to give them an unintended advantage, allowing multinationals to corner profitable segments of the British auto industry.[74] Wilks links the relative decline of the British automobile industry to the presence of these foreign firms. He suggests that "the competitive strategies and patterns of behavior of these multinationals play a large part in explaining the decline of the industry and their presence places clear constraints on individual policy-makers. . . . What is certain is that the industry's success, since the mid sixties, has been inseparable from the success of these companies."[75] Wilks adds that permissive government policies in the 1960s made the industry dependent on American ownership.

Although I do not dissent from the spirit of Wilks's explanation, I place a different emphasis in explaining the industry's demise. American multinationals manifestly did assume control of the industry in the

[73]Stephen Wilks, *Industrial Policy and the Motor Industry* (Manchester: Manchester University Press, 1984), p. 64.
[74]Ibid., p. 88.
[75]Ibid., p. 87.

1960s and may well have contributed to its decline. But the explanation for the emergence of multinational corporations as dominant firms *and* for the industry's decline precedes the 1960s. It is located in the liberal ideology and institutional structure of the British state that have encouraged the growth of foreign direct investment since the 1920s. Here I provide a more general explanation for the industry's development, one that can account for the emergence of dominant multinationals, their prior and subsequent behavior to the 1960s, and the industry's decline. In a sense I hope here to explain both the cause and the effect of the expansion and contraction of American investment.

Just as the liberal state was willing to tolerate and often encourage foreign direct investment by American firms, so it left firms characterized as paternal industrialists free to seek market niches unencumbered by political constraints. Furthermore, all foreign multinationals, specialist producers, and aspiring domestic mass producers knew they would be underwritten by the state if they extended their commitments beyond their capabilities. As a result of these state policies, it was precisely those automobile firms unsuccessful in the postfascist German context that were given the political latitude to succeed in Britain. The burden of British state policies was primarily borne by those firms which had benefited most in the German context—that is, aspiring domestic mass producers. Government policies protected unsuccessful firms, which would not face liquidation because they could rely on state aid.

As a result, the major winners in the British auto industry were the richer, larger subsidiaries of multinational corporations. Classic liberal economic theory might assume that unbridled foreign direct investment leads to more productive, competitive domestic producers, but it also assumes a relatively equal distribution of economic resources, political burdens, and unlimited market competition with the ultimate threat of elimination. Where domestic firms have inferior resources, are subject to political burdens not imposed on the subsidiaries of foreign firms (for instance, the threat of nationalization), and yet do not face the threat of elimination from the market through bankruptcy, the result will be very different. Indeed, in the British auto industry, these conditions generated a prescription for the development of foreign producers who have been (albeit marginally) more efficient and a lot more profitable (due to increased economies of scale) than domestic firms. In Germany, in contrast, the presence of multinationals combined with the imposition of constraints on their behavior produced efficient domestic firms able to compete internationally.

Rich foreign multinationals accorded national treatment threaten the nation with two forms of potential drain. The first is economic, initiated when multinationals begin to shift profits abroad rather than reinvest them locally. The process accelerates when multinationals respond to the changing terms of trade by shifting production locations. Wilks points to dramatic evidence of the effects of Ford's and Vauxhall's decisions to withdraw manufacturing from Britain. In 1969 Ford's percentage of production devoted to exports was 47 percent, Vauxhall's 42 percent. By 1974 these percentages had fallen to 25 percent and 21 percent respectively. By 1979 British Ford's recorded loss of £20 million hid an actual £268 million trading deficit caused by the use of Ford's British facilities for assembly, sales, and service rather than manufacturing.[76] Indeed, by the early 1980s Ford's market leadership in Britain was based on imports.[77] The second drain is on the political autonomy of the state, which becomes more reliant on the subsidiaries of foreign multinationals to implement employment, investment, and manufacturing policies.[78] Repeated government negotiations to preserve jobs often fail, as at Vauxhall where the company reduced employment levels by nearly 30 percent in the early 1980s, a period Wilks describes as "an employment catastrophe."[79] Even when government officials have succeeded, the negotiations have been conducted with "a pistol at their head."[80]

In the 1930s and 1940s Morris and Austin were the two major British producers. Ford had elected to make Britain the base for its primary European subsidiary and built the Dagenham plant in the early 1930s, unaware of the impending effect of the Depression on demand. Still, Ford was well placed to assume market dominance with any surge in demand. In addition to Austin, Rootes and Standard operated as major armaments, military vehicle, and aero-engine producers. Of the major producers, only Morris, owned and run by the enigmatic Lord Nuffield, refused involvement as a defense contractor. All firms producing military supplies, including the American subsidiaries, were subject to the same contractual agreements. None benefited exceptionally on the basis of profit per unit.

Unlike the American subsidiaries, whose plants were located in the south of England—Ford at Dagenham and Vauxhall at Luton—Britain's indigenous producers were clustered in the Midlands. Unexpectedly, the Midlands proved more accessible to air raids, and many plants

---

[76]Ibid., pp. 72, 112.

[77]Ibid., p. 245.

[78]For fuller discussion see Simon Reich, "Roads to Follow: Regulating Direct Foreign Investment," *International Organization* 43 (Autumn 1989), pp. 543–84.

[79]Wilks, *Industrial Policy*, pp. 75 and 248.

[80]Ibid., p. 132.

suffered severe damage from German bombing in the 1940s. It had been assumed that Ford's Dagenham plant was strategically vulnerable, but a combination of camouflage, a sophisticated air defense system on the southern English coast, and luck saved the plant from serious damage.

At the end of the war Austin and Morris were best placed among indigenous British producers to grow. Both had contributed to the war effort, and either could have dominated the British market if the government had skewed the distribution of scarce resources in its favor. It probably would have been easier for Austin to assume this role because unlike Morris, Austin had constructed a fully integrated plant and was therefore not reliant on suppliers of components to complete the production process. But the British state refused to make either firm a national champion by discriminatory policies. The government had the perfect discriminatory weapon—the allocation of sheet steel—in the hands of the Ministry of Supply. But ministry officials scrupulously stated criteria for distribution to avoid any accusations of favoring indigenous firms. When Ford's and Vauxhall's management did challenge the Ministry of Supply, its embarrassed civil servants apologized and increased Ford's allocation of sheet steel at the expense of Austin, despite Austin's superior production record.[81]

Not only did state policies not help indigenous firms develop at the expense of American subsidiaries, they actually impeded their development. Most critical were concerns about nationalization. With the nationalization or "socialization" of parts or all of Britain's coal and steel industries, railway system, and health services, the owners of indigenous auto companies feared they would be next. Despite the assurances of government spokesmen, industrialists such as John Smith at Standard and Leonard Lord at Austin remained distrustful.

State policies inadvertently provoked underinvestment by the management and owners of indigenous automobile firms. Fearing their firms would be confiscated and they would receive insufficient compensation, as they felt had happened in the steel and coal industries, the boards of the major indigenous auto manufacturers awarded their stockholders huge dividends in the late 1940s and throughout the 1950s. The situation was complicated by the fact that many of these firms were managed by their owners; nationalization would threaten these people's jobs and their fortunes. As a result, managers and owners implemented short-term policies that drove their companies into the ground. Long-term considerations were sacrificed to extract as

---

[81]"Note on the Meeting Held in the Permanent Secretary's Room, 3:30 PM, 8 April 1952," MinSupp 14/332, PRO.

much revenue as possible, for industrialists and shareholders were determined to extract every ounce of revenue they could. Consistent dividend awards of approximately 50 percent of earnings effectively denied these companies the finance necessary for recapitalization.

The only firms that did not make high dividend payments were Ford and Vauxhall. As subsidiaries of American firms they operated under different constraints. First, their management was accountable to the board of their parent companies which, quite reasonably, would not have considered such dividend levels to be fiscally prudent. Indeed, it was a desire to exert greater central control that prompted Ford's parent company in the 1950s to set up an international division to centralize decision making and to repurchase 100 percent ownership of the British subsidiary's outstanding stock from the British public in 1960. These moves effectively ended any debate about dividend awards. At the same time they opened up the potential for the rapid drainage of investment capital. Second, foreign ownership in a liberal state made the subsidiaries beneficiaries of all the rights and privileges of domestic firms without the obligations. In this instance, they did not face the same fear of impending nationalization. Multinationals may face such a prospect in the Third World, but they generally do not in a liberal state.

D. G. Rhys stresses that the development strategy of Ford and Vauxhall differed from that of other major auto producers in Britain.[82] Unlike their British counterparts, Ford and Vauxhall awarded relatively low dividends in the 1950s and retained profits for reinvestment.[83] Indeed, in the mid-1950s Vauxhall and Ford funded the two most expensive investment programs in the auto industry to date. Vauxhall's program, dating from 1953, cost £38 million; Ford's cost a staggering £75 million. In comparison, the investment program of the British Motor Corporation (BMC) after 1952 cost £25 million—a third of Ford's spending for a company that relative to Ford was already undercapitalized.[84] And Ford spent nearly as much in one year on capital investment—£20 million in 1957—as BMC spent in the entire decade.[85] British firms had to rely on British capital markets for funds, unlike the American subsidiaries, which could use their own surpluses and could borrow from their parent companies. British capital markets were predicated on assumptions favoring short-term rather than long-

---

[82]D. G. Rhys, *The Motor Industry: An Economic Survey* (London: Butterworth, 1972), p. 32.

[83]For examples see ibid., p. 23.

[84]Ibid.; Graham Turner, *The Car Makers* (London: Eyre & Spottiswoode, 1963), pp. 21–24, 39.

[85]For Ford's modernization project see Ford Motor Company Annual Report 1956; *Ford Bulletin* 21 (10 January 1958).

term returns.[86] Vauxhall and Ford subsequently cornered a growing
share of the British market because with their higher level of capitalization, they could take better advantage of economies of scale. The success of lower dividend payments and higher investment programs was
reflected in the 1960s and 1970s, when Ford and Vauxhall held a
dominant position in the large, lucrative, mass-volume "fleet sales" segment of the British market, supplying businesses that provided their
employees with company vehicles. This segment constituted in excess
of 45 percent of annual car sales in the British market.[87]

The issue of protectionist barriers reemerged in the postwar period.
The initial, brief removal of the McKenna duties justifiably provoked
fear of a flood of imports. As soon as evidence suggested these fears
were warranted, similar tariff measures were reimposed, severely limiting imports and thus effectively insulating the market. This move left
American subsidiaries free to compete head on with the small British
mass producers for control of the market. The American multinationals recognized the opportunity and went on the offensive, taking
advantage of surplus capital to expand aggressively. Chrysler entered
the British market and expanded horizontally by purchasing Rootes.
Ford adopted a different approach; it expanded vertically through the
purchase of suppliers. One example was the purchase of Briggs in
1953. Vauxhall took a third route, simply increasing its capacity to
produce. By 1967 the three American subsidiaries had expanded to
control over 50 percent of the British market and were more profitable
than ever.[88] In contrast, the sustained decline in the international competitiveness of British exports meant that the remaining British companies experienced a severe cut in profits.

The British state's response to the financial problems of indigenous
producers was predictable. It implemented measures designed to bail
out the losers. It organized successive rounds of defensive mergers,
generally combining relatively healthy with unhealthy companies in the
hope the former would rescue the latter. The state bought the cooperation of these firms by offering state financing.[89] The consistent result

[86]For the short-term returns problem associated with liberal capital markets see John
Zysman, *Governments, Markets, and Growth: Financial Systems and the Politics of Industrial
Change* (Ithaca: Cornell University Press, 1983), pp. 55–80.
[87]Britain's unique tax structure traditionally encouraged employers to provide workers with the tax-free benefit of a company car to compensate for high levels of taxation
on personal income. Firms purchasing such cars looked chiefly for reliable performance
and low servicing costs. Both Ford and Vauxhall sought to provide such a vehicle;
artificial barriers traditionally prevented foreign firms from competing directly in this
market segment. New tax laws in the 1980s under Margaret Thatcher have reduced the
tax advantages of a company car and therefore eroded the value of fleet sales.
[88]Rhys, *The Motor Industry*, p. 27.
[89]Ibid., p. 26.

of this policy was that small inefficient units became large inefficient units.

Concentration began in 1952 with the state's orchestration of the merger between efficient Austin and unprofitable Morris to form BMC. This merger recognized both the growth of Ford as the dominant British producer and the general decline of British auto exports. It boosted the new company's share of sales to a market-leading 40 percent, but the share remained static for the rest of the decade while Ford's share continued to expand. Indeed, according to Rhys "the most significant features of the UK motor industry in the post-war period was Ford's growth and BMC's relative decline." Austin and Morris were merged but not rationalized; nor were they protected or favored against competing American subsidiaries. Their plants produced different models that competed in the same market segment, and they could not achieve sufficient economies of scale to become price-competitive with Ford. Instead of enhancing productivity, the new arrangement infected Austin with Morris's inefficiencies.

The state recognized the new company was stagnating and subsequently offered incentives to profitable, small niche producers to merge with unprofitable, larger producers. One by one, the successful specialist producers, owned by conservative businessmen who had traditionally remained distant from the rest of the industry, were purchased by the state at inflated prices. These new acquisitions were then irrationally clustered with large firms whose outdated, ill-designed products were the result of years of undercapitalization. The refusal of the state to either rationalize these new entities to make them more efficient or discriminate against foreign subsidiaries to make them less efficient had the effect of dragging down the profitable specialist producers with the unprofitable large ones. As in Germany, paternal industrialists disappeared as owners. But here their demise was relatively less painful: they disappeared as a result not of state coercion but of state enrichment. The classic example was William Lyons, who owned the Jaguar company. Lyons had staunchly resisted government interference in his company but could not resist the government's financial lure. Jaguar was purchased by the government and merged with BMC. Lyons was kept in charge of the Jaguar division, but although he controlled the manufacturing process at his unintegrated plant, he now had no power over investment decisions. The result was persistent undercapitalization and a steady demise that reached its nadir in the early 1980s. Jaguar was eventually privatized and then sold to Ford at the end of the decade. Similarly, the profitable Leyland truck company purchased ACV (another heavy goods manufacturer) and Standard-Triumph and Rover, two specialist car producers, in a seemingly irrational series of mergers encouraged by government. This new combine then merged with the unprofitable BMC to form the British Leyland Motor Corporation (BLMC) in 1968. While concentration without rationalization was occurring, successive governments used only policies based on incentives and never denied Chrysler, Ford, or Vauxhall the right to invest.

Yet Daniel Jones has suggested that the policies of the British government after 1964 were discriminatory.[90] Our differences are more terminological than substantive, because Jones fails to distinguish between intervention and discrimination. Jones suggests that the new Labour government, elected in 1964, pursued discriminatory policies. His evidence is that it encouraged this series of mergers and takeovers. Government action certainly constituted intervention, but a refusal to favor these new firms and a corresponding willingness to fund or "bail out" American investment suggests there was no discrimination.

No evidence suggests the Labour government even contemplated limiting market, investment, or production rights for American subsidiaries. On the contrary, as Wilks notes, all the evidence suggests the Labour government believed that the sustained, unbridled activities of Chrysler, Ford, and Vauxhall would have a positive economic effect. Indeed, he suggests it was the particularly permissive decisions of that very government which shifted dominance of the auto industry to the Americans.[91] Even if British governments had considered discriminatory policies, they lacked the capacity to enforce them. The initial postwar attempt to form a peak association for the industry, the National Advisory Council for the Motors Manufacturing Industry (NACMMI), had proved a failure. By the early 1960s there was no such organ, although a private trade association, the SMMT, still existed. Furthermore, the government lacked both an articulated sectoral policy and the micro-level instruments to implement such a policy. It relied on macro-level instruments, and even its attempts to create policy forums at the national level met with stubborn resistance from the private sector. Events concerning both British Leyland and Chrysler exemplify this lack of capacity to organize and implement discriminatory policies. Jones himself points to the absence of discriminatory tools, concluding that successive governments were heavily dependent on the companies themselves for information about the industry in general and assessments of each company's prospects—effectively delegating the decision-making of the sovereign state to the companies themselves.[92]

[90]See Daniel T. Jones, *Industrial Adjustment and Policy: Maturity and Crisis in the European Car Industry* (Lewes: Sussex European Research Center, 1981), p. 45.
[91]Wilks, *Industrial Policy*, p. 87.
[92]Jones, *Industrial Adjustment*, p. 51.

The Labour government faced a problem common to British governments from the 1950s to the 1980s. It sought to assist domestic producers to improve their profitability, but its efforts were impaired by two factors. The first was the government's beliefs: specifically, that the health of indigenous producers was unrelated to the presence of American subsidiaries and that the presence of these subsidiaries helped improve the industry's aggregate economic performance. The second was the government's institutional limitations. It had only a limited capacity to assist these firms, mainly through incentive programs. And given its noncoercive character, it would not even link funding to demands for rationalization, let alone discriminate against Chrysler, Ford, or Vauxhall. The result was the only possibility for governments dominated by liberal ideology—a contradictory policy that attempted to increase the competitiveness of British-owned producers while simultaneously underwriting uncompetitive firms. Workers and managers at individual firms did not have to be economically efficient; they were secure in the knowledge they would be "bailed out." Defensive mergers did not provide a solution; nationalization followed; and the inevitable effect of this prescription was financial ruin.

Strictly speaking, Jones's claim that governments after 1964, particularly the Labour government, were discriminatory might be true if the Labour party had opposed American investment or if Labour governments had confined its activities on bailouts, mergers, and acquisitions to domestic firms. But neither was the case. The Labour party in opposition favored Chrysler's purchase of a minority share in Rootes, shadow chancellor James Callaghan suggesting that everyone welcomed American investment.[93] Once in power, the Labour government sanctioned Chrysler's controlling interest in Rootes, dismissing concerns about whether it served the national interest. According to Wilks some Labour ministers, most notably Harold Lever, then undersecretary of state at the Department of Economic Affairs, thought the Chrysler purchase represented "a potentially very favorable solution to the Rootes problem." Such beliefs reflected a "startling faith in the integrity of international corporations which has been such a consistent feature of the public utterances of successive governments."[94]

Ironically, many politicians in the Labour government of 1964 were leading actors in the negotiations to bail out Chrysler a decade later. By 1975 Chrysler accounted for 18 percent of the British market, impressive given the limited time it had been in Britain. The company's strategic economic and political importance was clear: it exported 55

---

[93] James Callaghan cited in Wilks, *Industrial Policy*, p. 90.
[94] Both quotes taken from Wilks, *Industrial Policy*, p. 95.

percent of British production and had 25,000 employees concentrated in two areas, Linwood near Glasgow and Coventry. Wilks estimates that Chrysler was indirectly responsible for another 30,000 jobs. Thus a Chrysler bankruptcy would have increased unemployment in Glasgow by 15 percent and in Coventry by 82 percent.[95] Faced with bankruptcy, Chrysler threatened to withdraw production from Britain completely unless it received government funding.[96] Prime Minister Harold Wilson was not disposed to provide such funding because he felt the government was being unduly pressured. But parochial considerations concerning employment predominated. John Starrels describes the rapid evolution of Prime Minister Wilson's position, from obstinate refusal to agreement that the government would underwrite projected losses of £72.5 million for 1976, award Chrysler a loan of £55 million for capital expenditure for 1976, and guarantee a further loan of £35 million from several leading London banks. Chrysler reciprocated by promising to maintain employment levels, increase competitiveness, and raise product quality. Apparently the prime minister was reminded by some members of his cabinet of such pragmatic considerations as the relationship between employment and votes in marginal electoral districts.[97] Chrysler's foreign ownership was never a significant factor. The effect of the Chrysler decision was to distance the government from indigenous producers, particularly British Leyland, because it made it clear there was no national champion, only a nonpartisan employment strategy that reemphasized the traditional arms-length criterion of contact between all firms and the state. Furthermore, Wilks suggests, the government's decision to bail Chrysler out "placed the future of the industry, at least implicitly, in the hands and with the strategies of the multinationals."[98]

These state policies, built on the principle of egalitarian treatment coupled with a willingness to underwrite all failing firms, had discouraging effects on the attitudes of both domestic management and labor. First, they encouraged dull, uncreative management; managers were not accountable to their boards of directors in the same way the managers of multinational corporations were. As a result, domestic management generally lacked the innovative capacity of the dynamic managers of American subsidiaries, particularly Ford. Second, state policies encouraged a labor force throughout the industry to believe

[95]Ibid., pp. 119–20, 127.
[96]John Starrels, "The Dilemmas of Government Intervention: Chrysler, the Labour Government, and Britain," paper delivered at the APSA meeting, Chicago, September 1976, p. 4.
[97]Ibid., pp. 6, 10; Jones, *Industrial Adjustment*, p. 49.
[98]Wilks, *Industrial Policy*, pp. 154, 186. For the Chrysler affair see pp. 132–50.

there was no relationship between sustained industrial action that reduced output and quality and a company's existence (and so, jobs). Vauxhall escaped this problem until the 1970s, because it generally had the best industrial relations record of any producer in the country. A worsening of industrial relations significantly contributed to the downturn in its economic fortunes. Ford historically shared this problem (see Chapter 3). However, Ford generated a level of profits high enough to offset the worst effects of industrial action in the 1950s, 1960s, and 1970s. When the Labour government finally attempted to maintain the Social Contract in the mid-1970s through statutory controls, Ford auto workers broke the national agreement through strikes. Poor industrial relations no doubt contributed to the decision of Detroit management in the 1970s to relocate production to Belgium, Spain, and, ironically, West Germany, at a cost to jobs and profits in Britain. Ford had set up a European headquarters in 1967 that effectively eliminated competition between its European subsidiaries and developed a standard European product range. It subsequently coordinated production and sales, maximized economies of scales, and shifted production away from labor plants with poor industrial relations. The British plants became victims of this capacity.[99] As Wilks states, "the American companies had taken the strategic decision to supply continental Europe with cars from their continental factories and could not be relied on to take advantage of the opportunities theoretically offered by membership of the EEC."[100] The steady relocation of jobs abroad coincided with the growth of Ford as an importer of cars, primarily from Spain and Germany. The firm that traditionally sold the largest number of cars in the British market became the largest importer.[101] By the early 1980s over 20 percent of sales in the British auto market were of "captive imports" of foreign multinational producers. Between 1968 and 1982 imported cars grew from 8.3 percent of sales to 57.7 percent.[102]

The policies of Ford and Vauxhall contributed to Britain's capital drain in the 1960s and 1970s. As Wilks suggests, "the industry's success, since the mid sixties, has become inseparable from the success of these companies."[103] Ford under its new Dearborn (as opposed to formerly British) ownership no longer reinvested on the scale of the 1930s and 1950s. Indeed, in 1982 Ford registered a £265 million trade deficit.[104]

[99]Ibid., p. 240.

[100]Ibid., p. 112.

[101]Karel Williams, John Williams, and Dennis Thomas, *Why Are the British Bad at Manufacturing?* (London: Routledge & Kegan Paul, 1983), p. 44.

[102]Wilks, *Industrial Policy*, pp. 70, 237.

[103]Ibid., p. 87.

[104]Ibid., pp. 72, 259.

Meanwhile, despite the assistance received in the mid-1970s and promises to maintain British employment levels, Chrysler ignored government protests and sold its British operation to PSA/Talbot, the French firm, in 1978—breaking all the terms agreed when it had received government assistance two years earlier. The British government had the right to block this deal under their 1976 agreement with Chrysler but characteristically did not want to discourage further multinational investment. It accepted the fait accompli. PSA then transformed its new British subsidiary from a producer to a minor assembler by closing the main Linwood plant and reducing employment from 22,000 in 1978 to 6,000 in 1983. PSA, as inheritor of the 1976 agreement, also broke agreed terms without any serious repercussions.[105] Vauxhall also contributed to the drain on British capital. Its Luton plant assembled imported kits for sale in the domestic market rather than for export.[106] In both Ford and Vauxhall, part of the profits from British sales accrued in West Germany, a policy ironically designed to bolster sagging earnings levels there. These events substantiate the suggestion that the British state's "policy on multinational corporations had always been ambivalent in tone but overwhelmingly liberal and permissive in content."[107]

The development of Ford and Vauxhall into effective multinational actors that have contributed to Britain's capital decline was accompanied by decline of the indigenous mass producers. BMC expanded its capacity between 1952 and 1965 from 300,000 to a million units per annum.[108] Yet the British market demanded diversity; because of the large number of competing models it offered and the buildup of surplus capacity, BMC was unable to effect economies of scale. Concentration without effective rationalization made BMC unable financially to compete with either American subsidiaries or imports.[109] Eventual entry into the EEC (which stimulated the import of foreign cars into Britain), the continued growth of Ford's and Vauxhall's market share, the removal of tariff barriers in formerly exclusive colonial markets, the introduction of Japanese cars, and the oil shortage were all factors that precipitated a crisis by the mid-1970s. Between 1972 and 1975 BMC sales plunged from 700,000 to 450,000 cars per year.[110] By the late 1980s that figure had halved again. Wilks describes this decline of

[105]Ibid., pp. 252–59.
[106]Williams, Williams, and Thomas, *Why Are the British Bad at Manufacturing?*
[107]Wilks, *Industrial Policy*, p. 260.
[108]Williams, Williams, and Thomas, *Why Are the British Bad at Manufacturing?* p. 54.
[109]Graham Turner, *The Leyland Papers* (London: Eyre & Spottiswoode, 1971), pp. 97–98.
[110]Williams, Williams, and Thomas, *Why Are the British Bad at Manufacturing?* p. 55.

the British auto industry since the late 1960s as being of "a unique order of magnitude."[111]

While sales were falling at home, foreign markets no longer provided export outlets. British producers could no longer rely on an exclusive sterling bloc market. They had briefly enjoyed a boom in American sales in the early postwar period, but the development of subcompacts by the American companies and new competition from German and Japanese automakers precluded reentry into the American market. Europe did not provide an alternative. BMC had been forced to spend money repaying debts rather than developing a European dealer network. The lack of a network discouraged volume sales in Europe. BMC had no export market to offset declining home sales.[112]

Both management and labor at BMC were criticized for short-sighted, short-term decisions that had led the company to this crisis. However, it was a broader framework of ideological proclivities and institutional structures that prompted state policies and these responses. In a liberal regime the state, capital, and labor reacted to each other's behavior in a predictable manner. First, the state provided a £25 million loan to encourage the merging of Leyland and BMC to form the British Leyland Motor Corporation in 1968. Then the new company was given an additional £10 million grant in 1970 to purchase machine tools. When the company finally collapsed, in 1975, it was nationalized by the state to bail it out. Then the Ryder Report encouraged government to fund an increased productive capacity, through an injection of £2,800 million, without considering whether there was demand for this new production.[113] Ironically the Labour government chose at the same time to rescue Chrysler; in hindsight, a simpler, cheaper solution would have been to let Chrysler go bankrupt and then integrate its resources into British Leyland, creating the new capacity recommended by Ryder. But refusal to underwrite a loser would be inconsistent with the behavior of a liberal state.

The Ryder Report's recommendation to expand British Leyland's capacity did not take into account that expansion would create efficiency only if accompanied by rationalization. Successive British governments appear to have made no attempt to coordinate events at BL across the company's different plants, let alone coordinating company activities with those in other sectors.[114] As Jones points out, the absence of effective state machinery has made successive governments reliant

111Wilks, *Industrial Policy*, p. 71.
112Williams, Williams, and Thomas, *Why Are the British Bad at Manufacturing?* p. 57.
113Ibid.
114See Jones, *Industrial Adjustment*, p. 26.

upon the company to provide information and needs assessment—
hardly the basis for impartial decision–making.[115] The evident failure
of the Ryder Report's recommendations by 1977 led to the appointment of Sir Michael Edwardes as chief executive. He was specifically
instructed to rationalize the company—the first occasion on which a
government had contemplated rationalization. Edwardes was a private
entrepreneur, leased from another firm rather than employed as a
state bureaucrat, and his reputation as a maverick conveniently created
the image of someone removed from the state. Thus the eventual
rationalization of production within British Leyland appeared to be
carried out not by government officials but by the private sector. Edwardes was not politically accountable to the electorate, and his activities were politically distanced from the government, which legitimated Edwardes's actions by claiming they were simply dictated by
market forces.[116] The government could and did disassociate itself
from unpleasant political and economic repercussions, casting itself in
the benign role of providing financial assistance toward recovery
rather than enforcing harsh redundancies. For although Conservative
governments have gone into office rigidly resistant to the idea of
providing public funds for the automobile industry, they, like Labour
governments, have succumbed and bailed out British auto companies.
Just as the Edward Heath government had performed the Great U-
Turn and nationalized Rolls Royce in the early 1970s, so the apparently
intransigent Margaret Thatcher government decided to provide BL
with £1,205 million in funding in 1979 and £990 million over the
period 1981–83. The justification in this latter instance was that the
money would prepare the company for sale to the private sector.

The latest chapter has been written only recently under the Thatcher
government. As with Rolls-Royce and Jaguar, the Thatcher government returned the sole remaining British mass producer to private
ownership. Yet having initially sworn that the company's funding
would end in 1983, Thatcher, that staunch resister of public funding,
continued to finance the restructuring of BL and its reemergence as
Austin-Rover and then underwrote £800 million worth of debt as a
condition for its sale to British Aerospace. Just as significantly, Thatcher, generally regarded as very nationalistic, was willing to sell the last
remaining British mass producer to a foreign firm. Both in preliminary
negotiations with British Aerospace and subsequently, when that deal
briefly appeared threatened, she explicitly acknowledged her willingness to sell the new Austin-Rover to whoever made the best offer—

[115]Ibid., p. 51.
[116]Ibid., pp. 48–49.

including General Motors, Ford, and Volkswagen. The attitude was demonstrated by her encouragement of the sale of Aston Martin and Jaguar to Ford, and Lotus to General Motors.

The Thatcher government's solution to reduced American investment was not expanded domestic production but expanded Japanese investment. Nissan, Toyota, and Honda all invested in British production facilities in the 1980s, as a way of combatting domestic content restrictions and gaining access to the EEC after 1992. Not surprisingly, they chose to locate plants in Britain because it provided the most hospitable environment in Europe. The Thatcher government has been willing to fight on behalf of Japanese producers to subdue French protectionism. It successfully forced the François Mitterrand government to conform to the Community's 60 percent domestic content requirement when the French arbitrarily imposed a higher limit to keep Japanese cars manufactured in Britain out of the French market. Margaret Thatcher took up the cudgel on behalf of Japanese officials who kept a diplomatic silence. Meanwhile, the status of Austin-Rover as the last exclusively British-owned mass producer was diluted by a deal it struck with Honda. After an initial series of joint ventures with Honda, Austin-Rover gave Honda a 20 percent holding in the British company in exchange for a 20 percent holding in Honda's new British component manufacturing business. Honda plans to build a plant and assume responsibility for the production of 100,000 Honda-Rover cars by 1992.[117] By that year Nissan, with a single British plant, will be the largest exporter of cars from Britain.[118]

The state's behavior in the auto industry has demonstrated consistent themes since the 1930s. A propensity toward national treatment in practice meant that foreign firms were accorded all the rights and privileges and none of the obligations of domestic firms. Foreign firms could agree, for instance, to maintain employment levels in exchange for financial assistance and then flagrantly break those accords without repercussions. The state clearly believed that increased foreign investment was compatible with increased domestic prosperity. It repeatedly demonstrated an unwillingness to use coercive or discriminatory measures, either to disadvantage American subsidiaries in relation to their British competitors or to discipline them when they reneged on agreements. The only intention of state policies toward Chrysler, Ford, and Vauxhall was to provide assistance. Indigenous firms did not benefit from discriminatory state policies, but this did not mean they were poorly treated—at least in the sense that they were protected by the state from market forces whenever it was within the state's power to do

[117]*Manchester Guardian Weekly*, 23 July 1989.
[118]"Motor Industry Survey," *The Economist*, 15 October 1988, p. 10.

so. A pattern of underwriting developed whereby successive British governments dealt with the shrinking markets of British mass producers through aimless funding schemes and the merging of profitable with unprofitable firms.

There were two unintended consequences of state policies. The attempt to make domestic auto firms larger and therefore prosperous had the opposite effect. The streamlining that the British state sought through mergers resulted merely in enlargement without consolidation, rationalization, or centralization; it was functionally a pallid response to the coerced, effective integration of domestic producers that the fascist German state enforced in the 1930s and 1940s. But the British state lacked the coercive power, the nationalist ideology, the will, or the instruments to replicate the fascist pattern. Furthermore, the willingness to bail out losers created a tenuous link between government policies and corporate prosperity. Both management and labor made decisions and pursued strategies inconsistent with their company's long-term economic prosperity. Conservatives generally blamed labor unions for the high number of strikes and generally poor industrial relations. Critics from the left blamed mismanagement, such as the inordinately high dividend payments to stockholders in the 1940s and 1950s, for declines. Both explanations are partially correct. But state policy explains both labor relations and investment decisions. Both labor and management behaved in a fiscally irresponsible manner because the state periodically underwrote their behavior. At the same time the state was unwilling to create the conditions that might have promoted growth—and therefore might have encouraged fiscal prudence and labor tranquility. It was not *that* the state intervened, it was *how* the state intervened that explains the behavior of capital and labor and the demise of indigenous producers.

Stemming from an egalitarian, noncoercive ideology, a limited institutional structure created a liberal state that resisted impulses to create a British equivalent of the German core in the automobile industry. A British national champion was never taken seriously because it would have entailed not only promoting the favored firm but depriving the competition. The overwhelming dominance of liberal ideology makes it doubtful that the British state even understood this as an option. The result was an eventual drift into oblivion.

COMPARABLE COUNTRIES

This section considers the applicability of the argument to three other advanced industrialized states: Italy, Japan, and France. The first

277

two undoubtedly were fascist regimes. France is an intriguing case. Does fascism imposed by occupation have the same effect as indigenous fascism on a country's economic structure?

Japan

The pattern of development of the Japanese automobile industry closely resembles what we have seen in Germany. If there are differences between Germany and Japan, it may be that Japan is a stronger case, making it plausible explicitly to link state policy 1930–45 and postwar prosperity for the economy as a whole rather than just the automobile industry. Chalmers Johnson suggests that although the development of the Japanese economy dates from the Meiji Restoration of 1868, the 1930s was the watershed in the nation's economic development. Relations between government officials and the executives who headed the large combines known as *zaibatsu* were personal and informal in the late nineteenth century, and state policy became laissez-faire in the first three decades of the twentieth century, but state policy in the 1930s became authoritative and dominated economic organization.[119] This new state intervention largely circumvented the zaibatsu's traditional role, creating and sponsoring new industrial units.

Johnson suggests that from "1935 to 1955 the hard hand of state control rested heavily on the Japanese economy. The fact that MITI refers to this period as its 'golden era' is understandable, if deeply imprudent."[120] This was the period when elite bureaucrats learned how industrial policy worked. They extended their activities into previously unchartered territories. As the postwar purge during the Occupation hardly touched the economics ministries, these bureaucrats were able to apply their knowledge in MITI policies, stimulating Japan's economic growth in the 1950s.[121] The emphasis on this period by Japan's leading postwar bureaucrats cannot be understated, and Johnson's description of their candid views deserves to be quoted at length:

> Nakamura Takafusa locates the "roots" of both industrial policy and administrative guidance in the controlled economy of the 1930s, and he calls MITI the reincarnation of the wartime MCI and MM. Arisawa Hiromi says that the prosperity of the 1970s was a product of the "control era," and no less a figure than Shiina Etsusaburo, former vice-minister, twice MITI minister, and vice-president of the Liberal Democratic party, credits the experiences of the old trade-and-industry bureaucrats in Manchuria in the

[119]Johnson, *MITI and the Japanese Miracle*, pp. 33, 85.
[120]Ibid., p. 29.
[121]Ibid., pp. 32–33, 40.

1930s, his own and Kishi Nobusuke's included. Tanaka Shin'ichi—who was one of the leading officials of the Cabinet Planning Board (Kikaku-in) before it was merged with the MCI to form the MM, and who became a postwar MITI official—argues that wartime planning was the basis for the work of the postwar Economic Stabilization Board (Keizai Antei Honbu) and MCI. And Maeda Yasuyuki, one of the leading scholars of MITI, writes that "the heritage of the wartime economy is that it was the first attempt at heavy and chemical industrialization; more important, the war provided the 'how' for the 'what' in the sense of innumerable 'policy tools' and accumulated 'know-how.' "[122]

The change in the structure of the Japanese economy was dramatic, and its legacy outlasted the war and, as these comments suggest, the occupation. The Ministry of Commerce and Industry (MCI) formed in 1925 became the Ministry of Munitions (MM) in 1942. It was reconverted to the MCI on the eve of Japan's surrender for fear that any bureaucrat associated with arms production would be tried as a war criminal. Johnson concludes that "however one evaluates the decade and a half from 1930 to 1945, Japan's government was much more bureaucratic and state dominated at the end of this period than it had been at the beginning."[123] The American decision to rule Japan indirectly, allowing the postwar Japanese government an autonomy of policy, proved critical. While other ministries were purged, the economics ministries went unscathed. The combination of autonomy and effective continuity enhanced the MCI's power in the occupation period. Johnson suggests that "in fact, the occupation years, 1945–1952, witnessed the highest levels of government control over the economy ever encountered in modern Japan before or since, levels that were decidedly higher than the levels attained during the Pacific War."[124]

State power grew in the 1930s through parliamentary legislation and imperial ordinances; institutional continuity survived from the 1930s to the 1950s despite often bewildering changes in the names and organizational structure of departmental bureaucracies; and the reorganization and growth of the scope and domain of the state's powers affected Japan's economic growth rates in the "economic miracle" of the 1950s. This is not the place to recapitulate Johnson's argument. But in sociological terms, fundamental to these changes in the 1930s was the growth in influence of both the military and an elite group known as "reform bureaucrats" who were located in the Cabinet Research Bureau and were specifically attracted to Nazi ideology—particularly its

[122]Ibid., p. 33.
[123]Ibid., p. 40.
[124]Ibid., p. 41.

emphasis on building national defense, its antiliberalism, nationalism, and statism. These bureaucrats survived in Japan's postwar bureaucratic elite. In ideological terms growth in state control of the economy rested on the increased popularity of the concepts of "industrial rationalization" and "excessive competition." Their precise meanings remained obscure, but each became synonymous with enhanced state control and a preference for cooperation rather than competition. Finally, in institutional terms the growth of the state's economic power rested on a series of laws that initially shifted power from the Diet (legislature) to industrial elites and then, when "self-control" failed to stimulate what the bureaucracy considered to be appropriate economic policies, from the private sector to the state executive—a realm increasingly dominated by the military. The first critical piece of legislation in this two-stage process was the Industries Control Law of April 1931, which established the existing cartels as self-governing associations. Although the MCI could dissolve it and although membership was voluntary, the MCI (as later in Germany) could force nonparticipants to abide by the terms of the cartel. The second was a series of laws in the mid-1930s designed to provide special government funding, tax exemptions, and protective measures for individual industries or energy sources. Industries that benefited from these laws included petroleum, aircraft, machine tools, shipbuilding, light metals, and, most pointedly, automobile production.[125] The third piece of legislation was the National General Mobilization Law of 1938. This law "authorized the complete reorganization of the society along totalitarian lines. . . . The law, in fact, became a carte blanche for the executive branch to do anything that it and its various clients could agree on; its policies extended not just to industry and the economy but also to education, labor, finance, publishing, and virtually all social activities even remotely related to the war effort."[126] It formed the basis for Japan's attempt to institute the Economic New Structure policies that emulated Hitler's New Order policies in fixing all prices, wages, rents, and economic indexes, and thus eliminating the last vestiges of autonomous market pricing. Many aspects of this law applied to the MCI's control over the economy during the Occupation, in the Temporary Materials Supply and Demand Control Law of October 1946, and then in the "foreign-currency budgets" of the 1950s and early 1960s, which were, according to Johnson, the main instruments of control during what he terms the "high speed growth era."[127]

125Ibid., pp. 108–10, 124–25, 133.
126Ibid., p. 39.
127Ibid., pp. 140, 147.

Johnson points to four factors in assessing the relevance of the 1930s to the postwar miracle. First, he notes the continuity of economic problems that Japan faced over these three decades—specifically the issues of competitiveness, industrial reorganization to achieve economies of scale, the application of technological developments, and the effort to increase productivity. Second, he suggests that the character of state policies, as applied to the economy, developed in this period:

> During the period from the creation of MCI to the passage of the Important Industries Control Law in 1931, the Japanese invented and experimented with the first of their three characteristic approaches to industrial policy, approaches that have remained in their repertoire to the present day. The first approach was the attempt to replace competition with self-control of an industry by the enterprises already established in it. The institutional form of this approach, state-licensed cartels, remains big business's preferred form of industrial policy down to the present day. Its major weakness, the tendency of cartelization to lead to zaibatsu domination and monopoly, was already fully visible by 1931; and this weakness in turn elicited demands for the opposite of self-control, namely state control, that dominated the rest of the 1930s.[128]

Thus the characteristic choice between self- and state control was mapped out as the government sought to avoid zaibatsu dominance. The result was a postwar system that, according to Johnson, has resembled a corporatist system, although Johnson notes that the state's role entails more than mediation. If this is an accurate appraisal, the Japanese version of corporatism reflects the values and institutional structure of state corporatism rather than societal corporatism.[129]

The third area of continuity is the emphasis placed on "industrial rationalization," meaning long-term rather than short-term profitability through a combination of superior organization, promotion of peaceful labor relations, and cost-cutting. Johnson says that this "is the most continuous feature of Japanese industrial policy throughout the Showa era." MCI's greatest achievement was a cooperative government-business relationship that stressed the competitive development of the Japanese economy relative to foreign ones.

Fourth, and perhaps most important for my argument, Johnson notes that the ideas and institutions developed in the 1930s did not merely constitute a symbol for succeeding generations. Survival was ensured by a continuity of personnel. "One of the most startling facts about the history of industrial policy is that the managers of the post-

[128]Ibid., p. 113.
[129]Ibid., p. 196.

war economic 'miracle' were the same people who inaugurated industrial policy in the late 1920s and administered it during the 1930s and 1940s." Japan therefore "did not experience a radical discontinuity in its civilian bureaucratic and economic elites."[130] In fact, Johnson points out that all of MITI's vice-ministers during the 1950s entered the bureaucracy between 1929 and 1934.[131]

In sum, and consistent with an argument I made in the opening chapters of this book, Johnson stresses that historical continuity is rooted primarily in political rationality and conscious institutional innovation rather than parochial cultural factors or vestiges of feudalism. Johnson's emphasis on the 1930s as a period when innovations in institutions and ideas started a series of continuities parallels my discussion of Germany in Chapter 2. But if anything, Johnson more forcefully argues for this continuity in the economic policies of the Japanese state through to the mid-1970s.[132]

Johnson's seminal work on Japan has been warmly welcomed by some but extensively criticized by others as interpretatively inaccurate and empirically flawed. Two influential works tend to support his general propositions about the nature and historical development of the Japanese state. The first is Ira Magaziner and Thomas Hout's study, which confines itself to describing and analyzing the state's role in postwar Japanese industrial policy. While rejecting a monolithic "Japan Inc.," they provide evidence generally confirming his view of the centrality of the state in the policy process.[133] Kozo Yamamura's more nuanced analysis of postwar Japanese economic policy also complements Johnson's approach. Yamamura emphasizes the willingness of the occupational authorities (Supreme Command of Allied Powers) to later negate reformist policies they had pursued in the immediate postwar period. These policies, predicated on the principles of economic democracy, in practice largely amounted to imposing a competitive market structure and a "just and equal tax law." The Americans' motives, according to Yamamura, were largely punitive. But the Japanese abandoned these policies in the early and mid-1950s with American consent as U.S. concern about the Korean War and the possible loss of Japan as an ally outweighed the issue of sanctions. The result emphasized economic growth rather than economic democracy, and Japan reverted toward the organizational structure developed in the prewar fascist period, which consisted of cartelization that excluded zaibatsu

---

[130]Ibid., p. 113.
[131]Ibid., p. 114.
[132]Ibid.
[133]Ira Magaziner and Thomas Hout, *Japanese Industrial Policy* (Berkeley: Institute of International Studies, University of California, 1980), pp. 35–54, especially p. 47.

involvement. One consequence was a speed-up in industrial concentration and mergers as the "economic hegemony" of the traditional zaibatsu, initially challenged in the 1930s, was broken. Another was the re-establishment of policy priorities initially specified in the fascist period that served Japan's specific needs—principally capital accumulation, rationalization, and export growth to achieve economic independence—rather than American ideological principles.[134] Despite pluralist critiques of his work, on such matters Johnson's work still serves as the benchmark for analysis of Japan.[135]

The general tendencies described by Johnson were mirrored at the level of the auto sector. In the three decades before the 1930s the national government paid little attention to the automotive industry. Production was the exclusive province of the private sector.[136] Domestic producers consisted of a variety of small firms that manufactured in numbers too small to use mass production methods and whose products reflected a low level of technological sophistication. As a result, Japanese consumers preferred American and European imports. Both the military and the MCI tried to encourage the large zaibatsu to develop truck production for military application, but zaibatsu leaders, recognizing the generally hostile character of the government's policies, ignored their suggestions, despite the incentives offered under the Military Vehicle Subsidy Law of 1918. They claimed they would not be able to compete with American imports.[137] Consequently, between 1914 and 1926 Japanese domestic production totaled 884 vehicles whereas 15,771 were imported. In the mid-1920s Ford and General Motors both set up Japanese assembly facilities to replace direct imports. Japan Ford was initially capitalized in 1925 at a figure of 4 million yen ($1,739,130) and added the same amount to match GM's capitalization level four years later. Both firms remained completely under foreign ownership. The scale of their assembly facilities dwarfed domestic producers, and they dominated the domestic market within five years. By 1934 these two firms accounted for almost 90 percent of

[134]Kozo Yamamura, *Economic Policy in Postwar Japan: Growth versus Economic Democracy* (Berkeley: University of California Press, 1967). For a summary see pp. 52–53, 68–69, 85–86, 106, 127, 180.

[135]Two examples are Richard J. Samuels, *The Business of the Japanese State: Energy Markets in Comparative and Historical Perspective* (Ithaca: Cornell University Press, 1987); Michio Muramatsu and Ellis Krauss, "The Conservative Policy Line and the Development of Patterned Pluralism," in Kozo Yamamura and Yasukichi Yasuba, eds., *The Political Economy of Japan*, vol. 1: *The Domestic Transformation* (Stanford: Stanford University Press, 1987), pp. 516–54.

[136]Phyllis Genther, "Complex Interactions: Government-Business Relations in Japan's Auto Industry" (unpublished manuscript), p. 26; Michael Cusumano, *The Japanese Automobile Industry* (Cambridge: Harvard University Press, 1985), p. 16.

[137]Genther, "Complex Interactions," p. 28.

Japan's market, overwhelming Tokyo Gas and Electric, Ishikawaji Ship-building, and Kaishinsha—Japan's three major domestic producers—which concentrated on military production because it gave them a guaranteed market.[138] But the military authorities did not create a strong industry, merely a dependent one. By the early 1930s every Japanese car firm had either closed down or was on the verge of bankruptcy, giving credence to Michael Cusumano's assessment that in the early 1930s the domestic Japanese auto industry was "starting from scratch."[139]

By the late 1920s extended economic recession and a worsening balance of payments initiated a popular upsurge in nationalism and increased government concern about the effect of imports on Japan's current account deficit. To this concern was added a renewed awareness of national defense, given the military's incursion into Manchuria.[140] The early 1930s therefore were a watershed in government policies. The state sought to institute protective measures. In 1931 a government committee on rationalization made the first determined attempt to assist domestic producers by recommending the minimal tariff on imports be raised. The following year tariff rates of 35 percent on engines and 40 percent on parts were imposed. After restricting direct imports, the state imposed measures that sought simultaneously to develop strong domestic producers and restrict Ford and GM. Government policy, however, was designed to omit the zaibatsu by sponsoring alternative entrepreneurs.[141] Initially formed in May 1931, the Survey Committee for the Establishment of the Automobile Industry was composed of members of government and the business and academic communities. It recommended that domestic firms standardize their product parts and take responsibility for exclusive production in market segments. They also developed plans for a mass-produced "people's car" to be named the Isuzu. Mirroring Hitler's idea of developing the Volkswagen, this notion ran into identical problems: no domestic firm was large enough to produce a competitive, good-quality vehicle, and private-sector producers feared the car would reduce their markets. Despite company mergers orchestrated by the government to facilitate mass production, by 1934 attempts to standardize production through mergers or cooperation had failed. Still, they had a dramatic effect, prompting reorganization among existing producers and some new entrants. Particularly notable were mergers that produced the Isuzu logo for the first time (although the car did not match the government's intent in price or quantity), the incorporation of Nissan in

138Ibid., pp. 31–34.
139Cusumano, *The Japanese Automobile*, pp. 2 and 16.
140Genther, "Complex Interactions," pp. 38–39.
141Magaziner and Hout, *Japanese Industrial Policy*, p. 68.

1933, and the establishment of Toyota as a subsidiary of Toyota Automatic Loom in 1937.[142]

Isuzu (officially incorporated as a company in 1937), Nissan, and Toyota initially developed as government attached new importance to the relationship between the auto industry, national defense, and economic welfare. What followed was a series of measures, enthusiastically sponsored by the military and supervised by the MCI, specifically designed to squeeze out American subsidiaries. The critical measure was the Automobile Manufacturing Enterprise Law of May 1936. It required firms producing more than 3,000 cars per year to be licensed by the state and to be majority owned by Japanese nationals. Licensees were given five-year exemptions from income taxes, local and business revenue taxes, and import duties on machinery, equipment, and materials purchased abroad. In addition, licensees were exempted from undesirable aspects of the commercial code relating to the issuance of new stocks and bonds to raise capital. In exchange, the licensees had to give the state supervisory rights over business plans concerning mergers and the production of military vehicles or equipment.

The law severely restricted Ford and GM, but three further measures were even more explicitly aimed at curtailing their operations. First, Ford's and GM's future production was limited to 1934–35 levels, 12,360 vehicles for Ford and 9,470 for GM. Second, import duties on finished vehicles, components, and units were raised to 50 percent. Third, Japan's foreign exchange regulations were revised to make it difficult for American subsidiaries to pay for the parts they imported. According to Cusumano, these measures had a major impact. They essentially created a monopoly for the only three licensed domestic producers primarily devoted to auto production—Toyota, Nissan, and, more marginally, Isuzu. The American subsidiaries responded by attempting to merge with either Nissan or Toyota, but these moves were thwarted by government and military opposition under the Exchange Control Law. When Ford tried to build its own production plants, it was initially denied the right to purchase land in Yokohama, then denied a building permit.[143]

After the 1936 law further measures were designed to hurt the American subsidiaries and assist Nissan and Toyota. The Temporary Measure Law Relating to Exports, Imports and Other Matters of September 9, 1937 henceforth controlled imports, exports, and the consumption, manufacture, and processing of trade-related goods. The introduction of the Materials Mobilization Plan laid out guidelines for

[142]Genther, "Complex Interactions," pp. 38–44.
[143]Ibid., pp. 48–50.

the use of materials, prohibiting car production in favor of truck production for national security purposes. The cumulative, intended effect of the government's measures, according to Ira Magaziner and Thomas Hout, was to drive GM and Ford out of Japan by 1939.[144] The effect of legislation on market share reveals why they left; Nissan and Toyota accounted for as much as 85 percent of auto production from the mid-1930s until the late 1950s, whereas European and American firms had accounted for 95 percent of production in the decade preceding 1935.[145] Most domestic dealers switched from Ford and GM to Nissan and Toyota, quickly creating a sales and service base for the new firms.[146] Given an additional advantage by government measures such as a favorable allocation of resources, Toyota and Nissan quickly surpassed existing domestic firms in terms of volume and profits through the introduction of foreign technology and mass production techniques. The effects of core sponsorship are indicated by production figures. Toyota's production of four-wheeled vehicles expanded from 20 in 1935 to 16,302 in 1942 and Nissan's from 940 in 1934, to 19,688 in 1941, combining for a total market share of 75.5 percent between 1935 and 1940, and 84.1 percent between 1940 and 1945.[147] The state's measures were astonishingly effective in creating a core and a periphery in the Japanese auto industry, just as they had been in Germany. Here there were two central members of the core, Nissan and Toyota (Isuzu was more marginal), while the periphery was composed of small domestic firms, many of which were forcibly merged or eliminated. From this period onwards, as Phyllis Genther notes, Toyota and Nissan rose to dominance and many small producers were pushed out of the market because they could not meet the authorities' requirements or obtain raw materials. "Government-business interactions geared to protecting the industry increasingly meant protecting the large companies, not all the producers in the industry," as these new heirs to the zaibatsu cooperated with the authorities. The same firms have remained dominant to the present day.[148]

Beyond these immediate considerations relating to the auto industry, the 1936 law was important because it provided a licensing system that let the Japanese government experiment for the first time with promotional and protectionist measures, such as restrictions on imports, local production, and foreign direct investment and encouragement of

[144]See Magaziner and Hout, *Japanese Industrial Policy*, p. 68; Johnson, *MITI and the Japanese Miracle*, p. 132.
[145]Cusumano, *The Japanese Automobile*, pp. 7, 17.
[146]Genther, "Complex Interactions," p. 60.
[147]Ibid., p. 52.
[148]Ibid., pp. 59–60.

firms to acquire foreign technology and invest in new plant and equipment. The state's measures became increasingly restrictive and supervisory in a process sustained through the war and ensuing occupation. The MCI prohibited most car production. Furthermore, it established price and distribution controls on other forms of motor vehicle in 1939, through a Materials Mobilization Plan that remained in effect until 1949. In 1941 the MCI set up a control association for the auto industry, the Automobile Manufacturers Industrial Association, to supervise production levels and distribution of materials, labor, and credit among firms and their suppliers. This association was structured like a cartel except, as in Nazi Germany, its function was to implement state policy rather than formulate its own.[149] Members of this cartel formed the basis of Japan's postwar production of trucks and passenger cars.

Between 1941 and 1945 both the government and the firms poured money into capital goods, particularly heavy machinery for truck production. The MCI gave way to the Ministry of Munitions, which controlled the allocation of raw materials and the manufacture and distribution of production. Executives at Nissan and Toyota were very nationalistic and supported the war effort, cooperating in the development of new technologies.[150] Genther suggests that in the decade and a half after 1930 both the Japanese state and the leading producers learned valuable general lessons that they applied in the postwar period. Among these was the belief that without protection, the domestic market would be dominated by direct imports or foreign direct investors, severely retarding the development of Japanese producers. Such dependence on foreign production would invariably lead to a chronic trade deficit and a foreign exchange shortage. Ford and GM were therefore specifically refused reentry to the Japanese market. Conversely, this period had demonstrated that government assistance could have a positive effect on industrial development. Two strong companies emerged out of a multitude of small and extremely weak domestic producers as a result of government policies, providing the foundation for postwar growth.[151]

Toyota and Nissan escaped the total destruction suffered by many Japanese producers; only Toyota's main plant was significantly damaged. Under the Occupation the executives of these two firms suffered contrasting fates, based on the nominal capitalization of their companies. The General Headquarters of the American forces decided to purge firms with a nominal capitalization of over 100 million yen.

[149]Cusumano, *The Japanese Automobile*, p. 18.
[150]Genther, "Complex Interactions," p. 60.
[151]Ibid., pp. 61–62, 71.

Nissan's capitalization was just over this level, so it lost all its top executives; Toyota's was 97 million yen, so it retained all of its executives. Still, both companies did exhibit a continuity in personnel from prewar through wartime to the postwar period. Ninety percent of Nissan's board of directors in 1965 had joined the company before 1945.[152]

Nevertheless, Toyota and Nissan suffered from similar problems in the latter 1940s. Twice-weekly meetings of officials from the MCI (reconstituted on the eve of surrender), the Ministry of Transport, and the leading manufacturers were convened. A new manufacturers' organization, the Japan Automobile Manufacturers Association, was formed, and it assumed an allocative function for scarce raw materials. Membership was confined to four firms that had produced the vast majority of Japanese military trucks and tanks—Toyota, Nissan, Diesel Motors, and Mitsubishi Heavy Industries (which produced tanks). Only the first three could legally recommence production of trucks at once because the terms of the Automobile Manufacturing Law of 1936 restricting who could produce remained in effect until 1946.[153]

These firms faced problems typically associated with scarce resources, reconstruction of a defeated economy, the threat of foreign competition, and the imposition of allied limitations on production. They also faced the prospect of surplus Allied inventories being sold off cheaply on the domestic market.[154] It was evident that industry leaders required government assistance just to survive. They therefore took the initiative in seeking government support, establishing the National Automobile Industry Revival Conference in April 1947. The conference called for a sectoral policy that would give auto production priority by assuring supplies of raw materials. The MCI responded with a five-year plan that outlined policies designed to end price controls, achieve import substitution, and embark on an export policy.[155] Under the Reconstruction Finance Bill the major producers received extensive government loans critical to their survival; as Cusumano states, "only huge loans from government and private banks kept Nissan, Toyota and Isuzu operating during the late 1940s."[156] Ignoring compelling arguments to neglect these auto firms from Bank of Japan and Ministry of Transport officials, first the MCI and then MITI, its successor, introduced measures to promote an industry they saw as critically important to Japan's future. So against their best economic judgment, the Bank of Japan, the Japanese Development Bank, and

152Cusumano, *The Japanese Automobile*, pp. 57, 74.
153Ibid., p. 74.
154Ibid., p. 19.
155Genther, "Complex Interactions," pp. 85–86.
156Cusumano, *The Japanese Automobile*, p. 19.

the Industrial Development Bank of Japan funded Nissan, Toyota, and Isuzu to keep them out of bankruptcy. Despite mass dismissals designed to increase productivity, the industry tottered on the brink of elimination until the huge demand created by the Korean War eliminated existing inventories, increased production, and provided foreign currency.[157] But it was only MCI and MITI that sustained these firms in the first postwar decade.

First, MITI resisted domestic opposition from within and outside government which either thought other heavy industries (such as shipbuilding or steel) should be favored or believed Japan should invest in light industries. Second, MITI promoted the belief that without the prewar system of tariffs, Japan would again be flooded by imports. Import controls were reintroduced in 1954, and central government agencies were advised to buy only domestic passenger cars. Finally, MITI dealt with the biggest threat, the possibility of recurrent direct foreign investment, by limiting the conditions under which smaller Japanese firms, disadvantaged by government policies, could sign agreements with foreign firms. In the Basic Policy for the Introduction of Foreign Investment into Japan's Passenger Car Industry, MITI explicitly warned foreign firms they might not be able to repatriate earnings and severely limited the conditions for joint ventures. Applications by firms such as Rootes and Chrysler to form joint ventures with small Japanese firms which were themselves seeking to break Nissan and Toyota's dominance were rejected outright, or MITI laid down conditions so constraining that the foreign partner withdrew. MITI's administration of policies governing joint ventures tended to favor the core producers. Genther notes that "while the government supported the development and protection of the passenger car industry, it did not protect all producers or would-be producers."[158]

By the early 1950s a collection of government measures had ensured both the industry's survival and Nissan's and Toyota's privileged position as leading producers. Some measures seemed general in nature although in effect they helped the privileged core firms. In addition to a 40 percent tariff and restrictions on foreign capital investment, imports were also constrained by a maze of currency exchange requirements and controlled by the Foreign Investment Law of 1951. Even autos produced in joint ventures were counted as foreign imports. Other measures more explicitly picked winners and losers. MITI proved highly discriminating in its application of loans, special depreciation measures, exemptions from import duties, authorizations for the im-

[157]Genther, "Complex Interactions," p. 96.
[158]For government policies see ibid., pp. 112–31. The quotation is from p. 131.

port of essential technologies, and subsidies from Japan's Development Bank. The bank even broke with historical precedent by negotiating a loan from the World Bank in 1956 for funds specifically intended for Toyota.[159] Thus, at the micro-level, government policies were explicitly discriminatory in who they did and did not support.

Three trends seemed well established by the middle of the 1950s. First, policies originally formulated in the 1930s had survived the Occupation and continued to be used effectively. The general thread of continuity that Johnson identified in Japanese economic policy is certainly illustrated by the auto industry. Foreigners were kept out, and the position of two national champions, whose rapid emergence the state had sponsored in the 1930s, was sustained largely by government's continued efforts. By 1955 Nissan and Toyota accounted for 69 percent of production.[160] New entrants to the industry in the 1950s, such as Honda and Mazda, found their potential blocked if it was at a cost to Nissan and Toyota's welfare. They often responded by ignoring or rejecting government policy where they could; it is no coincidence that the first Japanese car manufacturer to invest in a manufacturing plant within the United States was Honda. Meanwhile, government policies on tariffs, foreign direct investments, imports, loans, and subsidies survived demands for liberalization in the 1960s. Despite repeated negotiations with Japanese firms, Ford and GM were kept out of the Japanese market.

The second trend, according to Genther, was paradoxically toward a reduction in the state's ability to achieve its intended goals. An effective illustration of the point was the failure of the state to resurrect its people's car project along the lines achieved by Volkswagen in the 1950s.[161] MITI's attempts to rationalize the industry through mergers and an explicit division of labor that would have segmented the market so as to benefit Nissan and Toyota proved just as unsuccessful. Unbridled state power was replaced by private-public cooperation. But the nature of that cooperation, and who the state cooperated with, reflected trends developed earlier. The Japanese state could no longer dominate all auto producers, but it tended to share a cooperative relationship with core producers and an adversarial one with peripheral producers. As Genther suggests, there was no uniform response to government programs among producers. Rather, "these programs produced many types of reactions among the producers, depending on their size and on the specific reorganization program."[162] This shift to

---

[159]Ibid., pp. 138–41.
[160]Ibid., p. 208.
[161]Ibid., pp. 155–60.
[162]Ibid., p. 242.

a reduction in state power and the contrasting relationships between the state and core and peripheral producers are consistent with events in Germany. As in Germany, the state conceded a degree of power to social representatives in the shift away from fascism to a variant of liberal democracy, through the formation of quasi-public institutions. But while it could no longer impose its will uniformly, the Japanese state could still use discretionary power to the advantage of core producers, as in the allocation of automobile exports to the United States under the terms of the Voluntary Export Restraint agreement in the early 1980s.

The third trend by the mid-1950s was toward growth and prosperity. Toyota and Nissan benefited from government protection, as Cusumano notes, but they did not become more uncompetitive—contrary to classic liberal economic theory.[163] Government efforts over three decades had consolidated an industry in which a couple of producers had been given such great advantages that, given appropriate global market conditions, they were sure to flourish. And if those conditions did not prevail for an extended period, as in the late 1940s, it was apparent there were no lengths to which the Japanese state would not go to preserve those firms so that they could prosper in the future.

Italy

Events in the fascist period are clearly reflected in postwar Italy, in the auto industry's structure and in state policies concerning the treatment of foreign multinationals and domestic firms. As in Germany and Japan, so in Italy the advent of a fascist regime and its new policies significantly altered the structure of the auto industry. Consistent with the Japanese pattern of development, the new Italian state excluded foreign finished products and direct investment by foreign subsidiaries while developing a favored firm. In this case the recipient of the state's largess was FIAT.

Prior to the March on Rome and the fascist seizure of power, Italy's domestic auto firms had struggled against foreign competition in a sustained, open market. Citroen, the French firm, was the dominant importer and Ford had laid the groundwork for future production based on the guiding principles adopted in Britain, France, and Germany. Upon seizing power, the fascists' first acts relevant to the auto industry were designed to insulate inefficient producers from foreign competition. During the course of the 1920s tariffs were instituted on imported autos, the duty ranging between 122 percent and 142 percent depending on the size of the engine. To supplement these tariffs a

---

[163]Cusumano, *The Japanese Automobile*, p. 215.

quota system was instituted, denying market access to those producers willing to pay the tariff. The quota limited foreign producers to 3 percent of the market. In tandem these measures gave domestic producers a virtual monopoly on sales in Italy. This system of tariffs and quotas, introduced by Benito Mussolini's fascist regime, outlasted the regime. It was maintained by liberal democratic Italian governments until well into the 1960s and provides one indication of the sustained significance of fascist reforms.[164]

Protectionist measures were supplemented by state policies designed to end foreign direct investment and to drive existing foreign firms manufacturing in Italy, particularly Citroen as the largest foreign direct investor, out of the Italian market.[165] Ford had been the only American producer to establish a subsidiary in prefascist Italy. Ford hoped its Italian subsidiary could coexist with a fascist regime, despite Mussolini's calls for autarky. Initially Ford was the target of much government rhetoric but little effective policy. But the issue of its presence in Italy came to a head in 1929 when the company signaled its intention to rapidly expand its share of the Italian market by first purchasing a large area of land at Livorno as a site for an assembly plant and then opening new sales offices in Bologna, Genoa, and Naples. Giovanni Agnelli, part-owner and president of FIAT, personally protested Ford's actions to Mussolini. The Italian leader expressed his sympathy and suggested that Agnelli negotiate a suitable agreement with Ford. Ford officials and Agnelli were both reluctant negotiators, and lethargic efforts by both sides soon petered out. The fascist government then adopted more direct methods. In November 1929 it passed a decree specifically forbidding the construction of the Ford plant without government consent. Officials made it clear to Ford that such consent would be withheld for an indefinite period. Efforts by General Motors to build production facilities in Italy met a similar response.[166] Mussolini's intentions were subsequently made clear in his suggestion to a Ford representative that "it was not the desire of the Italian Government to permit any big volume of imported automobiles, but rather to foster a 100 per cent Italian manufacture thereof."[167] In Germany Ford initially responded to this sort of treatment by trying to buy an indigenous firm, and likewise, in Italy, Ford responded to the 1929

[164]See Romano Prodi, "Italy," in Raymond Vernon, ed., *Big Business and the State: Changing Relations in Western Europe* (Cambridge: Harvard University Press, 1974), p. 57.

[165]Jones, *Industrial Adjustment*, p. 113.

[166]Daniel Roos, Alan Altshuler, et al., *The Future of the Automobile* (Cambridge: MIT Press, 1984), p. 18.

[167]These data, including the quote, are from Wilkins and Hill, *American Business Abroad*, p. 230.

decree by seeking to merge with a domestic firm, hoping to gain political respectability. Ford officials entered into negotiations with the firm of Isotta Fraschini. Isotta Fraschini's owners were delighted, but Mussolini intervened to thwart the merger.

With an imported Ford now costing two-and-a-half times its American price, Ford's market share dropped dramatically, to 6.6 percent by 1930. Finally, Ford succumbed to government pressure and in effect abandoned the Italian market. It maintained a nominal sales network, using imported cars from Dagenham, but made no serious sales effort and suffered a loss of $699,000 in 1931–32 as FIAT's share of the Italian market was growing. By 1936 Percival Perry conceded that Ford's efforts in Italy were a disaster. Further government restrictions prevented Ford from liquidating the company by threatening forfeiture of assets. Ford decided to maintain its sales network, and the Italian operation consistently registered losses until 1939.[168] The company then decided that indefinite long-term costs were a greater burden than large short-term costs, and so closed down the dealer network and forfeited its assets.

In fact, Mussolini's treatment of Ford proved to be a serious strategic mistake. Instead of maintaining Ford and using its resources, Mussolini foreclosed the firm's development, thereby losing access to a military resource. Ford trucks proved so effective in the desert that Erwin Rommel later praised them and ordered they be captured and used by the Axis powers whenever possible. Ironically, Ford subsidiaries in and around North Africa, notably in Egypt, later sold trucks imported from Dearborn to the Italian government for use in the imperial campaign, but Henry Ford personally intervened when he discovered they were being used in war—increasing the Italian government's hostility to Ford.[169]

After 1939 Ford's Italian stock holding company amounted to no more than a title, which, in the postwar period U.S. Ford purchased from its Italian subsidiary as part of a global campaign to integrate ownership.[170] Yet Ford did not attempt to return to Italy as a producer until 1969, when it tried to take over Lancia. As had happened four decades earlier, Ford's plans were frustrated by government intervention that denied it the right to take over a domestic firm.[171]

The treatment of domestic firms was quite different from that accorded foreign firms. Quotas and tariffs were very effective in excluding foreign imports and, coupled with an aggressive policy toward

[168]Ibid., pp. 230, 260.
[169]Ibid., pp. 258–59.
[170]Ibid., p. 378.
[171]Jones, *Industrial Adjustment*.

multinationals, sealed up the Italian market. These protectionist measures assured Italian producers of a domestic monopoly that raised their profit levels. The money financed domestic capital investment and the formation of foreign subsidiaries, contributing to increased economies of scale. FIAT provides an example of the successful implementation of this policy, with postwar investment in Latin America as a source of profits and increased economies of scale from such mass-produced models as the FIAT 500.

Fascism's effects on the structure of domestic relations both among auto producers, and between the firms, the banking community, and the state, are even more significant at the micro-economic level. The industry was much like the British prior to Mussolini, with a variety of small companies. Fascist rule consolidated the formation of a national champion.[172] Although Alfa Romeo was the first auto firm to come under state ownership in 1933, FIAT remaining under the private ownership of the Agnelli family, the fascist state was far more concerned about FIAT because of its size. FIAT was therefore the primary target and beneficiary of the government's auto policy while Alfa Romeo shifted to aircraft production in preparation for Mussolini's imperialist foreign policy. Giovanni Agnelli, as a fervent supporter of Mussolini, welcomed this close relationship and cultivated it as a way of spreading his influence.[173]

Government policies were mainly funneled through the Istituto per la Ricostruzione Industriale (IRI), founded as a publicly funded holding company in 1933.[174] The IRI was originally conceived as a way of bailing out unprofitable banks and strategic industrial concerns, as well as a public utility company, but it soon took on a more activist industrial role. It insisted on acquiring 50 percent ownership in FIAT from the Agnelli family and assumed control of Alfa Romeo.[175] As a result, FIAT and Alfa benefited from exclusive access to the state.[176] Furthermore, they were singled out for special treatment, receiving an assured supply of iron and steel.[177] The government took the opportunity to adopt a more directive role in FIAT and supervised the opening of its new Mirafiori plant in Turin in 1939.

[172]Louis T. Wells, "Automobiles," in Vernon, ed., *Big Business and the State*, p. 234.

[173]Roland Sarti, *Fascism and the Industrial Leadership in Italy, 1919–1940* (Berkeley: University of California Press, 1971), p. 40.

[174]On the IRI see M. V. Posner and Stuart J. Woolf, *Italian Public Enterprise* (London: Duckworth, 1967), pp. 43–53.

[175]For the IRI under fascism see Kevin Allen and Andrew Stevenson, *An Introduction to the Italian Economy* (London: Robertson, 1974), pp. 217–22.

[176]See Wells, "Automobiles," in Vernon, ed., *Big Business and the State*, pp. 233–34.

[177]Sarti, *Fascism and the Industrial Leadership*, p. 109.

FIAT became the dominant Italian producer under fascism, and it assumed the mantle of national champion after 1945. Its fascist past was discredited, but the structure of relations between firm and state was sustained and, if anything FIAT adopted a role as instrument of the state even more pronounced than that of Volkswagen in Germany, Nissan and Toyota in Japan, or, as we shall see, Renault in France. FIAT assumed control of Autobianchi in 1963 and Lancia in 1969, for example, in moves specifically designed to frustrate foreign takeovers. But despite FIAT's postwar position as a private sector company, public-sector officials have often insisted on maintaining significant influence, periodically straining relations with the Agnellis.[178]

The benefits of the mantle of national champion were tangible. Its monopoly in a protected market made FIAT the only firm selling mass-produced cars in Italy. But products became outdated without the stimulus of competition. Overwhelming protection was replaced by greater exposure to competition in the 1960s and 1970s, when a monopoly over Latin American markets broke down through rival investment by European producers and the monopoly in Italy was ended by EEC membership. Increased competition severely curtailed the firm's profits, and the government responded to a slump in sales of crisis proportions. In the early 1980s government allocated extensive funding over a three-year period that provided the basis for FIAT's reemergence in the late 1980s as one of Europe's most competitive producers.[179]

In the pattern of protectionism and favoritism in Italy from the early 1920s to the late 1970s one can identify the influence of fascist state policy. The Italian pattern does not perfectly match the French, German, and Japanese varieties but bears similar characteristics. Italian fascism began earlier. As in the other countries, the fascists treated foreign firms brutally, and the state cultivated domestic mass and specialist producers. The structure of the industry was revolutionized through macro- and micro-level policies that survived the return to democracy and were embraced by right-wing democratic parties. It is conventional to consider Italy's fascist regime the longest-lasting but the shallowest in its effect on the structure of society. Such a view ignores the influence of state policy on economic structure.

France

France is the most problematic and deviant of the four fascist regimes. This assessment is not too surprising: the country was physically

[178]Jones, *Industrial Adjustment,* p. 53.
[179]Ibid.

divided by an occupying power that imposed a fascist regime, even
though the country had a large, indigenous fascist movement and regime leaders were French. Nevertheless, if the issue whether fascism
was indigenous or imposed is crucial, as Peter Katzenstein suggests,
then one would expect France's auto industry to resemble the industrial
structure of small states rather than those of the postfascist regimes of
Germany, Italy, and Japan. Yet despite variations, the pattern of events
in France resembles that in countries with indigenous fascist regimes.
Moreover, a discernibly similar structure suggests that fascist state policy did indeed have a significant effect on the auto industry in both the
Vichy and the postwar periods. My specific argument about the auto
industry is consistent with Robert Paxton's general argument about the
revolutionary effect of the Vichy regime on the French bureaucracy—
and how that legacy reemerged in the Fifth Republic.[180] According to
Paxton, the civil service was rationalized and emphasized technocratic
values; the bureaucracy extended its influence to local levels. To the
statist tradition was added a more authoritative, directive element. The
new economic order was built around a corporatist notion of self-
regulation by business, which in practice tended to favor the development of big business—consolidating a move toward efficiency and
greater productivity through rationalization, concentration, and modernization in order to supply the German economy with greater resources.[181] Paxton says that "France was being dragged through the
Occupation in the direction of concentrated industry and rationalization. The 1930s' emphasis upon preventing overproduction was already giving way to the postwar emphasis upon seeking higher productivity. Corporatism had become central planning and *dirgisme*."[182] In
his most controversial claim, Paxton concludes that the boom of the
1950s and 1960s originated in the discrediting during the Vichy period
of the values and structures of the ancien regime. Many of his generalizations about radical restructuring apply to the French auto industry.

In the prewar period Ford was the only American subsidiary to produce in France. It set up a manufacturing plant as it had done in
Britain and Germany, largely as a response to tariffs imposed from
1916 onwards—in this case between 70 and 220 percent—to curtail
American imports. Fewer imports and Ford's new local plant resulted
in the growth of aggregate French production from 18,000 automobiles in 1919 to 254,000 in 1929.[183] Although the majority market

[180]Robert O. Paxton, *Vichy France: The Old Guard and New Order, 1940–44* (New York:
Knopf, 1972), p. 193.
[181]Ibid., pp. 213–16.
[182]Ibid., p. 20.
[183]Patrick Fridenson, "French Automobile Marketing, 1890–1970," in Akio Okochi
and Koichi Shimokawa, eds., *The Development of Mass Marketing* (Tokyo: University of
Tokyo Press, 1981), pp. 133–34.

share was then divided between Renault, Peugeot, and Citroen, concentration and rationalization were consolidated during the Vichy regime. The integration of small domestic firms that had held just over a third of France's market in the early 1930s was so complete that in the postwar period the periphery was little more than the American multinationals. Domestic producers were consolidated into four major firms: Renault, Citroen, Simca, and Peugeot.

Renault emerged as the chief wartime producer under the ownership and control of Louis Renault. He collaborated with both Vichy and German leaders, and his company received extra materials and machinery and was streamlined to provide the Germans with cars and tanks.[184] Many competitors were closed down or, as in the case of Ford (the only American multinational in France in the Third Republic or under Vichy), were left intact while assets were shipped to Germany. Discrimination crippled Ford during the war, in stark contrast to the British subsidiary.[185] Maurice Dollfus, head of the French Ford subsidiary, was placed under the direct authority of Robert Schmidt, head of the Cologne plant. Robert Schmidt, under orders from the Nazis, confiscated the best machinery from the French Ford plant at Asnières and shipped it to Cologne.[186] Dollfus struggled through to the end of the war, keeping the company in existence as a minor producer of armaments for the Germans. The Asnières plant suffered heavily in the last year of the war, from strategic Allied bombing and the Allied invasion. Even firms that did survive (with the exception of Renault) suffered heavily from German confiscation. Peugeot is one example: three hundred specialist machines were taken from its plants and shipped to the Volkswagenwerk, thereby depleting a productive capacity already affected by shortages of raw materials.[187]

Despite the wartime problems, Ford's prospects seemed bright in 1945 to visitors from Detroit. A new plant was built at Poissy.[188] Yet Ford's French subsidiary encountered consistent political hostility from the new French state. Perhaps production for the Germans—which had led to heavy bombing—was partially responsible for this antagonism.[189] The appointment of François Lehideux, who had exercised control over the entire French auto industry under Vichy, as Ford's managing director in 1948 probably aggravated the firm's relationship with the French government. This hostility was fundamental in the

[184]Paxton, *Vichy France*, p. 343.
[185]Jones, *Industrial Adjustment*, p. 36.
[186]Letter, Dollfus to Edsel Ford, 27 November 1940, Accession 6, Box 361, Edison Institute.
[187]See BIOS Report, Number 768, IWM.
[188]Wilkins and Hill, *American Business Abroad*, p. 342.
[189]Ibid., p. 331.

parent company's decision to sell its French operation to Simca in 1954.[190] When Ford tried to come back in 1964, it was denied permission to build a plant by Charles de Gaulle's French government and built a plant in Belgium instead.[191]

Chrysler purchased Simca in 1963 as a way of gaining entrance to the French auto market. Daniel Jones suggests that "the [French] state was unsuccessful in blocking Chrysler's takeover of Simca between 1958 and 1963 because the shares were already privately owned." However, once the shares were purchased, Chrysler found its attempts to integrate the company into its European operations thwarted at every turn by French governments.[192] General Motors did not even get this far, only contemplating investment in France in 1964. Like Ford, it sought to build a plant in Strasbourg, but de Gaulle rejected GM's request to invest in France. Like Ford, it had to settle in Belgium instead.

In the postwar period, unlike before the war, Jones suggests, "hostility to foreign firms has been a continuous feature of car industry policy in France." Even after joining the EEC, the French government retained the right to limit foreign investment. Foreign firms have the right to purchase up to 20 percent of the shares of a French firm but require permission from a committee of the Ministry of Finance to purchase more. This committee can veto acquisitions it considers "harmful to French interests or contrary to the government's industrial strategy."[193] The rules were relaxed only in 1980 for acquisitions made by firms based in EEC states. The last time an American auto producer seriously considered investment was in the early 1980s when Ford suggested it build an assembly plant in the depressed Lorraine region. The government rejected the idea, maintaining its exclusion of foreign investment.

In sum, American firms after Vichy could not create their own subsidiaries and were subject to harassment when they attempted to invest in domestic firms. Stipulations and pressures, coupled with tariffs and quotas, effectively sealed off the French market from either investment by American capital or the import of American-owned products.

The other side of the coin has been the French state's treatment of domestic firms. The characteristics of postwar state behavior, favoring select domestic firms, bear some similarities to those identified in Germany. After the war Louis Renault had his assets confiscated, and the company was nationalized in 1946. Nevertheless it remained largely intact, typical of the continuity of Vichy innovations throughout

[190]Ibid., p. 393.
[191]Jones, *Industrial Adjustment.*
[192]Ibid.
[193]Ibid., p. 37.

French industry.[194] Under new state ownership Renault took on most favored status, a French national champion despite its discredited past. The new government punished the perpetrators of the company's restructuring, but successive governments of the left and right retained the internal changes and new relationship between firm and state developed during Vichy. The newly rationalized Renault benefited from its exclusive access to the state.[195] It was protected from domestic rivals and international competitors while being nurtured by the French state.[196]

Successive French governments used high protective tariffs and quotas to exclude American firms from the marketplace, and Renault dominated the French market in the 1950s and 1960s.[197] The other French producers—Peugeot, Citroen, and Simca—also benefited from the exclusion of American firms. Nevertheless, some French producers struggled because they were still recovering from the war and did not receive the postwar benefits granted to Renault. As Patrick Fridenson suggests, Renault's government ownership and an insulated market did not guarantee the success of the French auto industry.[198] The characteristic government solution for an ailing French firm was to organize a merger. One example is the case of Citroen. The government orchestrated two deals whereby the struggling Citroen was taken over by Peugeot and Renault assumed responsibility for Berliet, Citroen's commercial vehicle division.[199] Unlike in Britain, however, concentration was accompanied by rationalization to achieve greater economies of scale.

The government continued its close relationship with Renault after the war. The company's senior management has traditionally been appointed in close consultation with the government, which has influenced basic strategy and removed obstacles in the path of Renault's goals.[200] Renault has had ready access to loan capital from government when needed and has benefited from "negotiating favorable tax treatment and alleviating the burden of social security payments," enabling "Renault to restrain prices and increase its market share."[201] Renault has traditionally had direct access to high-level government officials to resolve conflicts over such issues as speed of expansion and location of new plants. This exchange of information has often been accompanied

[194]Ibid., p. 252.
[195]See Charles Albert Michalet, "France," in Vernon, ed., *Big Business and the State*, pp. 107–9.
[196]Wells, "Automobiles," in Vernon, ed., *Big Business and the State*, p. 234.
[197]Ibid.
[198]Fridenson, "French Automobile Marketing," p. 142.
[199]Jones, *Industrial Adjustment*, pp. 37–38.
[200]Ibid., p. 38.
[201]Ibid.

by an exchange of personnel, particularly between the auto producer and the Ministry of Industry, which has resulted in shared priorities among senior industrialists and civil servants.[202] These shared views were reflected in, for example, the slow reduction of trade barriers even after France had joined the EEC, to 17.6 percent in 1968 and 11 percent in 1972.[203]

The French treatment of American multinational corporations resembled both the Italian and the Japanese response—throwing them out of the market altogether. As in Germany, Italy, and Japan, the state in France distinguished between favored and other firms among domestic producers. It favored Renault. While other firms benefited from macro-level policies, they did not benefit from micro-level policies as much as Renault, which was clearly given preferential treatment. Renault has consistently been able to rely on the support of its government, secure in the knowledge that it will be protected from hostile takeovers and competition from foreign subsidiaries. But with fewer producers than Germany or Japan and a completely insulated market, France could afford to sustain all its producers while making one firm the national champion.

Clearly, each country has unique characteristics that were reflected in its auto industry before and after the experience of fascism. In France the state was centralized long before the Vichy regime. Vichy's contribution was not so much to create a new source of state power as to sharpen the state's economic instruments, particularly those which could be used to discriminate—pointedly against American producers and subtly in favor of a national champion that had first become preeminent during Vichy. The French may have disowned the Vichy experience as an alien phenomenon, but they gladly retained the structure of relationships it created in the auto industry. On the micro-level this pattern preserved Renault's special status, reflected in subsidies and the funding of expansion. On the macro-level, for at least the first two postwar decades, the French market remained insulated from foreign competition. Now, although EEC membership has brought greater competition, tariffs and quotas ensure Renault remains heavily protected from two of its major potential competitors, American and Japanese producers.

The nature of state policies and structure of the French auto industry suggest that Vichy is a hybrid case in this analysis. The influence of fascism is clearly reflected in the state's new discriminatory treatment of foreign direct investors and its favoritism toward Renault. Yet the

---

[202]Ibid., pp. 39–40.
[203]Fridenson, "French Automobile Marketing," p. 141.

core-periphery distinction between Renault and other domestic producers is not so emphatic, reflecting less discrimination (and, correspondingly, greater egalitarianism) than in Germany, Italy, or Japan. Like Britain, France supported all its domestic firms by creating a floor in the postwar period. The French example perhaps illustrates the different implications of imposed and indigenous fascism, highlighting state policies that discriminated powerfully against foreigners but not as powerfully among domestic firms.

CONCLUSION

This chapter has briefly examined the automobile industry in five countries since the 1920s. Three of those countries, Germany, Italy, and Japan, were unquestionably ruled by indigenous fascist regimes. France was ruled by an externally imposed fascist regime. The Vichy regime was predicated on German power and staffed by native Frenchmen who enthusiastically cooperated with the Germans. In terms of the effect of state policy on the structure of the automobile industry the source of the fascist regime may have made a difference. French policies during Vichy departed radically from those of the Third Republic and resembled those of Germany, Italy, and Japan in some respects. The structure of relations between the state and foreign firms in France resembled that in other fascist states and, as in those states, was reflected in the postwar auto industry. In prefascist France, Italy, and Japan liberal foreign direct investment policies and egalitarian treatment created an environment in which American subsidiaries thrived; fascist regimes then introduced policies explicitly designed to encourage American firms to abandon these markets and the capital they had invested locally. Indeed, state policies in these countries were perhaps more extreme than in Germany, where American subsidiaries, though repressed, were at least allowed to continue in existence. In France, Renault certainly benefited more than other domestic firms, though a core-periphery distinction among domestic firms was not so pronounced.

The one country that deviated from this pattern of discrimination and repression was Britain. In the prefascist period the British auto industry bore important similarities to its counterparts in these other four countries: numerous small producers were protected from foreign imports by high tariff barriers. In Britain, as in the other four countries, American firms had responded by investing in local production facilities and had thrived. Although American firms did not have the market dominance they enjoyed in Japan, for example, the potential was there. Yet while the structure of the auto industry was radically altered elsewhere in the fascist period, and the change was sustained in the postfascist period, it was retained in postwar Britain. Only in the 1960s did the undesirable effects of a sustained liberal policy toward foreign direct investment become apparent, when the terms of trade turned against sustained foreign investment and American firms in Britain shifted from exporters to importers. However, events in this period can be explained by policies dating over the prior four decades. The comparison of prewar conditions in Britain, France, and the Axis powers supports the proposition that fascist state policy had a significant, lasting effect on the structure and aggregate welfare of the auto industry and the prosperity of individual companies.

The four countries ruled by fascist states were in no sense identical, of course. Each one's domestic structure in general and the structure of each auto industry in particular differed from the others in important ways before, during, and after fascist rule. Germany, for instance, permitted American subsidiaries to continue manufacturing throughout the fascist period, although it imposed new political cadres as company executives, curtailed the free flow of investment capital, and strictly allocated resources, production, employment, and sales. Yet Germany and the other three share important similarities that distinguish them from Britain. All were ruled by fascist states that ruthlessly pursued discriminatory policies. Not only were American subsidiaries repressed and often driven out, but favored domestic firms received the benefits of consolidation, centralization, and, most important, rationalization. These states developed both an understanding of the process of, and acquired the economic instruments for, intervention—a fact only explicitly acknowledged in Japan by postwar elite bureaucrats. Never ruled by fascists, the British neither integrated the concept of discrimination into their dominant ideology nor acquired the institutional tools necessary to impose selective policies. These omissions were reflected in postwar policies—particularly in the defensive consolidation of the domestic auto industry without centralization and rationalization and in the failure to protect indigenous producers against market dominance by American subsidiaries.

CHAPTER EIGHT

The Consequences
of Fascism

Political scientists have understandably tended to focus their studies of fascism on its causes. World War II and the Holocaust generate questions that demand answers. Why Hitler? Why Germany? Why Auschwitz?—all were reasonable questions even if effective answers remained beyond our grasp. But all choices involve a trade-off. Questions about fascism's causes meant neglect of questions about its consequences. The absence of empirical research created a vacuum filled by the myth of the fresh start: a slate had been wiped clean, a new, distinct West German economy had arisen "from the ashes" as the product of a liberal democratic economic system. Germans had to live with national shame, but Germany was divided, and the new German economy was historically detached from the old.

In a way this view suited everybody. It suited West Germans and their leaders who were keen to distance themselves from economic advances paid for by Nazi atrocities. It suited the new Communist leaders of East Germany who, like the Soviets, sought to propagate the idea that fascism was a natural outgrowth of capitalism. The Nazi state was a different political creature from the innocent German Democratic Republic. The tendency to delink the postwar economy from that of the Third Reich also suited the Western Allies. If history is written by the winners, then Britain, France, and the United States wanted the world to believe their victory had been complete and decisive, and nothing should spoil that idea. In the Cold War climate the Western allies particularly wanted the USSR and its satellites, their potential new adversaries, to believe that the conquering Western powers brought opponents to their knees and then restructured their societies and economies. Political science had its own version of fighting the new enemy, as comparativists replaced fascism with communism as the new totalitarian threat.[1]

The success of reforms in the western zones of Germany through the 4 Ds—demilitarization, decartelization, decentralization, and denazification—went unquestioned. A few historical studies of individual companies and some general studies of the postwar reforms provided credible supporting evidence, although the company studies were based on scant empirical material and the more general ones concentrated on constitutional changes.[2] More broadly, a common view developed that the economic miracles of the German Federal Republic, Japan, and, to a lesser extent, Italy in the 1950s and 1960s were all the results of reform and new capitalization. Their economies arose "like a phoenix from the ashes." The photographs of bombed-out production facilities at Volkswagen's Wolfsburg plant provided evidence to support this view. Indeed, explanations were developed that stressed the cleansing effects of total destruction. They found their cumulative theoretical expression in Mancur Olson's *Rise and Decline of Nations*, which employed a sophisticated deductive model to demonstrate the rehabilitative effects of wholesale destruction on the capacity of entrepreneurial capitalism to generate high growth rates.[3] One popular variant stressed that the destruction of the old Axis powers had required each country to develop a new capital base, supposedly paid for by the Allies. German, Italian, and Japanese prosperity was paid for by countries that had defeated them in war: "The Allies won the war but the Axis powers won the peace."

Other social scientists and historians of Germany and Japan stressed continuities that predated fascism. The postwar successes of the Federal Republic and Japan were somehow linked to late development, to late unification in Germany and the Meiji Restoration in Japan. A parallel approach was offered by scholars who emphasized long-term structural factors in Britain's economic decline.[4] To political scientists, it appeared that history could be conveniently packaged into landmark dates around which parsimonious explanations could be generated.[5] Alexander Gerschenkron's sophisticated analysis, linking the contribu-

[1]See Carl Friedrich, *Constitutional Government and Democracy* (Boston: Ginn, 1946), preface.

[2]For the former see, for instance, Walter H. Nelson, *Small Wonder: The Amazing Story of Volkswagen* (Boston: Little, Brown, 1965); for the latter see John D. Montgomery, *Forced to Be Free: The Artificial Revolution in Germany and Japan* (Chicago: University of Chicago Press, 1957).

[3]Mancur Olson, *The Rise and Decline of Nations: Economic Growth, Stagflation, and Social Rigidities* (New Haven: Yale University Press, 1982).

[4]Eric Hobsbawm, *Industry and Empire* (Harmondsworth: Penguin, 1978).

[5]This approach has been taken to its extreme in the recent literature, notably in works that sought to explain Britain's and the United States' rise and decline as hegemonic

tion of the timing of Germany's entry into the world political economy to the structure and role of the state, was expanded by Barrington Moore's cross-national comparison in his model of three roads to modernity. But the essence of these arguments was distorted by a tendency to redefine these factors as critical variables that could do much to explain the structure of modern economies—and, by implication, their propensities for prosperity. The result has been arguments that are underspecified and overdetermined.

This book challenges both traditional explanations of Britain's and West Germany's relative postwar prosperity, those that stress causes which either predate or postdate fascism and World War II. It does so by directly linking economic robustness to the continuities and changes that characterized state policies in each country in the 1930s and 1940s. In this period the British state solidified and consolidated a set of values and institutions. In Germany, however, political changes revolutionized the state's dominant values and the nature and scope of its institutions. The difference is reflected in contrasting public policies after 1945.

I have focused on the automobile industry for two reasons. First, the automobile industry was the basis for Germany's economic miracle. If the argument works for the auto industry, it helps explain postwar German prosperity, even if it only applies to one industry. Second, the automobile industries in Britain and Germany were remarkably similar in the late 1920s and early 1930s yet differed drastically in the late 1940s, 1950s, and 1960s. This difference was due to the divergence in state policies.

Two aspects of change, between Weimar and the Third Reich, and continuity, between the Third Reich, the Occupation, and the Bonn Republic, are evident. First, the principles governing the state's economic behavior shifted, from encouragement of active, integrative, but nondiscriminatory behavior in the Wilhelmine and Weimar periods to the sanctioning of discriminatory behavior in the Third Reich. This tendency may have been diluted with the defeat of National Socialism, but was nevertheless still evident in the Bonn Republic, notably in the discriminatory behavior of Finance Ministry officials (with the collusive assistance of favored firms and the larger banks). Even the labor unions made unique contractual concessions to Volkswagen. As a result, American subsidiaries had to subordinate their interests to an industry-wide

---

powers. See Robert Gilpin, *U.S. Power and the Multinational Corporation: The Political Economy of Foreign Direct Investment* (New York: Basic, 1975), and his *War and Change in World Politics* (New York: Cambridge University Press, 1981), both of which take a structural approach to explaining historical development.

agreement that specialist producers, with their high value-added products, could afford. Meanwhile Volkswagen, their main competitor, was exempted from the agreements and independently negotiated more favorable terms. State officials demonstrated coercive tendencies when they subverted Opel's and Fordwerke's attempts to break free from these cartelistic arrangements by negotiating individual contracts, confirming Leo Panitch's view that, buried in the concept of cooptation, corporatism has a repressive component.[6] Ludwig Erhard himself was initially intent on eradicating any form of intervention but was drawn to intervene. By the early 1960s he had shifted emphasis from the reformist "social market economy" to the corporative, "formed" society.

The second change initiated in the Third Reich was in the nature of the state's institutions. Increased autonomy encouraged the state to develop more diverse capacities. The state moved from a primarily integrative role to a more directive, authoritative one. This tendency was reflected in a generally manipulative treatment of cartels and, more specifically, its behavior toward the automobile industry. There any relation between market forces and production, prices, and distribution was abandoned in favor of the state's authoritative allocation of resources. Again, the postwar period saw the state abandon more coercive instruments, such as certification and standardization, but the initial maldistribution of material resources under the Allies and then of financial resources under the Bonn Republic was performed with allocative instruments that originated in the Third Reich. Even Erhard, the disciple of classical liberalism, thought it appropriate to negotiate the price of cars with Volkswagen. These changes in the values and instruments of the state caused a further change, in the distribution of wealth among producers and in the industry's aggregate wealth.

No comparable changes occurred in the dominant values of the British state or its instruments, and so in the nature of its policies. An egalitarian ideology was sustained, and with it a reliance on macroeconomic instruments rather than the sensitive sectoral instruments suited to implementing discriminatory policies. As a result, a potential American dominance of Britain's auto industry in the early 1930s materialized after the war, generating policies whose effects reached their zenith in the 1960s as Ford, Vauxhall, and Chrysler dwarfed indigenous producers in terms of market share. Despite the undesirable results of five decades of generous policies to foreign investors, for the welfare of indigenous producers, for the balance of payments, and for the state's autonomy, British governments continued to give American

---

[6]Leo Panitch, "Recent Theorizations of Corporatism: Reflections on a Growth Industry," *British Journal of Sociology* 31 (June 1980), p. 163.

subsidiaries loans, grants, and tax breaks. While British Leyland needed all the help it could get, the state gave financial assistance to Chrysler. Stephen Wilks suggests that the contemporary problems of the British car industry can be traced to government policies toward foreign multinationals in the 1960s. While I share the spirit of Wilks's interpretation, I believe the policies of the 1960s were consistent with those at the industry's formation early in the century. This consistency can largely be explained by the fact that Britain escaped the traumas of Weimar, fascism, and military defeat. Political stability in the face of the economic challenge of the Depression, the political challenge of the indigenous fascist movement, and the military challenge of the Axis powers reinforced a conviction about the superiority of British values, institutions, and methods. They did not serve Britain well in the new context of the postwar world economy.

Political scientists, employing interest-based explanations, have long recognized the tendency of liberal states to emphasize the costs of change and push the costs of adjustment on others whenever possible. Concerns about political costs are always amplified by the domination of the incumbent government's behavior by short-term electoral considerations. The political and economic costs of avoiding change, however, are significantly increased, I suggest, the longer they are postponed. The German fascist state disregarded such concerns. It implemented the required changes by rationalizing production and, more important, politically restructuring the industry. Perhaps only a state as powerful as a fascist state could do so; the liberal British state could not.

This book does not constitute a traditional sectoral study because it does not treat the auto sector as monolithic. By examining firms that benefited and firms that suffered from state policies I have sought a dynamic explanation of one industry's development, an explanation that stresses the importance of process.

CONTRASTING PATTERNS

The details of Ford and Austin in Britain and Fordwerke and Volkswagen in Germany bear out my general expectations. Volkswagen was an intended, unqualified beneficiary of Nazi state policies; Fordwerke's growth and development were first stopped and, after 1933, reversed. Once the private sector's reluctance to help the Volkswagen project became apparent, the DAF assumed all engineering, financial, and political responsibilities for design, construction, and personnel. The motive behind Volkswagen's development was unquestionably political;

the state intended to subsidize the car in order to raise the "social wage" of the laboring masses and thereby legitimate the Nazi government. Indeed, by defining Volkswagen as a public utility the state codified its disinterest in profits. But an unintended consequence of the state's activities was to create a firm perfectly positioned to take advantage of sustained demand for a cheap, reliable car after the war. Of course, this outcome was contingent: the Wolfsburg plant could have ended up in the Soviet zone, or the British Treasury could have lost its fight with the Board of Trade and Ministry of Supply and the plant could have been dismantled. But although random factors may play a role in determining outcomes, in this instances they did not derail Volkswagen.

In contrast, the Nazis intentionally stifled Fordwerke's development. Although the company posed no challenge to Opel's dominance in the early 1930s, it seemed well-positioned to prefigure what happened in Britain in the 1950s when sales and profits grew at the expense of small, unprofitable mass producers. Yet explicitly coercive state policies, instituted soon after 1933, aborted this potential. Ford's Cologne plant languished, excluded from state contracts and grants despite Hitler's admiration of the parent company's achievements in the United States and the unrelenting efforts of executives and owner to curry favor with the fascist state. Furthermore, state policies on standardization and domestic ownership crippled Fordwerke in the 1930s. In a triumph of ideology over pragmatism, in the wartime allocation of scarce resources Fordwerke was consistently treated as producer of last resort, even though these policies sometimes hurt Germany's military efforts.

Details about the relative treatment of Fordwerke and Volkswagen under the Third Reich would be interesting but inconclusive if we could not demonstrate any bearing on postwar prosperity. But evidence does substantiate the existence of such a relationship. It strongly suggests that Volkswagen retained the material benefits it accumulated during the Third Reich. Volkswagen was no "phoenix from the ashes"; rather, the vast bulk of its hitherto unprecedented assembly of capital survived destruction and was essential to the firm's postwar expansion. Furthermore, the contrasting treatment of Fordwerke and Volkswagen continued (albeit in a diluted form) in the discriminatory policies of the Allied authorities and the new Bonn Republic. Both firms were located in the British sector, and the British Treasury had an agenda different from that of the Western Allies. The French authorities focused on reparations, hoping to confiscate machinery formerly owned by the DAF. The Americans were more concerned about political reform and the introduction of a federal system.

The Treasury's dominance over policy placed an emphasis on relieving the British exchequer of the burden of supporting the German population. Relief could most easily be secured by reinvigorating the German economy. Volkswagen was considered a cornerstone of the new German economy, and so the Treasury, in cooperation with the CCG, made strenuous efforts to find it resources and profitable markets. These policies repeatedly conflicted with the interests of Fordwerke, whose access to markets and resources suffered in a zero-sum allocation game. Volkswagen's unlimited access to resources and guaranteed government contracts provided the initial basis for its exponential growth in the 1950s. Under terms agreed with the British, responsibility for Volkswagen was awarded to the new Finance Ministry, which for over a decade effectively resisted Erhard's neoliberal efforts to privatize Volkswagen. Erhard had relatively little influence over Finance Ministry policy because, despite his prestige, his real power lay in the Economics Ministry. And thus, despite impeccable antifascist credentials, the Finance Ministry triumvirate of Minister Fritz Schäffer, Staatssekretär Alfred Hartmann, and Heinz Maria Oeftering (who was also a Volkswagen director) colluded with Heinrich Nordhoff to replicate the discriminatory policies that had advantaged Volkswagen in the Third Reich. Of course, these policies were not so crude or so explicit, but they maintained the same relationships between state and firms as those instituted under fascism and reinforced during the Occupation. Statist intervention helped Volkswagen sustain fabulous levels of growth by making research and development grants available, encouraging high levels of capital reinvestment, and facilitating bilateral agreements among selected producers including Volkswagen, Audi, NSU, BMW, Daimler-Benz, and Porsche. Volkswagen was the fulcrum in these agreements, providing the adhesive for the core of the German auto industry. Volkswagen enjoyed an intimate, collusive relationship with the state because it shared interests with both the state and other core firms; also it was resourceful enough to effectively implement these policies. Joint research, production, and marketing agreements between core firms conflicted with the basic principles of the Federal Republic's new antitrust laws, but the evidence suggests that the purpose of this unofficial "cartel within an industry" was to undermine the competitive position of American subsidiaries.

The Finance Ministry officials were ousted at the end of the 1950s when Erhard extended his political power from the Economics Ministry to the CDU. He presented control over the Finance Ministry to the party as a referendum on his leadership and won. But cumulatively Nordhoff and the Finance Ministry officials had entrenched relations in the auto industry that systematically favored certain indigenous producers, guaranteeing that American multinationals would not overwhelm the German market as they did the British. On the contrary, they ensured that Fordwerke and Opel would remain on the defensive, and as domestic and foreign markets grew, Volkswagen was uniquely positioned to fill the vacuum created by Opel's demise, which dated from the Nazi era.

Events in Britain followed a different course. In the early 1930s American subsidiaries had been more dominant in Germany than in Britain; British Ford could not match Opel's domestic market share. But the construction of Dagenham in the early 1930s gave Ford the potential to assume dominance—a potential unfulfilled until the 1950s because of Depression, war, and government constraints. Yet Ford and Vauxhall repeatedly benefited from the egalitarian principles upon which British state policy was predicated. In practice these policies gave them all the benefits associated with indigenous production but did not burden them with corresponding obligations. Successive British governments and their bureaucracies repeatedly refused to discriminate against American subsidiaries and in favor of indigenous firms, even when presented with motives, instruments, and evidence that such a course would reduce national dependence on foreign capital. Conversely, however hard Austin worked to achieve the explicit goals of the British state—to break the defense contractors' cartel in World War I, to fulfill government contracts in World War II, to secure American dollars in an export drive in the late 1940s or in the Korean War effort in the early 1950s—it received not the slightest advantage.

It was almost too easy for Ford. The louder their executives complained about maltreatment, the more inclined British officials were to prove that Ford was receiving fair treatment, even if that occasionally meant flagrantly transgressing their own egalitarian principles by in effect favoring foreign firms. Ford's initially distant relationship with the British state (characteristic of the firm's global culture) was replaced by cooperation and trust. Its executives were periodically integrated into the decision-making apparatus of the state, doubling as ministry officials during World War II and taking a leading role in rewriting the PEP report on the future of the British auto industry in 1950. Ford was always treated as a faithful friend of Britain.

This cordial relationship between American subsidiaries and British state is an interesting contrast to two alternative sets of state-firm relations. First, compare this close relationship with the British state's indifference toward indigenous producers, particularly Austin. Austin's persistent efforts to assist the state went unrecognized and unrewarded. Its eventual disenchantment led to an alienated, almost poisoned relationship based on mistrust and suspicion. Second, contrast this relationship with state-firm relations in Germany, where American subsidiaries were treated with hostility rather than gratitude. Only the executives of Volkswagen and coopted indigenous partners such as BMW and Daimler-Benz were integrated into the state apparatus.

I have examined the relations of only two states with Austin, Ford, Fordwerke, and Volkswagen in detail. Yet these cases provide a basis for expanding the analysis. Many of the contrasting patterns of relations with the state identified in the study of these four firms were replicated among other British and German firms. Evidence about Opel provides critical support for the argument because although it started from a vastly different position in terms of market share and importance to the state, it converged with Fordwerke's position during the Third Reich. Furthermore, the contrasting fates in the early 1960s of BMW and Borgward, as a coopted partner and a paternal industrialist, substantiate the expectations generated by the argument.

The consistency of policy in Britain should not detract from its interest. As the state helped indigenous firms "circle the wagons," encouraging defensive mergers and providing financial assistance, it simultaneously pursued economic policies that pushed these firms toward eventual oblivion. It underwrote losers, creating fiscal irresponsibility among management and labor, but refused to use discriminatory instruments to create an environment for expansion. Bail-outs became more common as earlier, generous state policies toward American multinationals had their full effect in the 1970s and 1980s. It nationalized firms without rationalizing or centralizing them, preserving an inability to achieve economies of scale. And it allocated scarce material and financial resources to American subsidiaries at a cost to British firms.

These policies sowed the seeds of a decline unprecedented in its swiftness and steepness. Conservatives have emphasized government intervention as its principal cause. One pointed example is Peter Dunnett's study, which claims that the decline of the sector can be directly traced to interventionist, macro-level state policies. Dunnett's polemical argument defines the options as simply whether the state intervenes or not, and he claims the industry would have been better off had it not.[7]

---

[7]Peter J. S. Dunnett, *The Decline of the British Motor Industry: The Effects of Government Policy, 1945–1979* (London: Croom Helm, 1980). A statistical study by Jones and Prais strongly contradicts this position and claims that demand was more stable than Dunnett supposes. Stable demand suggests that inconsistent use of macro-economic policy does not explain poor performance by British automobile producers. However, consistently poor use of macro-economic tools, or a consistent reliance on only macro-economic tools, *could* provide an explanation. The latter form of explanation is consistent with my claims. See Daniel T. Jones and S. J. Prais, "Plant Size and Productivity in the Motor Industry: Some International Comparisons," *Oxford Bulletin of Economics and Statistics* 40 (May 1978).

By contrast, I suggest that the choice is not whether to intervene but how and why. All states intervene, it is how they intervene that is important. The British state's egalitarian principles bolstered foreign firms that were not likely to remain domestic producers in the long term because their locational investment decisions were wholly dominated by economic considerations and they had options. An eventual and inevitable change in the terms of trade led to a change in their investment strategy. The British state's policies irreparably damaged firms that were most vulnerable to political pressure and whose investment decisions were most influenced by national loyalty. Austin would have been valuable to the British economy in the long term because it would have been the most cooperative and, more important, the most enduring domestic producer.

I extended the argument to other advanced industrialized countries that were formerly fascist to see if the auto industry's development during and after the fascist regime more closely resembled that of liberal Britain or of fascist Germany. Italy and Japan were clear examples of indigenous fascist control while France was a more complex case because of the country's occupation and division. The policies of the Italian and Japanese states closely resembled those implemented in Germany. The only variation was that, if anything, the Japanese and Italians repressed the multinationals more than the Germans did, and the American presence was completely eradicated in both countries. Interestingly, neither government ever permitted them to return. Otherwise, the resemblance between the policies of the Japanese, Italian, and German governments and the effects of those policies were striking. Like the Germans, both the Italian and the Japanese fascists nurtured their own privately owned national champions in creating an industrial core, giving credence to Peter Hayes's claim that fascism is "capitalism harnessed to politics."[8] In all three countries these firms were strategic levers for the sustained periods of economic growth that followed in the 1950s and 1960s. And despite national differences in the prefascist period, similar fascist state policies led to a convergence in the structure of their national auto industries after the war.

Was France ever truly fascist? This book has no more than a marginal contribution to make on this recurrent question. Whether fascism was indigenous or imposed, its effects on the automobile industry were, in some dimensions, comparable to those in Germany, Italy, and Japan. As in Germany, so in France the Ford subsidiary was subjugated, although it was not eliminated under the Vichy regime. Of course France was

---

[8]Peter Hayes, *Industry and Ideology: IG Farben in the Nazi Era* (New York: Cambridge University Press, 1987), p. 79.

under German control, but even after the war Ford was treated with such hostility that it was eventually forced to leave. Thus American investment disappeared from France as it had done in Japan and Italy. And as in Italy and Japan, once it left neither Ford nor its American competitors were allowed to return. Similarly, the Vichy regime created a new, privately owned national champion in Renault, which, after forcible nationalization in 1946, retained its special, most favored status in the postwar period. But France's defensive postwar mergers were reminiscent more of Britain than of Germany, carried out under the protection and guidance of the state. The shared fascist experience in France, Germany, Italy, and Japan therefore seems to have been more important than anything that preceded it as a formative influence on state policy in the auto industry in some respects, notably in its hostility to foreign firms. That aspect is what separated France from Britain's sustained liberalism. But in another important aspect French policies resembled the British. In analytic terms the French case is a hybrid that suggests important implications for the distinction between indigenous and imposed fascism.

CONTINUITY AND CHANGE IN POLITICAL ECONOMY

One recent trend in political economy has been to divide twentieth-century history into neat decades built around generalizations, concepts, or events—an approach that offends de Tocqueville's notion of institutional continuity. The 1950s was the decade of reconstruction and the economic miracle; the 1960s of unprecedented institutionalization of corporatist interest intermediation; the 1970s of stagnation and attempts at structural adjustment; and the 1980s of the end of Keynesianism and the triumph of conservative monetarism. The popularity of state theory has ensured that recent studies have included a heavy dose of historical analysis, but much of this work has confined itself to invoking critical patterns of development traceable to events in earlier centuries. These tendencies achieve specific goals and often provide useful theoretical insights.[9] But one by-product is the tendency to ignore possible links between interwar and wartime events and those of the postwar period. Causal relationships across decades rather than centuries have been largely neglected. As a result, the significance of fascist governance has been downplayed. The most notable exception is Mancur Olson's analysis, but he consigns to fascism only a rehabilita-

---

[9]See John Zysman, *Governments, Markets, and Growth: Financial Systems and the Politics of Industrial Change* (Ithaca: Cornell University Press, 1983).

tive economic role by virtue of its part in the destruction of indigenous institutionalized relationships. Few works have stressed the activist contribution of fascism to postfascist development in liberal democracies. David Schoenbaum suggests that the scholarly focus has been on German-Nazi continuity—that is, continuity between the Second and Third Reichs—and, by implication, not on Nazi-German continuity— that is, between the Third and Fourth Reichs.[10]

One of the few exceptions to this tendency to ignore the relationship between interwar, wartime, and postwar politics is David Friedman's *Misunderstood Miracle*. Although Friedman does not share my focus on the importance of fascism, he does stress the importance of the links between the interwar period and postwar Japan in the historical evolution of Japan's machine tool industry.[11] Another, less explicit example is Peter Katzenstein's *Small States in World Markets*, which links the events of the 1930s to the postwar structure of policy making in the "seven dwarfs."[12]

In German studies two works have made notable contributions to this type of analysis. The first is David Schoenbaum's historical analysis of the revolutionary aspects of Nazi rule. His work examines both the ability and the inability of National Socialism to restructure German society and to solve Germany's problems. Yet by implication his analysis emphasizes, in the structure of German society after 1945, a congruence between tendencies that predated fascism and those that emerged under National Socialism.[13] But perhaps the work that best exemplifies an enduring capacity to relate the structure of Germany's state and society across the decades of the twentieth century is Ralf Dahrendorf's *Society and Democracy in Germany*.[14] Dahrendorf places a unique stress on the revolutionary, modernizing role of National Socialism in Germany: "However, brutal as it was, the break with tradition and thus a strong push towards modernity was the substantive characteristic of the social revolution of National Socialism."[15] Dahrendorf claims this revolution was necessary in dismantling the old order and eventually shifting to liberal democracy.[16]

In emphasizing the role of fascism in the destruction of German

---

[10]David Schoenbaum, *Hitler's Social Revolution: Class and Status in Nazi Germany, 1933–1939* (New York: Anchor, 1967).
[11]David Friedman, *The Misunderstood Miracle: Industrial Development and Political Change in Japan* (Ithaca: Cornell University Press, 1988), pp. 37–126.
[12]Peter J. Katzenstein, *Small States in World Markets: Industrial Policy in Europe* (Ithaca: Cornell University Press, 1985).
[13]See Schoenbaum, *Hitler's Social Revolution*, pp. 275–89.
[14]Ralf Dahrendorf, *Society and Democracy in Germany* (New York: Norton, 1967).
[15]Ibid., p. 382.
[16]Ibid., p. 383.

institutions, Dahrendorf expressly recognizes that the Third Reich was not simply a stage but more of a phenomenon. And in a statement recognizing Nazi legacies that seems almost designed to address Olson's subsequent analysis, Dahrendorf suggests that "if National Socialism was not an historical episode but the German revolution, it must have left its traces in the subsequent phase. This is indeed the case, although these traces are obscured by that other heritage of Nazi rule, . . . total defeat. . . . Which was the path prescribed to German society after the war in respect to the task of mastering the problems already mentioned? Which path was precluded for it? In answering these questions, the lasting result of the social revolution of National Socialist Germany became evident."[17] From the perspective of the subsequent Federal Republic, he tries to provide an answer to these questions. "Between the Federal Republic and the Weimar Republic lies the indistinguishable social revolution of National Socialism, which has transferred the very structures in which the effective equity of citizenship rights was anchored."[18] Part of those equity rights was the state's treatment of capital, and the German propensity changed in the Third Reich and was sustained in the early Bonn Republic. Dahrendorf reflects this notion in the claim that Germany's postwar development was not liberal and free of state control, even under Erhard. He says that "the area of government intervention by direct measures of planning and indirect measures of fiscal policy remained as wide as that of state-ownership."[19]

The argument presented in this book complements Dahrendorf's analysis. In general terms it highlights the powerful relationships formed in the Nazi era, noting that Erhard's initial attempts to dissolve such relationships through liberal reform failed as he retreated to the Nazi conception of "organic" relationships defined within the boundaries of a corporativistic "formed society." However, paradoxically, there never was an organic relationship between the state and the whole of society in the Third Reich, only one between the state and those the state selected to include. The point is evident in the Nazi treatment of Jews, Catholics, homosexuals, and Gypsies. Like the German state in the Third Reich, although perhaps less consciously, the Bonn Republic was drawn to a discriminatory web. On a less general scale I have sought to identify the configuration of political relationships formed between state and individual firms in the interwar auto industry. Although this analysis is confined to one industry, it too

[17]Ibid., p. 395.
[18]Ibid., p. 414.
[19]Ibid., p. 416.

suggests that fascist state policy acted as a modernizing force whose influence on the postwar period cannot be understated or ignored. This pattern of fascist restructuring appears to be replicated in the auto industries of other countries governed by fascist regimes.

This book's findings generate reasonable questions about the breadth and scope of the influence of fascist state policy on postwar economic prosperity. One question focuses on the applicability of the pattern identified in this book to other industries; another concerns the longevity of the structure of relations within the auto industry. The current lack of empirical research precludes any great speculation. But superficial evidence regarding other industrial sectors in Germany suggests that the Nazi state had a weighty influence. One example may be the German textile industry, whose international and domestic economic significance has consistently grown in the postwar period.[20] I am less unsure about the duration of the influence of this new configuration on the automobile industry. I rely on primary empirical material that traces the network of core relationships between state, firms, banks, and occasionally unions until the early 1960s. These claims about Germany work, I believe, only until the mid-1960s, and indeed Katzenstein has recently described the period of German postwar political history that ended then as the "first German Republic."[21]

After the mid-1960s the automobile industry's core relationship began to fragment under the combined effect of domestic changes in the political system and external, systemic pressures. There were two main source of domestic change within the German political system. The first, more gradual source was a series of institutional changes, such as the development of cooperative federalism and parapublic institutions, whose origins can be found in the 1950s and early 1960s but whose influence was fully felt for the first time only in the mid-1960s. The second, precipitant source was the reemergence of the Social Democrats as a political force. Together these electoral and institutional factors decentralized and "tamed" the power of the German state.[22] Decentralization created impediments to the unity of the core coalition. For example, the eventual privatization of Volkswagen deprived the state of the pivot around which it could build strategic bilateral core relations. Similarly, the rise in the political significance of regional gov-

---

[20] For the textile industry see Werner Hagemann, "Zur Entwicklung der Bekleidungsindustrie," in Ernst Melzer, ed., *Die Bekleidungsindustrie* (Darmstadt: Elsner, 1955), pp. 1–15.

[21] Peter J. Katzenstein, "Stability and Change in the Emerging Third Republic," in Katzenstein, ed., *Industry and Politics in West Germany: Toward the Third Republic* (Ithaca: Cornell University Press, 1989), p. 343.

[22] Peter J. Katzenstein, *Policy and Politics in West Germany: The Growth of a Semi-Sovereign State* (Philadelphia: Temple University Press, 1987).

ernments was reflected in their greater importance to the welfare of individual firms, evident in Bavarian assistance to BMW as early as 1967. The new visibility of the *Länder* tended to fragment core relations by driving a wedge between the successful specialist producers of the south German "auto bloc" in Bavaria and the mass producers in the industrial regions of the north, notably Lower Saxony, which operated under increasingly difficult conditions as demand shrank in the 1970s.

As the state's capacity to unify the core was weakening, several factors simultaneously helped fragment the interests of core members. The sources included different regional imperatives. Beyond that, the coalition was predicated on the assumption that sustained periods of growth would occasionally be punctuated by limited cyclical downturns, sustaining high profits, wages, and job security. Wage restraint could be implemented by union leaders only for limited periods, in exchange for the promise of future rewards. Furthermore, the labor cushion provided by the *Gastarbeiter* (foreign workers) in periods of reduced employment disappeared. The public outcry over IG Metall's refusal to help protect foreign workers from expulsion during the Volkswagen crisis in the mid-1970s led to new legislation giving them the same job security as German natives. These new factors initially strained two dimensions of the core coalition; within labor, between native workers and foreigners used as *Lumpenproletariat;* and between labor and capital in core firms. In the early 1970s cyclical downturns began to be overwhelmed by systemic, structural ones—as reflected in the Volkswagen crisis of 1973–74. Currency fluctuations that raised the value of the Deutsche mark, the new competition posed by Japanese firms and the newly industrializing countries to German firms in traditional export markets, and higher relative labor rates all decreased the competitiveness of German firms. American multinationals could swiftly shift production between subsidiaries and thus remain competitive by taking advantage of cheaper labor (for example, Ford in Spain). German core firms faced more effective impediments to internationalization, however, as Volkswagen discovered when it decided to form an American manufacturing subsidiary to combat currency fluctuations.

Furthermore, the relationship between core firms was strained by a breakdown in the traditional segmentation of the market caused by increased international competition. Volkswagen had always mass-produced cheap cars, BMW sport cars, motor bikes, and small sedans, and Daimler-Benz big sedans. These three firms divided market production and shared an interest in collectively and cooperatively competing against American subsidiaries and foreign firms. New competition, however, forced Volkswagen to move "up-market," producing more sophisticated autos, and Daimler-Benz and BMW to move "down-market," with smaller or cheaper versions of traditional models. Daimler-Benz and BMW were also indirectly encouraged to down-size by American government requirements that encouraged producers to build efficient models or face sanctions. A sufficient overlap developed between Audi's and Volkswagen's luxury models and Daimler-Benz's and BMW's cheaper models to obscure what had once been clear distinctions. The firms that had once been collaborators thus became partial competitors. The core began to dissolve its network of relations, reducing the disadvantage borne by peripheral producers.

WEST GERMANY AND BRITAIN IN THE 1970S AND 1980S

Despite changes in the structure of the German state in the 1960s, this argument has implications for the 1970s and 1980s. In discussing the German auto industry's ability to adjust successfully to new demands and constraints, Wolfgang Streeck recently suggested that the West German state has no tradition of industrial policy or selective intervention. Furthermore, he claimed, the German state had not provided research and development funding; on the contrary, the state's contribution to the success of domestic firms was its emphasis on supply-side liberalism. The government had traditionally confined itself to safeguarding the market through free international trade and the promotion of domestic competition. Volkswagen, said Streeck, had always been run like a private enterprise and had never received significant public subsidies. And while this tradition contributed to its successful adjustment, the British state's supposed tradition of selective intervention contributed to its industry's lack of such capacities.[23] Although these "traditional" differences were insufficient to explain the variation between the two countries, Streeck suggested they were major contributors.

Obviously the argument of this book contrasts starkly with Streeck's assessment. Its theoretical approach inverts his argument about the causes of success and failure in West Germany and Britain; its empirical evidence challenges his historical claims. Similarly, I suggest that the contemporary West German auto industry and its individual producers cannot be divorced from the "tradition" I have identified in this book. Streeck focuses on the contemporary period and tends to ignore the political forces that first shaped the market. Furthermore, although the

[23]Wolfgang Streeck, "Successful Adjustment to Turbulent Markets: The Automobile Industry," in Katzenstein, *Industry and Politics*, pp. 134–36.

core coalition fragmented in the 1970s and 1980s, its remnants can still be glimpsed in the German state's discriminatory policies toward what were formerly core and peripheral firms. Take, for example, Bonn's response to foreign attempts to purchase Daimler-Benz, a firm with great economic and symbolic importance to the national economy.

GM's repeated attempts to buy Daimler-Benz in the 1960s and early 1970s were rebuffed by the company; domestic ownership seemed assured. But in the mid-1970s the Quandt family, which owned 14 percent of Daimler-Benz shares, unexpectedly sold their holdings to oil-rich Kuwaiti investors. Soon after this sale, Friedrich Flick announced he was going to sell 29 percent of his 39 percent holding to an undisclosed Iranian investor (subsequently presumed to be the Shah of Iran) for $1 billion. This development brought the traditional network among core members and the state to the surface. Unlike GM's bids, this time the threat to domestic ownership was serious and rallied the banking community and the state to Daimler-Benz's defense.[24]

The Deutsche Bank, Daimler-Benz's traditional benefactor, invoking what the Dresdner Bank described as distinctly "nationalistic overtones," purchased Flick's 29 percent share "to prevent their dispersal abroad and to ensure the corporate independence of Daimler-Benz." This purchase was at the time the largest financial deal in German postwar history. The bank elected to hold the shares until they could be sold to "appropriate" purchasers. The government's enthusiasm for the Deutsche Bank's purchase, according to the *New York Times*, "suggest[ed] considerable behind-the-scenes maneuvering by Bonn officials to prevent a repetition of the Kuwait sale." In fact, Chancellor Helmut Schmidt's only concern was how long it would take for the Deutsche Bank to resell the shares. Economics minister Hans Friedrichs promised legal steps to prevent a repetition, and government spokesman Armin Grünewald added that he now felt that the door had been barred for a foreign takeover of Daimler-Benz.[25] The next day the government announced legal controls on the sale of majority shareholdings in major industries to foreigners—a law specifically designed to keep core companies in German hands.[26] Once again the state had coordinated activities to preserve the domestic ownership of a core German firm. Daimler-Benz has since developed into the largest firm in the FRG.

Similar examples of core relations can be found in the state's involve-

[24]George Heaton, "Government Structural Policies and the Automobile Industry," paper prepared for the International Automobile Program, International Policy Forum, Hakone, Japan, May 1982, p. 10.
[25]For this information see *New York Times*, 15 January 1975.
[26]*New York Times*, 16 January 1975.

ment in Volkswagen during the crisis of the mid-1970s;[27] in the 1981 federal court decision that upheld Volkswagen's monopolistic relationship with repair dealers because the company "provided the consumer with better service," despite antitrust laws;[28] and in IG Metall's continued willingness to negotiate exclusive, favorable labor agreements with Volkswagen. These instances reflect vestiges of the structure of relationships from which core firms benefited in the first two decades of the Bonn Republic.

The implications of my argument are more transparent for Britain in the 1970s and 1980s. Traditional patterns are still evident there—no surprise, given my stress on continuity in Britain. This claim, however, contradicts much that has been written about the "Thatcher Revolution." While conservatives and socialists claim that the last decade has provided a watershed in British politics, the evidence from the British auto industry has a depressingly familiar ring. Thatcher governments have encouraged foreign investment despite its demonstrably detrimental effects on indigenous producers and the British economy in general.

Chrysler had threatened to withdraw production from Britain in 1975 but then promised to maintain production and employment levels in exchange for financial assistance from the British government.[29] In 1978, however, Chrysler broke the terms of the signed agreement and sold its British operation to the French firm PSA/Talbot. Although the British government had the capacity and the right to block this deal under their agreement with Chrysler, it characteristically did not do so for fear of discouraging further multinational investment. PSA then ran down its British operation, transforming its new British subsidiary from a producer to a minor assembler, and closing the main Linwood plant and reducing employment from 22,000 to 6,000 between 1978 and 1983. PSA, as the legal inheritor of the terms of the 1976 agreement, also broke the agreement without reprisals, providing support for Stephen Wilks's suggestion that the British state's "policy on multinational corporations had always been ambivalent in tone but overwhelmingly liberal and permissive in content."[30]

Ford and Vauxhall have maintained a presence in Britain. Yet the accelerated decline in the size of their labor force and the new tendency

---

[27]Streeck, "Successful Adjustment."

[28]Heaton, "Government Structural Policies," p. 9.

[29]John Starrels, "The Dilemmas of Government Intervention: Chrysler, the Labour Government, and Britain," a paper delivered at the APSA meeting in Chicago, September 1976, p. 4.

[30]See Stephen Wilks, *Industrial Policy and the Motor Industry* (Manchester: Manchester University Press, 1984), pp. 252–59. The quotation comes from p. 260.

to use their plants for assembly rather than manufacture increased both domestic unemployment and British trade deficits.[31] In 1969 the percentage of production devoted to exports was 47 percent for Ford and 42 percent for Vauxhall. By 1974 these percentages had fallen to 25 percent and 21 percent respectively.[32] By 1979 British Ford's trade deficit of £20 million hid an actual £268 million trading deficit caused by the use of Ford's British facilities for assembly, sales, and service rather than manufacturing.[33] Vauxhall reduced employment levels by nearly 30 percent in the early 1980s—a decision Wilks describes as "an employment catastrophe"—and by the early 1980s Ford had become the largest net importer of cars to Britain.[34] More recent figures suggest that fully assembled imported cars are now about 55 percent of market sales in Britain, and by the beginning of the 1980s Britain produced fewer cars than Spain.[35]

Did British governments take this refusal to produce in Britain as an opportunity to invoke more aggressive, discriminatory policies? With the worst possibility realized—domestic companies in retreat and a rapid withdrawal of foreign direct investment—did they reassess their policies? The answer was resoundingly negative. First Labour governments and then Conservative ones maintained traditional attitudes and policies, encouraging a sizable foreign presence and increased foreign control over domestic resources. The Thatcher governments presided over the sales of Aston Martin and Jaguar to Ford and Lotus to GM. They were also willing to sell Austin-Rover to General Motors, Ford, FIAT, or even Volkswagen before finally concluding a deal with British Aerospace. Austin-Rover was sold to British Aerospace only with the proviso that the government, despite its anti-interventionist rhetoric, be willing to underwrite the company's losses. The Thatcher government demonstrated two traditional approaches: agreeing to write off the company's debt, and then encouraging the new board to sign a deal with Honda that exchanged a 20 percent ownership in Austin-Rover for a comparable share of ownership in Honda's new British components subsidiary. A fifth of Britain's last remaining mass producer was exchanged for a fifth of the British components subsidiary of Japan's third-largest producer.

Rather than use the withdrawal of American investment as an oppor-

[31]Karel Williams, John Williams, and Dennis Thomas, *Why Are the British Bad at Manufacturing?* (London: Routledge & Kegan Paul, 1983), p. 44.
[32]Wilks, *Industrial Policy and the Motor Industry*, p. 112.
[33]Ibid., p. 72.
[34]Ibid., pp. 75, 248.
[35]See "Motor Industry Survey," *The Economist*, 15 October 1988, p. 9; Wilks, *Industrial Policy and the Motor Industry*, p. 245; Daniel Roos, Alan Altshuler, et al., *The Future of the Automobile* (Cambridge: MIT Press, 1984), p. 22.

tunity to stimulate the redevelopment of domestic firms, British governments have focused most of their energies on searching for foreign sources of new domestic investment. They have been most successful in encouraging Japanese investment in Britain as a springboard for European exports. Thus Japanese multinationals have invested in Britain as a way of combatting EEC domestic content restrictions, and the British government's confrontations with its French counterpart over domestic content legislation has demonstrated that it is conscious of its role in subduing French protectionism. The logic of the decision to seek increased Japanese investment reflects the same attitude that formerly encouraged American investment. One sign of the decline of indigenous producers (recall that Britain was the largest exporter of cars in the late 1940s) is a 1988 report that suggested that Nissan, with a single British plant, is projected to be the biggest exporter of cars from Britain by 1992.[36]

Oblivious to the lessons of the past, successive Thatcher governments have continued to encourage foreign direct investment by offering foreign firms the benefits of national treatment. This tendency has, in fact, caused rare instances of Conservative parliamentary and extra-parliamentary rebellion—most notably over the allocation of defense contracts in the Westland Affair. But Margaret Thatcher has successfully fought to sustain a trend that began in the opening decades of the century and has culminated in the disappearance of an entire industry.

LESSONS FOR THE UNITED STATES

This is not a book about the United States, yet it has a lot to say about the principles of the American state. Assumptions about American exceptionalism now have to be replaced by a capacity for comparison. And the comparative evidence is not encouraging. The U.S. ideological propensity toward national treatment and the U.S. pattern of state policy toward foreign direct investment most clearly converges with the British pattern—where the effect on state autonomy and the balance of payments has been most adverse. This finding is not surprising, for both countries share liberal characteristics, and the United States has had to face the breakdown in the structural barriers that formerly insulated American producers from foreign competition.

American auto producers created a new production mix and a new form of industrial relations captured in the concept of "Fordism." Fordism synthesized mass production methods, anti-unionism, and rela-

[36]"Motor Industry Survey," p. 10.

322

tively high flat salaries.[37] Yet despite the development of unprecedented economies of scales, successive U.S. administrations implemented tariffs, dating from the Dingley tariff of 1897, that protected the infant American auto industry from rival European producers by classifying foreign autos as manufactured steel, subjecting them to a 45 percent duty.[38]

With the industry's development three factors made the issue of tariffs and foreign direct investment a moot point by the 1930s. The first concerned the relative price levels of domestic and foreign products. The effective economies of scale that resulted from the development of Fordism, the consolidation of the industry into a limited number of producers, and the development of a mass market gave American firms a competitive price advantage over European firms. The Europeans did not manufacture cars in quantities large enough to achieve those economies of scale. The second factor concerned the relative financial resources of American and foreign firms. The size and scale of investment involved in competing in the burgeoning American market inhibited European firms from developing a dealer network. The third factor was the unique aspects of American consumer demands. Cheap gas and America's large size and varied climate created unique market conditions. Consumers developed expectations about the nature of the product—such as a "soft" ride, even for mass-marketed cars—inconsistent with those of European consumers. Cheap gas relative to Europe enabled American consumers to afford big cars. Investment costs, relatively cheap cars, and distinct consumer demands combined to preclude foreign entry to the American market. The imposition of tariffs was functionally irrelevant from the 1930s onward. This situation lasted until the 1960s, when Volkswagen became the first European producer able to manufacture on a large enough scale and with enough resources (both courtesy of the Nazi regime) to create a niche in the marketplace. Even Volkswagen's heralded breakthrough in the American market was minimal in effect, its market share peaking at 5 percent in the 1960s.[39]

A change did finally expose the American market to foreign competition, however, a shift in control over the world's oil resources that resulted in the two oil crises of the 1970s. The culminative effect was significantly higher gas prices for American consumers, effectively destroying the market insulation enjoyed by indigenous auto producers.

[37]See Steven Meyer III, *The Five Dollar Day: Labor Management and Social Control in the Ford Motor Company, 1908–1921* (Albany: SUNY Press, 1981).

[38]See Mira Wilkins and Frank E. Hill, *American Business Abroad: Ford on Six Continents* (Detroit: Wayne State University Press, 1964), p. 37.

[39]See, for example, *New York Times*, 26 May 1963.

Domestic consumers now had an incentive to purchase smaller cars, and as their preferences changed the sale of imported cars from Europe and Japan, which had begun as a trickle in the early 1970s, grew to a flood. U.S. manufacturers initially refused to redesign their products. Poor management decisions by the Big Three, combined with a new consumer awareness of the relatively poor quality of American-made cars, resulted in a swift decline in domestic market share. By 1980 the Big Three collectively lost $4 billion.[40] The problem was dramatized by the Chrysler Crisis of 1979, when the federal government had to guarantee commercial bank loans in order to bail the company out.[41]

The American government's response to this sectoral decline was a policy that was essentially no different from what British governments had attempted: the reimposition of formal trade barriers intended to limit the direct import of·finished products, complemented by policies designed to encourage direct capital investment by foreign competitors. Britain had historically used unilateral, formal tariff barriers in the adoption of the McKenna duties; the United States used an informal barrier, negotiating a bilateral Voluntary Export Restraint agreement (VER) with the Japanese government because Japanese firms accounted for the overwhelming bulk of imports. This agreement was first instituted in May 1981. The VER initially set a U.S. import ceiling of 1.68 million Japanese autos per annum, subsequently raised to 1.8 million in 1984 and then 2.3 million. The increases were primarily designed to accommodate GM and Chrysler imports of small Japanese-produced cars. Until 1985 the agreement was negotiated annually between the Reagan administration and the Japanese government, the latter arbitrating market share among Japanese producers. Since that time it has been respected if not negotiated, even though the Reagan administration and the U.S. firms had insisted in 1981 that the VER was a temporary measure to be respected for no more than three years. It is clear that, although Japanese firms have benefited financially from this agreement, which stimulated a steep rise in the price of Japanese cars that has more than compensated for lost market share, the United States initially formulated the agreement and has sustained it by the exercise of American power.[42] Japanese producers have re-

[40]See "The American Car Industry's Own Goals," *The Economist*, 6 February 1988.
[41]See as examples U.S. Congress, Senate Committee on Banking, Housing, and Urban Affairs, *The Chrysler Corporation Loan Guarantee Act of 1979: Hearings before the Committee on Banking, Housing, and Urban Affairs*, 96th Congress, 1st sess., 1979; and the committee's subsequent *Finding of the Chrysler Corporation Loan Guarantee Board*, May 1980.
[42]For the benefits enjoyed by Japanese firms as a result of the agreement see *New York Times*, 23 December 1981. See also U.S. Congress, *Issues Related to the Domestic Automobile Industry: Hearings*, Part 2, S.396, 1981.

peatedly stated that because of their competitive advantage, they prefer free exchange with potentially greater market share to smaller market share with higher prices.

The administration had both short- and long-term objectives. The short-term ones were to nurse domestic producers back to health and stop the flood of lost jobs. These goals have been achieved, and domestic firms achieved record profit levels in the mid 1980s.[43] The long-term objective was to force Japanese firms to locate a greater percentage of their production in the United States, an objective reflected in the debate prior to 1981. In the late 1970s Japanese firms, particularly Nissan and Toyota, staunchly resisted overtures by MITI officials to agree to a strategy of foreign investment, prompting a rare public attack on them by MITI minister Sasaki. The major exporters did begin to respond, albeit inadequately, in 1979 by covertly limiting exports to the United States to avoid politicization of the issue.[44] American industrialists accused both Toyota and Nissan of dumping cars in the U.S. market, and Doug Fraser, head of the United Auto Workers (UAW), threatened to call for a boycott unless Japanese firms built local manufacturing plants.[45] The Japanese eventually responded to the combined effects of pressure from their own government, American threats, and the VER by building American plants.

The Reagan administration faced a choice between domestic content legislation designed "to encourage the production in the U.S. by American workers of automotive products which are sold or distributed in interstate commerce"[46] and a VER. The administration preferred the VER, which primarily aided American business but did not require formal legislation, thus avoiding congressional involvement.[47] The *New York Times* suggested "the only alternative to these 'mild and temporary' restraints on Japanese sales, the Reagan team contends, was a

---

[43]See, for example, *New York Times*, 7 February 1989. For job losses in the 1970s and early 1980s see Wolfgang Streeck and Andreas Hoff, "Manpower Management and Industrial Relations in the Restructuring of the World Automobile Industry" (Wissenschaftszentrum, Berlin: International Institute of Management, Discussion Paper IIM/LMP 83–35).

[44]See Nobaru Fujii, "The Road to the U.S.-Japan Auto Crash," in *U.S.-Japan Relations: New Attitudes for a New Era, Annual Review 1983–1984* (Cambridge: Harvard Center for International Affairs, Program on U.S.-Japan Relations, 1984), pp. 40–41.

[45]Ibid., p. 36.

[46]U.S. Congress, House Committee on Ways and Means, *Fair Practices in Automotive Products Act of 1983: Hearings before the Subcommittee on Trade*, 98th Congress, 1st sess., 1983, HR 1234, Section (3)(8).

[47]For the proposed domestic content legislation see U.S. Congress, *Fair Practices in Automotive Products Act of 1983: Hearing before the Subcommittee on Trade, Committee on Ways and Means*, HR 1234, Section 2. This bill was later resubmitted as *Fair Practices in Automotive Products Act of 1983*, HR 5133.

tough congressional quota, which might even have become permanent."[48]

The result of these policies has been growing Japanese investment in the United States that resembles earlier American investment in Britain. Will the American state respond the way the British has? The federal government is officially neutral on this question. But in practice it has effectively endorsed the development as an intended consequence of its policies by politically pressuring the Japanese government, suggesting that congressional protectionist sentiment might cut Japanese exports to American markets. Japanese firms should therefore invest in the United States to protect their position in this market.

Japanese firms have been encouraged to invest in the United States not only by the federal government's coercive policies but also by enormous incentives offered by individual state governments to attract investment and raise employment. Honda was the first Japanese company to invest in Ohio, followed by Nissan in Tennessee and Toyota in Kentucky and California.[49] As Japanese firms complete the transition to multinational status, early indicators suggest that Japanese investment threatens to have the same deleterious effect on domestic producers and the U.S. economy that American investment had in Britain. Aggregate Japanese automobile production, whether imported or built in the United States, now accounts for 25 percent of the American market. Recent estimates suggest that when Japanese assembly plants in the United States are completed, in the early 1990s, combined U.S. and domestic production will give Japanese firms a 40–45 percent market share. These figures do not include Japanese cars imported by GM and Chrysler and sold under license.[50]

The influence of Japanese firms on the American auto market could therefore rival peak American influence on the British market within a decade. Without constraints on Japanese capacity or limits on the diffusion of investment capital abroad, the decline of the American auto industry could be as steep and swift as Britain's. With only three domestic producers, their strategic significance increases. Changing circumstances and state policies suggest that the federal government may have to repeat the Chrysler plan, underwriting other losers. But next time such an effort may prove less successful, for one critical factor in Chrysler's recovery in the early 1980s, the ability to reduce the Japanese presence in the American market, cannot now be repeated.

[48]See *New York Times*, 1 May 1981.
[49]See Martin Tolchin and Susan Tolchin, *Buying into America* (New York: Times Books, 1988), p. 25.
[50]See "Motor Industry Survey," p. 8.

Debates about state intervention often focus on either the normative desirability of intervention or the effectiveness of intervention in achieving social and political goals. In either case, it is universally assumed that because states intervene for political reasons, economic outcomes will be suboptimal. This book suggests that both fascist and liberal states intervene, and both do so for political reasons. The principles upon which states decide to intervene, and the methods they therefore use to do so, however, are crucial for the economic consequences of their behavior. This book does not advocate fascism. It simply recognizes the influence of fascism on the structure of postwar economic power. Fascist regimes have long been recognized for their brutality, but not for their effectiveness in creating durable political relations and prosperous economic structures. I have sought to make that point. The consequences of fascism thus did not end with the defeat of the Axis powers. More broadly, state intervention is not antithetical to the organization of national prosperity. I thus pose questions about the rights of foreign investors and suggest that the answers are of major consequence. Among major industrial states there are now two major patterns of policy on the issue of foreign direct investment; in that sense, if in no other, we are still living with the consequences of fascism.

Index

General Electric Company (GEC) of
Britain, 193, 254–55
General Motors (GM), 241, 326
in Belgium, 120, 298
in Denmark, 120
in France, 120, 298
French government and, 298
in Italy, 292
Opel, relations with, 110, 113, 249
Opel purchased by, 28, 110, 150, 153,
246
U.S. government and, 67, 324
General Motors in Britain, 203. *See also*
Vauxhall
Austin Motor Company, attempts to
purchase, 208, 211
Austin-Rover, attempt to purchase,
275–76
British government and, 1, 217–18,
275–76, 321
Jaguar, attempt to purchase, 1
Lotus purchased by, 276, 321
Vauxhall purchased by, 77, 208
General Motors in Germany, 110–11.
See also Opel
Daimler-Benz, attempts to purchase,
319
German government and, 218, 319
General Motors in Japan
Japanese government and, 284–87,
290
market share of, 283–84
production levels at, 285
Genther, Phyllis, 286, 287, 289, 290
German Automobile Trustee Associa-
tion, 112
German Industrial Credit Bank, 119,
130
Germany, 74, 88, 211, 216, 224, 229,
231, 243, 268, 273, 274, 278, 282.
See also Bonn Republic; Weimar Republic; Wilhelmine period; *specific
auto companies*
Adenauer and auto industry, 29, 190–
92, 194, 195
Allied Occupation of, 3, 61–62, 65,
71–72, 131–39, 142, 144–48, 168,
171–86, 189, 190, 192, 253, 257,
303–6, 308–9
Bismarckian period, 9, 11, 20, 22, 26–
27
Cartel Law of 1923, 23, 24
cartels in, 21–28, 43, 45–46, 54, 150,
280, 287, 306, 309
Christian Democrats (CDU) in, 135–
36, 178, 187–90, 253, 309
Christian Social Union (CSU) in, 187–
88, 255

Communist party (KPD) in, 135–36
continuity and change in, 6–19
Control Commission for Germany
(CCG), 133–34, 144, 171–74, 176–
78, 185, 186, 191, 193, 309
Control Law 2, 176
Control Law 5, 133
Control Law 22, 135
Control Law 52, 174, 176, 185
Corporation Law of 1937, 44
corporatism in, 6, 30–32, 47–54, 62,
63, 66–67, 111, 261
DAF, 154–58, 160, 162, 166, 174,
176, 177, 257, 307, 308
Deutsche Reichspartei in, 180
domestic firms, government policy toward, 3, 4, 27, 29, 44, 45, 50–53,
65, 69–73, 75–76, 110–12, 118–20,
130, 134, 138–39, 141, 145–49,
151–201, 219, 223, 248, 251–63,
277, 284, 286, 287, 291, 295, 298,
300, 302, 305–12, 317, 319–20
Emergency Service Decree of 1938, 126
Employers' Association, 135–37, 143
fascism in, 2–7, 9–12, 14, 15, 17–21,
23–26, 29–32, 38–39, 41, 43–47,
49, 54–55, 60–62, 64–65, 67–69,
71, 73, 80, 109–31, 135, 138, 139,
141, 142, 144–49, 151–70, 177,
180–87, 189, 195, 199–201, 247–
53, 258, 260, 277, 279–80, 284,
287, 291, 295, 301–3, 305–16
foreign firms, government policy toward, 2–4, 29, 45, 51, 53, 65, 69–
72, 75–76, 80, 107, 109–39, 141–
42, 144–46, 148, 153, 159, 160,
164, 172, 175, 195, 196, 198, 199,
218, 247–51, 254, 257, 262, 263,
286, 292, 295, 300–302, 305–12,
319
4 Ds (decartelization, demilitarization,
democratization, denazification), 17,
18, 304
and the Holocaust, 18, 303
ideologies, institutions, and the study
of, 4–6
Indemnification Law of 1939, 122
Joint Export-Import Agency (JEIA),
183
Junker class in, 10–14, 16, 17
Level of Industry Plan, 134, 172, 174,
175
liberalism in, 54, 62, 66–67, 200, 291,
303, 306, 309, 315
Military Law, 52, 124, 133
Navy bills, 13–14
Prussian contributions to unification
of, 10–14

Japan (*cont.*)
European opposition to competition
from, 2, 276
Exchange Control Law, 285
fascism in, 49, 55, 277–91, 295, 301–
2, 312–14
foreign firms, government policy toward, 2, 281, 284–87, 289, 290,
295, 300–302, 312, 313
Foreign Investment Law of 1951, 289
Important Industries Control Law of
1931, 280, 281
Liberal Democratic party in, 278
liberalism in, 291, 301
Materials Mobilization Plan, 285–87
MCI (Ministry of Commerce and In-
dustry), 278–81, 283, 285, 287–89
Meiji Restoration, 278, 304
Military Vehicle Subsidy Law of 1918,
283
MITI, 278, 282, 289–90, 325
MM (Ministry of Munitions), 278–79,
287
National General Mobilization Law of
1938, 280
negotiations with World Bank, 290
Reconstruction Finance Bill, 288
Temporary Materials Supply and De-
mand Control Law of 1946, 280
Temporary Measure Law Relating to
Exports, Imports and Other Matters
of 1937, 285–86
U.S. Occupation of, 278–80, 282–83,
287–88, 290
Voluntary Export Restraint agreement
with U.S., 291, 324–26
Japan Automobile Manufacturers Asso-
ciation, 288
Japanese Development Bank, 288–90
Japan Ford:
Japanese government and, 284–87,
290, 313
market share of, 283–84
production levels at, 285
Johnson, Chalmers, 261, 278–83, 290
Jones, Daniel, 36, 269, 270, 274–75, 298
Junkers, Hugo, 43, 45
Jürgens, Ulrich, 194, 199

Kaishinsha, 284
Kantorowicz, Hermann, 9
Katzenstein, Peter, 296, 316
Small States in World Markets, 47–49,
314
Kayser, Frank, 205
Kehr, Eckhart, 8–9, 20–21
Kelsey Hayes, 98

Kennedy, John F., 195
Kilb, Hans, 254
Kissel, Wilhelm, 153, 155, 251
Knudsen, William, 82
Könecke, Fritz, 254
Kopf, Hinrich, 177
Korean War, 236, 283, 289
Austin Motor Company and, 203,
244, 310
British Ford and, 97
Krauch, Carl, 119, 121, 132
Kruk, Max, 251–52
Krupp, Gustav, 22
Krupp company, 133, 144

Labour party (Britain), 105, 204, 234–
37, 239, 244, 269, 272, 275, 321
auto industry seen as source of for-
eign exchange, 93, 229–32
Chrysler favored by, 270, 274
McKenna duties revoked, 210
union strikers supported by, 218
Lafferentz, Bodo, 157, 166
Lancia:
FIAT control over, 295
Ford Motor Company attempt to pur-
chase, 293
Lehideux, François, 297
Lehmbruch, Gerhard, 67
Lenz, Max, 7
Lever, Harold, 270
Ley, Robert, 155–57, 160
Leyland:
ACV purchased by, 268–69
British government and, 268–69, 274
British Leyland formed by BMC merger with, 269, 274
Rover purchased by, 268–69
Standard-Triumph purchased by,
268–69
Liberal Democratic party (Japan), 278
Liberalism, 314
in Britain, 5, 30–32, 36–38, 51–52,
63, 67–72, 74–75, 106, 150, 202–3,
236, 244, 261–63, 266, 270, 273,
277, 302, 307, 312, 313
characteristics of, 31–38
corporatism compared to, 47, 50–55
domestic firms, government policy toward, 35, 261–62
fascism compared to, 2, 38, 41–42,
44, 45, 53–55, 307, 327
foreign firms, government policy toward, 35–36, 261–62
in Germany, 54, 62, 66–67, 291, 303,
306, 309, 315
in Italy, 292

Nordhoff, Heinrich:
labor relations and, 181, 182, 185
at Opel, 154, 180, 249
at Volkswagen, 154, 180–82, 185,
188–89, 192, 195, 196, 198, 256,
309–10
North, Douglass, 32
NSU:
Audi-NSU formed by Auto-Union
merger with, 255
FIAT's attempt to purchase, 193, 255
German banking community and, 193
German government and, 309
Honda's attempt to purchase, 255
Volkswagen purchase of, 149, 199,
246, 255
Nuffield, Lord (William Morris), 213,
214, 219
at BMC, 241, 244
British government and, 211, 220–21,
264
as driving force behind Morris company, 203, 210–11, 264

Oeftering, Heinz Maria, 188–89, 191,
309
Olson, Mancur, 3–4, 61, 201, 313–15
Rise and Decline of Nations, 5, 304
Opel, 107, 114, 139
General Motors, relations with, 110,
113, 249
General Motors' purchase of, 28, 110,
150, 153, 246
German government and, 51, 110–11,
116, 118–20, 130, 138, 159, 199,
247–51, 306, 310, 311
labor relations/working conditions at,
51, 199
market share of, 108–12, 150, 152,
159, 246–50, 308, 310
production levels at, 110, 134, 152,
159, 247, 249, 250
profits and losses at, 51, 116, 247, 250
Volkswagen formation and, 111, 153–
54, 180
World War II and, 111, 167, 180, 248,
249
Opel, Dr. Wilhelm von, 153
Overy, Richard J., 152, 159, 227
Owen, Richard, 22

Panitch, Leo, 143, 306
Paxton, Robert, 296
Payton, Ernest, 209, 219, 222–23, 228
Peacock, Arthur, 207
Perry, Percival, 293
British government and, 81–82, 84,
91, 116, 216

on Fordwerke AG board of directors,
108, 114, 116, 130
as head of British Ford, 76–77, 79–
82, 84, 89–91, 93, 96, 216, 221
labor relations and, 79–80, 89, 90
Peugeot:
Citroen, merger with, 299
French government and, 299
market share of, 297
Piore, Michael, 58–59
Pohl, Hans, 252
Polanyi, Karl, 74
Popp, Franz, 153–55, 257
Porsche, Ferdinand, 152, 157, 166, 256
Porsche company
German government and, 309
Volkswagen collaboration with, 256
Preussag, 193
PSA/Talbot:
British government and, 273, 320
Chrysler Corporation in Britain pur-
chased by, 273, 320
employment levels at, 273, 320

Quandt family, 319

Rachfahl, Felix, 7
Ranke, Leopold von, 7, 18
RDA auto trade organization (Germany),
150, 152
Reagan, Ronald, 324–26
Renault, Louis, 297, 298
Renault company, 104
Berliet controlled by, 299
British government and, 239
French government and, 295, 297–
301, 313
market share of, 297, 299, 300
nationalization of, 298–99, 313
Rhys, D. G., 266, 268
Ritter, Gerhard, 8–10
Roberge, R. I., 137
Rolls-Royce, 99
Austin Motor Company collaboration
with, 239
British Ford collaboration with, 82–84
British government and, 275
nationalization of, 275
World War II and, 82–84
Rommel, Erwin, 85, 293
Rootes, William, 222
Rootes company, 220, 222, 232
British government and, 264, 270
Chrysler purchase of, 267, 270
Japanese government and, 289
market share of, 267
profits and losses at, 264
Roth, Karl Heinz, 252–53

United States (*cont.*)
competitive advantages of U.S. auto firms, 28, 75, 208, 232, 317, 323
Dingley tariff, 323
domestic firms, government policy toward, 67, 323–26
foreign firms, government policy toward, 2, 38, 197–98, 322–26
Japan, Occupation of, 278–80, 282–83, 287–88, 290
Lend-Lease program, 88, 92
liberalism in, 34, 36, 38, 261–62, 322–27
Sherman Act, 197
Voluntary Export Restraint agreement with Japan, 291, 324–26

Vauxhall, 111
British government and, 203, 216, 232, 235, 238, 264, 265, 267, 269, 270, 276, 306–7, 310
employment levels at, 264, 320–21
General Motors purchase of, 77, 208
labor relations/working conditions at, 272
market share of, 213, 267, 306
production levels at, 267
profits and losses at, 69, 203, 235, 266, 267, 272, 273
World War II and, 220, 221
Versailles Treaty, 27, 251, 256–57
Vitger, Erhard, 109, 116, 120–21, 132, 136, 144
Völkischer Beobachter, 44
Volkswagen (VW), 58, 97, 104, 203, 210, 290, 317–18
Austin-Rover, attempt to purchase, 276
Auto-Union purchased by, 149, 199, 246, 255
British government and, 276, 321
Daimler-Benz, attempt to purchase, 199
Daimler-Benz collaboration with, 255, 256
employment levels at, 52, 161, 163–65, 170, 183
formation of, 111, 119, 149–56, 180, 248, 251, 257, 307–8
German banking community and, 147, 155, 158, 162, 174, 219, 254
German government and, 29, 44, 50–53, 73, 75–76, 119, 130, 134, 138–39, 141, 145–49, 151–201, 219, 223, 248, 253, 255, 257, 284, 295, 305–9, 311, 320

labor relations/working conditions at, 51–53, 138, 164–66, 169–71, 181–83, 199–200, 305–6, 317, 320
market share of, 50, 75, 152, 180, 195–96, 249
NSU purchased by, 149, 199, 246, 255
Porsche collaboration with, 256
privatization of, 316
production levels at, 138, 152, 161–63, 168–70, 172–75, 180, 189
profits and losses at, 29, 57, 139, 156–57, 166–67, 174, 180, 183, 189, 196
Savers Fund, 157–58, 176–77, 179, 191
in U.S., 197–98, 317, 323
World War II and, 152, 160–70, 253, 304
Volkswagen of America Inc., 197–98
Von Schell, Colonel, 116, 159

Wanderer, 150, 247
Wehler, Hans-Ulrich, 10–17, 21–22, 26, 40
Weimar Republic, 8, 17, 148, 155, 305, 307, 315. *See also* Germany
auto industry and, 26, 27, 61–63, 109, 117, 118, 135, 138, 146, 151
cartels and, 23, 150
downfall of, 11, 12, 14
Weltpolitik, 7, 12
Werlin, Jacob, 157, 166
West Germany. *See* Germany
Whitney, Sir Arthur, 209
Wilhelmine period, 5–6, 8–11, 13–15, 19–22, 26, 27, 30, 49, 181, 305
Wilkins, Mira, 79, 81–82, 91, 136
Wilks, Stephen, 262, 264, 269–72, 274, 307, 320, 321
William II, Kaiser, 14
Wilson, Harold, 271
Wolseley:
Austin and Morris, proposed merger with, 210–11
Morris purchase of, 211
Womack, James, 50
World War I, 5–11, 15, 126, 251
Austin Motor Company and, 203, 205–7, 214, 217, 219, 310
British Ford and, 76, 81–82
World War II, 11, 61, 279, 303
Alfa Romeo and, 294
Austin Motor Company and, 203, 214–16, 219–28, 265, 310
Borgward and, 258
British Ford and, 82–92, 221, 264–65, 310

Index

World War II (*cont.*)

Daimler-Benz and, 167, 251–53

Fordwerke AG and, 119–31, 249

French Ford and, 120, 297

Italian Ford and, 293

Morris and, 220–21, 265

Nissan and, 287–88

Opel and, 111, 167, 180, 248, 249

Rolls-Royce and, 82–84

Toyota and, 287–88

Vauxhall and, 220, 221

Volkswagen and, 152, 160–70, 253, 304

Wyatt, Richard, 240

Yamamura, Kozo, 282–83

Zschopauer, 150, 247

Zeitlin, Jonathan, 223–24

Zentralestelle für Finanzwirtschaft (ZfF) (Germany), 162

Zysman, John, 235

341

Cornell Studies in Political Economy

EDITED BY PETER J. KATZENSTEIN

Library of Congress Cataloging-in-Publication Data

Reich, Simon, 1959–
  The fruits of fascism : Postwar prosperity in historical perspective / Simon
Reich.
     p. cm. — (Cornell studies in political economy)
  Includes bibliograhical references.
  ISBN 0-8014-2440-2 (alk. paper). — ISBN 0-8014-9729-9 (pbk.: alk. paper)
    1. Germany (West)—Economic conditions.   2. Germany—Economic conditions—
1918–1945.   3. Germany (West)—Politics and government.   4. Germany—Politics
and government—1933–1945. I. Title. II. Series.
HC286.5.R39   1990
330.94'086—dc20
                                                         90-55136